THE CAMBRIDGE COMPANION TO
BIBLICAL NARRATIVE

The Cambridge Companion to Biblical Narrative offers an overview and a concise introduction to an exciting field within literary interpretation of the Hebrew Scriptures and the New Testament. Analysis of biblical narrative has enjoyed a resurgence in recent decades, and this volume features essays that explore many of the artistic techniques that readers encounter in an array of texts. Specially commissioned for this volume, the chapters analyze various scenes in Genesis, Exodus and the wilderness wanderings, Israel's experience in the land and royal experiment in Kings and Chronicles, along with short stories like Ruth, Jonah, Esther, and Daniel. New Testament essays examine each of the four Gospels, the book of Acts, stories from the letters of Paul, and reading for the plot in the book of Revelation. Designed for use in undergraduate and graduate courses, this *Companion* will serve as an excellent resource for instructors and students interested in understanding and interpreting biblical narrative.

Keith Bodner is Professor of Religious Studies at Crandall University in New Brunswick. Previous publications include *1 Samuel: A Narrative Commentary* (Sheffield Phoenix, 2008), *After the Invasion: A Reading of Jeremiah 40–44* (Oxford University Press, 2015), and *The Theology of the Book of Kings* (Cambridge University Press, 2019). Along with Brent A. Strawn, he is the author of "Solomon and 666 (Revelation 13.18)" in the journal *New Testament Studies*; he also served as co-editor for a three-volume collection that includes *Characters and Characterization in the Book of Judges* with Benjamin J. M. Johnson. Recent books are *The Psalms* (Oxford University Press, 2024) and *The Economy of Grace in the Parables of Jesus* (Baker Academic, 2025).

CAMBRIDGE COMPANIONS TO RELIGION

This is a series of companions to major topics and key figures in theology and religious studies. Each volume contains specially commissioned chapters by international scholars, which provide an accessible and stimulating introduction to the subject for new readers and nonspecialists.

(continued after index)

THE CAMBRIDGE COMPANION TO
BIBLICAL NARRATIVE

Edited by

Keith Bodner
Crandall University, Canada

CAMBRIDGE
UNIVERSITY PRESS

CAMBRIDGE
UNIVERSITY PRESS

Shaftesbury Road, Cambridge CB2 8EA, United Kingdom

One Liberty Plaza, 20th Floor, New York, NY 10006, USA

477 Williamstown Road, Port Melbourne, VIC 3207, Australia

314–321, 3rd Floor, Plot 3, Splendor Forum, Jasola District Centre,
New Delhi – 110025, India

103 Penang Road, #05–06/07, Visioncrest Commercial, Singapore 238467

Cambridge University Press is part of Cambridge University Press & Assessment,
a department of the University of Cambridge.

We share the University's mission to contribute to society through the pursuit of
education, learning and research at the highest international levels of excellence.

www.cambridge.org
Information on this title: www.cambridge.org/9781108841290

DOI: 10.1017/9781108888882

First published 2025

A catalogue record for this publication is available from the British Library

A Cataloging-in-Publication data record for this book is available from the
Library of Congress

ISBN 978-1-108-84129-0 Hardback
ISBN 978-1-108-81028-9 Paperback

Contents

Contributors

David L. Barr is Emeritus Professor of Religion and former Chair of the Departments of Religion, Philosophy, and Classics at Wright State University in Dayton, Ohio. His primary research areas include Jewish and Christian apocalypticism, the book of Revelation, and stories as told in the New Testament writings. He is the author of *Tales of the End: A Narrative Commentary on the Book of Revelation* (Polebridge Press, 2012) and *New Testament Story: An Introduction* (Wadsworth, 2009), and editor of *Reading the Book of Revelation: A Resource for Students* (SBL, 2003) and *The Reality of Apocalypse: Rhetoric and Politics in the Book of Revelation* (SBL, 2006).

Stephen B. Chapman is Associate Professor of Old Testament at Duke University and Editor-in-Chief of the *Journal of Theological Interpretation*. He is the author of *1 Samuel as Christian Scripture: A Theological Commentary* and *The Law and the Prophets: A Study in Old Testament Canon Formation* (Wm. B. Eerdmans, 2016), as well as numerous essays. He co-edited (with Marvin A. Sweeney) *The Cambridge Companion to the Hebrew Bible/Old Testament* (Cambridge University Press, 2016) and is the founding editor of the *Touchstone Texts* commentary series, with recent volumes on Isaiah 53 and the Lord's Prayer.

Lynn H. Cohick is Distinguished Professor of New Testament and Director of the Houston Theological Seminary at Houston Christian University. Lynn enjoys studying women's lives in the ancient world, and the Apostle Paul and his epistles within their larger Jewish and Greco-Roman contexts. Her publications include *The Letter to the Ephesians* (NICNT, Eerdmans, 2020), *Christian Women in the Patristic World: Their Influence, Authority, and Legacy in the Second through Fifth Centuries* (co-authored with Amy Brown Hughes; Baker Academic, 2017), *Philippians* in *The Story of God Bible Commentary* (Zondervan, 2013), and *Women in the World of the Earliest Christians* (Baker Academic, 2009).

Scott S. Elliott is Professor in the Department of Philosophy, Religion, and Leadership at Adrian College, Michigan. He is the author of *Reconfiguring Mark's Jesus: Narrative Criticism after Poststructuralism* (Sheffield Phoenix, 2011) and *The Rustle of Paul: Autobiographical Narratives in Romans, Corinthians, and Philippians* (T&T Clark, 2020), and co-editor of *Bible and Theory: Essays in Biblical Interpretation in Honor of Stephen D. Moore* (Lexington/Fortress Academic, 2020). His work centers on literary readings of biblical writings and on popular adaptations of biblical material in novels, comics, and film.

Rachelle Gilmour is Bromby Associate Professor of Old Testament at Trinity College, University of Divinity (Melbourne, Australia). She is author of *Divine Violence in the Book of Samuel* (Oxford University Press, 2021), *Juxtaposition and the Elijah Cycle* (T&T Clark, 2014), and *Representing the Past: A Literary Analysis of Narrative Historiography in the Book of Samuel* (Brill, 2011). She is also editor, with Mark G. Brett, of *Political Theologies in the Hebrew Bible* (Brill Schönigh, 2023) and is currently preparing a commentary on 1 Samuel 1–15 for the International Exegetical Commentary on the Old Testament/Internationaler Exegetischer Kommentar zum Alten Testament series (Kohlhammer).

Laura Carlson Hasler is Assistant Professor of Religious Studies and Jewish Studies and holds the Alvin H. Rosenfeld Chair in Hebrew Bible at Indiana University Bloomington. She is the author of *Archival Historiography in Jewish Antiquity* (Oxford University Press, 2020). She is currently writing a monograph on theories of divine violence and economics in the postexilic prophets.

Cameron B. R. Howard is Associate Professor of Old Testament at Luther Seminary in St. Paul, Minnesota. She is the author of *The Old Testament for a Complex World: How the Bible's Dynamic Testimony Points to New Life for the Church* (Baker Academic, 2021) and is a frequent contributor to WorkingPreacher.org. Her research interests include the political backgrounds of the Hebrew Bible and the biblical ethics of work.

Carmen Joy Imes is Associate Professor of Old Testament at Biola University in Southern California. She is the author of *Bearing YHWH's Name at Sinai: A Reexamination of the Name Command of the Decalogue* (Eisenbrauns, 2018), *Bearing God's Name: Why Sinai Still Matters* (IVP, 2019), and *Being God's Image: Why Creation Still Matters* (IVP, 2023), and the editor of *Praying the Psalms with Augustine and Friends* (TUMI, 2020). Her passion is to make the Old Testament more accessible to modern readers. To this end, she speaks, blogs, appears on podcasts, and creates videos for her YouTube channel.

Marian Kelsey is Teaching Associate in Hebrew Bible at the University of Nottingham. She researches the interrelationship of text, belief, and community in the formation of the biblical texts, both in the historical context of the ancient Near Eastern world and in their legacy in contemporary Western culture. She is particularly interested in inner-biblical allusion, literary motifs, and biblical reception in art and literature.

Adriane Leveen is Senior Lecturer in Hebrew Bible at Hebrew Union College–Jewish Institute of Religion, having previously taught at Stanford University. Her books include *Biblical Narratives of Israelites and Their Neighbors: Strangers at the Gate* (Routledge, 2017) and *Memory and Tradition in the Book of Numbers* (Cambridge University Press, 2008). She has published in a number of scholarly journals, including *Prooftexts, Journal for the Study of the Old Testament*, and the *Harvard Theological Review*. Her passions include teaching biblical prophets and the book of Job. She is co-founder of Jewish Climate Action Network NYC, Bronx Jews for Climate Change, and facilitates JTREE

USA. Professor Leveen is married to Dr. Arnold Eisen, Chancellor Emeritus of the Jewish Theological Seminary.

Tremper Longman III is Distinguished Scholar and Professor Emeritus of Biblical Studies at Westmont College. He has authored and co-authored more than thirty books, including a commentary on the book of Genesis. His earliest writings include works on literary theory and methodology, including *Literary Approaches to Biblical Interpretation* (Zondervan, 1987), a subject to which he has recently returned with *The Old Testament as Literature: Foundations for Christian Interpretation* (Baker Academic, 2024). Tremper lives in Alexandria, Virginia, with his wife Alice and near his three sons and their families, including six granddaughters.

Matthew J. Lynch is Associate Professor of Old Testament at Regent College in Vancouver. He is the author of *Flood and Fury: Old Testament Violence and the Shalom of God* (IVP Academic, 2023), *First Isaiah and the Disappearance of the Gods* (Eisenbrauns, 2021), *Portraying Violence in the Hebrew Bible: A Literary and Cultural Study* (Cambridge University Press, 2020), and *Monotheism and Institutions in the Book of Chronicles* (Mohr Siebeck, 2014). Matt is a founder and co-host of the OnScript and Biblical World podcasts.

Kara J. Lyons-Pardue is Professor of New Testament at Point Loma Nazarene University in San Diego, California. She is the author of *Gospel Women and the Long Ending of Mark* in the Library of New Testament Studies (T&T Clark, 2020). She co-edited and contributed to a collection of essays called *Following Jesus: Prophet, Priest, King* (The Foundry, 2018). At present, she is writing a commentary on Mark's Gospel for the Commentaries for Christian Formation series with Eerdmans.

Raj Nadella is the Samuel A. Cartledge Associate Professor of New Testament at Columbia Theological Seminary. He is the author of *Dialogue Not Dogma: Many Voices in the Gospel of Luke* (Bloomsbury, 2011) and co-editor of *Christianity and the Law of Migration* (Routledge, 2021). He is currently co-editing the *Oxford Handbook of Bible, Race and Diaspora*. His work has appeared in publications such as WorkingPreacher.org, Sojourners and the *Huffington Post*.

Elizabeth E. Shively is Professor of Christian Scriptures at Baylor University's Truett Seminary. For eleven years formerly, she taught New Testament at the University of St. Andrews (Scotland). She is the author of *Apocalyptic Imagination in the Gospel of Mark: The Literary and Theological Role of Mark 3:22–30* (De Gruyter, 2012) and is currently preparing a monograph on Gospel genre for Oxford University Press, a theology of Mark for Cambridge University Press, and a commentary on the Gospel of Mark for the NIGTC series (Eerdmans).

Matthew L. Skinner is Professor of New Testament at Luther Seminary in Saint Paul, Minnesota. His teaching and writing attends to questions about how biblical writings conveyed, interpreted, and shaped people's theological ideas in their ancient contexts. He is currently writing a commentary on the Acts of the Apostles and has already published two books on Acts for general audiences: *Intrusive God, Disruptive Gospel: Encountering the Divine in the Book of Acts* (Brazos, 2015) and *Acts: Catching Up with the Spirit* (Abingdon, 2020). He is also the author of *A Companion to the New Testament* (three volumes; Baylor University Press, 2017–18).

Tyler Smith has been a postdoctoral fellow at the University of Ottawa and the University of Salzburg since completing his PhD at Yale in 2016. He is the author of *The Fourth Gospel and the Manufacture of Minds in Ancient Historiography, Biography, Romance, and Drama* (Brill, 2019) and has published a number of articles on narrative and cognition in Greco-Jewish and early Christian literature.

Introduction

The State of the Art of Biblical Narrative

KEITH BODNER

Among the most innovative and dynamic fields of study in recent days is the analysis of biblical narrative. Using a number of literary methodologies and approaches, the lengthy narrative sections of the Hebrew Bible and the New Testament have been subject to fresh appraisal in recent decades, with impressive results. Not so long ago, historically orientated and form-critical approaches were the dominant paradigm, and a majority of questions posed by scholars were related to matters such as identifying sources, sifting through layers of redactional sediment, or hypothesizing about the diachronic development of various biblical texts. In part a reaction, but also something of a recovery operation, scholars and interested professionals of late have steadily been advocating a renewed appreciation for the intrinsic literary power of these ancient stories. With compelling plots, deft characterization, and an array of subtle and often sophisticated literary techniques, biblical narrative has an appeal that even moves beyond traditional faith communities and contributes to other forms of intellectual discourse and the study of cultural history. In the field of comparative literature, the Bible has a place alongside the great classics of the university curriculum, further enhancing an interest in the poetics of biblical narrative. Consequently, the study of Hebrew Bible and New Testament narrative has evolved into much more than a recovery operation or a protest movement, and its own set of approaches has generated a host of new perceptions and ways of reading that are increasingly commending themselves to different kinds of audiences.

This *Cambridge Companion* is a user-friendly resource for appreciating the world of biblical narrative and showcases some of the fine scholarship that is currently available in the field. Several other volumes in this series focus exclusively on methods and history of interpretation or as introductions to various sections of the Bible. By contrast, the emphasis in this collection both lies in textual analysis and close readings that illustrate the workings of biblical narrative and gives examples of what narrative criticisms look like, along with an appraisal of the kinds of interpretive questions that are germane to the study of literary prose. It should be acknowledged that many commentaries in major series (such as the Old Testament Library and New Testament Library, Yale Anchor Bible, Hermeneia, and even the International Critical Commentary) increasingly utilize insights drawn from narrative criticism. Consequently, this volume helps to show how the study of narrative – with its unique emphases on the development of character, modulations in point of view, voice of the narrator, expository dialogue and oration, temporal indicators, and spatial movements – has influenced recent commentaries and other secondary studies, along with other interpretive trends and approaches currently in practice. An assumption shared by the contributors to this volume is that the literary study of biblical narrative is a complementary approach from which other methodologies and reading strategies can variously benefit. It is therefore envisioned that this *Cambridge Companion* will be a useful resource for working scholars and for anyone seeking an informed and up-to-date appraisal of how the study of narrative can be used alongside different modes of inquiry.

A feature of this volume is that the narratives of the Hebrew Bible and the New Testament are treated together. Most introductory works separate the two, and there are practical reasons for such a division. But because there are numerous points of continuity (as well as some creative divergences), approaching the New Testament narratives more organically and in continuity with the Hebrew antecedents has a certain value for the reader. Although treating the two Testaments (written in different languages, centuries apart) is not without its challenges, there are enough advantages to outweigh the obstacles. Even indirect analysis can underscore how New Testament narrative utilizes many similar literary techniques, and this illuminating area of study merits further discussion down the road. Furthermore, instead of a series of topical chapters dealing with matters such as characterization, point of view, irony, or spatial settings, in this volume the essays are organized around books of the Bible in roughly canonical order. Such a structure has some obvious strengths, as there is at least a degree of familiarity and ease of reference for the reader. Also, various topics can be addressed (whether *plot dynamics* in Genesis, *ironic reversal* in Exodus, or *character development* in the books of Samuel) as they actually appear in the unfolding of the text. Whatever the drawbacks of this kind of treatment, it nonetheless facilitates an awareness of the macroplot of the larger story into which the numerous books have been gathered. Recent narrative study of the Bible has fostered a renewed appreciation of this larger storyline with all of its intricacy and artfulness, and this volume aims to reflect such advances and share that vibrancy with new generations of readers.

A natural place to start is in the beginning, for in many ways the book of Genesis sets the literary tone to come. The first eleven chapters narrate the beginnings of the cosmos and humanity and lead to the dispersal at the Tower of Babel, and then chapters 12–50 recount childless Abraham and Sarah's sojourn from Ur of the Chaldeans to the land of Canaan where there is an astonishing divine promise of land and offspring, followed in due course by the vicissitudes of the Jacob cycle and the account of Joseph sold as a slave into Egypt with its surprising denouement. The opening essay in Chapter 1 by Tremper Longman III functions as a synopsis of literary analysis of biblical narrative in general, and the book of Genesis in particular, featuring engagement with some prominent scholars (Robert Alter, Meir Sternberg, Jan P. Fokkelman, David Clines, and Adele Berlin, among others) and a useful discussion of how the study of narrative poses alternative questions to other historical-critical kinds of approaches. The story of creation is inaugurated with a divine word that mitigates chaos, before moving to the spatial setting of the garden in the east and the tantalizing introduction of the serpent. Longman reflects on the early portrayals of humanity and the major events of fratricide, flood, and the founding narrative of the city of Babylon (Babel), which looms large in the later plot. He notes that the form of the story is significant, for the reader is shown not only the consequences of sin, but also God's efforts toward restoration. Such themes continue with the migration of Abraham, the marriage of Isaac and Rebekah, Jacob's displacement from and return to Canaan, and the final images of a coffin in Egypt that calls out for a sequel.

Turning the page from Genesis, the initial sentences in the book of Exodus report the exponential growth of the Israelites in the land of Egypt, yet matters take an ominous turn as the people are enslaved by an unnamed new king. The divine promise in Genesis is thus imperiled, but in due course the reader encounters the birth of a child who will play a key role in the forthcoming storyline. A series of signs and wonders occurs in the land of Egypt, events that are a preface to the miraculous rescue that sets in motion the movement to Mount Sinai where laws of covenant are received along with instructions for building a sanctuary of worship for the liberated community. In Chapter 2, Adriane Leveen offers an overview of Exodus and focuses attention on several important facets of the text, including the complex career of Moses (starting with his infancy as he is saved from the waters of the

Nile by an ark, prefiguring his role in delivering the nation through the waters of the Red Sea). Leveen also invites the reader to wonder if the legal and tabernacle sections of Exodus are crafted with more literary artistry than is often supposed, and her analysis of the golden calf debacle has implications for interpreting the people of Israel as a collective character.

Navigating the wilderness narrative before and after Mount Sinai poses a number of challenges. The serious obstacles for the Israelites in this stretch of the story include a scarcity of resources in a foreboding desert, an array of military antagonists, as well as their own doubts, lack of resolve, and conflicted longings to return to Egypt rather than press on toward the land of Canaan. In Chapter 3, Carmen Joy Imes explores a large section of text – parts of Exodus, Leviticus, and Numbers – starting with a statistical reminder than only thirteen percent of the Torah takes place in Canaan, and so travel is an important motif. Along this road the reader encounters some strange places, intriguing characters, and memorable events ranging from talking donkeys and fiery snakes to water from a rock and rebels who are swallowed up by the earth. It turns out that wandering through the wilderness with various campsites and the tent of meeting is actually prime real estate for literary analysis, and Imes suggests that there is a more organized structure in this material than might be expected.

The books of Joshua and Judges recount the story of Israel in the land of Canaan, replete with options for faithfulness alongside numerous snares and temptations. After the death of Joshua there is no leader of any stature, adding another layer of challenge for the twelve tribes who have been delivered from Egypt and are struggling to take possession of their inheritance. In Chapter 4, Cameron B. R. Howard notes an essential coherence of the long narrative in this next phase of the biblical text: "A storyline can be traced through the Pentateuch and into these so-called 'historical books,' a roughly chronological account of ancient Israel that continues right through Joshua and Judges and carries on into 1 and 2 Samuel and 1 and 2 Kings, ending with an account of the destruction of Jerusalem and exile of Judah to Babylon." In her treatment of Joshua, she comments on the figure of Joshua himself, the theme of border crossing, and the remarkable characterization of Rahab, the Jericho prostitute who hides the two spies and misleads the king before cutting a deal to survive along with her family. Judges contains some gruesome accounts, but also some highly nuanced literary art, and Cameron's essay includes analysis of the shades of ambiguity in the infamous relationship between Samson and Delilah.

A controversial turning point in Israel's political history is the request for a king in 1 Samuel 8, a decision that casts its shadow over the remainder of the nation's tenure in the land. In Chapter 5, Stephen B. Chapman illustrates how the events before and after this decision are powerfully rendered on the narrative canvas of 1 and 2 Samuel. In the wake of the prophet Samuel, whose birth-story and career as a judge frame the request for a king, Chapman probes the two pivotal figures who dominate the landscape in quite different ways. Saul of Benjamin has undoubted potential, but his volatile reign poses awkward questions about how someone chosen by God can experience such a disastrous royal tenure. David of Judah rises to prominence amidst popular acclaim (and is perhaps the first rock star in world literature), but his reign is later engulfed by the flames of civil war and the virtual implosion of his house. Yet God has promised that David's house will endure, although that promise is sorely tested in the multi-voiced book of Samuel and beyond. Chapman concludes by returning to the beginning ("The Samuel narrative is one of the Bible's greatest literary achievements, a cornerstone of Western civilization, and a crucial scriptural text for the Christian tradition"), as he offers a few examples of the effect of these stories – with all their imaginative freight and rich artistry – on both faith communities and wider culture.

The consolidation and wealth of the Solomonic empire is the primary focus in the early chapters of Kings. But as Rachelle Gilmour notes in Chapter 6, despite the impressive achievements and construction of the Jerusalem temple during Solomon's administration, the ominous threat of exile can nonetheless be discerned even at early points in his reign: "The contrast between the glory and splendour of King Solomon's succession and reign at the beginning of the book of Kings and the 'exile' or captivity of King Jehoiachin by the Babylonians at the end," she writes, "points to one of the central themes of the book: the collapse of the monarchy descended from the line of David." Gilmour's synthesis of 1 and 2 Kings considers not only some of the major players (Jeroboam, Ahab, Manasseh, and Josiah) and events (the division of the kingdom, Assyrian demolition, and Babylonian siege of Jerusalem) in the book of Kings, but also some of the minor episodes and interludes that suggest that exile is not the end of the Israelite story. The final lines of 2 Kings 25 describe the survival of Jehoiachin, a Davidic heir previously taken into captivity but released by the Babylonian monarch who gives him a seat at the royal table in an ironic twist on David's own succession of Saul in the distant past.

A pair of short stories provide an opportunity for the reader to study narrative poetics on a smaller canvas, and in Chapter 7 Marian Kelsey surveys some literary issues in the books of Ruth and Jonah. First, a host of intriguing issues arise in the journey of Ruth from her nation of Moab to the land of Judah, including the role of direct speech, the motif of famine, allusive echoes to the story of Tamar in Genesis 38 and other ancestral episodes, and the ethnic hostilities that fester at the margins of this narrative. Kelsey reveals shades of comparison and contrast at the heart of Ruth's profile in the story. Second, the book of Jonah affords an opportunity for the literary interpreter to probe the fantastic portraits of the king of Nineveh and the great fish, the technique of delayed exposition, the role of the psalmic collage in chapter 2, and the ambiguous conclusion in the book's final sentence. The Jonah narrative also features intertextual conversations with other prophetic texts, and Kelsey suggests that this sequence of allusions "function together to illustrate Jonah's failure to assume the normal roles of a prophet, especially the roles of intercession and warning. In turn, the use of the allusions in Jonah creates a lens through which the reader then views the earlier stories: the reader understands the earlier stories differently in light of the book of Jonah."

The Babylonian invasion of Jerusalem in 586 BC left an indelible mark on the people of Israel, with the destruction of the temple and traumatic deportation that followed in its wake (2 Kings 25; cf. Jeremiah 52). Deep in the spatial and temporal settings of exile, the books of Esther and Daniel both manifest a high degree of narrative aesthetics, albeit, as Laura Carlson Hasler delineates in Chapter 8, in varying ways from other materials seen so far in the Hebrew Bible. The story of Esther takes place against the opulent backdrop of the Persian court, with a satirical portrait of the mighty Xerxes, and in the figure of Haman a complex allusion to the ancient grudge of Israel versus the Amalekites in the days of the Exodus can be glimpsed. If the book of Esther presents a vision of the subversion of imperial power – all without any overt mention of divine involvement – then the book of Daniel unfolds a series of episodes where younger Judahites participate in similarly risky enterprises. Replete with echoes of earlier narratives and rich with dialogue and miraculous surprise, the first half of the book sets the stage for a series of visions that radically depict the rise and fall of empires and eventual triumph of the disenfranchised. In Hasler's discussion, the reader can witness the several traditions and variant texts that indicate a vigorous interpretive wrestling as these stories developed and were used by different reading communities.

At first glance, 1 and 2 Chronicles may not seem to be the most fertile site for literary analysis, and the fact that it starts with the most extensive and exhausting genealogy in the Bible may not be overly appealing to some contemporary audiences. Its placement in the Christian Bible immediately following 2 Kings poses another problem, as some readers might demur that the Chronicler repeats lengthy sections of Israel's royal history while excluding the more salacious bits, such as the adulterous scandals, the murderous mayhem, and the prophetic intrigues of Samuel and Kings. But as the last book of the Hebrew Bible, Chronicles has its own artistic repertoire, with its selective retelling of stories heard elsewhere in the Bible, particular focus on the Jerusalem temple as the virtual center of the world, and unique emphases on speeches of foreign rulers and structural patterns of exile and return. In Chapter 9, Matthew J. Lynch reflects on a renewed interest in the storytelling techniques of Chronicles, concluding that these last books of the Hebrew Bible present a complex work of narrative art: "Appreciating its literary merits requires us to set aside some of our modern expectations about how a good story begins, how it proceeds, and how it retells. Chronicles *begins* with a long genealogy, one that asks us to share the joy of 'all Israel' as they find their place among God's people and the nations, and to anticipate some of the key themes and emphases in Chronicles (e.g., worship and the promises to David's house)."

Turning to the New Testament, what kinds of narrative-critical readings of the book of Matthew have been undertaken in the past, and what avenues can be further explored in the days ahead? In the past, literary interpreters have been drawn to significant episodes in the book and intrigued by the types of names included in the opening genealogy, the visit of Magi from the east, fulfilment of oracles from Israel's prophetic tradition, temptation in the wilderness and the Sermon on the Mount, parables of hidden treasure and moments of transfiguration, along with the layers of conflict and opposition en route to the centripetal and climactic passion narrative. In Chapter 10, Scott S. Elliott compares the literary milieu of Matthew with the other three Gospels, and provides a helpful overview of recent narratological approaches to this first book of the New Testament and its contours: "upon closer inspection, one finds in it a different sort of narrative. It is a narrative that is deeply infused with Jewish storytelling techniques, and reflects an image of early followers of Jesus characterized by a particular way of reading, interpreting, and understanding the Old Testament in relation to Jesus and vice versa, one that embodies and enacts a certain sense of divine presence and of time." There are a number of elements within the gospel genre that are unique to Matthew, unfolding a portrait of Jesus as the fulfillment of the Davidic promise amidst rejection and misunderstanding.

Probably the earliest of the four canonical Gospels, the book of Mark is also the shortest, but it has a range of fascinating interpretive issues for the narrative critic, such as: the abrupt beginning with the tapestry of prophetic quotations and baptism by the Jordan, the sense of immediacy that pervades the early chapters, the motif of secrecy, and the technique of intercalation (that is, when a narrative unit is split by inserting another scene or episode, often with an ensemble of minor characters). Moreover, a freight of intertextual echoes conveys the impression that a new exodus is at hand, and the lengthy flashback sequence of Herod's alarm in Mark 6 has been a notable scene for narrative analysis. Of particular interest to literary theorists is the mysterious sense of an ending in 16:8: "So they went out and fled from the tomb, for terror and amazement had seized them, and they said nothing to anyone, for they were afraid." In Chapter 11, Elizabeth E. Shively and Kara J. Lyons-Pardue reflect on this fear factor and emotive register as part of Mark's literary enterprise, demonstrating how this thematic thread is woven into the larger narrative tapestry. They further consider the material in 16:9–20, and their concluding words are as provocative as the ending(s) to the narrative itself: "both ancient and modern audiences may share in the implications of Mark's key challenge, which is that the good news of Jesus's resurrection is to be met not with emotions that generate unbelief and inaction, but with emotions that elicit reverence, belief, and proclamation."

The story in Luke begins with a night shift in the Jerusalem temple and ends with a communion meal hosted by the risen Jesus after a journey to the otherwise obscure village of Emmaus. Addressed to a recipient with a Greek name, Theophilus, the book of Luke is the longest document in the New Testament, and presumably addressed to a predominantly Gentile audience. But by commencing the narrative with a supernatural encounter in the Jerusalem temple, the book of Luke shows (rather than tells) how the arrival of the Messiah is a story of atonement and reconciliation with implications for both the people of Israel and all of humanity. In Chapter 12, Raj Nadella provides an overview and wider perspective as "Luke deftly weaves in narrative elements from Greco-Roman literary traditions but also presents the gospel narrative as a historical account contemporaneous with Roman history in ways that have theological implications." He then moves in for a close-up on the pivotal section in Luke 10–19 that is sometimes referred to as *the gospel for outsiders*, the centerpiece of which is the parable in 15:11–31 of a father with two sons. Luke has a number of unique parables, such as the mercy of a Samaritan to a wounded victim on the side of the road, and a rich guy clothed in purple who ignores a needy person at his gate. But Nadella's analysis of the parable of the prodigal sons inquires how the history of Israel – with the tropes of inheritance, rebellion, exile in a distant land, and chastised restoration – might be refracted through the lens of this story located in the multi-layered middle section of the book of Luke.

By most accounts, the book of John is the last of the Gospels to have been written, and in recent years there has been lots of literary interest in the prologue with its binaries of light and darkness, allusions to the wilderness in the Nicodemus dialogue, the Samaritan women and the type-scene of the woman at the well familiar from the Hebrew Bible (e.g., Genesis 29; Exodus 2), and the portrayal of Peter's threefold denial and restoration. In terms of structure, commentators frequently draw attention to the seven "I am" statements and prominent feasts such as Passover or Tabernacles. Furthermore, it is variously argued that there are seven signs in the first half of the book that include events like feeding the multitude (with memories of manna in the desert) and walking on water. What is the purpose of these signs, and how do they contribute to the overall configuration of the story? In Chapter 13, Tyler Smith discusses the complexity of John's sign language, noting that in Cana of Galilee "the actual transformation of water into wine is not emphasized; instead, John emphasizes what leads up to and what follows from the sign," and the equivocation of the parents of the man born blind when they are confronted by the authorities. Smith remarks, "Although the Johannine signs never seem to elicit the ideal belief response hoped for in the gospel's purpose statement – those who come to belief almost without exception go on to show shortcomings in their understanding of Jesus – they are nevertheless a key dynamic in the interplay between Jesus and those to whom he reveals himself." The reader is thus challenged to consider these signs as part of a drama of belief that is at work in this narrative.

Similar to Luke's prologue, the book of Acts is addressed to Theophilus, and it seems reasonable to assume that Acts is the sequel. In Chapter 14, Matthew L. Skinner surveys the unique story of Acts that traverses vast distances and diverse cultural settings: "Not only does the book tell a geographically expansive tale, but it also brings a wide spectrum of people onto the narrative stage: as Jesus' followers follow his command to bear witness to him near and far, they encounter nameless people who rely on begging to survive and powerful Roman officials, zealous converts and insidious apostates, a seamstress and a fabric dealer, virtuous military officers and violent mobs, as well as audiences both superstitious and sophisticated. The sheer scope and variation within the plot mark Acts as a complex story that rewards those who interpret it with attention to its narrative dynamics." In the course of Skinner's analysis, numerous questions might arise in a reader's mind. For instance, is *persecution* a primary mechanism that drives the plot of Acts? Should it be approached as a classic underdog story, for how can a tiny and beleaguered group share a message that eventually reaches the imperial city of Rome in the closing verses of the last chapter? How should the conversion of Saul of Tarsus be interpreted, and how might the various minor characters (such as Gamaliel, the Ethiopian eunuch, Philip the evangelist, Gallio the proconsul of Achaia, or King Agrippa and his sister Bernice) be assessed from a literary viewpoint? Indeed, the open-ended conclusion of the story invites ongoing reflection on this expansive narrative.

To what degree can a story be reconstructed from the letters of Paul, and can such a story be subject to narrative-critical analysis? As a corollary, to what extent can stories within the letters be extracted and interpreted? When thinking about the application of literary tools to the Pauline correspondence, one could consider the issue of Thessalonica. In Acts 17 Paul visits the city for a brief period, where there is violence and hostility, and the reader may imagine that the Thessalonian believers merely drift from the scene. But when reading Paul's letter to this same group, it appears rather that they have flourished and have become a model for communities throughout the region. In Chapter 15, Lynn H. Cohick carefully outlines a theoretical framework that considers several different viewpoints, and then uses Paul's letter to the Philippians as an example. When hearing the letter against the backdrop of Acts 16, Cohick concludes that we "discover a shared story, and Paul's views of events that shaped both their paths. As readers today, we reconstruct that story to better understand Paul's message. Paul's letters make sense within the larger narrative of God's purposes told in the Jewish Scriptures, in creation and the promised new creation, and most assuredly in the Christ story. The meta-narrative of God's redemptive work in the world through Christ includes several substories that animate Paul's letters."

The book of Revelation has exercised enormous cultural influence, and from the outset a great story is promised: an imprisoned leader of the early Christian movement on the island of Patmos receives a visit by *one with eyes like blazing fire and the ruler of the kings of the earth*, who commissions him to write seven letters before unveiling a kaleidoscopic vision with universal import. Is this text the exclusive domain of dooms-day speculators with an eschatological abacus, or can Revelation be read as a narrative, and if so, what are some of the central literary features that the reader confronts in the book? In Chapter 16, David L. Barr reads the Bible's last book for its plot, and notes, "Narrative criticism seeks to consider consciously how the action is presented, how the characters are portrayed, how the storyteller is portrayed, how those who hear the story are imagined, how the time of the events in the story is measured, how the setting is located in space, how the story begins and ends, and much more." Suffused with allusions and images derived from the Garden of Eden, dreams of Daniel, and schematics of Ezekiel's temple, and pop-ulated with rebooted characters like Balaam and Jezebel, Barr samples recent studies of Revelation that have explored the question of whether an overarching narrative arc can be discerned: "Read as a narrative, the Apocalypse of John invites us to listen in on a hidden world – one far distant from ordinary reality. It is a world of monsters and mayhem, bloodied Lambs and spotless brides, of worlds vanquished and of worlds created anew. The full force of this narrative is best felt in an oral pre-sentation, wherein the audience re-experiences John's visions." Readers are confronted with a fresh possibility that, instead of a straight-line progression, there is a spiral-shaped or even a spherical plot at work, as doors of perception are opened and Revelation can be viewed as a majes-tic coda to the biblical story.

As a collection, the essays in this *Cambridge Companion* provide a glimpse of the kind of work on biblical narrative that is available today, along with an introduction to the diverse forms and repertoire of tech-niques used by a cadre of ancient writers across spectrums of time and place. There is an invitation for both new readers and seasoned veter-ans to attend to questions of how a plot is developed, shades of indirect characterization through voice inflection or posture, nuances of dialogue that darken or illuminate scenes that are fraught with background, shifts in spatial landscapes or temporal horizons, ironic overtures and the gen-eration of suspense, variations in point of view, intertextual echoes, and unfinalized endings that combine to provide a virtually inexhaustible literary experience. Vast stretches of narrative have not been treated in this volume, implying that there is much more that can be done in the future. By assembling this group of scholarly voices on various sections of a sprawling text, we hope to have offered a useful conversation about the imaginative depths and sophistication of biblical narrative.

1 The Literary Worlds of Genesis

TREMPER LONGMAN III

Few books have been the subject of more literary reflection and analysis than the book of Genesis. Genesis plots the story of the beginning of the cosmos, the earth, humanity, God's elect people, and more, spanning the time from creation through the account of the founding ancestors of later Israel (Abraham, Isaac, and Jacob) and ending with Joseph and his eleven brothers, who will provide a bridge to the continuing narrative of the founding of the people of Israel (Exodus) and beyond.

A literary approach to Hebrew narrative did not begin with Robert Alter's pivotal book *The Art of Biblical Narrative*,[1] but certainly the argument can be made that his work energized and motivated a transition from an obsession with historical approaches to concern for the final form of the text.[2] Alter used passages from Genesis more than any other book to illustrate the artistic quality of biblical narrative.[3] Examples of point of view, characterization, management of dialogue, type scenes, and more drawn from the book of Genesis pepper Alter's work. Other pioneering students of biblical narrative also found themselves attracted to the book of Genesis, including Meir Sternberg, J. P. Fokkelman, and Adele Berlin.[4] While some believed that biblical studies was experiencing a paradigm shift away from historical (diachronic)

---

[1] Robert Alter, *The Art of Biblical Narrative* (New York: Basic Books, 2011 [orig. 1981]).

[2] The case can also be made that for a period of about a decade and a half (1980–1995), the almost monolithic focus on historical approaches turned into a monolithic focus on the final form. For a while it seemed as if every book had the word "literary" or equivalent in the title.

[3] As confirmed by a look at his "Bible Reference Index." Alter, *The Art of Biblical Narrative*, 251–53.

[4] Meir Sternberg, *The Poetics of Biblical Narrative: Ideological Literature and the Drama of Reading* (Bloomington: Indiana University Press, 1985); J. P. Fokkelman, *Narrative Art in Genesis: Specimens of Stylistic and Structural Analysis* (Sheffield: JSOT Press, 1991; J. P. Fokkelman, "Genesis," in *The Literary Guide to the Bible*, eds. Robert Alter and Frank Kermode (Cambridge, MA: Harvard University Press, 1987), 36–65; Adele Berlin, *Poetics and Interpretation of Biblical Narrative* (Sheffield: Almond Press, 1983). Mention should also be made of M. Fishbane, *Biblical Text and*

interests in the text and toward literary (synchronic) ones, eventually the field realized that the two interests were not mutually exclusive. Today, insights drawn from literary studies are often embedded in commentary and exposition of the text along with the results of other approaches, including historical critical/grammatical analysis.

Still, there is great value in studies that for heuristic purposes bracket, without denying, the diachronic dimension of a narrative text like Genesis to explore the literary strategy of its final form. That is the purpose of the present chapter, though our goal must be modest considering space constraints. Considering the literary riches of the narratives of Genesis, even a large monograph would be insufficient to present the literary qualities of the book, so we will settle here for an overview of the shifting nature of the different parts of the book, indicating the subtle changes in characterization, point of view, setting, theme, and more, while also noting the coherence of the plot of the book as it moves from creation to the death of Joseph. Our description will allow for occasional, brief looks at specific passages.

The overall plot of Genesis moves along largely chronological lines (*sujet* and *fabula* roughly the same,[5] though there are exceptions to that observation). Nonetheless, there are significant differences of narrative style between the various major sections of the book. Some scholars describe only two major sections, the primeval history (Gen. 1–11) and the story of the ancestors, combining the Joseph story with that of Abraham, Isaac, and Jacob (Gen. 12–50). We will see, however, that in terms of narrative style there is enough difference between the accounts of the three ancestors and Joseph to encourage us to speak of three major parts. But before entering into discussion of the three, we need to recognize and address two preliminary issues: the composite nature of the book of Genesis and the role of the *toledot* formula in providing an alternative structure to the book.

The narrative of Genesis may be approached by two different literary strategies, one often called diachronic and the other synchronic. A diachronic study seeks to tease out the literary sources that preceded the

Texture: A Literary Reading of Selected Texts (New York: Schocken Books, 1979), where half the book provides literary case studies from the book of Genesis.
5   The terms come from Russian Formalism (see M. Sternberg, *Expositional Modes and Temporal Ordering in Fiction* [Bloomington: Indiana University Press, 1978]). *Fabula* refers to the "chronological or chronological-causal" sequence of the "raw material" of the story, while the *sujet* is "the actual disposition and articulation of these narrative motifs in the particular finished product" of the story (p. 8).

present final form of the book as we have it today.[6] Utilizing various criteria (different names for God, doublets, double-naming, different theological emphases), source critics detect fissures or gaps in the narrative that they believe allow one to separate the earlier sources from one another. Certainly the best known, though certainly not the only, of these diachronic approaches is the Documentary Hypothesis, first popularized by Julius Wellhausen,[7] various versions of which are still debated today among scholars. Perhaps the most confident and widely held conclusion of this type of study separates a later P (Priestly) document from an earlier non-Priestly document, sometimes divided into a J (Yahwist) source and an E (Elohist) source.[8]

As opposed to a diachronic study of the narrative of Genesis, a synchronic study reads the text as we have it before us, not in an earlier more hypothetical form. In such a study, a fissure or gap or tension in the text, while conceivably the result of bringing together different sources produced at different time periods and/or by different writers, now becomes a gap to be either filled by the interpreter or left in tension.

Some have argued that the mere ability to provide a reasonable narrative interpretation of the final form of the text renders the diachronic project not only speculative, but also wrong-minded. After all, if the different sequence of creation found in Genesis 1:1–2:4a (P) and in Genesis 2:4b–25 (J) can be explained by observing that there are literary or stylistic reasons for the difference and that neither account is interested in giving the "actual" sequence, then what need do we have for a diachronic explanation at all?

However, a rejection of a diachronic study based on a synchronic analysis is premature. Indeed, value can be found in both approaches. While one can imagine not only the discernment of earlier sources but also the synchronic analysis of those sources,[9] this present study is interested only in the analysis of the narrative of Genesis in its final form. Indeed, in his classic study of biblical narrative, Robert Alter, while primarily engaged in a synchronic study, referred to the narrative as "composite."[10]

---

[6]   And these might have derived from even earlier oral traditions.

[7]   Julius Wellhausen, *Prolegomena to the History of Ancient Israel* (Gloucester, MA: Peter Smith, 1983 [or in German in 1883]).

[8]   David M. Carr, *Reading the Fractures of Genesis: Historical and Literary Approaches* (Louisville, KY: Westminster John Knox, 1996).

[9]   Harold Bloom (with D. Rosenberg), *The Book of J* (New York: Grove Weidenfeld, 1990).

[10] Alter, *The Art of Biblical Narrative*, 1131–54, devotes a whole chapter to the topic of "composite artistry."

We will conduct our overview of the narrative of Genesis in three parts: the primeval history (Gen. 1:1–11:26), the ancestor narrative (Gen. 11:27–37:1), and the Joseph story (Gen. 37:2–50:26). Our rationale for this three-part division derives from the different narrative strategies, which we observe and describe later. That said, we want to acknowledge that this is not the only way to structure the book of Genesis. Indeed, an argument can be made that the book itself makes explicit a structure based on the recurring *toledot* formula found throughout the book. Eleven times we encounter the formula "this is the account of x," where x is typically a person's name, though in the first instance we have the "account of the heavens and the earth" (2:4, see also 5:1; 6:9; 10:1; 11:10, 27; 25:12, 19; 36:1, 9; 37:2). Many questions surround the significance and interpretation of these *toledot* formulae, but our only purpose here is to acknowledge that there is more than one way to structure the book as we proceed now to explore the narrative strategy of the primeval history, the ancestor narrative, and the Joseph story.

THE PRIMEVAL HISTORY (GENESIS 1:1–11:26)

In the beginning God created the heavens and the earth. Gen. 1:1

The first sentence of Genesis signals the narrative strategy of the first eleven chapters of the book that in many ways will differentiate it from the following sections.[11] In this first verse, the unnamed narrator who will take us through the book reveals himself as omniscient and omnipresent. The narrator here informs the reader of something that happened at the very beginning of time. As the story progresses, the narrator not only describes the creation of the cosmos, the earth, and its creatures, but does so by telling us what God said to bring it all into functioning order (more about the role of dialogue later).

Third-person omniscient narration is not foreign to even modern secular narrative. In a book like Genesis, and throughout Hebrew narrative where this type of narrative is the norm,[12] it is hard not to think of the narrator as divine. Is God the one telling the story?

---

[11] The well-known debate over whether to translate Genesis 1:1–2 as a single sentence (NRSV) or as two (NIV, NLT, ESV) is not germane to our comments about narrative style.

[12] The so-called memoirs of Ezra (Ezra 7–10; Nehemiah 8–10) and Nehemiah (Nehemiah 1–7 and 11–13) being the obvious and rare exceptions.

That God is also a, or perhaps better, the primary character in the book of Genesis does not, in our opinion, invalidate that conclusion. We will come back to the question of characterization in Genesis 1–11; for now we want to note that the adoption of third-person omniscient narration allows the story to begin before even the creation of the first humans and continue through time. This strategy allows the writer to speak of things that no human being could have experienced or could have learned through their own study or even through the passing down of traditions.

In other words, in Genesis 1–11 the omniscient narrator allows for a cosmic point of view. Indeed, one of the features that will differentiate the primeval history from Genesis 12 and following is the wide-angle lens, to use a camera analogy, with which the narrator tells the story. The whole world is the subject of these stories, in particular those of the creation, the flood, and the Tower of Babel. That does not mean that within this broad scope the narrator cannot focus momentarily on a more limited subject, whether it is Adam and Eve in the garden of Eden (Gen. 2–3), the murder of Abel by Cain (Gen. 4:1–16), or the enigmatic account of the "sons of God" and the "daughters of man" (Gen. 6:1–4). But these stories fit into the broad scope of Genesis 1–11 that has a broad lens as it surveys God's creatures from their creation up until the time of Abraham.

Indeed, the contrast will become apparent at Genesis 11:27 and following, when narrative time dramatically slows as well the narrator's point of view. We will describe this transition more carefully in the next section. That Genesis 1–11 covers such a vast tract of time with such a broad focus not only leaves readers with many questions about which we can only speculate, but may also indicate that these stories are really only, but importantly, background for the next section that begins with the call of Abraham.

When we consider the plot of Genesis 1–11, we first of all start with the recognition that these chapters contain different episodes, with their own plots, that contribute to a bigger plot that continues beyond Genesis 11 and indeed will continue through the rest of the biblical narrative. Again, bracketing historical questions, one can discern a plot that starts in Genesis 1 and continues through the stories of Ezra and Nehemiah.[13]

Genesis 1–2, the account of creation, presents what Sternberg would call "exposition."[14] In spite of their possible separate origins, Genesis

---

[13]   For Christian readers, the plot continues into the New Testament and culminates in the book of Revelation.

[14]   Sternberg, *Expositional Modes*, 1–34.

1 and 2 now stand side by side, and the question is how do these two creation stories relate to each other? One way is to think of Genesis 2 as providing a kind of second telling of creation with a focus on what Genesis 1 claimed happened on Day 6. In any case, at the end of Genesis 2 everything has its proper place in God's creation and the focus of the story, Adam and Eve, live in harmony with God, with each other, and with creation. Indeed, Genesis 1 introduces us for the first of many times to a word that will be thematic in the book of Genesis when we learn that at their creation God "blessed" them (1:22, 28; 5:2). Blessing here indicates this state of being in relationship with God, with all the good benefits that flow from that.

Genesis 3 tells the story of the shattering of that blessed life in the garden. That is, Genesis 3 presents the complication of the plot. By their rebellion against the one command God gave Adam (2:17), Adam and Eve fractured their relationship with God, leading to harm in their relationship with each other and with the rest of creation. In essence, though the term is not used in the chapter, when we see the alienation and fragmentation that are the consequences of this refusal to obey God, we cannot but conclude that the original blessing is now gone.

Even so, as the plot continues, we see that this is not the end of the story. The complication now yearns for resolution. That move toward resolution or reconciliation is signaled in Genesis 3 itself as God provides clothing for Adam and Eve. They are no longer naked and unashamed, but rather than just leaving them in that condition, God provides what has been called a token of grace for them, a signal that God will continue to be in relationship with them.

Indeed, as others have pointed out, the three main stories that follow the account of Adam and Eve's rebellion share the same basic plot. They are stories of sin, judgment, and grace. As Adam and Eve sinned by eating the prohibited fruit, so Cain sinned by killing Abel (4:8), humanity as a whole on the eve of the flood sinned by its pervasive wickedness (6:5), and finally people sinned by gathering together after God had scattered them to build a city with a tower "that reaches to the heavens" (11:4).

In all four stories, this sin is first met by a divine speech announcing judgment (3:14–19 [Adam and Eve]; 4:10–12 [Cain and Abel]; 6:7, 13–21 [Flood]; 11:6–7 [Tower]) and concludes with a description of the execution of that judgment (3:22–24 [Adam and Eve]; 4:16 [Cain and Abel]; 7:6–24 [Flood]; 11:8 [Tower]). The fourth element of these stories are what might be called "tokens of grace," symbols of God's continued involvement with his rebellious creatures. Besides the gift of clothing to Adam and Eve mentioned earlier, these tokens include the mark put on Cain to preserve him from the hostility of others (4:15) and the survival of Noah and his family at the time of the flood (6:8). Interestingly, there appears to be no token of grace in the Tower story. Such a departure from the plot structure of the previous three major stories in Genesis 1–11 attracts our attention, but we will delay our comments on this absence until we come to the transition to the ancestor narratives.

Before going on to other literary features of Genesis 1–11, I want to make an observation that could be repeated throughout, and that is that the way the story is told is not simply a matter of ornamentation. We can appreciate how the narrative unfolds to be sure in and of itself, but we cannot help noticing that how the story is told contributes to its message or meaning. The very structure of these stories has theological significance, in other words. In these chapters, which are a prelude to the ancestor narratives that follow, we learn that humans are recalcitrant sinners, God judges sin consistently, but he also continues to work toward restoration.

Having considered the function of the narrator and point of view as well as plot, we turn our attention now to characterization in Genesis 1–11, and again we will observe both continuity and some discontinuity between these opening chapters and what follows.

The first character to whom we are introduced in Genesis is none other than God, who remains the main character throughout the book. Here we are not so interested in describing God as a character as much as to offer some comments on how God, and indeed other characters, take shape in Hebrew narrative. We will begin with some comments based on Genesis 1 where we are first introduced to God.

First, of course, the narrator controls what we learn about God. Genesis 1 presents God as the one who created "the heavens and the earth." As we read the chapter, we read that he changes a formless watery mass (1:2) to a finished product over a period of six days, after which he rests on the seventh day.

The narrator not only tells the story, but also moves the plot forward and shapes the characters not just through narration per se but by presenting the speech of the characters. Alter spoke of this literary feature of Hebrew narrative as "narration-through-dialogue,"[15]

---

[15]   Alter, *The Art of Biblical Narrative*, 63–87, quote from 69.

and since characterization and plot are integrally combined we could also say "characterization-through dialogue." In Genesis 1, God speaks creation into existence even though there is no one to whom he is said to speak.[16] God's speaking creation into order (e.g., "Let there be light") followed by the narrator's report ("and there was light," 1:3) presents God as the sovereign creator who can command creation into existence.

God is, not surprisingly, the most complex character in Genesis 1–11, but the narrator introduces us to a host of other characters: Adam, Eve, the serpent, Cain, Abel, and Noah among the most notable. While these characters play major roles in their particular episodes, they are not nearly as well developed or rounded as the characters we will encounter later in Genesis, particularly Abraham, Jacob, and Joseph. And as in Hebrew narrative generally, the narrator is spare in presenting physical description and motivation or even in providing evaluation of characters' actions. At times, this lack is due to irrelevance to the story (so when a physical description does appear it must be important to the story and not gratuitous), but at other times the narrator's reticence invites a close reading of the story.

For instance, many readers question why God rejects Cain's sacrifice while accepting Abel's. God's response to Cain's anger, "If you do what is right, will you not be accepted?" (4:7) begs the question what is "right." But an attentive reader will recognize that, while Abel brought a high-quality sacrifice ("fat portions from some of the firstborn of his flock," 4:4), Cain brought an ordinary offering ("some of the fruits of the soil," 4:3). While it is not explicit (the narrator shows rather than tells), the reader can reasonably conclude that the differing quality of their offerings reflects their different attitudes toward God.

We conclude our look at Genesis 1–11 with two examples where the structure of the story reveals that the composer weaves how the story is told with the message of the story. We chose one example from the beginning, the days of creation, and one from the end, the Tower of Babel.

The six days of creation as presented in Genesis 1 have an interesting parallel relationship to each other. The first three days describe the creation of realms of habitation, while the second three creation days describe the inhabitants of those realms. Day four (sun, moon, and stars) fills day one (light and darkness), day five (birds and fish) fills

---

[16] But perhaps we should take note of Genesis 1:26, though who the "us" refers to is a matter of extensive debate.

day two (sky and sea), and day six (animals and humans) fills day three (land), as the following chart indicates:

Day 1	Day 2	Day 3
Light and Darkness	Sky and Sea	Land
Day 4	Day 5	Day 6
Sun, Moon, and Stars	Birds and Fish	Animals and Humans

Observing this structure supports the idea that the composer was likely not interested in giving what was thought to be the actual sequence of creation, but rather knowingly gave a figurative depiction of creation based on the analogy of the work week which ended on the seventh day, a day of rest.

Fokkelman's close reading of the Tower of Babel story (11:1–9) has revealed its intricate design.[17] He begins his study by noting word plays throughout this short episode. Certain word groups are bound together by their similar sound: "let's make bricks" (*nilbĕnâ, lĕbēnîm*); "bake them thoroughly" (*niśrepâ, śĕrēpâ,*); "tar" and "mortar" (*hēmār/hōmer*). There is also an alliteration between "brick" (*lĕbenâ*) and "for stone" (*lĕ'âben*). These nearly similar sounds give the story a rhythmic quality that draws the reader's attention not only to the content of the words but also to the words themselves. Other repeated words also sound alike: "name" (*šēm*), "there/that place" (*šām*), and "heaven" (*šāmayîm*). "The place" (*šām*) is what the rebels use as a base for storming "heaven" (*šāmayîm*) in order to get a "name" (*šēm*) for themselves. God, however, reverses the situation because it is "from there" (11:8) that he disperses the rebels and foils their plans. The ironic reversal of the rebels' evil intentions is highlighted in more than one way by the artistic choice of words. Fokkelman lists the numerous words and phrases that appear in the story with the consonant cluster *lbn*, all referring to the human rebellion against God. When God comes in judgment, he confuses (*nbl*) their language. The reversal of the consonants shows the reversal that God's judgment effected in the plans of the rebels. This reversal is also reflected in Fokkelman's analysis of the chiastic structure of the story (Figure 1.1).

Unity of language (A) and place (B) and intensive communication (C) induce the men to plans and inventions (D), especially to building (E) a city and a tower (F). God's intervention is the turning point (X). He

17   Fokkelman, *Narrative Art in Genesis*, 11–45.

```
A    11:1
   B    11:2
      C    11:3a
         D    11:3b
            E    11:4a
               F    11:4b
                  X    11:5a "But the LORD came down"
               F'    11:5b
            E'    11:5c
         D'    11:6
      C'    11:7
   B'    11:8
A'    11:9
```

Figure 1.1 Chiastic structure of Genesis 11:1–9

watches the buildings (F') people make (E') and launches a counter plan (D'), because of which communication becomes impossible (C') and the unity of place (B') and language (A') is broken.

ANCESTOR NARRATIVES (GENESIS 11:27–37:1)

> I will make you into a great nation,
>   and I will bless you;
> I will make your name great,
>   and you will be a blessing.
> I will bless those who bless you,
>   and whoever curses you I will curse;
> and all peoples on earth
>   will be blessed through you. (Gen. 12:1–3)

The ancestor narratives begin with the *toledot* of Terah (11:27–25:11), which is the story of Abraham and encompasses the *toledot* of Isaac (25:19–35:29),[18] which really focuses on Jacob. Interestingly, there is no *toledot* of Abraham and thus no extended focus on Isaac. Isaac is the least fully developed character among the three patriarchs. He is Abraham's son and Jacob's father; he also serves as a link between the two as he receives the promise from his father and passes it on to his son Jacob.

And it is the promises that Abraham receives from God in 12:1–3, contingent on his going to the land (Canaan) God shows him, that propel the plot of the ancestor narratives. As we mentioned in the previous

---

[18] Though his name is not changed to Abraham from Abram until Genesis 17:5, I will use Abraham throughout.

section, the Tower of Babel story departed from the structural pattern of the previous three episodes in having no token of God's grace, leading to the question whether God was once and for all done with his rebellious human creatures.

God's call to Abraham answers with a definitive no. The primeval history, describing the pervasive sinfulness of humanity, sets the stage for this pivotal moment in the narrative. And, not surprisingly, with this call, narrative time radically slows and the scope of the narrator's interest moves from a focus on the whole world to a focus on one person and those immediately around him. While the previous eleven chapters cover the unspecified, but presumably lengthy, period of time from creation to the time of Abraham, the next twenty-four chapters follow the life of Abraham, beginning when he is seventy-five years old. This retardation of time and expansion of scope signals the significance of Abraham, and that significance is centered on his reception of the promises.

Indeed, as David Clines pointed out years ago, the theme of the ancestor narratives centers on the promises as we follow Abraham's life.[19] Most of the episodes in his life concern his reactions to threats and promises and the fulfillment of these promises. God told Abraham that he would make him a great nation, implying land and many descendants, and that he would bless those descendants, but also "all peoples on earth ... through you" (12:3).

The ancestor narratives, those concerning Abraham as well as Isaac/Jacob, are composed of episodes, relatively short narratives that seem to follow the chronology of their lives, but do not exhibit the type of narrative cohesion of short stories. In this, we can see similarity with the primeval history and a contrast with the Joseph story. Still there is a kind of thematic cohesion to the episodes of the story in that they give different vignettes as they follow whether Abraham responds with faith and trust or with fear and manipulation when it looks like God is not going to follow through on the promises even though Abraham has obeyed him and gone to the land he would show him.

Of course, the main challenge to Abraham's faith in terms of God's willingness or ability to fulfill his promises concerns descendants, which we have suggested is a necessary ingredient for God to make Abraham a "great nation" (12:2). If there were any doubt about that, they are alleviated by the latter promise to make Abraham's descendants as numerous

---

[19] D. J. A. Clines, *The Theme of the Pentateuch*, 2nd edition (Sheffield: JSOT Press, 2002 [orig. 1978]).

"as the sand on the seashore" (22:17; cf. 32:12) or the stars in the heavens (15:5; 22:17; cf. 26:4).

But, of course, to ultimately have numerous offspring, Abraham has to begin with one heir, and he and Sarah do not quickly or even over a long period of time produce an heir. Since Abraham is already seventy-five and was married to Sarah by the time he received the promise, it is possible that he knew she was barren (11:30) and may have received God's promise with hope that she would now give birth. Perhaps, though, it also motivated him (remember that Hebrew narrative often does not give explicit motivations) to bring along Lot, even though God's command included leaving his "father's household" (12:1). In other words, short of producing an heir themselves, Abraham may have thought that his legacy would live through his nephew. If so, we have a good explanation as to why the narrator devotes attention to the fate of Lot.

Even if it is correct to say that Lot plays the role of backup plan, Abraham makes his disappointment known to God after God comes to him to encourage him not to be afraid. Abraham's lack of confidence is displayed through his speech: "Sovereign LORD, what can you give me since I remain childless and the one who will inherit my estate is Eliezer of Damascus? ... You have given me no children; so a servant in my household will be my heir" (15:2–3). In the light of the challenge of Sarah not conceiving, Abraham responds with fear, and his fear leads him to try to manufacture an heir by suggesting that his household servant will serve in that role.[20] In response, God again reaffirms his promises, performing a ritual that underlines his commitment.[21]

While Abraham may have at that time responded with belief, according to the narrator ("Abram believed the LORD, and he credited it to him as righteousness," 15:6), the very next chapter sees Abraham back to his doubting and manipulative ways as he acts on Sarah's suggestion that he sleep with her slave, Hagar, and "build a family through her" (16:2). In response, once again God comes back to reassure Abraham that no,

---

[20] Some evidence exists that in the absence of a child, an aging couple could appoint their household servant an heir so that in return for taking care of them in their dotage, the heir would inherit the property. See M. J. Selman, "Comparative Customs and the Patriarchal Age," in *Essays on the Patriarchal Narratives*, eds. A. Millard and D. J. Wiseman (Winona Lake, IN: Eisenbrauns, 1983), 91–140.

[21] Evidence exists that the ritual of passing through the divided parts of animals was a way of taking a self-maledictory oath that affirmed a person's commitment to follow through on a promise.

the heir Abraham has in mind is not Ishmael, the son of Hagar, but a child born to Sarah (17:16–19).

Divine reassurance of progeny would come again in the context of the story of the judgment on Sodom and Gomorrah, which may also have the purpose of once-and-for-all demonstrating that Lot will not be the heir.[22] Abraham receives three visitors, one of whom is Yahweh, who are on their way to those two wicked cities. As he extends them hospitality, Yahweh reaffirms that Sarah will soon have a son, to which news Sarah laughs, thinking herself and Abraham much too old to conceive (18:10–15). We will return to this episode in connection to other promises shortly.

We can see how narrative tension surrounding the promise of descendants has been building since the beginning of the narrative. Throughout, Abraham has responded with skepticism and doubt as well as manipulative actions to try to fulfill the promise of an heir in other ways than through Sarah. But that tension comes to an apparent resolution a year later, as the divine visitor announced. The birth of a child in Abraham and Sarah's old age is reported briefly and simply, including the fact that Abraham is now one hundred years old (21:1–7). The implication is clear, however; the birth of this child, while the result of natural human conception, could only have taken place as a result of divine intervention.

But what looks like resolution is not one after all. Like the ending of Beethoven's Fifth Symphony, the apparent crescendo does not bring the piece to a close but to more tension before the final resolution.

After a period of some unspecified years, though enough that Isaac has grown at least to adolescence, indirectly indicated by his being able to carry the kindling (22:6), God issues the horrifying command to "take your son, your only son, whom you love – Isaac – and go the region of Moriah. Sacrifice him there as a burnt offering on a mountain I will show you" (22:1). While the narrator relieves some of the readers' anxieties by stating that God is testing Abraham, he does not inform us what Abraham's internal response is to the order. As we have pointed out, this third-person omniscient narrator could have chosen to tell the reader what was in the mind of a character, so we need to ask what is the effect of keeping the reader ignorant. As we read the command followed by a quick and to-the-point description of Abraham's obedience, we can reasonably conclude that the narrator wants us to understand

---

[22]   Laurence A. Turner, *Announcements of Plot in Genesis* (Eugene, OR: Wipf and Stock, 2007), 80–82.

that at this point Abraham has come to utterly trust God and, while modern readers might question the ethics of the story, in the world of the story, this unquestioning obedience is a positive thing. So positive that God reiterates his intention to fulfill his promises to Abraham (22:15–18). Abraham's heir, Isaac, is now firmly in place and ready to inherit the promises upon the death of his father.

The promise that Abraham will father a great nation also implies land, so while the primary focus of the narrative follows the question of heir, land also features. God's command to "go ... to the land I will show you" (12:1) takes him to the promised land. When he arrives there, Canaanites are in the land, but God promises that "to your offspring I will give this land" (12:7). So Abraham journeys from place to place building altars to Yahweh, perhaps to be seen as symbolically and proleptically claiming the land. But a threat of sorts to the land promise arises almost immediately when the promised land is struck by famine. How will Abraham respond to this threat? By heading off to Egypt. Will he go with confidence and faith? No. In a self-protective move, his lying about the status of Sarah puts her (and the promise of descendants) at risk.

The very next episode also has land at the center of its interest. In this case, the crisis arises for a more positive reason. Abraham and Lot have grown so prosperous that they can no longer live in the same vicinity. While Abraham as Lot's uncle and also as the one who received the land promise could have determined the outcome, he does not grasp at the promise but gives Lot the option to choose the land. The narrator forewarns the reader of the later narrative of the destruction of those cities by telling the readers that "this was before the LORD destroyed Sodom and Gomorrah" (13:10). It is difficult to access the narrator's intention when he says that "Abram lived in the land of Canaan, while Lot lived among the cites of the plain" (13:12). Is the intention to imply that Lot purposefully chose to move out of the promised land and thus disqualify himself in the eyes of his uncle as heir?[23] Perhaps. though, the land promise is later defined as including this area (13:14–17).

The land promise surfaces time and again in the remainder of the Abraham narrative. As God reassures Abraham that a natural-born son rather than his household servant will be his heir, he also reaffirms his intention to give them the land in which he now lives as a foreigner (15:7), specifying in more detail than before its scope: "To your descendants I give this land, from the Wadi of Egypt to the great river, the

---

[23]   The position of Turner, *Announcements of Plot*, 67.

Euphrates – the land of the Kenites, Kenizzites, Kadmonites, Hittites, Perizzites, Rephaites, Amorites, Canaanites, Girgashites, and Jebusites" (15:18–20). The same is true when God again appears to Abraham to assure him that he will have descendants with Sarah; indeed, the promise expands to include multiple nations (17:6), though the focus is still on the land that his future son's descendants will receive: "The whole land of Canaan, where you now reside as a foreigner, I will give as an everlasting possession to you and your descendants after you" (17:8). As the three visitors discuss disclosing God's designs on Sodom and Gomorrah, the Lord reminds the other two that "Abraham will surely become a great and powerful nation" (18:18). And in the aftermath of Abraham's aborted sacrifice of Isaac, the angel tells him, "Your descendants will take possession of the cities of their enemies" (22:17).

As with the promise of descendants, by the end of Abraham's life there are only glimmers of fulfillment of the promise of land. When he dies, while setting up altars through the land, he possesses two relatively small parcels of land. By treaty with the Philistine king Abimelek, he owns a well that he dug in the region of Beersheba (21:22–34) and a field with a cave that he purchased from the Hittites as a grave site when Sarah died (23:17–20).

We finally turn to the third promise given to Abraham at the beginning of this story, that God will bless Abraham and in turn he will be a blessing to the nations. How does that theme display itself in the narrative?

By the time God promises Abraham that he will both receive and impart blessing to the nations, "blessing" is a *Leitwort*, a repeated word that connects to a major theme, in the book of Genesis. Thus, it is important to circle back to Genesis 1–11 for some background.

On the sixth day of creation God created humans, endowing them with his image. God then "blessed them" as he instructed them to be fruitful and multiply, as well as to "fill the earth and subdue it" (1:28; see also 5:2). In a substantial article on the root *brk*, Michael L. Brown suggests that "that which is blessed functions and produces at the optimum level, fulfilling its divinely designated purpose."[24] I would suggest that this blessing flows from a harmonious relationship with God that results in a harmonious relationship with others and ultimately with the creation itself. Though the word does not occur in Genesis 3, the

---

[24] Michael L. Brown, "BRK," in *New International Dictionary of Old Testament Theology and Exegesis*, edited by Willem A. VanGemeren, vol. 1 (Grand Rapids: Zondervan, 1997), 759.

harmony of the garden is clearly shattered when Adam and Eve eat the fruit from the tree of the knowledge of good and evil. Their relationship with God, with each other, and with creation is fractured, but as we observed earlier, God signals his desire to work toward reconciliation, the restoration of blessing, through presenting Adam and Eve with clothing (a token of grace and continued relationship).

The next occurrence of the root *brk* comes in 9:1 as the narrator informs the reader that "God blessed Noah and his sons, saying to them, 'Be fruitful and increase in number and fill the earth.'" This is just one of a number of literary allusions back to Genesis 1 that intend to communicate that humanity is off to a fresh start. With the flood, the earth once again is "formless and empty" (1:2), and so Noah functions as kind of a second Adam. Unfortunately, as with the first Adam, Noah and his sons soon show that humanity continues to rebel against God (Gen. 9:18–29). Harmony continues to elude the relationship between God and his human creatures.

It's on this background that God calls Abraham and promises to bless him and all people on earth through him.[25] In addition, God will bless those who bless Abraham. In other words, God now seeks to restore the creation blessing, now broken by human sin, through the agency of Abraham and his descendants.

As we read the various episodes that constitute the story of Abraham, however, we note times when Abraham brings trouble rather than blessing to other nations. When he flees Canaan because of the famine, he lies about Sarah and, as a result, "the LORD inflicted serious diseases on Pharaoh and his household" (12:17). In a similar scene later in life, Abraham brings trouble, not blessing, on the court of Abimelek, king of Gerar (20:1–18). However, Abraham, while seeking his own self-interest in regard to Lot, does bring blessing on the kings of Sodom, Gomorrah, Admah, Zeboyim, and Bela when he pursues the five foreign

---

[25] Though not the place to get into the issue, I am aware of the debate over whether the niphal form of the verb should be translated passive (as here), reflexive, "all families of the earth will bless themselves by you," or middle "and all families of the earth will find blessing through you." We agree with Anderson, citing Gruneberg, "that the reflexive sense misses the fact that this is a promise from God to Abraham and not to the nations, while the middle sense is without any linguistic corroboration. A passive sense captures the fact that Yhwh directs this word of promise to Abraham, who will be the instrument of bringing bless to all," J. E. Anderson, *Jacob and the Divine Trickster: A Theology of Deception and Yhwh's Fidelity to the Ancestral Promise in the Jacob Cycle* (Siphrut 5 Winona Lake, IN: Eisenbrauns, 2011), 42, citing K. N. Gruneberg, *Abraham, Blessing and the Nations: A Philological and Exegetical Study of Genesis 12:3 in Its Narrative Context* (BZAW 332; Berlin: de Gruyter, 2003), 84.

kings who have just plundered their kingdoms, leading the mysterious Melchizedek, King of Salem, to bless Abraham in the name of "God Most High, Creator of heaven and earth" (14:19). Though Abraham exhibits a mixed record of blessing the nations during his life, still in the aftermath of the story of the sacrifice of Isaac, the Lord promises, "and through your offspring all nations on earth will be blessed" (22:18). Indeed, we might also see this idea that Abraham will be a conduit of blessing to the nations in God's promise to him concerning Ishmael, that he will bless him and that he will be "the father of twelve rulers, and I will make him into a great nation" (17:20).

Most of the occurrences of the blessing theme during Abraham's life, though, are connected to offspring. God promises that his blessing on Sarah will issue forth in her giving birth to a son, making her "the mother of nations" and promising that "kings of peoples will come from her" (17:16). And to Abraham, also in the aftermath of the Akedah, God accounts, "I will surely bless you and make all your descendants as numerous as the stars in the sky and as the sand on the seashore" (22:17).

ISAAC AND JACOB

The *toledot* of Terah, begun in 11:27, concludes appropriately with an account of the death and burial of Abraham (25:1–11). Since, as we have already commented, *toledot* focuses on the child or children of the person named in the formula, we might expect that the *toledot* of Terah would be followed by a *toledot* of Abraham. But the narrator surprises us in two ways. First, we have a short *toledot* of Ishmael (25:12–18), surprising because Ishmael was not the son chosen to perpetuate the promises given to his father. This brief *toledot* precedes the longer *toledot* of Isaac, the chosen son (25:19–35:29), a pattern repeated in the final part of Genesis, where two *toledot* (36:1–8, 9–43) precede the lengthy *toledot* of Jacob (37–50). This pattern of short *toledot* of non-chosen descendants shows that these characters are not ignored, but certainly not central to the message of the book, supporting the point made so well by Kaminsky that non-elect should not be considered anti-elect unless they turn against God and his chosen human agents.[26]

The second surprise is that that there is no *toledot* of Abraham, but rather after the short Ishmael *toledot*, there is a *toledot* of Isaac, which focuses on Isaac's children Esau and especially Jacob. That there is no

---

[26]   Joel Kaminsky, *Yet I Loved Jacob: Reclaiming the Biblical Concept of Election* (Nashville: Abingdon, 2007).

toledot of Abraham, which would focus on Isaac, highlights the relatively minimal role that Abraham's son plays in the narrative. Almost exclusively, he is treated as the son of Abraham or the father of Jacob rather than a character in his own right. He even plays a relatively minor role in the choice of his wife, Rebekah, since Abraham sends his servant up to Haran to bring back the appropriate choice. Touchingly, the account ends when the narrator tells us that "she became his wife, and he loved her; and Isaac was comforted after his mother's death" (24:67).

There is, however, no doubt that Isaac was the chosen recipient of the promises given to Abraham. That is obvious in the narrative even before he was born (17:19, 21) and is repeated in the one episode that does focus on Isaac, but even this story, wedged between episodes that focus on Jacob and Esau, replicates episodes from Abraham's life, namely lying about the status of his wife to a foreign king during a famine and making a treaty with the Philistine king Abimelek during a dispute about water rights (26). But in this context, God speaks directly to Isaac, assuring him that he is the recipient of the promises (26:1–5, 24) and thus he becomes the conduit to the next generation, which is where the *toledot* of Isaac places its emphasis.

Once again, we can only give a glimpse of the narrative richness of this part of Genesis. Like the Abraham narrative, the story of Jacob is composed of several episodes, but is filled with intrigue and character development.

When the childless Rebekah finally gets pregnant, she gives birth to twins who "jostle" within her. When she inquired of God, God announces that:

> Two nations are in your womb,
>> and two peoples from with you will be separated;
> one people will be strong than the other,
>> and the older will serve the younger. (25:23)

Esau (25:25, hairy) also called Edom (25:30, red) is the firstborn, named for his physical appearance at birth. He grows up as a person of adventure, a hunter who loves fresh game. Jacob, named for grabbing the heel of his brother as he leaves the womb but also signifying that he is a deceiver, is content at home winning the favor of his mother.

Readers enter the narrative knowing what God has told Rebekah, that the older, Esau, will serve the younger, Jacob. The first story we read about the men when they have grown is how flippantly Esau sells his birthright to Jacob because of his physical need for food. The narrator makes clear the significance of this act: "So Esau despised his birthright" (25:34). Whether there is any legal significance to this sale is beside the point; we now know that Esau puts his material, physical needs ahead of more serious, spiritual considerations, thus making the reader less sympathetic to him when he becomes the object of Rebekah's and Jacob's deception.

Still, one wonders whether the narrator wants us to be fully sympathetic to Rebekah and Jacob either, when they devise the ruse to get Isaac, who is preparing to pass the blessing on to Esau, to give it instead to Jacob. In her defense, Rebekah heard from God that it is the older who will serve the younger, but should that divine message have led them to wait on God rather than to try to manufacture the outcome? That God often chided Abraham for attempting to do that in regard to an heir makes one raise the question. The fact that the deception leads to all kind of plot complications that we cannot pursue here supports that idea.

Again, we can only skim the surface and be suggestive as to the narrative depth of this material, and will content ourselves by pursuing only one other thread. Even if we should consider the method of Jacob's acquisition of the promises problematic, we should have no doubt that he does receive them. Isaac confers them (27:27–29) and God confirms them at the place renamed Bethel as he travels up to Haran (28:13–15). Jacob remains a complex figure through the rest of the *toledot* of Isaac. While arguably, after wrestling with the mysterious divine figure, he perhaps develops in the direction of maturity, having his name changed from Jacob (deceiver) to Israel (struggling with God), he nonetheless on occasion continues to deceive (e.g., 33:12–20), perhaps explaining why the narrative does not make a definitive switch to that name as it did when Abram's name was changed to Abraham. But still he is the one who bears the promises into the next generation, which becomes the subject of the final *toledot*, the one that bears his name (37:2), but that today is more popularly known as the Joseph story.

THE JOSEPH STORY

> You intended to harm me, but God intended it for good ... the saving of many lives. (Gen. 50: 20)

Genesis 37:2–50:26, the *toledot* of Jacob, concerns Jacob's twelve sons, with a primary focus on Joseph and a secondary focus on Judah. While the promises of Genesis 12:1–3 have passed from father to son for two generations after Abraham, now the assumption is that they pass to the twelve sons all together, or at least they are all considered to be among the chosen who will eventually become a great nation who will be blessed and will be a blessing to the nations. It is at the end of his life that Jacob actively confers blessings on his sons. There is a special emphasis on the blessing of Joseph (48:15; 49:22–26) that manifests itself in his blessing both Ephraim and Manasseh. In Genesis 49, even though Jacob announces a difficult future for some of his sons (notably Reuben, Simeon, and Levi), the narrator concludes his pronouncements by saying, "All these are the twelve tribes of Israel, and this is what their father said to them when he blessed them, giving each the blessing appropriate to him" (49:28).

As we noted a difference of narrative strategy or style from the primeval history to the ancestor narratives, we also note a difference between the latter and the Joseph story. The ancestor narratives were more loosely associated episodes, while the Joseph narrative displays increased literary cohesion with smoother transitions between scenes. Rather than a series of vignettes, Genesis 37–50 comes across more like a short story as it follows the vicissitudes of Joseph, the eleventh son of Jacob (see later on Genesis 38).

Of course there are plot connections to the previous chapters. By the time we come to Genesis 37 we know that Jacob's family suffers significant dysfunction due to his propensity to favoritism. The latter began with his preference for Rachel over Leah that has now morphed after her death into a preference for her son Joseph. This preference is symbolized by Jacob's gift of an ornate coat that sets Joseph apart from his brothers (37:3), and then Joseph only accentuates filial animosity by describing to the family two dreams that have the obvious implication that he will be the dominant brother in the future. While the dreams are true, he has not yet come to the realization that his leading role in the family is not to rule but to serve, and that this service will result in his suffering.

Thus, it is not surprising that, when they get an opportunity, the brothers plot to get rid of Joseph. As he goes to visit them as they shepherd the flocks, they agree to throw him into a cistern. The omniscient narrator tells us the thoughts of the oldest brother Reuben, who should have simply nixed the plot, that he planned to come back and rescue him. But before he could, Judah, who perhaps even more than Joseph will mature in character in the course of the narrative, convinces his brothers in Reuben's absence to sell Joseph as a slave to passing Ishmaelites. They then break their father's heart by telling him that

Joseph has been killed by an animal. All that is left is his blood-stained ornate robe (we will note how clothing plays an important role in the storytelling in terms of both plot and character).

Space does not permit a detailed laying out of the plot, but let's just say that much of the early part of his story details how Joseph suffers one injustice after another. He enters into the service of Potiphar, an important Egyptian official, whose wife falsely accuses him of rape (Genesis 39). In prison he meets the chief cupbearer and the chief baker, high-level Egyptian officials, who tell him their dreams which he interprets successfully, telling the baker that he will be executed and the cupbearer that he will be restored to Pharaoh's service. As the latter departs the prison, Joseph requests his help to get him out of prison, after which the cupbearer promptly forgets him until Pharaoh himself has two dreams.

When Pharaoh tells him his dreams, Joseph interprets them in a way that helps him prepare for a coming severe famine. Joseph rises to a high position in Egypt, and at this point the focus of the narrative turns back to Joseph's family in famine-hit Canaan. Jacob hears there is grain in Egypt and orders his sons to go down and buy some. We now learn there is a new favorite, Benjamin, the son to whom Rachel gave birth as she died. Jacob does not allow the other ten to take him with them in case they lose him.

Joseph immediately recognizes them, but he does not reveal his identity to them. Indeed, he accuses them of being spies. Why? The reticent narrator simply says that "he remembered his dreams about them" (42:9), but what is it about the dreams? If it's that they anticipated his present superior position to them, how does that explain his actions? If it is rather their angry, jealous reaction to the dreams, then perhaps that explains his caution, but he is really in no danger from them in Egypt where he is second in power.

His motivation is revealed in his actions over the next couple of chapters as he manipulates matters to recreate a situation that mimics the moment years ago when they sold him into slavery. His accusation that they are spies leads them to tell him about the family and the son left at home. Thus, he demands, "You will not leave this place unless your youngest brother comes here" (42:14). After negotiating that Simeon serve as hostage, they return with grain (and their payment) to Jacob.

Jacob, though, remains adamant that Benjamin will not go to Egypt, even apparently if it means the loss of Simeon, and we might at this point remember the episode in Shechem (Genesis 34) where Jacob finds himself in conflict with Simeon and his brother Levi.[27] Reuben, who has already shown that he is an ineffectual firstborn (37:21-22, 29), asks his father to entrust Benjamin to his care, and if he fails Jacob can kill his two sons (42:37). One can imagine that Jacob, in spite of his flaws, might not think killing his grandsons would compensate for the loss of Benjamin. The narrator is putting Reuben in a bad light for a contrast with Judah, who will now play a pivotal role moving forward.

Soon, lack of food moves Jacob to instruct his sons to go back to Egypt. Judah insists that they will only go if Benjamin comes with them. Instead of offering that Jacob kill his sons, he steps forward to say that he will be personally responsible and if anything happens to Benjamin he "will bear the blame" before him for the rest of his life (43:9). Jacob relents and allows them to go.

When they arrive, Joseph again manipulates matters by placing his diviner's cup into Benjamin's grain sack so that after they leave Joseph sends his steward out to "discover" it there. Joseph has thus successfully recreated a situation similar to the one that led to his slavery. How will the brothers react? Will they be callous toward their brother and their father and simply cut their losses and run?

At this pivotal moment in the plot, Judah steps forward, good to his word to his father. In a speech whose length calls attention to its significance (44:18–34), he offers himself in Benjamin's place. At this point, Joseph, recognizing that his brothers have changed, reveals himself to them. He then invites them to go and get Jacob and bring him down to Egypt.

We have now rehearsed enough of the storyline to get a hint at least of the masterful plot and character development of this final section of Genesis. In terms of the latter, we have seen how the firstborn Reuben is an ineffective leader. Judah's character, on the other hand, develops in a remarkable way. At the beginning of the narrative, he is insensitive to his father and his brother when he devises the plan to sell him to the Ishmaelites.

The characterization of Jacob can also explain the function of Genesis 38. Past scholars have thought that this story about Judah's marrying a Canaanite and eventually unknowingly sleeping with his daughter-in-law had no place in the Joseph narrative. It seemed an intrusion. On the contrary, though, it serves the purpose of further

---

[27]   Though, interestingly, the narrator appears to signal his disappointment in Jacob and at least relative approval of the actions of Levi and Simeon by giving them the last word. See Longman, *Genesis* (Grand Rapids: Zondervan, 2016), 428–31.

darkening Judah's reputation early in the story, so that by the time he steps forward to offer himself as a substitute for Benjamin, we see a tremendous transformation that suggests he is ready for leadership among the brothers.

Joseph's character is harder to evaluate. Of course, God uses him (see later on Gen. 50:19–20), but how are we to think about him? What signals is the narrator sending us? On certain points, readers might differ in a similar way to how different interpreters assess the life of David.[28] We have already commented on the introduction to Joseph, where he relates the account of his dreams to his family in a way that was insensitive, provoking his brothers' jealousy (37:5–11).

When the brothers throw Joseph into a cistern and then sell him to the traders going down to Egypt, the narrator only reports the brothers' thoughts and words. We do not hear Joseph's reaction to the treatment that he receives. The emphasis is on the brothers' abuse and deception. In particular, as we commented, this scene in particular sullies Judah's character.

When we next encounter Joseph, he is serving in the household of Potiphar. Here the narrator emphasizes God's presence with Joseph that results in the prosperity of Potiphar's household (39:2–3). Because of the presence of this descendant of Abraham, God brought blessing on this Egyptian household (39:5–6; cf. 12:3). When Potiphar's wife tries to lure him into her bed, Joseph resists, citing his loyalty to Potiphar and to God (39:9). Once again an item of clothing gets him in trouble, as Potiphar's wife uses the cloak she snatched from him as he ran away to implicate him (39:16–18).

Joseph is sent to prison, and God's presence with him now brings prosperity to the prison (39:20b–23). The narrator presents him as the model prisoner, and his interaction with the cupbearer and the baker demonstrates that he is a skilled interpreter of dreams. Though the cupbearer promptly forgets him after being restored to Pharaoh's court (40:23), he remembers him when Pharaoh has disturbing dreams.

Joseph's success at interpreting Pharaoh's dreams as anticipating seven years of plenty followed by seven years of famine brings him into

---

[28] For instance, note the difference between the dark portrait of David described by S. L. McKenzie, *King David: An Autobiography* (Oxford: Oxford University Press, 2000), Baruch Halpern, *David's Secret Demons: Messiah, Murderer, Traitor, King* (Grand Rapids: Eerdmans, 2001), and Cephas T. A. Tushima, *The Fate of Saul's Progeny in the Reign of David* (Eugene, OR: Wipf and Stock, 2011), with a more positive picture given by Paul Borgman, *David, Saul, and God: Rediscovering an Ancient Story* (Oxford: Oxford University Press, 2008.

a position of power, symbolized by a change of clothing (41:42–43) as he is selected as the point person for preparation for the famine and then for distribution when the famine hits. It is at the point that Joseph achieves power that interpreters begin to diverge on how to assess Joseph's actions.

On the one hand, Joseph's anticipation of the famine results in his gathering grain so that when the shortage comes he can sell it to the people of Egypt, perhaps another way a descendant of Abraham brings blessing on a foreign nation. But then as the famine persists and the people of Egypt run out of money to pay for the grain, Joseph offers a plan whereby they first sell their livestock, then their land to Pharaoh (47:13–26). He even institutes a perpetual requirement in the future that they work the land that no longer belongs to them and give one-fifth of the harvest to Pharaoh. In other words, Joseph "reduced the people to servitude" (47:21) and in return for their lives the people agree to "be in bondage to Pharaoh" (47:25).

How is the reader expected to react to this?[29] On the one hand, these actions do save their lives. But on the other hand, he does it in a way that reduces them to a life of servitude to Pharaoh. Is this a blessing or a curse? Is Joseph a benefactor or a bad actor? Of course, there is another consideration to keep in mind. The story is about Egypt, after all, the Egypt that would reduce the Israelites to bondage. While there are questions about when the story was written, all agree it was post-exodus. Could this be a way of characterizing later Egyptian kings as the most ungrateful type of people? The later Pharaoh is described as one who has forgotten all about Joseph (Exod. 1:8), Joseph whose plan led to the institution's tremendous power in the first place. Could this be a story about how a descendant of Abraham brought a curse on a nation that would later curse it (Gen. 12:3)? And his actions also provide rescue for God's chosen family, who themselves journey down to Egypt, at which time Jacob blesses Pharaoh (47:7).

In a similar vein, we could also explore what Joseph's treatment of his brothers indicates about his character. By deceiving them into a situation where they have to make a choice between their own safety and the safety of Benjamin, the favorite son of Jacob, is he being wise and careful? Or is he being manipulative and vengeful? Both readings can find support from the text.

---

[29] I was prompted to reassess my more positive reading of Joseph at this point of the story by Robert F. Cochran Jr. of Pepperdine Law School, who has since published, "Biden, Abortion, and the Temptations of Status: Biblical Lessons from Another 'Ordinary Joe,'" *Public Discourse*, 25 May 2021, www.thepublicdiscourse.com/2021/05/75993/.

We conclude our study of Joseph and his brothers with a scene that provides a thematic lens through which Joseph views his life and through which the readers can now re-evaluate the preceding story. Upon burying Jacob, Joseph's brothers now worry that Joseph will finally take out retribution on them for their earlier actions. They report that before he died, Jacob wanted Joseph to forgive them. That Jacob did not tell this directly to Joseph indicates that they are fabricating this request. They also offer themselves as slaves to Joseph. To this, Joseph responds, "You intended to harm me, but God intended it for good to accomplish what is now being done, the saving of many lives" (50:20).

As Joseph looks back over his life, he remembers that his brothers betrayed him, Potiphar's wife framed him, the cupbearer forgot him. But in all that he sees the hand of God, while not exonerating their evil actions ("You intended to harm me"), but God took those very acts and used them to bring him to a position where he could rescue God's chosen family.

CONCLUSION

As stated at the beginning of the chapter, Genesis provides a rich display of literary features as the book plots the story of God's interaction with his creation and in particular with his chosen people from the very beginning of time through the life of Joseph. Indeed, the book's ending provides closure by concluding with an account of Joseph's death (Gen. 50:22–26). Nonetheless, the report of his death also signals an eventual continuance of the plot as Joseph makes the Israelites swear to take his embalmed body back to the promised land when God eventually comes to their aid. Genesis thus ends on a cliffhanger, with Joseph's coffin in Egypt setting the reader up for a sequel.

2 Exodus

The Journey to Sinai

ADRIANE LEVEEN

The book of Exodus tells a tale that begins in oppression and slavery, hard labor and suffering, replaced by a daring escape orchestrated by YHWH (a biblical Hebrew name for God), whom the slaves do not yet know, under the leadership of Moses the prophet. Once freed, the former slaves journey to a mountain deep in the wilderness to encounter their God in a frightening and awe-inspiring revelation. Revelation leads to covenant, *brit* in Hebrew, between God and the newly freed children of Israel. At Mt. Sinai God gives Moses and the people the Ten Commandments, laws, rituals and instructions to build a portable sanctuary. The people respond by building a molten calf that nearly leads to their destruction.

This essay examines how the biblical writers imagined this timeless tale of a suffering people freed by God to become God's servants rather than Pharaoh's slaves, as well as the obstacles in achieving that goal. I will closely examine and highlight the literary artistry of three passages within Exodus – Moses' birth and maturation, God's revelation at Mt. Sinai and the creation of the molten calf in the wilderness camp. I will argue for the centrality and interconnection of each story, both to one another and to the larger project of creating a people Israel in a new and enduring relationship with a God they are just learning to know.

Exodus, the second of the Five Books of Moses – the Torah – provides the crucial beginning for the collective return journey from Egypt to the Promised Land. The narrative arc of Exodus begins in its first chapter with the enslaved descendants of Jacob in Egypt and ends in its last chapter at the newly built portable sanctuary at the foot of Mt. Sinai (40:34) in the presence of God. Its importance not only to the other books of Torah but also to the rest of the Hebrew Bible cannot be overstated:

No other event in the history of Israel is given so much attention by biblical writers as is the Exodus – as many as one hundred and

twenty references in a variety of literary genres including narrative, law, prophecy and psalm, as well as extensive coverage in the
Pentateuch.[1]

J. P. Fokkelman identifies the focus of Exodus 1–15 on the physical
birth of the people Israel while chapters 16–40 imagine the spiritual
birth of the people. He refers to these two stages as "Liberation and
Covenant."[2] I will argue that the spiritual birth of the people begins
with Moses' birth story right from the start but that Liberation is necessary for Covenant. God's encounter with Moses at the burning bush
leads to the people escaping from slavery into freedom, from Egypt to
Mt. Sinai, where they directly witness YHWH and enter the covenant.
The molten calf episode emphasizes God's absence which Moses must
regain on behalf of the people. Thus the journey begun in Egypt and ending at Sinai captures a dynamic series of events expected of a narrative: a
beginning crisis that sets the story in motion; a daring plan in response;
obstacles that must be overcome; characters who help or hinder; a cli-
matic crisis that is resolved; and, if lucky, fulfillment in the end.

PART ONE: EGYPT AND MIDIAN

Exodus is referred to in Hebrew as *Shemot*, 'Names', because it begins
with the names of the ancestors of the twelve tribes of Israel. Eleven sons
come down to Egypt with their father Jacob. They are preceded by their
brother Joseph who is second only to Pharaoh and whose story stretches
over the last chapters of Genesis. After the deaths of that generation,
their descendants continue to flourish: "And the children of Israel were
fruitful and *swarmed* and *multiplied* and mighty, very much, and the
land was filled with them" (Exod. 1:7).[3] Verse 7 invites the close reader
to identify specific words (italicized) that lead us back, via allusion, to
the creation story in the first chapter of Genesis. "Swarming" is used
in Genesis 1:20–21 to describe the waters that swarm with the living
creatures that God has just created. In Genesis 1:22 they receive God's
blessing before human beings to be "fruitful and multiply and fill the
waters." God's blessing to humankind occurs in Genesis 1:28: "Be fruitful and multiply and fill the land." At the end of the flood story, God

---

[1]   Yair Zakovitch, "*And You Shall Tell Your Son…*": *The Concept of the Exodus in the
      Bible* (Jerusalem: The Magnes Press, 1991), 9.
[2]   J. P. Fokkelman, "Exodus," pages 56–65 in *The Literary Guide to the Bible*, eds.
      Robert Alter and Frank Kermode (Cambridge: The Belknap Press, 1987), 56.
[3]   All translations mine unless otherwise noted.

announces to Noah in Genesis 9:7: "As for you, be fruitful and multiply and swarm all over the land." The writers have relied on intertextual allusions, reusing words strongly associated with the creation of the world and, after the near destruction of the flood, its recreation. These allusions allow the writer at the beginning of Exodus to announce a new creation, that of the children of Israel.

Verses 8–10 signal an ominous shift in the fortunes of the children of Israel as a new king rises over Egypt who does not know Joseph. He fears that their rapid growth could overpower the Egyptians from the inside or that they might join forces with the enemies of Egypt from the outside. A mere three verses deftly characterize a new king whose anxieties, even paranoia, lead him to act aggressively against a perceived threat, the people Israel, by enslaving them. The biblical writer often astonishes the modern reader through such concise use of language: Joseph gone, a new king, fear, oppression.

The writer has embedded in the encounter between the children of Israel and this new king a careful word choice that conveys a moral lesson and a warning to the reader: "And Egypt forced labor upon the children of Israel *ruthlessly*" (1:13). "Ruthless" is used here and in verse 14: "And they embittered their lives in hard labor, in mortar and bricks and all labor of the field, with all their labor as they labored – *ruthlessly*." The word reappears in Leviticus 25:43, 46 and 53 to describe what one shall *not* do to one's servants. The rules in Leviticus describe treatment of Israelites by fellow Israelites. They must treat their servants differently and are tasked with being more lenient than Egypt treated the children of Israel. According to Ezekiel 34:4, the Israelites are condemned and now in exile precisely because they treat the vulnerable *ruthlessly*.

This word study links the present moment of suffering in Egypt with the promise that in the future Israelites will be free and must not be *ruthless* in that freedom over their servants. Otherwise, they risk the punishment that Ezekiel describes in exile. Hopping from Exodus to Leviticus to Ezekiel, one can observe the Hebrew Bible in conversation with itself. At the same time, we are now in the midst of a crisis begun by Egypt's new king that calls for God's response.

The last section of chapter 1 shifts our attention to the midwives, important characters who will lead us directly to the birth of Moses and his plight. Not content with oppressing the enslaved children of Israel, Pharaoh becomes increasingly determined to rid Egypt of this people and orders the two midwives, Shiphrah and Puah, to kill all male Israelite infants. Specifically naming these two women draws our attention to them. Thinking on their feet, they disobey Pharaoh and are rewarded by God in 1:20 for their loyalty as necessary partners in God's actions on behalf of this vulnerable people. Consider how remarkable is this story, placed in the very first chapter of Exodus. The midwives become the first example in Exodus of those who bravely stand up to power and an authoritarian leader's genocidal tendencies on behalf of victims. They provide the model for Moses and Aaron who later defy this pharaoh. Overwhelming power can be met with acts of defiance.

Paying attention to details of Moses' birth allows us to recognize that his individual story foreshadows the subsequent story of the people. His birth and escape precede their rebirth through escape. His sudden encounter of God anticipates their equally momentous encounter of God at Mt. Sinai. Moses' story begins in Exodus 2:2–3:

> And the woman conceived and bore a son and saw him, that he was good and she hid him for three months. And when she could no longer hide him she took for him a wicker basket [*teva* in Hebrew] ... and put in it the child and placed it in the reeds on the banks of the Nile.

Not surprisingly, "and the woman conceived" puts Moses' mother in the line of those matriarchs in Genesis who conceived and bore sons. Genesis repeatedly uses the phrase to tell the story of the birth of all humankind followed by the particular people Israel, but in Exodus the phrase is used only once. This sole use signals that the birth of Moses is unique to the degree that his character will now dominate the remainder of the Torah as he leads the people out of Egypt and into the wilderness.

Birth is the central motif of this first section of the larger narrative. We have already been introduced to the midwives and now we learn of an actual birth. Moses' sister looks after him and his mother nurses him once Pharaoh's daughter has drawn him out of the Nile. Moses is saved by the brave acts of five women – the midwives, his mother, his sister and the daughter of Pharaoh. Ironically, Pharaoh's own daughter thwarts her father's genocidal impulses.[4]

These verses also contain allusions to Genesis. Upon seeing the baby, Moses' mother declares that he is *good*, in an echo of God's

---

4   Keith Bodner goes further, pointing out "an intriguing symmetry: the twelve sons named at the outset are enabled to survive, as it were, by various actions of the 'twelve daughters' of Exodus 1–2 (namely, the pair of midwives, the mother and sister of Moses, Pharaoh's daughter, and the seven daughters of the priest of Midian)." Keith Bodner, *An Ark on the Nile: The Beginning of the Book of Exodus* (Oxford: Oxford University Press, 2016), 44 n. 7.

declarations in Genesis 1 during the seven days of creation that "it was good." *Teva*, the Hebrew term for basket, used in Exodus 2:3 and 5, is used in only one other biblical story, that of the flood in Genesis 6–9. Noah's ark is a *teva*. Just as the world's survival depended on Noah, now the survival of the Israelites depends on Moses. The daughter of Pharaoh explains why she names the infant Moses: "for from the water I drew him out" (2:10). Her act foreshadows God's saving the people by means of water as they leave Egypt.

The next verse, 2:11, presents Moses, already a young man, in the role of Israelite savior. Going out to see his "brothers," Moses witnesses an Egyptian brutally beating an Israelite. Moses kills the Egyptian. It is not clear if Moses knows that the Israelites are his "brothers," but as Aviva Zornberg suggests, at that moment he makes a "subjective choice. It leads him to kill the Egyptian, responding to violence with violence."[5] Fleeing from Pharaoh after his action becomes known to save his own life, Moses finds himself at a well in the land of Midian.

Moses begins his life in Midian by saving the seven daughters of a local priest, Jethro, from a group of menacing shepherds as they attempt to water their flock (Exod. 2:17). Jethro invites the Egyptian outsider into his tent in thanks for saving his daughters. While he is dressed in the Egyptian clothes in which he fled Pharaoh, the reader realizes what Jethro does not – that Moses is actually an Israelite about to settle in the tents of a Midianite. Zipporah, daughter of Jethro, becomes his wife and they have a son. The past soon reasserts itself in the name Moses gives that son – Gershom – which literally means "a stranger there." While naming his son, Moses acknowledges, "I have been a stranger in a foreign land" (Exod. 2:22). This brief speech suggests that Moses as an Egyptian has long been an outsider to himself. Thanks to Jethro, Moses has found Midian to be a land in which he can flourish and find perspective.[6] And yet Midian does not settle his question of identity. Neither Egyptian nor Midianite, Moses will only accept that he is part of the children of Israel when he encounters YHWH for the first time.

The passage (Exod. 3:1–6) is worth quoting in full:

And Moses was shepherding the flock of his father-in-law, the priest of Midian, and he drove the flock into the wilderness and came to

---

[5] Avivah Gottlieb Zornberg, *Moses: A Human Life* (New Haven and London: Yale University Press, 2016), 108.

[6] For details of their relationship, see Adriane Leveen, "Inside Out: Jethro, the Midianites and a Biblical Construction of the Outsider," *Journal for the Study of the Old Testament*, Vol 34.4 (2010): 395–417.

the mountain of God at Horeb. And an angel of YHWH *appeared* to him in flames of fire in the midst of a bush and he *saw* and behold, the bush was ablaze in fire but the bush was not consumed. And Moses said, "I shall turn aside and *see* this great *sight* – why is the bush not burned?" And YHWH *saw* that he had turned aside to *see* and God called to him from the midst of the bush and said, "Moses, Moses," and he said, "Here I am." And [God] said, "Don't come close. Remove your sandals from your feet for this place on which you stand – it is holy ground." And [God] said, "I am the God of your fathers, God of Abraham, God of Isaac and God of Jacob," and Moses hid his face for he was afraid to look at God.

Torah often depicts a human encounter with God in the wilderness, a liminal place, betwixt and between, removed from familiar people and settings, alone and humbled by the vastness of wilderness. So it is with Moses.

Moses' encounter with God at the burning bush at the foot of the mountain marks the site as holy. While called Horeb, the mountain is thought by many to be identical with Sinai. The association to Sinai emerges from the bush, *sneh* in Hebrew, which shares two of the three Hebrew letters that spell Sinai. Not only does the scene foreshadow the eventual return of the people Israel to Mt. Sinai in their own encounter with God in Exodus 19, but in 3:12 God tells Moses explicitly that he will bring the people to this mountain.

Moses *sees* that the bush is not consumed. A version of the Hebrew root for seeing appears six times in these six verses, indicating that it is a key word of the passage. A key word is often used in a short passage to convey a message to the reader. Not only is the verb important to this passage, but *seeing* has also been important in the two chapters that precede Moses' encounter with God. Moses' mother sees that he is good, the daughter of Pharaoh sees him and rescues him, and Moses sees the oppression of his brothers. *Seeing* illustrates how observation can lead humans to have compassion for others. The prior acts of seeing pave the way for Moses' arrival at the burning bush where he now *sees* God. Moses' seeing in verse 3 is *seen* by God in verse 4 as a sign of Moses' willingness to be engaged. Only then does God call out to him.

Fire is an apt image for God's presence as it gives light and keeps one warm. But fire can also burn and destroy. Life- and death-giving properties express the writer's understanding, and perhaps fear along with awe, of God's powerful and mysterious attributes. In the Hebrew Bible God does on occasion use fire to destroy (e.g., Lev. 10:2, Num.

11:1). Here God overturns the natural order with divine power through a fire that would normally consume a bush but does not.

God explains a great deal to Moses in the four verses that follow. Specific words are italicized to highlight the brief passage's structure:

> And YHWH said: I have surely *seen* the affliction of My people in Egypt and *their cries* I have head because of their taskmasters; for I know their pains. And I shall descend to rescue them from the hand of Egypt and take them up from that land to a land that is good and spacious; ... And now, behold, the *cry* of the children of Israel has come to me and also I *see* the oppression with which Egypt oppresses them. And now, come and I will send you to Pharaoh and you shall bring out my people the children of Israel from Egypt. Exod. 3:7–10

Note that two words, *seeing* and *cries*, in verse 7 are repeated in reverse order in verse 9, when God reiterates having heard the *cries* and *seen* the oppression to confirm that God is ready to intervene against Egypt. Verses 7 and 9 frame the verse that they surround, drawing the reader's attention in verse 8 to God's promise in consequence. God will rescue these people. Verse 10, outside the neat frame, concludes with God's strategy – to send Moses back to Egypt to implement God's promise as stated in verse 8. Verse 10 also neatly introduces the role of the prophet, one who serves as God's intermediary in speaking truth to power. Such a careful structure reflects the writer's skill in highlighting a particular point. We discover that the suffering of the children of Israel has become intolerable to God who is ready to act.

God's rhetoric is powerful, but Moses' response in 3:11 is surprising: "Who am I that I should go to Pharaoh and take out the children of Israel from Egypt?" Moses refers to the children of Israel impersonally rather than as his people, hinting at his continued confusion over his identity. His reluctance also becomes a refrain in later prophetic passages modeled after this initial divine call and human response. As put by Martin Buber, "And now begins the great duologue in which the God commands and the [hu]man resists."[7] Numerous biblical prophets respond to God's call as did Moses, reluctant and perhaps frightened. It takes God's reassurance, insistence and, at times, demand for a human being to accept the prophetic call.

In Exodus 3:12 God responds simply to Moses' reluctance: "I will be with you." Moses then asks God for a name. God responds in verse

---

[7] Martin Buber, *Moses: The Revelation and the Covenant* (New York, Hagerstown, San Francisco, London: Harper Torchbook, 1958), 46.

14: "I am that I am," *Ehyeh-Asher-Ehyeh,* a unique name used nowhere else in the Torah.[8] The phrase and the name YHWH share the same root for the verb "to be." God's name asserts God's existence, suggesting "to be" in its different tenses – was, is and will be – to express God's continual presence in the life of the people Israel. God's reassurance is needed by Moses, for in the last verses of the chapter God describes Pharaoh's future resistance to Moses, necessitating the Ten Plagues and God's ultimate success.

Moses is neither placated nor reassured. He anxiously questions whether the Egyptians and the Israelites will believe his words. God reveals divine powers through a series of acts – turning Moses' rod into a snake, making the skin of Moses' hand diseased and then, once he confronts Pharaoh, turning the Nile into blood. Moses remains unconvinced, offering another objection: he is not a man of words. God remains undeterred, reassuring Moses in 4:11–12 that God gives humans the ability to speak. Finally, Moses begs God to send someone else.

This initial dialogue between the two reveals Moses' deep reluctance to serve in the role God is sending him to perform. God reveals an insufficient appreciation of Moses' apprehension and only now appears to recognize how deep seated is Moses' reluctance. Each is learning how to be in what is new for both – a divine–human relationship. Their encounter sets the stage for the later collective encounter with God by the children of Israel with its own series of missteps.

In response to Moses' objection, God appoints Moses' brother Aaron to accompany him in confronting Pharaoh. At the end of this divine–human exchange, Moses says his farewells to Jethro and returns to Egypt, this time with his wife and son. On the journey back, God reiterates the earlier plan to Moses but adds a new detail in 4:23: the firstborn son of Pharaoh will be killed before Pharaoh lets the people go.

God then inexplicably attacks Moses. Acting quickly, Zipporah saves Moses' life by circumcising their son.[9] Moshe Greenberg suggests that this event is a "premonition of things to come depicted in intensely personal terms," a reference to the final plague God described in 4:23.[10] Perhaps God wants Moses to concretely confront the horror of

[8]   Gary A. Rendsburg, "Moses the Magician," pages 243–258 in *Israel's Exodus in Transdisciplinary Perspective;* eds. T. E. Levy et al., (Switzerland: Springer International Publishing, 2015) 244.

[9]   For Zipporah's role, see Ilana Pardes, *Countertraditions in the Bible* (Cambridge: Harvard University Press, 1992) and Claudia Camp, *Wise, Strange and Holy* (Sheffield: Sheffield Academic Press, 2000).

[10] Moshe Greenberg, *Understanding Exodus* (New York: Behrman House, 1969), 117.

death, whether his own or that of his son, before he inflicts the same on Pharaoh and his son. But no explanation can do away with the ominous threat of God's unpredictability, even directed at Moses.

God's unsuccessful encounter with Moses in order to take his life in 4:24 is followed, thanks to Zipporah, by Aaron's successful encounter with Moses the next day in 4:27. Together they return to Egypt to begin the terrifying mission God has sent them to perform.

Aviva Zornberg beautifully sums up Moses' life until this point.

> He lives within closed spaces, hidden in his mother's house; in the box, in the river; in the palace; burying the dead Egyptian in the sand; hearing God calling him from within the Bush, hiding his hand within his bosom. God urges him to "bring forth" what is incubating within him: to utter, to redeem, to expose to the light. The submerged is to emerge ... Everything is a risk, to the limit of life itself.[11]

Moses is now ready to take on the greatest human power in his world, Pharaoh, on behalf of a far greater power, YHWH, whom Moses has learned he must follow whether he wants to or not and in whom he must place his trust. This first part of the narrative arc of Exodus concludes with Moses back where he began, in Egypt.

Before moving on, let me highlight a few of the literary techniques present in the first four chapters of Exodus that allow the writer to set the stage for the rest of the book. These include intertextual allusions to Genesis that announce a new creation; the use of naming to reveal a key detail of the later plot or a character's inner experience; the strategic use of framing and structure to draw our attention to a central point; and finally, the presence of foreshadowing in Moses' biography that anticipates the story of the new nation about to leave Egypt.

AN INTERLUDE BETWEEN BIRTH AND REVELATION

The journey out of Egypt is long and dramatic. Chapters 5–11 describe the Ten Plagues that finally force Pharaoh's hand. The plagues prove both to the Egyptians and to the Israelites that divine powers are greater than those possessed by the most powerful human figure, Pharaoh. That showdown culminates in the dramatic exodus of the children of Israel after a night of terror that includes the slaying of every firstborn Egyptian in the land, including Pharaoh's son (Exod. 12:12).

---

[11] Zornberg, Moses, 23.

The events of the plagues and the liberation have been memorialized within the Jewish community in a retelling of the story on Passover every year. Exodus 12–13 commemorate that story by describing the details of the people's last night in Egypt along with the regulations and rituals of the Passover festival. Thus is collective memory shaped by story and ritual that allow one to remember the past in the present.

Exodus 14–15 also contribute to the collective memory of the exodus by narrating the actual march out of Egypt to the edge of the Reed Sea and then across its waters. These chapters mingle story and a victorious poem that celebrates God's rescue of the Israelites from the waters while allowing the Egyptian army and Pharaoh to drown. Human nature quickly reasserts itself. The people begin to complain in chapters 16–17 of thirst and hunger. God tries to placate them by providing water, quails and manna, a wafer-like substance that nourishes them through their wilderness wandering. But these divine acts appear insufficient to retain the people's fidelity. God seeks a more successful way to form the Israelites into a people united to serve YHWH by appearing before them at Mt. Sinai.

PART TWO: ON TOP OF MT. SINAI

Exodus 19 opens with the people's arrival in the wilderness of Sinai where Moses first encountered God, an encounter that forced his return to Egypt to take the people out of slavery precisely to this holy place. Buber describes their arrival: "The hour has come. The sign promised to Moses by the voice which spoke from the burning bush is now about to be fulfilled."[12] The people camp at the foot of the mountain as Moses goes up to God at the top. As he climbs, Moses physically acts out the role God has given him as mediator between heaven and earth, the divine vision and instruction to the people. Chapter 19 makes the relationship between God and the people under Moses' leadership explicit by introducing God directly to them and establishing a covenant between them. God calls out and the people respond. Chapters 20–24 provide the details and obligations of that covenantal relationship.

God opens the episode in grand rhetorical style:

"You have seen what I did to Egypt and *how I lifted you on the wings of eagles* and I brought you to me. Now if you will truly listen *to my voice and observe my covenant* you will be to me a

---

[12]   Buber, *Moses*, 101.

treasure from among all the peoples; for mine is all the earth, and you will be to me a *kingdom of priests and a holy nation.*" These are the words which you shall speak to the children of Israel. Exod. 19:4–6 (italics mine)

The moment of liberation recalled by God calls for something grand. The poetic "on the wings of eagles" elevates God's rhetoric, allowing it to soar, captivating the listener and stirring the heart far more than the familiar formula: "who took the children of Israel out of Egypt."

Verse 5 declares that if the people follow God's voice and accept the covenant, they will become God's "treasure." A closer look at the word reveals its use through different biblical books, expanding its meaning over time. In the present chapter the term is one of endearment by God for the people. It is used again in Deuteronomy 7:6 and 14:2 to reiterate that God cherishes the people. Deuteronomy 26:18 again reminds the people that they are God's treasure. Years later the prophet Malachi in 3:17 assures them that God continues to cherish them as a "treasure," just as a father has compassion on his child. Psalm 135 praises God for having chosen Israel as God's treasure. Together these verses, spread throughout the Hebrew Bible from the Five Books to the Prophets and the Writings, illustrate just how persistently the people Israel held on to the belief that they were God's treasure. Ecclesiastes 2:8 defines treasure as that of the gold and silver of kings but goes on to warn that such material wealth is futile. 1 Chronicles 29:3 describes the treasure of David as gold and silver but hastens to explain that David gives it to the House of God. Throughout these verses the people should understand that it is God's view of them as a treasure that is essential for their flourishing, not gold or silver.

The use of "a kingdom of priests and a holy nation" in Exodus 19:6 suggests that just as priests devote their lives to God, so too must the children of Israel. In contrast to later priestly hierarchy, each Israelite, not just the priests, can aspire to holiness, thus introducing an egalitarian spirit into the relationship with God.

Exodus 19:4–6 offers the reader in miniature the events of the larger narrative before and after Sinai: God's rescue, the covenant and the resulting transformation of all the people into God's treasure.

Divine revelation in 19:16–25 ensures that God's promise to the people in 19:4–6 becomes reality. The mystery of the Divine Presence is presented in a way that dramatizes the overwhelming confusion, anxiety and experience of sacredness that the event conceivably produces in the minds of the people, of God and the reader. A choreography of revelation plays out against a backdrop of lightning and the overwhelming sound of thunder.

That sound is captured in verse 16 through the use of the word "voice," *kol*, both for thunder and the shofar blast. Verses 18–19 use "voice" again at the central moment: "And Mt. Sinai was all in smoke for descending upon it was YHWH in fire and the smoke rose like the smoke of a kiln and all the mountain greatly shook. And the *voice* of the shofar grew very loud. Moses spoke and God answered him in *Voice*."

The Voice cries out. What do the people hear? It is unclear. Note the use of one word for three different sounds – thunder, shofar blast and the voice of God. Its overlapping meaning in such a dense passage creates purposeful ambiguity, especially since the last voice is that of God at the moment in which the shofar's blast is at its most powerful. Such sounds force the interpreter to concede uncertainty over what is, or even can be, heard and deciphered. Perhaps each participant hears something different in the cacophony of sound. Benjamin Sommer puts the effects of reading Exodus 19 this way: "the extraordinary event ... was witnessed through a fog ... the narrative of that event could not be articulated in human words; further, one senses that the text combines multiple recollections of an essentially unreportable event."[13]

Just as sound is muffled and hearing strained, so too do the fire and smoke allow God to be shrouded in obscurity. Details such as lightning and thunder, understood as weapons of divine battle, along with the shofar call that summons troops, remind the people of a familiar trope from the cultures surrounding Israel: gods as divine warriors. While images from the outside are creatively used to describe the God of Israel in familiar ways, room is left for their combination with other roles kept separate in polytheistic systems. The biblical God is envisioned as creator, warrior and lawgiver, allowing the reader to imagine God in multiple ways. The moment at Sinai also adds another dimension to God's characterization. By battling Pharaoh and freeing the people Israel before coming down to Earth on the top of Mt. Sinai, God enters history, however briefly. The children of Israel are obligated in turn to make the reality of God present in their lives both personally and collectively in concrete ways.

The path to fulfillment of the divine vision can be found in the details of the Ten Commandments, literally translated from the

---

[13]   Benjamin D. Sommer, *Revelation and Authority: Sinai in Jewish Scripture and Tradition* (New Haven: Yale University Press, 2015), 33.

Hebrew as "words," and in a body of law known as the covenant code in Exodus 20–23. Chapter 24 concludes this section in a covenantal ceremony of acceptance. The establishment of a divine–human covenant is based on the model of a king who establishes a treaty with the people he conquers. The formal ceremony includes the identification of the king, the details of the covenant between king and conquered, a warning if the agreed-upon rules are broken, and specifying where the written rules will be deposited. These formal steps are replicated in this section of Torah. God identifies Godself, lays out the conditions and laws of the covenant, warns Israel of what will happen if they break the covenant, and instructs Moses to deposit the covenantal tablets in the sanctuary about to be built. The Ten Commandments declare God's singularity; call for an avoidance of sculptured images of God; warn the people not to blaspheme God's name, to keep the Sabbath and to honor one's parents; and prohibit murder, adultery, theft, bearing false witness against one's neighbor and coveting a neighbor's house or wife. These Ten Commandments reflect universal religious values shared with other faiths.

The covenant code contains a variety of laws targeted specifically to the children of Israel. These include, more or less in the order that they appear, the treatment of slaves; the consequences of murder, kidnapping and insulting one's parents; damages for injuries caused by an ox; an array of civil and criminal laws; agricultural mishaps; sexual violations; the proper treatment of strangers and the poor; various holidays and dietary restrictions. The code attempts to cover different facets of individual and collective behaviors encountered in agricultural and urban settings that need either to be curtailed and punished because they are damaging, or to be encouraged for the collective good. The series of laws are concrete rather than abstract, designed to be enacted in reality. The people might not see a transcendent God but will know what God wants of them: follow these laws and achieve God's vision of a harmonious and just community.

Three verses are particularly appealing. "And do not wrong a stranger and nor oppress, for you were strangers in the land of Egypt, and any widow or orphan you shall not ill-treat" (22:21–22). Chapter 23 adds to the command: "and a stranger you shall not oppress, for you know the inner nature of a stranger for you were strangers in the land of Egypt" (23:9).[14] The stranger, widow and orphan would be vulnerable

---

[14] "Inner nature" for *nefesh*, Robert Alter, *The Hebrew Bible* (New York: Harper Collins, 2018), 310 n. 9.

in any community and without obvious protection, so the law protects them, both physically and economically. Perhaps even more remarkably, protection is justified through empathy. You get the experience of the vulnerable since you were once vulnerable (and could be again). Richard Elliot Friedman comments:

> Why, according to these sources, should we be good to aliens? Because we know how it feels. We know the alien's soul. So we shall not persecute foreigners, we shall not abhor them, we shall not oppress them, we shall not judge them unfairly, we shall treat them the same as we treat ourselves, we shall love them.[15]

The final scene in the revelation narrative occurs in chapter 24 at the end of the laws in a ritual ceremony confirming the covenant. Moses repeats all that he has heard from YHWH to the people. They answer in one voice: "All these words that YHWH has spoken, we will do" (Exod. 24:3). Moses writes them down. Animal sacrifices follow, after which Moses dashes blood of the sacrificed against the altar. Blood, evidence of life and death, has a cleansing function within priestly spaces. Informed consent, a gift to God (the sacrifices) and purification by blood are necessary steps in the ceremonial dimension of covenant.

Once the ceremony is concluded, Moses and a group that includes Aaron and his sons along with seventy elders of Israel ascend (presumably the mountain) in 24:9. Two astonishing verses describe what happens next:

> And they saw the God of Israel. Under God's feet was a likeness like a pavement of sapphire, like the sky for purity. And toward the elders of the children of Israel God did not raise a hand and they beheld God and ate and drank. Exod. 24:10–11

The elders are granted an extraordinary encounter with God whom they see, in contrast to the obscured view of God earlier granted to the entire people. The two events preserve different conceptions of God and who gets to "see" God. In Exodus 19 all the people, told that they are holy, experience God's presence even if obscured by smoke and fog. In Exodus 24 an elite group of leaders are granted a fuller vision of God. I understand the different possibilities for seeing God as fragments of ancient visionary reports that a later writer collected and preserved in Torah. God is presented through a flame of fire at the burning bush, veiled at the top of the mountain and directly to the elders.

[15]   Richard Elliott Friedman, *The Exodus* (New York: Harper One, 2017), 202.

God next commands Moses to climb to the top to receive the stone tablets, Torah and the divine commandments:

> And Moses ascended the mountain and the mountain was covered in cloud. And the Glory of YHWH dwelled on Mt. Sinai and the cloud covered it six days and God called to Moses on the seventh day from the midst of the cloud. And the appearance of the Glory of YHWH in fire consumed the top of the mountain in the eyes of the children of Israel. And Moses went into the midst of the cloud and ascended the mountain and Moses was there on the mountain forty days and forty nights. Exod. 24:15–18

The children of Israel are able to see a fire that consumes (in an echo of the burning bush), so they know that God is there but they do not see God directly. Moses, on the other hand, must walk through the cloud and the fire to face God. Perhaps an explanation for the next episode, the creation of the idolatrous calf, can be found in the people's fear that Moses would not survive an encounter on the fiery Mt. Sinai.

PART THREE: IN THE ISRAELITE CAMP

Though the episode with the molten calf in chapter 32 is actually separated from Moses on top of the mountain in chapter 24 by the detailed instructions for building the wilderness sanctuary, 32:1 begins as if it comes right after the end of chapter 24: "When the people saw that Moses was delayed from coming down the mountain, the people gathered against Aaron and said to him, 'Get up, make us a god who will go before us since that man Moses who took us out of the land of Egypt – we don't know what happened to him'" (Exod. 32:1). The long wait for Moses to return fuels the anxious uncertainty of this people who agreed to a covenant with YHWH. They know that God took them out of Egypt, led them to Mt. Sinai and gave them laws to live by. But apparently YHWH has left unanswered other pressing questions such as where God is located and in what form does God appear. Without Moses, their doubts take over. Since the relationship with a distant God has become increasingly difficult to fathom, the people demand a concrete god from Aaron. He complies immediately and without hesitation. In a mere six verses the reader learns that the great acts of God detailed so dramatically on behalf of the people have left them unmoved. Their panic leads to a false idol, death for some and God's ominous alienation.

Aaron casts a mold for a molten calf out of gold gathered from the people. They exultantly declare in verse 4, "This is your god, Israel, who took you up from the land of Egypt." The claim rings of parody since until then the people have repeatedly heard that God took them out of Egypt. Meanwhile, at the top of Mt. Sinai God describes the scene to Moses in a battle of possessives. In verse 7 God shifts responsibility on to Moses and orders him to hurry down, for *"your* people, whom *you brought up from Egypt,* have become corrupted."* Now they are Moses' people. Now it is Moses who has taken them up from Egypt. God is ready to destroy them all except for Moses.

Not to be outdone nor fazed by God's threat, Moses swiftly responds in verse 11: "Why does YHWH turn your anger against *your people who you took out from the land of Egypt?"* In such a simple way the writer captures the dynamic between Moses and God. Who is ultimately responsible for this people, and for how long? Surely it is God who liberated them and established a covenant with them. God cannot discard them at the first sign of trouble. This scene captures the essence of the prophetic role. Moses must stand up to God on behalf of the people. Therefore Moses addresses God's reputation and loyalty to the ancestors of this difficult people as the reasons for maintaining God's covenant with them and succeeds in keeping God's anger at bay.

However, it does not end there. As Moses descends the mountain with the written commandments on stone tablets in his hands, the sight of the people worshipping the idol so enrages him that he breaks the tablets. Breaking the tablets makes the covenant legally null and void. In his prophetic role, Moses now stands up for God. His reaction is immediate, rebuking his brother and calling the Levites to kill those responsible.[16] This is a very difficult passage to read. No mercy exists for the culpable who remain unsure of YHWH. Perhaps the episode is meant as a deterrent, teaching the people that the covenant is, literally, deadly serious. They have just learned what will happen if they break it. God has proven to be more dangerous than they understood.

Yet Moses dares to return to the mountaintop, determined to seek forgiveness on behalf of the people. If God does not forgive the people's sin, then Moses will no longer participate in God's mission: "erase me from your scroll which you have written" (32:32). He links his own fate inextricably with that of the children of Israel as a model for God to do the same. As a prophet, Moses acts again on behalf of the people. Whether intentionally or not, the story captures the gap between God's plans and human partners who are challenged by a God they cannot see.

---

[16] For an interesting discussion of the Levites, see Friedman, *The Exodus,* 50–51, 64, 200.

God assures Moses that the covenant will continue but is still angry enough with the people to remain at a distance. Exodus 33 describes three opportunities used by Moses to overturn God's decision and keep God fully engaged with the people during the rest of the journey. Each interaction captures different aspects of a divine–human encounter.

Exodus 33:7–11 depicts Moses heading outside the camp to a tent of meeting. The tent's location and function preserve a different, minor tradition within the Hebrew Bible in contrast to the much more referenced *Mishkan* or sanctuary, placed in the very center of the Israelite wilderness camp. Anyone who seeks God can go out to the tent of meeting. As Moses goes to meet God, "all the people rose and stood, each at the opening of their tent and gazed after Moses until he came to the tent" (33:8). The appearance of a pillar of cloud at the entrance to the tent indicates that God and Moses are speaking. Each person bows low in acknowledgment at their own tent. In contrast to Exodus 32, when the people wondered what had happened to Moses, 33:7–11 allows them to witness the encounter between Moses and God. The most interesting verse describes a divine–human encounter that the people desperately want to reestablish: "And YHWH would speak to Moses face to face like a man would speak to his neighbor" (33:11).

The next exchange is an abrupt exchange between God and Moses that does not appear to take place at the tent of meeting. Moses argues that if he is such an intimate of God, why does God insist on remaining distant? Moses quickly includes the children of Israel in the question: "And now, if I really have found favor in your eyes, make your ways known to me so that I know ... and look, this nation is *your* people" (33:13). Moses beautifully uses his special relationship with God to secure the divine commitment to the people. God grants the wish in verse 14: "I [literally 'my face'] will go in the lead." Moses has secured God's commitment.

The third interaction emphasizes God's unique relationship with Moses. In a gesture of great intimacy, God vows to pass God's goodness before Moses. But since a human being cannot see God's face and live (verse 20), God devises a plan to place Moses in the cleft of a rock, cover his face as God's glory passes by and then remove God's hand so that Moses can see God's back. God concludes in verse 23, "but my face you shall not see." What? Verse 11 has just described how God and Moses speak face to face like a man and his neighbor! I will return to this contradiction.

Each exchange with God reconfirms that the divine presence will remain with the children of Israel in spite of God's fierce anger over the molten calf. "Face" weaves the three encounters together and expresses their main concern: knowledge of and closeness to God. "Face" appears twice in verse 11 (face to face like a human and his neighbor), verses 14 and 15 (God's face), verse 19 (Moses' face) and verses 20 and 23 (God's face). The result communicates a more nuanced understanding of the possibilities. God is present for individuals and agrees to a collective presence among the people, but retains a unique relationship with Moses. All three exchanges have in common the reassurance that God will not abandon God's people in spite of the molten calf.

But harmonization fails to cover up the clear contradiction in chapter 33. Put bluntly, can a human being see God or not? Yes and no. By preserving contradictory traditions, chapter 33 presents different models of holiness and of the human experience of God that coexist in the final form of Exodus. The three versions of the relationship share a great longing for intimacy with God. But tensions exist between intimacy and fear of the dangerous God of chapter 32. Even the intimacy God promises Moses at the end of Chapter 33 has its limitations, as put by Zornberg:

> what God offers Moses is both less and more than he desires. The back, not the face: no fullness of divine presence, but intimations, traces, interpretations that passionately connect Moses with God and His words. What opens up is the dynamic space of being *with* God.[17]

Exodus 34 concludes the larger narrative arc I have mapped in this essay between God, Moses and the children of Israel. The relationship between God and the people, so recently threatened, is formally restored in a renewal of the covenantal ceremony established in Exodus 19. By describing chapter 34 as a third revelation, Fokkelman reminds us of the other two:

> As a text that articulates a large spiritual vision, Exodus is defined by the three climaxes of revelation on the mountain of God, in 3:1 [the burning bush] called Horeb, in 19–24 and 33–34 Sinai. The divine revelation in Exodus concerns God ... both [God's] name and [God's] nature.[18]

Chapter 34 covers much ground in depicting a renewal of the covenant. The first set of tablets, written by God's hand, are replaced by a second set that Moses will carry up the mountain, carved (as we learn in 34:27–28), by Moses' hand. God's acceptance of a second set of tablets

---

[17] Zornberg, *Moses*, 98.
[18] Fokkelman, "Exodus," 62–63.

suggests divine magnanimity. Remember that Moses threw the tablets down in Exodus 32, nullifying the covenant. Now, in a gracious act of forgiveness, God accepts the new tablets written in Moses' hand, signaling a readiness to renew the covenant with the children of Israel.

God descends in a cloud in 34:5 on the top of Mt. Sinai, pausing to "firmly stand" with Moses before declaring the divine qualities. That stationary moment with Moses strikes me as an expression of God's commitment and even love for this prophet who has borne so much on God's behalf. God calls out: "*YHWH YHWH*, a compassionate and gracious God, slow to anger and great in loving kindness and truth" (34:6). Here God emphasizes the Divine Self not as the liberator from Egypt but as the One who can forgive. Perhaps God has learned that divine mercy and compassion are more efficacious for the success of the covenant than God's punishing rage.

GOD'S DWELLING

The story of Moses' birth develops into a series of dramatic, sometimes troubling, encounters between the unruly people Moses must lead and God. All are chastened by the experience but remain covenant partners. It ends, after chapters of instructions for how to build the *Mishkan*/sanctuary and its implementation, with the arrival of God's presence in the completed sanctuary. Surely the journey is not only a physical one with all its attendant hardships, but also a spiritual achievement for the people Israel and their God. The last verses of the book confirm the result:

> And the cloud covered the Tent of Meeting and the *Kavod* [glory or presence] of YHWH filled the *Mishkan* … the cloud of YHWH was on the *Mishkan* during the days and fire would appear at night, in view of all the house of Israel throughout their journeys. Exod. 40:34, 38

SELECTED FURTHER READING

Bodner, Keith. *An Ark on the Nile: The Beginning of the Book of Exodus.* Oxford: 2016.

Buber, Martin. *Moses: The Revelation and the Covenant.* N.J.: 1993.

Camp, Claudia. *Wise, Strange and Holy.* Sheffield: 2000.

Fokkelman, J. P. "Exodus." Pages 56–65 in *The Literary Guide to the Bible.* Eds. Robert Alter and Frank Kermode. Cambridge: 1987.

Friedman, Richard Elliott. *The Exodus.* New York: 2017.

Greenberg, Moshe. *Understanding Exodus.* New York: 1969.

Leveen, Adriane. "Inside Out: Jethro, The Midianites and a Biblical Construction of the Outsider." Pages 395–417 in *Journal for the Study of the Old Testament*, v. 34.4 (2010).

Pardes, Ilana. *Countertraditions in the Bible*. Cambridge:1992.

Rendsburg, Gary A. "Moses the Magician." Pages 243–258 in *Israel's Exodus in Transdisciplinary Perspective*. Eds. T. E. Levy et al, Switzerland: 2015.

Sommer, Benjamin D. *Revelation and Authority: Sinai in Jewish Scripture and Tradition*. New Haven: 2015.

Zakovitch, Yair. *"And you shall tell your son…"* *The Concept of the Exodus in the Bible*. Jerusalem: 1991.

Zornberg, Avivah Gottlieb. *Moses: A Human Life*. New Haven and London: 2016.

3 Reading the Wilderness Narratives

CARMEN JOY IMES

If you have ever stood on the edge of the Grand Canyon, you know what it is to feel dwarfed by the sheer size of the wilderness and the impossibility of taming it. Attempting to navigate the wilderness with ancient Israel feels similar. Although we will limit ourselves to the so-called "Sinai narratives" plus the journey stories on either side, we still have much ground to cover. A road trip from Egypt to Canaan that should have taken a few weeks became a forty-year ordeal, spanning the Books of Exodus, Leviticus, and Numbers. Never mind the actual wilderness of the Sinai Peninsula, attempting to read these chapters can feel like walking in circles. What follows can function as a hiker's map, helping you make sense of these foundational stories.

Have you ever realized that only a fraction of Israel's foundational narratives takes place inside the land God promised to Abraham and his descendants? Only 13 percent of the Torah takes place in Canaan, while 31.5 percent occurs at Sinai, 25.5 percent on the plains of Moab, and 8.5 percent on the road to these locations.[1] We will focus on the journey from Egypt to Canaan, which includes the wilderness and Sinai narratives from Exodus 15 to the end of Numbers. When I say "wilderness," do not picture the lush unspoiled wilderness of the Canadian Rockies or the rolling green of the Appalachian Mountains. The land the Israelites traversed was hot and dry, an unfriendly desert. The trip from Egypt to Canaan would test their mettle and refine their faith.

However, the Torah itself is literary masterpiece. The following diagram attempts to capture some of the symmetry and patterning of these narratives (Figure 3.1). While Genesis and Deuteronomy each has its own unique character, Exodus and Numbers mirror each other in an uncanny way. Leviticus presents its instruction as a literary sandwich,

---

[1] Of the Torah's 187 chapters, twenty-four are in Canaan, fifty-nine at Sinai, forty-eight in Moab, and sixteen on the road. Egypt, Midian, and Mesopotamia are the other major locations.

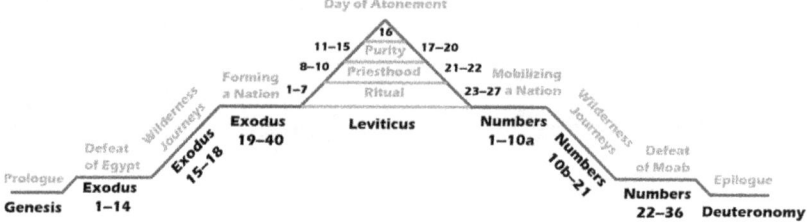

Figure 3.1 Structure and symmetry of the Torah.

or chiasm, forming the center of an elaborate complex of stories that take place at Sinai (Exod. 19–Num. 10), framed by wilderness journeys with paired incidents on either side (Exod. 15–18 and Num. 10–21).

EXODUS

Exodus 15b–18: Egypt to Sinai

The wilderness narratives officially begin in Exodus 15:22, with Pharaoh defeated at the Sea of Reeds and Israel heading into the "wilderness of Shur."[2] The Israelites find only bitter water, but God makes it fit to drink, suggesting that he can heal them as well if they obey his commands (verse 26). Six weeks after leaving Egypt, they move on to the "wilderness of Sin" (unrelated to our English word "sin;" Exod. 16:1). God provides for their hunger in a way that invites them into a new rhythm of work and rest – six days of collecting manna followed by a day of Sabbath rest. God teaches them week by week to rely on and rest in his miraculous provision.

The narrator does not recount every stop on Israel's journey (Exod. 17:1, cf. Num. 33), but chapter 17 includes two incidents at Rephidim: God's provision of water from a rock in answer to Israel's thirst and Joshua's victory against the Amalekites. Chapter 18 withholds the specific location in order to achieve a sophisticated literary design. Although they are "in the wilderness ... encamped near the mountain of God" (18:5), the narrator does not call it Sinai. Moses is already teaching the people God's decrees and deciding their disputes. However, the incident appears *before*

---

[2] Note that although English versions always call it the "Red Sea," the Hebrew Bible consistently refers to this body of water as the "Sea of Reeds." The proper starting place for our journey is debatable. In Exodus 12, the Israelites leave Egypt (see verse 51). Exodus 13 describes the first stage of their journey, led by a pillar of cloud. However, in Exodus 14, Pharaoh changes his mind and pursues them. The Israelites cross the Sea of Reeds and YHWH decisively conquers the Egyptian army. Most of Exodus 15 is a song of celebration for this victory. All Scripture quotations are from the NRSV unless otherwise noted.

the official arrival at Sinai in order to provide a literary frame around the Sinai narratives. As he will again in Numbers 10–11, Moses struggles under the burden of leadership and receives help from a Midianite family member. This pair of narratives is one of many. Reading Numbers feels like *déjà vu*. The overall effect of this design is a chiasm that extends even beyond the wilderness journeys, with the Sinai narratives in the center:[3]

Exod. 5–15 YHWH's showdown with Pharaoh, king of Egypt
   Exod. 14:19–20 Angel of YHWH protects Israel from Egypt's army
      Exod. 15 Song of victory over Pharaoh, king of Egypt
       Exod. 15:22–25 Springs of water provided
         Exod. 16:1–17:6 Food; Sabbath; opposing Moses; water from rock
         Exod. 17:8–16 Joshua wins battle with Amalekites
           Exod. 18:1–6 Moses' family (conflict?)
             Exod. 18:13–18 Moses' leadership burden
               Exod. 18:19–27 Assisted by Midianite kin (Jethro)
                 Exod. 19:1–2 Arrival at Sinai
                  SINAI NARRATIVES (Exodus 19–Numbers 10)
                 Num. 10:11–13 Departure from Sinai
               Num. 10:29–32 Assisted by Midianite kin (Hobab)
             Num. 11 Moses' leadership burden
           Num. 12 Moses' family (conflict)
         Num. 13-14 Joshua and Caleb; battle with Amalekites/Canaanites lost
         Num. 15:32–21:9 Sabbath; opposing Moses/Aaron; water from rock; food
       Num. 21:16–18a Springs of water provided
      Num. 21:18b–35 Song of victory over Sihon, king of Ammon
   Num. 22:21–35 Angel of YHWH protects Israel from Moab's curses
Num. 23–24 YHWH's showdown with Balak, king of Moab

---

[3]   Chiasm adapted and expanded from L. Michael Morales, *Who Shall Ascend the Mountain of the Lord? A Biblical Theology of Leviticus*, NSBT (Downers Grove: IVP Academic, 2015), 26. Wilderness narratives are in bold type. See also Frank Moore Cross, *Canaanite Myth and Hebrew Epic: Essays in the History of the Religion of Israel* (Cambridge, MA: Harvard University Press, 1973), 308–16. Two more incidents contribute to this mirroring effect, although they do not appear precisely in the right locations to be included in the chiasm:

Exod. 13:17–28	Taking the long route to avoid war
Exod. 16	Manna and quail provided
Num. 11	Manna and quail provided
Num. 20:14–21	Taking the long route to avoid war

The cumulative effect of this impressive chiasm is threefold. First, by framing Sinai on either side with similar stories, otherwise separate books join to tell a single story. While each of Exodus, Leviticus, and Numbers is a coherent work of its own, together they exhibit intentional literary design. Second, the importance of the Sinai narratives in the center is plain. Just as a mat and frame draw the viewer's attention to the painting itself, so the wilderness narratives direct our gaze to these central narratives. Third, the telling of such similar stories in Exodus and Numbers invites comparison. The wilderness narratives in Numbers are more expansive than their counterparts in Exodus and often incorporate instructional material. After Sinai, Israel's grumbling prompts harsher judgment from YHWH. Prior to Sinai, they are still learning how to trust YHWH; after Sinai, they have no excuse. YHWH has repeatedly demonstrated divine provision, protection, and power on their behalf and has clearly expressed how they should live in response.

EXODUS 19–NUMBERS 10: THE SINAI NARRATIVES

Exodus 19–24: Covenant Revealed and Ratified
In Exodus 19, the Israelites arrive at Mount Sinai. In the chapters that follow, Moses makes repeated trips up and down the mountain to meet with YHWH and to relay messages to the Israelites. YHWH begins by announcing the new identity of the nation and the vocation that will result from their obedience.[4]

> You have seen what I did to the Egyptians, and how I bore you on eagles' wings and brought you to myself. Now therefore, if you obey my voice and keep my covenant, you shall be my treasured possession out of all the peoples. Indeed, the whole earth is mine, but you shall be for me a priestly kingdom and a holy nation. (Exod. 19:4–6)

The narrative location of this pronouncement is significant: *before* the giving of the law and *after* Israel's deliverance from Egypt. The law is not how Israel will qualify for salvation. Rather, it is Israel's means of fulfilling their vocation as YHWH's people. The Israelites sign on willingly (19:8).

Geography is also important. Israel's divine encounter at Mt. Sinai fulfilled YHWH's promise to Moses (3:12). Just as Moses fled from Pharaoh, crossed the wilderness, met YHWH at the mountain,

---

4   Leon R. Kass, *Founding God's Nation: Reading Exodus* (New Haven, CT: Yale University Press, 2021), 293.

and received a commission for service (3:1–4:17), so the Israelites fled from Pharaoh, crossed the same wilderness, met YHWH at the same mountain, and received a commission for service (19:4–6). Obedience to God's law would enable them to fulfill their role as God's "treasured possession," a term reserved for a trusted treaty partner who represents the sovereign.[5]

YHWH delivers the core stipulations of the covenant – the Ten Commandments, or "Ten Words" – directly to the Israelites (19:25; 20:1), after which Moses approaches God on the mountain to receive further instructions. The next section, or "Covenant Code" (Exod. 20:22–23:33), sets expectations for the community regarding worship and interpersonal relationships. This code is not the final word on every topic; YHWH provides for future guidance in 23:21–22.

At God's invitation, the people confirm their commitment to this new covenant relationship with a special ceremony in Exodus 24. Moses sprinkles blood from the sacrifices on the people to indicate their inauguration as a kingdom of priests (24:8; cf. 19:5).

Exodus 25–31: Tabernacle Plans

Again, at God's invitation, Moses ascends the mountain to receive the stone tablets. While there, YHWH gives him detailed instructions about how to build the tabernacle. Narrative time is significant in these chapters. The presence of God envelops Moses for six days before God speaks. On the seventh day God calls to Moses (24:16). "The LORD said to Moses" occurs seven times in this section, organizing YHWH's tabernacle instructions into seven speeches. This literary design is no accident; the seventh speech is a reminder to keep the Sabbath.[6] To the careful reader, the narrative implies that building the tabernacle mimics God's creative work in Genesis 1. In Genesis, God brought order to creation. Here, YHWH invites the Israelites to participate in the work (and rest!) of creation by bringing order to their worship.

The first speech stretches from 25:1 to 30:10 and includes the tabernacle furnishings, priestly garments, and the priestly ordination

---

5   Carmen Joy Imes, *Bearing YHWH's Name at Sinai: A Reexamination of the Name Command of the Decalogue,* BBRSup 19 (University Park, PA: Eisenbrauns, 2018), 118.

6   Daniel I. Block, "Eden: A Temple? A Reassessment of the Biblical Evidence," in *From Creation to New Creation: Biblical Theology and Exegesis,* eds. Daniel M. Gurtner and Benjamin L. Gladd (Peabody, MA: Hendrickson, 2013), 18; Carmen Joy Imes, "The Lost World of the Exodus: Functional Ontology and the Creation of a Nation," in *For Us, but Not to Us: Essays on Creation, Covenant, and Context in Honor of John H. Walton,* eds. Adam E. Miglio et al. (Eugene, OR: Pickwick, 2020), 134–37.

ritual. YHWH summarizes the purpose of this consecrated place and its functionaries: "I will dwell among the Israelites, and I will be their God. And they shall know that I am the LORD their God, who brought them out of the land of Egypt that I might dwell among them; I am the LORD their God" (29:45–46). The next six speeches are much shorter and deal with atonement money (30:11–16), the washbasin (30:17–21), anointing oil (30:22–33), sacred incense (30:34–38), the designated artisans, Bezalel and Oholiab (31:1–11), and the importance of keeping the Sabbath (31:12–17). These seven speeches conclude with a definitive statement that God had "finished speaking" (31:18; cf. Gen. 2:1).

Another notable feature of the tabernacle instructions is their placement *before* the golden calf incident. The tabernacle instructions anticipate the need for a system to restore the Israelites to their status as a holy nation and cleanse them from their sin. Even before they commit idolatry, YHWH implements a plan for forgiveness and the restoration of national holiness. Moses is on the mountain for "forty days and forty nights" (24:18), the typical length of a test of faith. Moses' absence tests the obedience of the rest of the nation, who fail miserably.

Exodus 32–34: Apostasy and Presence

The people quickly lose patience while Moses is on the mountain meeting with YHWH. They demand a new deity in a form they can see (32:1). Aaron tries unsuccessfully to rein in their idolatrous worship by dedicating their festival to YHWH (32:5), but it is too late. They replace YHWH with a prohibited calf idol (32:8; cf. 20:3–6).

Meanwhile, on the mountain, YHWH's righteous anger burns against them (32:7–10). Although Moses successfully intercedes on their behalf, when he descends the mountain his own anger flares (32:11–20). As his breaking of the stone tablets symbolically demonstrates, Israel has already broken the covenant. Aaron minimizes his involvement (32:21–24), but the Levites demonstrate their fidelity to YHWH by killing the idolaters (32:25–29). Moses ascends the mountain again to intercede for the people (32:31–32). Their apostasy prompts a new crisis: God's decision not to accompany the people to Canaan (32:33–33:6).

Here the narrator offers a parenthetical picture of Moses' usual practice of meeting with YHWH outside the camp in the tent of meeting (33:7–11). If Moses leads the people from Sinai *without* YHWH's accompaniment, he will be unable to have this regular fellowship with God. For the second time, Moses rejects God's offer of a privileged status not shared with the nation ("you" is singular in 33:14; cf. 32:10). His identification with the people is so strong that he refuses to lead them without the presence of God. In Moses' second forty-day stay on the mountain, YHWH reveals himself more fully to Moses, agrees to accompany them, and reiterates the basics of covenant faithfulness (34:4–28).

Exodus 35–40: Building the Tabernacle

The rest of Exodus depicts the Israelites' obedience in carrying out God's commands. Moses issues three speeches, prefacing tabernacle work with a reminder about the importance of keeping the Sabbath (35:1–3). Although the building project is important, it does not supersede the need to rest. Moses' second speech invites contributions of materials from every Israelite and labor from skilled workers (35:4–19), followed by their response (35:20–29). Men and women participate together in this creative and generous work and provide more than enough (36:2–6).

Moses' third speech introduces Bezalel and Oholiab to the community as those who will oversee the artistic design of the tabernacle (35:30–36:1). The narrative account of the building process may seem repetitive, but its role is significant. In chapters 36–39 the Israelites carefully obey all that God commanded in chapters 25–31, creating a narrative frame around the golden calf incident and Moses' intercession. The repeated phrase, "as the LORD had commanded Moses," emphasizes the artisans' careful attention to divine instruction (Exod. 39).

YHWH commands Moses to erect the tabernacle on the first day of the new year, signaling a new era with the creation of sacred space (40:1). God's assembly instructions move from the Most Holy Place to the outer curtains (40:2–15), while Moses' fulfillment begins with the outer curtains and moves inward (40:17–33). Leviticus 8 presents a detailed version of the anointing and consecration of tabernacle and priesthood. Here, the result is anti-climactic: God's glory descends, but Moses can no longer enter the tent of meeting (40:35). Leviticus offers the solution to that problem.

LEVITICUS

Leviticus may not be a story in the conventional sense, since it consists mostly of procedures relating to ritual and moral purity. However, the presence of just one letter in Hebrew stitches Leviticus into the wider narrative. It is the Hebrew letter *vav*, which means "and." Whoever is responsible for the text of Leviticus deliberately sought to connect it to the surrounding narrative.

The book of Exodus ends with the completed shell of the tabernacle at Sinai filled with God's glory. That final episode is strong on setting (when and where), but light on character (who) and plot (what and why). By connecting Leviticus to Exodus with the word "and," the narrator supplies a timeless *who, what,* and *why* for the tabernacle. Members of the congregation are to bring sacrifices. Priests are to take their sacrifices and offer them in the prescribed way. These rituals are to populate the sacred space of the tabernacle for generations to come.

The final sentence of Leviticus reinforces this thin narrative setting: "These are the commandments that the LORD gave to Moses at Mount Sinai for the people of Israel on Mount Sinai" (Lev. 27:34). While the implementation of these commands will span generations, their origin is clearly set at Sinai, making them foundational for Israel's life and worship. Leviticus is not just a manual of tabernacle worship. It carries forward the wider story. Numbers, the next book of the Torah, also begins with "and." It reads, "And YHWH spoke to Moses in the tent of meeting in the Desert of Sinai on the first day of the second month of the second year after the Israelites came out of Egypt" (Num. 1:1, author's translation).

Numbers is far more storied than Leviticus. It picks up where the narrative left off in Exodus, but implicitly acknowledges the contribution of Leviticus. The pressing problem at the end of Exodus was that Moses was unable to enter the completed tabernacle. Until this point, Moses had been Israel's designated mediator, able to approach God directly on Mount Sinai. When God's glorious presence descended to the tabernacle, Moses' entry was barred. *This* is why Leviticus was necessary – to achieve proximity with the deity again. In Numbers, God speaks to Moses *in* the tent, indicating that Leviticus has resolved the purity problem of Exodus.

Leviticus is not exactly a story, but it intersects the broader Sinai narratives and plays a role in the overall plot development. The instructions offer regular reminders of the characters involved: "YHWH said to Moses," or, "YHWH said to Moses and Aaron." Although the book is not a robust narrative, it is also not purely procedural. A few key narratives punctuate these ritual instructions to carry the storyline forward. The first is the priests' ordination, followed by stories of success and failure (Lev. 8–10). Leviticus bears traces of character, setting, and plot. Even ritual instructions respond to narrative events.

As many have noted, the entire book is a giant chiasm. Rituals at either end frame priestly instructions, which frame purity instructions, with the Day of Atonement as the central focus of the book. Each section carries the plot forward. We will explore them in order.

1–7 Ritual Sacrifices
    8–10 Priests Ordained
        11–15 Ritual Purity
           16 Day of Atonement
        17–20 Moral Purity
    21–22 Priestly Standards
23–27 Ritual Festivals

Leviticus 1–7: Ritual Sacrifices
The first step in solving the problem of barred entry to the presence of God is the implementation of a sacrificial system whereby worshippers may offer a tangible sign of repentance. These ritual-heavy chapters include a narrative introduction and conclusion and regular reminders that "the LORD spoke to Moses" (4:1; 5:14; 6:1, 8, 19, 24; 7:22, 28). Leviticus 1:1 situates the book at the tent of meeting, with YHWH calling to Moses from inside. The content of YHWH's instructions, which Moses is to pass along to the Israelites, are the rituals that follow.

The organization of these chapters and the purpose of each offering is not obvious. The first five chapters appear to address laypeople, while the last two address priests. The instructions for laypeople fall into two parts: (1) God-focused sacrifices, including the burnt, grain, and peace offerings that appease YHWH with a pleasant aroma (Lev. 1–3). (2) Sacrifices that cleanse the worshipper, namely the purification and reparation offerings that bring forgiveness for sin (Lev. 4–5). The concluding summary in Leviticus 7:37–38 highlights the characters and setting for these instructions:

> This is the ritual of the burnt offering, the grain offering, the sin offering, the guilt offering, the offering of ordination, and the sacrifice of well-being, which the LORD commanded *Moses on Mount Sinai*, when he commanded *the people of Israel* to bring their offerings *to the* LORD, *in the wilderness of Sinai*. (Emphasis added)

The book of Leviticus affirms the effectiveness of these sacrifices to cleanse the community from sin pollution. This ritual system is the first step toward addressing estrangement from God. However, these sacrifices cannot perform themselves. The tabernacle requires holy agents – priests set apart and trained for this work.

Leviticus 8–10: Priestly Ordination, Ministry, and Failure
The priestly ordination in Leviticus 8 fulfills God's previous instructions to Moses (Exod. 29; 40:9–15). Exodus assures us of Moses' compliance

(Exod. 40:16), but the narrator reserves the details until Leviticus. In the intervening chapters (Lev. 1–7), YHWH gives Moses instructions regarding various sacrifices. Prescribing the sacrifices first ensures that the priests' ordination sacrifices are intelligible.

Ritual texts take on a timeless character due to their prescriptive and iterative nature. However, the narrator explicitly presents the ordination as a narrative involving Moses, Aaron, and Aaron's sons at the time of the tabernacle inauguration. The first thing to notice is the characters: Moses is the primary actor in the drama. Although Aaron and his sons are the focus of the ritual, they do almost nothing. Moses washes them. Moses dresses them. Moses anoints them. Moses performs the sacrifices (a purification offering to obtain forgiveness, a burnt offering to appease God, and an ordination offering). Moses acts as priest, inaugurating a new stream of authorized leadership in Israel.

Another thing to notice is the significance of the setting: the ordination ceremony lasts seven days and takes place at the "entrance" to the tent of meeting. Rituals in any culture include an element of liminality. "Liminal space" (from the Latin *limen*, or threshold) is "in-between space," neither here nor there. To ordain these men to the priesthood involves a separation from the community at a location straddling the boundary of sacred space (8:2–9). The seven-day ritual implies the creation of something new: a holy priesthood. As we will see, sacred time in Israel always comprises patterns of seven.

By the end of Leviticus 8, Aaron and his sons are properly dressed and consecrated for their new roles. Chapter 9 takes place entirely "on the eighth day," the priests' first day on the job (9:1). Moses directs the activities while the priests fulfill their duties. First, Aaron offers purification and burnt offerings for himself, to ensure his own holiness (9:2, 8–14). Next, he offers purification, burnt, grain, and peace offerings on behalf of the people (9:3–4, 15–21). The goal is to facilitate the presence of God among them: "so that the glory of the LORD may appear to you" (9:6b). Done properly, these sacrifices will qualify the Israelites to be in God's presence.

It works! As soon as Aaron completes his sacrificial duties, he pronounces a blessing over the people (9:22–23). The blessing appears in Numbers 6:24–26, followed by a statement that tells us what it accomplishes: "So they shall put my name on the Israelites, and I will bless them" (Num. 6:27). Aaron is the divinely designated mediator: he cleanses the people so they can approach the presence of God, and he confers YHWH's name upon them so they know their vocation to represent God. The blessings of Aaron frame Leviticus 9:23: "Moses and

Aaron entered the tent of meeting." This is precisely what Moses could *not* do in Exodus 40:35. Immediately after the blessing, God's fiery glory appears and consumes the offerings on the altar. Everyone is overjoyed (9:24). The sacrificial system is operating as designed.

This is a satisfying conclusion, and the chapter division in our Bibles offers a sense of closure. However, the Hebrew narrative carries on without a pause. The next scene is devastating. Aaron's sons, Nadab and Abihu, evidently let their special status go to their heads. They innovate, taking censers with unauthorized incense into the tent of meeting (10:1). The same fiery holiness of God that consumed the burnt offerings in the previous scene is now directed at the renegade priests, and they die instantly.

After dealing with the corpses, Moses instructs the priests not to defile themselves by mourning. Then, for the first time in Leviticus, God addresses Aaron directly, without Moses' mediation, warning the priests not to drink alcohol on duty (10:8–9). They need their full powers of discernment and are responsible for teaching YHWH's decrees to others. The placement of these instructions suggests that Nadab and Abihu may have been under the influence of alcohol.

Leviticus 10 closes with the resumption of priestly ministry from chapter 9. Aaron and his remaining sons pick up where the ceremony left off by eating the grain offered on the altar. Aaron innovates slightly by not eating his share of the sin offering. As he explains to Moses, the flagrant disobedience of his sons made it seem inappropriate to consume his share. This innovation reflects fear of God, rather than arrogance, so it is acceptable.

The deaths of Nadab and Abihu raises a pressing problem that the rest of Leviticus endeavors to resolve.[7] God's presence is now accessible, but the priests and the people must maintain their purity to avoid further deaths. God's holiness is dangerous to those who approach in a state of impurity or rebellion.

Leviticus 11–15: Ritual Purity

The next section of the chiasm of Leviticus lays out instructions on ritual purity. Ritual purity is a foreign concept to most of the developed world today. It might help to think of it like a kind of spiritual germ. We understand the danger of germs, even though we cannot see them. The "uncleanness" Leviticus describes is not being dirty. "Uncleanness" has to do with impurity from physical contact with a substance inappropriate to bring into God's presence. Ritual impurity is not morally wrong.

---

7   Morales, *Who Shall Ascend?*, 153–54.

Just as getting sick implies no moral failure, so being ritually impure is not sinful. What *is* sinful is failing to honor God by approaching the divine presence in a state of impurity.

All the prescribed ritual inspections and procedures share a concern for sacred time (seven days) and sacred space (inside the camp). Unclean persons or substances are isolated for set periods. In the case of skin diseases, the person must await inspection outside the camp.

Leviticus 11–15 divides neatly into six speeches. The first speech (Lev. 11) outlines which meats are off limits for the Israelites. Animals fall into two categories – clean (which can be eaten) and unclean (which cannot be eaten). Leviticus 11 trains the Israelites to distinguish between these. The second speech (Lev. 12) details how long a woman is impure after childbirth.[8] The third speech (Lev. 13) concerns the proper diagnosis of skin diseases and moldy fabrics. Both interrupt the purity required to be in God's presence. The ceremony to restore someone after the skin disease has run its course in the fourth speech (Lev. 14:1–32) is quite elaborate. The sprinkling and daubing of blood seem to indicate a person's need for formal reinstatement as a member of the "priestly kingdom" (see Exod. 19:6; cf. 24:8). The fifth speech (Lev. 14:33–57) appears to be an addendum to deal with molds in houses. Given the narrative setting of Leviticus at Sinai, the people all live in tents. These instructions anticipate the day they will live in houses in Canaan. Now the priest takes on the role of building inspector in addition to health and clothing inspector.

The sixth speech about ritual purity (Lev. 15) concerns bodily discharges of men and women. The order proceeds from abnormal to normal male discharges, followed by normal and then abnormal female discharges (ABB'A'). Abnormal discharges of men and women frame the normal discharges of semen and menstrual blood. While normal emissions do not require a sacrifice, abnormal, chronic discharges do. Verse 31 expresses the point of these purity instructions: "so they do not die in their uncleanness by defiling my tabernacle that is in their midst." Impurity is unavoidable, but God teaches them to respond properly so that the divine presence is not dangerous.

Leviticus 16: Day of Atonement

At the center of the literary sandwich of Levitical instructions is the Day of Atonement. As already noted, instructions on purity frame

---

[8] The difference in length of time for birth of a boy or girl may simply take into consideration that a baby girl will herself one day give birth. Her life-giving potential extends the length of time the woman must wait to bring her purification offering.

Leviticus 16; priesthood instructions frame the purity chapters, and ritual instructions frame the entire book. However, the Day of Atonement is not just the thematic center of the book, it is also the formal center, framed by eighteen divine speeches on either side.[9] This annual ritual is the crowning jewel of worship activity because it marks the high point of the liturgical year, cleansing the entire community of impurity. Although it is a procedural text, it is not generic; Aaron is the specified actor in this yearly drama and two narrative statements situate this ritual in a specific place and time:

> YHWH spoke to Moses *after the death of the two sons of Aaron who died when they approached YHWH.* YHWH said to Moses: 'Tell your brother Aaron that he is not to come whenever he chooses into the Most Holy Place behind the curtain in front of the atonement cover on the ark, *or else he will die.* (Lev. 16:1–2a, AT, emphasis added)

YHWH deliberately correlates the Day of Atonement with the deaths of Nadab and Abihu (Lev. 10) to address the problem introduced by their carelessness and to underscore how seriously Aaron must take these instructions. As high priest, he cannot approach YHWH whenever he desires. YHWH strictly regulates entrance into the central sanctuary of the tabernacle. Israelite worship is not a freestyle event.

Another narrative statement closes the chapter: "And Moses did as the LORD had commanded him" (16:34b). Although YHWH prescribes the Day of Atonement as a yearly ritual, the narrator grounds the ongoing practice of this ritual in its first fulfillment by Aaron, the high priest, with reference to the tragic events of his first day in office.

The ritual itself is elaborate, with Aaron's clothing and movements carefully choreographed to deal with impurity. Although many aspects of this ritual will seem familiar (e.g., sin offering, burnt offering, and sprinkling of blood), key differences distinguish it. Aaron does not wear his normal regalia. He wears only white linen garments and his headdress, perhaps to signal his humility in approaching YHWH. This ritual is the only time all year that anyone will enter the Most Holy Place, where God's presence is especially concentrated. Aaron burns incense in the tabernacle to shield himself from the divine glory as he enters, and he sprinkles blood on the ark – first bull's blood for priestly sin, and later goat's blood for the people's sin. He releases the second goat into the wilderness as a scapegoat, carrying the sins of the community. This

[9] Morales, *Who Shall Ascend?*, 28.

ritual cleanses the tabernacle itself of impurity so the community can
begin with a clean slate.

Leviticus 17–20: Moral Purity

Corresponding to Leviticus 11–15 on *ritual* purity, Leviticus 17–20 deals
with matters of *moral* purity. Unlike ritual purity, moral purity involves
sinful behavior. This section consists of four speeches, one per chapter.
These address the centralization of worship at the tabernacle and prohibition of eating blood (Lev. 17), prohibition of defiling sexual relations (Lev.
18), a wide variety of instructions pertaining to holiness (Lev. 19), and pen-
alties for sexual sin, child sacrifice, and magic arts (Lev. 20). The central
idea of these chapters is expressed in Leviticus 19:2: "You shall be holy,
for I the LORD your God am holy." YHWH's instructions are not arbitrary,
but call the covenant people to live in a way set apart from the surrounding
nations so they can exemplify God's holiness. The sexual relationships
prohibited here contrast with the sexual mores of Egypt and Canaan (18:3).
Obedience will result in a long tenure on the land (18:24–30).

Leviticus 21–22: Priestly Standards

This section contains five speeches regarding priestly ministry and corresponds with the section in Leviticus 8–10 on priestly ordination. The
speeches address the priests concerning proper behavior, eligibility for
service and eating sacred offerings, and criteria for a proper offering.
The priests must obey or, like Nadab and Abihu, their lives will be
in jeopardy (22:9). The section concludes what scholars often call the
"Holiness Code" (Lev. 17–22).

Leviticus 23–27: Ritual Feasts and a Difficult Case

Moses first addresses five speeches to the Israelites, prescribing festival days to celebrate. Every Jewish festival falls on the seventh day or
the seventh month or links with the Sabbath. These patterns of seven
coordinate the Jewish calendar with the memory of God's own rest after
creation, implementing a pattern of work and worship that anticipates
and relishes celebration.

Israel is to honor the *Sabbath* by ceasing from work every *seventh*
day. Passover falls on the fourteenth day of the first month of the Jewish
calendar (a *Sabbath*) and initiates *seven* more days of celebration for the
Festival of Unleavened Bread, concluding with another *Sabbath*.

Firstfruits falls on the day after a *Sabbath* and kicks off *seven*
weeks of counting until the Feast of Weeks fifty days later. The Feast of
Trumpets initiates the *seventh* month with a *Sabbath* marked by the

blowing of trumpets. The Day of Atonement falls on the tenth day of the *seventh* month, adding another *Sabbath* to the calendar. Finally, the feast of Tabernacles runs *seven* days (plus one) from *Sabbath* to *Sabbath* from the fifteenth to the twenty-second of the *seventh* month.

Leviticus 24 turns from yearly festivals to daily and weekly rituals in the tabernacle. In this speech, YHWH requires every Israelite to contribute oil to light the lamps in the Holy Place (cf. Exod. 27:20). Aaron and his sons are to keep the lamps lit daily (cf. Exod. 27:21). The same rare word designates the "lights" (*ma'or*) of the lamp and the "lights" (*ma'or*) of creation in Genesis 1:14, which God appointed to rule over day and night and whose purpose was "for signs and for seasons and for days and years" (Gen. 1:14, 16). These seven tabernacle lights represent God's presence in the tabernacle. Every Sabbath, Aaron places twelve loaves of bread on the table facing the lampstand. These loaves symbolize the twelve tribes of Israel, who symbolically bask in the presence of YHWH from one Sabbath to the next, illuminated by the lampstand.[10] Just as the yearly calendar is under the rule of the heavenly lights (Gen. 1:16), so the twelve tribes are under the rule of YHWH symbolized by the tabernacle lights.[11]

One final narrative punctuates the Levitical instructions (Lev. 24:10–23). It involves a difficult case, where the appropriate penalty for violation of covenantal instructions is not obvious. The crime itself is plain: a man has cursed YHWH, which clearly merits the death penalty. However, community leaders are unsure how to respond because the man is not a full-blooded Israelite. His mother is Israelite, but his father is Egyptian. In a way, this incident mirrors that of Nadab and Abihu in Leviticus 10. They dishonored God inside the tabernacle and died as a result. This man "designated the Name and disparaged [it]" (10:11, AT) outside the tabernacle.[12] The death penalty applied because the honor of YHWH within the community was of utmost importance. The tabernacle was not alone in its holy status. The name of God must also be treated as holy throughout the community (see Lev. 22:32).[13] At God's command, the community administers the death penalty outside the camp, eliminating the threat to God's honor (verses 14, 23). This brief episode conveys Israel's need for ongoing guidance as they encounter situations for which the existing laws are inadequate or ambiguous.

---

[10] See Morales, *Who Shall Ascend?*, 188–92.

[11] Leigh M. Trevaskis, "The Purpose of Leviticus 24 within Its Literary Context," *VT* 59 (2009): 304.

[12] For a discussion of the interpretive issues here, see Imes, *Bearing YHWH's Name at Sinai*, 82–83.

[13] Morales, *Who Shall Ascend?*, 192–94.

Leviticus 25 contains the last of the festival instructions. Although this speech takes place "on Mount Sinai" (25:1), it pertains to Israel's tenure in the land of Canaan. Whereas Leviticus 23 regulated the sacred yearly calendar, Leviticus 25 prescribes longer cycles of time: Sabbath years for the land every seven years, and a Jubilee after seven cycles of seven. God promises to provide as he did in the wilderness, with extra food every sixth year to last until the harvest of the eighth year (25:20–22). These cycles of years necessitate further regulations regarding rental or redemption of property and the hiring and redemption of servants. Three key concepts stand out: First, the land is only available as a temporary rental because it belongs to YHWH (25:23). Second, the Israelites will always be "foreigners and tenants" in the land (25:23, AT), but must treat each other "as though resident foreigners" (25:35, AT). Finally, the Israelites are YHWH's servants so they cannot become permanent servants of another (25:55).

Leviticus 26 closes the festival instructions by describing the blessings that result from obedience. By paying attention to ritual and moral purity, the people have set up their community in such a way that God can live among them (26:11–12). The consequences for ignoring these instructions are dire. YHWH will go to great lengths to restore the people to covenant faithfulness. If none of these works, then God will send them into exile so that the land can finally have its Sabbath (26:33–34). Confession and repentance are key to restoration (26:40–45). The narrative conclusion reminds readers of the setting and characters involved in this ritual drama: "These are the statutes and ordinances and laws that the LORD established between himself and the people of Israel on Mount Sinai through Moses" (26:46). Chapter 27 adds a single speech regarding proper procedure for dedicating something to YHWH. It provides a fitting conclusion to the book, since the entire body of instructions has as its goal the dedication of Israel to YHWH.

Leviticus resolves the problem facing Moses at the end of Exodus – barred entry to the tabernacle – and it unfolds in a way that addresses the problem illustrated by Nadab and Abihu's carelessness. To be a holy nation, the people must attend to the ritual and moral dimensions of purity, the sacred calendar, sacred priests, and sacred space.

NUMBERS

In Numbers, Levitical rituals give way to lists of difficult-to-pronounce names and totals of fighting men along with tribal offerings and camping and work assignments. As boring as these chapters may seem to us, they provide essential information regarding the organization of this new nation. In Exodus, the descendants of Jacob transferred their service from Pharaoh to YHWH. As they leave Sinai, they exhibit the sophistication of an ordered society. However, unlike the clear chiastic structure of Leviticus, Numbers is notoriously difficult to outline, in part because it forms a bridge between the holiness concerns of Leviticus and the pastoral concerns of Deuteronomy.[14] The other challenge is the wide variety of genres stitched together.

The first ten chapters take place at Sinai, continuing its narratives and preparing for departure. The entire block of Sinai narratives, stretching from Exodus 19 to Numbers 10, is signaled on either side by the blast of horns (rams' horns in Exod. 19:13 and silver trumpets in Num. 10:1–10). The rest of Numbers unfolds piecemeal as Israel navigates the wilderness. The narrative meanders from one incident to another, juxtaposing genres with no clear starting and stopping points. Reading Numbers mimics the liminal wilderness experience of the Israelites. We feel the people's dislocation and desire for clear signposts on their journey and a sense of closure. However, we have already noted the elaborate chiasm that results from reading Numbers alongside Exodus. If we feel lost in the wilderness, we need only step back and take a wider view. The organization is deliberate.

The book's Hebrew name reinforces this way of reading. While the English name "Numbers" spotlights the two military censuses in chapters 1 and 26 that mark the transition from one generation to another, the Hebrew title "In the Wilderness" (*bemidbar*) highlights how these events function together with Exodus 15–18 as bookends to the Sinai narratives.

Numbers 1:1–10:10: Staging at Sinai

Numbers 1–10 contains crucial information for the administration of Israel's worship and community life that did not fit the literary design or focus of Leviticus. The "Levites" mentioned in these chapters are support personnel for the tabernacle who do not offer sacrifices. The rituals are either camp-related, voluntary, or involve special cases. The festival regulations are an addendum to Leviticus and intended to address new issues. The ten chapters proceed as follows:

[14] See Nathan MacDonald, "Numbers," in *A Theological Introduction to the Pentateuch: Interpreting the Torah as Christian Scripture*, eds. Richard Briggs and Joel N. Lohr (Grand Rapids: Baker Academic, 2012), 120–21.

1–2 A military census and camp assignments

3–4 A priestly census and work assignments

5–6 Further ritual instructions related to the camp and special situations

7–8 Consecration of tabernacle and other Levite clans

9–10 Extra Passover instructions for travel; cloud and trumpets for traveling

One hallmark of this new nation is that each tribe has permanent standing in the covenant community. They all appear on the roster of a new nation. Each contributes soldiers for Israel's army (Num. 1). Each has an official campsite (Num. 2). None can marginalize or block another from tabernacle access. Every clan among the tribe of Levi has a designated role in the maintenance of the tabernacle and a designated place to camp (Num. 3–4). Each tribe contributes equally to the tabernacle (Num. 7). The repetition of each tribe's identical offering over the course of twelve days results in a literary parade, slowing narrative time as we observe each entourage. These administrative records play a crucial theological function: registering each tribe as a legitimate member of God's people. Having arrived at Sinai as a mixed multitude of uprooted families, they now possess a clear identity as the holy people of YHWH and a clear mission to represent YHWH among the nations by living holy lives.

Numbers 10:11–22:41: Sinai to Moab

A new date stamp marks the beginning of the wilderness narratives: "In the second year, in the second month, on the twentieth day of the month" (10:11). The Israelites leave Sinai in an orderly fashion and head to the desert of Paran. This new section of Numbers connects with the previous section via the list of the same tribal leaders from Numbers 1:5–16. Moses attempts to persuade a Midianite family member, Hobab, to guide them through the wilderness (10:29–32). This reference, together with Jethro's advice to Moses in Exodus 18, bookends the Sinai narratives. Although Hobab does not answer in the affirmative and disappears from the narrative, Moses' exhortation may serve a broader theological function: "if you go with us, whatever good the LORD does for us, the same we will do for you" (10:32). The path to blessing for any nation or individual depends upon joining the nation of Israel, the people whom God has determined to bless. Moses' statement may hint at a wider invitation to participate in the covenant community.

The cloud of God's presence guides Israel through the wilderness, giving the people everything they need to triumph over their enemies

(10:33–36; cf. Exod. 40:36–38). However, the journey is fraught with difficulties and setbacks because the people fail to trust God's provision. Numbers 11–12 recount three incidents in a row that follow a cycle of complaint, judgment, prayer, and naming that echoes similar narratives in Exodus 15–18. The climax of this section is Miriam's bout with leprosy, a consequence of Aaron and Miriam's failure to respect Moses' authority. While Miriam seems to bear the consequences alone, Aaron's distress over the situation is apparent (Num. 12:10–12). His inability to heal Miriam demonstrates his dependence on Moses' superior authority.

Next, Moses sends representatives from each of the twelve tribes to scout out the land of Canaan and bring back fruit (Num. 13). Their exploration is geographically thorough, but the narrator keeps us in suspense until they return to camp. Ten men assess the land through eyes of fear, rather than faith, and their despondency is contagious (13:31–14:2). Drawing on the ancient story from Genesis 6 about the Nephilim, they paint the Promised Land as a land of horrors:

> The land that we have gone through as spies is a land that devours its inhabitants; and all the people that we saw in it are of great size. There we saw the Nephilim (the Anakites come from the Nephilim); and to ourselves we seemed like grasshoppers, and so we seemed to them. (Num. 13:32–33)

Caleb and Joshua see things the other way around:

> The land that we went through as spies is an exceedingly good land. If the LORD is pleased with us, he will bring us into this land and give it to us, a land that flows with milk and honey. Only, do not rebel against the LORD; and do not fear the people of the land, for they are no more than bread for us; their protection is removed from them, and the LORD is with us; do not fear them. (Num. 14:7–9)

According to the ten spies, the land is vicious and will devour the Israelites. According to Joshua and Caleb, the land is "exceedingly good" and, because of YHWH's protection, the Israelites will devour its inhabitants. The stories we tell each other and ourselves have the capacity to inspire faith or fear. When God determines to destroy this faithless generation, Moses intercedes again – if God wipes out the Israelites now, the nations will wrongly conclude that God was unable to deliver on his promises (cf. Ezek. 36:20). The fate of the people who bear YHWH's name strongly influences YHWH's own reputation. In response to Moses' prayer, God strikes only the ten spies with a plague.

The rest of that generation will die of natural causes in the wilderness, cut off from the blessings they eschewed.

It may seem strange for a chapter of ritual instructions to follow this epic drama. However, Numbers 15 sounds a note of hope. All the supplementary offerings reflect the situation of a later generation who will harvest fields and produce wine. In contrast, those who sin defiantly ("high-handedly") are to be cut off from the community, a command followed by a narrative example of blatant disregard for God's instructions (15:30–31, 32–36).[15] The "Sabbath-breaker" incident may also be a theological reflection on the rebellion of the spies, who prevented Sabbath rest in the land for all Israelites and died as a result. Any time a community member ignores God's instructions, they align themselves with the unfaithful spies. To prevent apostasy, every Israelite is to wear tassels on their garments as a tangible reminder of the LORD's commands (15:37–41). The new generation has a choice whether to join their unbelieving parents or to follow the faith of Joshua and Caleb and experience abundance in the land. The blue thread in these tassels likely signals their role as a "kingdom of priests" (cf. Exod. 19:4–6), since the high priest wears a blue robe (Exod. 28:31). However, the next scene portrays the folly of imagining that every Israelite shares Moses' and Aaron's status. The narratives of Numbers 16–20 reinforce the themes of holiness and death.[16]

Korah (a Levite), Dathan, and Abiram (Reubenites) complain against Moses' and Aaron's priestly leadership, protesting that every Israelite is holy. The ensuing narrative dramatically demonstrates YHWH's choice of Aaron and Moses. In Numbers 13–14, the unfaithful Israelites feared that the land of Canaan would devour them; now the ground swallows the offenders and their households because their contempt for Moses and Aaron indicates contempt for YHWH (cf. 13:32, 14:11). As in Leviticus 10, fire from the altar consumes the men who joined their rebellion (16:35). Because the entire community blames Moses for the debacle rather than themselves, God sends a plague that kills many more (16:41–50). Numbers 17 resolves the unfinished business of Numbers 16 by affirming Aaron's authorization to approach YHWH (17:1–10).[17]

---

[15]   John Sailhamer, *The Pentateuch as Narrative: A Biblical-Theological Commentary* (Grand Rapids: Zondervan, 1995), 389.

[16]   Thomas W. Mann, *The Book of the Torah: The Narrative Integrity of the Pentateuch* (Atlanta: John Knox, 1988), 133.

[17]   Thomas W. Mann, "Holiness and Death in the Redaction of Numbers 16:1–20:13," in *Love & Death in the Ancient Near East: Essays in Honor of Marvin H. Pope*, eds. John H. Marks and Robert M. Good (Guilford, CT: Four Quarters,1987), 184.

Numbers 18 reiterates the responsibility of Aaron and his sons for the holiness of the tabernacle and the role of other Levites as support personnel. The goal is to avoid another incident like those recounted in chapters 16 and 17 (18:5, "so that wrath may never again come upon the Israelites"). Numbers 19 introduces the prescribed means of cleansing anyone or anything that has become unclean through contact with a dead body.[18] Given the fate of the entire generation to die in the wilderness, the placement of this ritual here is sensible. Again, the juxtaposition of ritual text and narrative results in a comprehensive paradigm for a holy nation.

Chapter 20 begins with a halfway-helpful chronological note "in the first month" (of which year?) and an equally ambiguous geographical note: "The Israelites, the whole congregation, came into the wilderness of Zin in the first month, and the people stayed in Kadesh" (20:1). It is a new year. They have already been at Kadesh; Moses sent the spies from "the wilderness of Paran, at Kadesh" (13:26). Is Kadesh now in a different desert? Probably readers are supposed to infer that an entire generation has passed away and Israel is arriving here a second time. Kadesh-Barnea sits roughly between the Desert of Paran and the Desert of Zin. Perhaps "Paran" indicates that the Israelites are south of Kadesh, and "Zin" indicates they are on their way north. In any case, when we examine the full itinerary in Numbers 33, we find eighteen campsites between Hazeroth and Kadesh not mentioned in the narrative (33:19–36). Since they arrive at Kadesh for the second time after leaving Ezion-geber, along the Sea of Reeds at the Gulf of Aqaba (33:36), it seems the Israelites have retraced their steps in preparation for a second attempt to enter Canaan.[19]

Like the last episode at Kadesh, which disqualified an entire generation from entering the land, this incident also proves decisive. As before, the people complain of thirst. This time Moses and Aaron disqualify themselves from entering the land by failing to follow God's instructions, overreacting to the complaint and taking credit for the miracle. The setting at Kadesh is suggestive thematically: not only does it evoke memories of the community's failure to trust YHWH at Kadesh in Numbers 13–14, but "Kadesh" hints at the root of the problem – Moses' and Aaron's failure to honor God as "holy" (*kdsh*, 20:12).[20]

---

[18]   Sailhamer, *Pentateuch as Narrative*, 394.
[19]   Contra Gordon J. Wenham, *Numbers: An Introduction and Commentary*, TOTC (Downers Grove, IL: IVP, 1981), 16–17; Morales, *Who Shall Ascend?*, 25–26. Both of these scholars see Kadesh as a location stretching from Numbers 13–20.
[20]   Noted by Mann, "Holiness and Death," 185.

The deaths of Miriam and Aaron frame this chapter as a narrative unit (20:1, 22–29) and envelop Edom's refusal to let Moses and the people pass through their land. The theme is death and delay.

Israel encounters resistance on their journey to Moab (21:1), just as they had on their way to Sinai (Exod. 17:8–16), both times after complaining of thirst.[21] While the Amalekites represented anyone opposing YHWH and his people, the people of Arad represent the Canaanites. Israel's success in battle here mirrors their success in Exodus 17 and reverses their defeat by both groups on their way to Kadesh due to their disobedience (Num. 14:45). As usual, the euphoria of success does not last long. On the next stretch of the journey, their complaints prompt God to send poisonous snakes (21:6). Just as God had used a staff-turned-snake to show his power before Pharaoh in Egypt (Exod. 6), now God instructs Moses to make a bronze snake (*nehash hanehoshet*) on a staff to prompt an expression of faith.[22]

The remainder of the trip to Moab goes more smoothly. God provides water without the people complaining (21:16–17), after which Israel defeats the Amorites and the army of Bashan (21:21–35) on their way to Moab.

Numbers 22–36: Staging on the Plains of Moab

Commentators disagree about where and whether Numbers transitions to a new literary section. As mentioned earlier, the structure of the entire wilderness saga is elusive. From my perspective, 22:1 represents a transition from the wilderness narratives to Israel's staging area on the plains of Moab, signaled by the first mention of their camp "across the Jordan from Jericho." Here they conduct a second census, numbering the new generation of fighting men. Moses issues reminders about ritual offerings and festivals, adding instructions about vows. They recap their journey with a look at where they have camped and where they will live in the land. The book closes with a retrospective statement that reinforces this section break, "These are the commandments and the ordinances that the LORD commanded through Moses to the Israelites in the plains of Moab by the Jordan at Jericho" (Num. 36:13).

As readers, we are privy to a series of events in Numbers 22–24 about which Israel is oblivious. Balak, King of Moab, is understandably terrified of the Israelites. Having heard of the defeat of Sihon and Og, he summons Balaam, a powerful diviner from Mesopotamia, requesting

---

[21] Noted by Sailhamer, *Pentateuch as Narrative*, 401–2.
[22] Sailhamer, *Pentateuch as Narrative*, 402.

that he curse the Israelites. Balak wants to obtain a tactical advantage over YHWH's people, but his endeavor is futile. No matter how he tries, Balaam is unable to curse the people God has determined to bless (22:12, 18, 35, 38; 23:12). Instead, he prophesies Israel's victory and pronounces a curse over their enemies (24:9). This episode is the counterpart to YHWH's confrontation of Pharaoh in Exodus 5–15.

Sadly, the following chapter shows that the Israelites are their own worst nightmare. God's relentless determination to bless the Israelites does not protect them from their own apostasy. Unable to curse them, Moabite women entice the men of Israel to participate in idolatrous feasts (25:1–3). The plague of God's judgement wipes out the last of the rebellious generation, setting the stage for a second census in chapter 26. The total number of fighting men is roughly the same, although some tribes have experienced a dramatic increase and others a dramatic decrease. The tribe of Simeon has the biggest drop, probably due to the rebellion of chapter 25, which displays the insolence of a Simeonite man (25:14). This census provides the basis for land distribution, with larger tribes receiving larger territories (26:52–56). The narrator leaves two sober warnings for the next generation by reminding readers of the rebellion that led to the death of the previous generation (26:8–11, 63–65).[23]

Numbers 27 follows the census with two pressing concerns to ensure a smooth transition to life in the land. First, a family with no male heir petitions for land rights and YHWH gives a new command about keeping land in the family. Second, YHWH selects a new leader – Joshua – to replace Moses, who will die outside the Promised Land.

Numbers 28–29 catalogues daily, weekly, monthly, and yearly offerings, including only those offerings designated for YHWH brought by the whole community.[24] Moses addresses these commands to the people, perhaps to ensure their support for a smooth transition to Joshua and Eleazar's leadership of Israel's sacred calendar. The monthly offerings are an addition to the worship calendar not mentioned in Leviticus. Moses continues the theme of the people's offerings with a postscript about individual vows to YHWH in Numbers 30. Vows made by men or previously married women are binding, but a wife or an unmarried woman is released from her vow if her father or husband forbids it.

YHWH gives Moses one final assignment: "Avenge the Israelites on the Midianites" (31:2). Moses has lived among them and had married a

---

[23] Mann, *The Book of the Torah*, 141.
[24] Timothy R. Ashley, *The Book of Numbers*, NICOT (Grand Rapids: Eerdmans, 1993), 561.

Midianite wife (Exod. 2:15–22). However, Midian joined Moab in trying to curse the Israelites as they passed through the area (Num. 22:7), and Midianite women were involved in seducing the Israelites (25:1–2, 6, 14–18). An army made up of equal numbers from each tribe attacks the Midianites. They divide the plunder between the soldiers (half), the people (half), the LORD (1/500 of the soldiers' share), and the Levites (1/50 of the people's share). Israel's attack fulfills Balaam's prophetic message: "Blessed is everyone who blesses you, and cursed is everyone who curses you" (24:9b) – which itself echoes God's promise to Abraham in Genesis 12:3.

Numbers 32 recounts the innovation of two tribes who decide to settle east of the Jordan. Their request for land precedes the description of land boundaries and cities of refuge in chapters 34–36. This focus on the Promised Land comes after a recap of Israel's wilderness travels, with a reminder of YHWH's instructions for those entering Canaan (Num. 33). While YHWH instructs Israel to drive out the current inhabitants of the land (33:52), the shedding of innocent blood is a serious offense, necessitating instructions for accidental and intentional murder in chapter 35. "Blood pollutes the land" (35:33) because God lives among them. Only those who accidentally kill someone will be able to take refuge in designated cities.

A final narrative concludes the book of Numbers. Chapter 36 closes a loophole in YHWH's decision to allow Zelophehad's daughters to inherit their father's property (Num. 27:5–11). The women must marry members of their own tribe in order to preserve the tribal inheritance. Like the last panel on the hull of a great ship, this final instruction equips the Israelites to "set sail" in Canaan.

The wilderness journeys recounted in Exodus, Leviticus, and Numbers prepare the family of Abraham, Isaac, and Jacob for their vocation as the people belonging to YHWH, who bear his name among the nations. Once enslaved, God liberated and commissioned them for this new work. God has provided sustenance, appointed leaders, issued instructions for an ordered society, authorized a place and means for proper worship, taught them to maintain the holiness of the community so God's presence can accompany them, organized an army, and established boundaries for their possession of a land of their own. Along the way, God has repeatedly demonstrated the veracity of his promises to Abraham:

> I will make of you a great nation, and I will bless you, and make your name great, so that you will be a blessing. I will bless those

who bless you, and the one who curses you I will curse; and in you all the families of the earth shall be blessed. (Gen. 12:2–3)

The fulfillment of these promises awaits the reader who continues the journey beyond the wilderness.

SELECTED FURTHER READING

Ashley, Timothy R. *The Book of Numbers. NICOT*. Grand Rapids: Eerdmans, 1993.

Block, Daniel I. "Eden: A Temple? A Reassessment of the Biblical Evidence." Pages 3–29 in *From Creation to New Creation: Biblical Theology and Exegesis*. Edited by Daniel M. Gurtner and Benjamin L. Gladd. Peabody, MA: Hendrickson, 2013.

Briggs, Richard, and Joel N. Lohr, eds. *A Theological Introduction to the Pentateuch: Interpreting the Torah as Christian Scripture*. Grand Rapids: Baker Academic, 2012.

Cross, Frank Moore. *Canaanite Myth and Hebrew Epic: Essays in the History of the Religion of Israel*. Cambridge, MA: Harvard University Press, 1973.

Imes, Carmen Joy. *Bearing YHWH's Name at Sinai: A Reexamination of the Name Command of the Decalogue*. BBRSup 19. University Park, PA: Eisenbrauns, 2018.

Imes, Carmen Joy. "The Lost World of the Exodus: Functional Ontology and the Creation of a Nation." Pages 126–41 in *For Us, but Not to Us: Essays on Creation, Covenant, and Context in Honor of John H. Walton*. Edited by Adam E. Miglio, Caryn A. Reeder, Joshua T. Walton, and Kenneth C. Way. Eugene, OR: Pickwick, 2020.

Kass, Leon R. *Founding God's Nation: Reading Exodus*. New Haven, CT: Yale University Press, 2021.

Mann, Thomas W. "Holiness and Death in the Redaction of Numbers 16:1–20:13." Pages 181–90 in *Love & Death in the Ancient Near East: Essays in Honor of Marvin H. Pope*. Edited by John H. Marks and Robert M. Good. Guilford, CT: Four Quarters, 1987.

Mann, Thomas W. *The Book of the Torah: The Narrative Integrity of the Pentateuch*. Atlanta: John Knox, 1988.

Morales, L. Michael. *Who Shall Ascend the Mountain of the Lord? A Biblical Theology of Leviticus*. NSBT. Downers Grove: IVP Academic, 2015.

Olson, Dennis T. *The Death of the Old and the Birth of the New: The Framework of the Book of Numbers and the Pentateuch. Brown Judaic Studies 71*. Chico, CA: Scholars Press, 1985.

Sailhamer, John. *The Pentateuch as Narrative: A Biblical-Theological Commentary*. Grand Rapids: Zondervan, 1995.

Trevaskis, Leigh M. "The Purpose of Leviticus 24 within Its Literary Context." *VT* 59 (2009): 295–312.

Wenham, Gordon J. *Numbers: An Introduction and Commentary. TOTC*. Downers Grove, IL: IVP, 1981.

4 Prospects and Perils in the Land of Promise

CAMERON B. R. HOWARD

The biblical books of Joshua and Judges present some of the Hebrew Bible's finest literary artistry, as well as some of its most disturbing content. Joshua presents a troubling account of divinely sanctioned invasion and conquest, while the stories in Judges descend into ever-more-violent tales, culminating in descriptions of horrific sexual violence against women. Recent scholarship affirms that admiration of the books' skillful composition cannot ignore their problematic subject matter. In her commentary on Joshua, Carolyn J. Sharp foregrounds this clash between art and ideology, regarding Joshua "not only as a gorgeously wrought piece of literature and as a theologically profound sacred text but also as an ethically challenging testament to issues of harm and distortion that confront readers and communities in every age."[1]

At the same time, it is precisely the narrative art of these texts that reveals fissures in their totalizing discourse. Claims of complete annihilation of the Canaanites in Joshua 1–12 are then immediately undercut by a catalog of the land that has not been conquered in Joshua 13. Similarly, an elaborate etiology in Joshua 9 justifies why the Gibeonites survive the conquest and are "hewers of wood and drawers of water for the community and for the LORD's altar to this day" (Josh. 9:27 Alter). In the penultimate speech of Joshua's life, he intermingles superlative language about the success of the conquest of the land with admonitions about the dangers of the peoples who remain there (Josh. 23). Despite a rhetoric pushing obliteration, Joshua does not accomplish an erasure of the enemy, but rather emphasizes their abiding presence.

The narrative structure of Judges, which involves repeating and eventually disintegrating patterns that introduce each judge and her or his exploits, proceeds episodically, rather than in the broader movements visible in Joshua. Moreover, the deeds of the judges, who are

---

[1]   Carolyn J. Sharp, *Joshua*, SHBC (Macon, Georgia: Smith & Helwys, 2019), 7.

overwhelmingly male and ostensibly the "heroes" of their book, also call attention to the many women of Judges, whose stories of violence and loss also constitute a through line in the text – what Mieke Bal describes as "countercoherence."[2] Using the work of Mikhail Bakhtin, Mark Lackowski argues that Judges is a "polyphonic" text, "whose Deuteronomic narrator is not the dominant, monologic voice in the text, but is dialogically placed alongside a chorus of voices (Israelite, Judahite, preexilic, exilic, postexilic, anti-monarchic, pro-monarchic) that clash and compete in a cyclical carnival."[3] These examples underscore that Judges, like Joshua, is marked by a multiplicity that resists totalizing readings.

Such inherent ambiguities in these texts do not suddenly resolve their profound ethical difficulties, nor do they neutralize the books' long and sordid history of interpretation. They do, however, point to fissures in the text, spaces where diverse readers have glimpsed light and possibility amid the clouds of violence. In this essay I will focus on two female characters – Rahab (Josh. 2) and Delilah (Judg. 16) – and the ways recent scholarship has highlighted the significant ambiguities in their characterizations. While many different literary devices will be identified in the discussion, including point of view, repetition, structure, and plot, it is the confluence of these elements in the realm of characterization that best amplifies the murmurs of ambivalence bubbling in this corner of the Hebrew Bible.

UNITY OR DIVERSITY

The first challenge presented to any reader attempting a literary analysis of Joshua and Judges – and indeed, of much of the biblical canon – is how to navigate the books' inherent tension between literary unity and textual diversity. Joshua and Judges are united in their setting; they relate the story of Israel's entrance into, and earliest days in, the land of Canaan. A storyline can be traced through the Pentateuch and into these so-called "historical books," a roughly chronological account of ancient Israel that continues right through Joshua and Judges and carries on into 1 and 2 Samuel and 1 and 2 Kings, ending with an account of the destruction of Jerusalem and exile of Judah to Babylon.

---

[2]   Mieke Bal, *Death and Dissymmetry: The Politics of Coherence in the Book of Judges*, CSHJ (Chicago: University of Chicago Press, 1988), 9–39.
[3]   Mark Lackowski, "Victim, Victor, or Villain? The Unfinalizability of Delilah," *JBRec* 6.2 (2019): 197–225.

Joshua and Judges also share with the books of Samuel and Kings an affinity for the theological outlook of the book of Deuteronomy, which, among other characteristics, emphasizes God's covenant love for Israel and advocates for centralized worship in Jerusalem. The books also feature a polemical disdain for foreign (especially Canaanite) women because of their perceived potential to seduce Israelite men into apostasies with their foreign gods. This anxiety is presented in Deuteronomy itself as a warning for Israel when it crosses into Canaan: "Do not intermarry with them, giving your daughters to their sons or taking their daughters for your sons, for that would turn away your children from following me, to serve other gods" (Deut. 7:3–4a). Encounters with non-Israelite women, or with men who have married them, appear over and over in Joshua through 2 Kings, culminating in the figure of Jezebel, the Phoenician wife of King Ahab, whose apostasies are so egregious to the narrator that the text revels in her murder and the obliteration of her corpse.

In his classic proposal for understanding Joshua–Kings as a "Deuteronomistic History" Martin Noth mapped out speeches at key junctures in the story across these books, suggesting a coherent narrative structure that stretches across them all.[4] Although many aspects of Noth's proposal have been challenged by subsequent scholars, especially regarding the idea of a solitary exilic author-redactor, Noth's observations of editorial coherence, as well as the ongoing analysis he inspired, remain particularly useful not only for redaction critics, but also for readers concerned with literary features in the final form of the texts. Given these points of overlap in chronology, setting, theme, and structure, it is altogether fitting to undertake a study of Joshua and Judges together as part of a larger literary unit whose features will form a helpful backdrop for our analysis.

At the same time, Joshua and Judges are discrete books, each with a particular focus. The book of Joshua spans Joshua's career as the Israelites conquer and settle in Canaan, while Judges recounts the exploits of Israel's pre-monarchic leaders once they are established there. Joshua introduces few characters in any great detail besides Joshua himself, while Judges brings together episodic portrayals of many different, complicated, colorful figures. The Deuteronomic emphases so prominent

---

[4] For a concise presentation of Noth's proposal and its relationship to major developments in the study of the Former Prophets, see Thomas Römer, *The So-Called Deuteronomistic History: A Sociological, Historical and Literary Introduction* (London: T&T Clark, 2007).

in Joshua are much more muted in Judges. Joshua displays a neatly chiastic structure: a prologue (chapter 1) and epilogue (chapters 23–24) envelop battle narratives (chapters 2–11) and accounts of land negotiations (chapters 13–22), with the list of conquered kings (chapters 12) at the center.[5] Judges, on the other hand, is more of a cycle that gives way to a downward spiral.[6] In what follows I will treat each book as its own narrative unit, but my analysis will remain mindful of the many points of connection.

JOSHUA

As I have described in part, the books of Joshua and Judges constitute portions of overlapping narrative arcs in the Hebrew Bible. They are at once both a continuation of the Pentateuchal story and the start of a fresh new narrative. The Israelites' entrance into the promised land in the opening chapters of Joshua is a response to the command, with its concomitant promises of blessing, that God first gave to Abram at Genesis 12:1: "Go ... to the land that I will show you."[7] The conquest of Canaan is also the dramatic culmination of the exodus event, when God comes down "to deliver them from the Egyptians, and to bring them up out of that land to a good and broad land, a land flowing with milk and honey, to the country of the Canaanites, the Hittites, the Amorites, the Perizzites, the Hivites, and the Jebusites" (Exod. 3:8 NRSV). In some respects, the book of Deuteronomy ends on a cliffhanger that requires the book of Joshua for its resolution: the people of Israel are poised to enter the promised land, but their leader Moses, who has shepherded them from Egypt through forty years of wilderness wanderings, dies there at the edge. Joshua must finish what Moses has started.

Yet Joshua 1 also marks a distinctly new beginning. It opens with an acknowledgment of Moses' death and then God's direct address to Joshua, the new leader. In fact, God leads with a repetition of the fact that Moses is dead and exhorts Joshua to cross over with all the Israelites into the land God is giving them (verse 2). The crossing of the physical border into Canaan is preceded by a narrative border, with new characters and a new stage in the plot. Indeed, border-crossing is a

---

5   Sharp, *Joshua*, 35.
6   See discussion of structure in "Judges" section, later in chapter.
7   Cf. the title of Johanna W. H. van Wijk-Bos' book *The End of the Beginning: Joshua and Judges*, A People and a Land (Grand Rapids: Eerdmans, 2019).

dominant theme in the book of Joshua, as commentators have widely noted.[8] The establishment and/or transgression of boundaries – both physical and metaphorical is – a primary concern throughout the narrative. The Israelites cross over the Jordan River into the land of Canaan. The conquered land is divided into allotments for the tribes of Israel. And introducing all of this talk of boundedness and transgression is the story of Rahab, a Canaanite woman who literally lives on a boundary line and embodies the narrative's many anxieties about insiders and outsiders, identity and belonging.

Rahab and the Spies (Joshua 2)

As Robert Alter has established, biblical narrative tends to be driven by plot and dialogue without elaborate scene-setting.[9] This propensity is observable in the story of Rahab's visit from two Israelite spies (Josh. 2), where key details about the setting are revealed by the narrator only when they become necessary for the plot. Characterization in this story similarly depends not on any descriptions of appearance or musings on personality, but on the words and actions of each character. At the same time, however, meaning is also constructed in Joshua 2 through intimation and allusion. The straightforward presentations of speech and action are supplemented by innuendo, wordplay, and strategic references to other biblical narratives, creating multiple layers of interpretive possibility.

A rousing speech from Joshua in the first chapter of the book marks the transference of authority from Moses to Joshua, his successor. The people affirm, "Just as we obeyed Moses in all things, so we will obey you. Only may the LORD your God be with you, as he was with Moses! Whoever rebels against your orders and disobeys your words, whatever you command, shall be put to death. Only be strong and courageous" (Josh 1:17–18 NRSV). Chapter 2 then opens with orders from Joshua to the spies, who appear immediately to disobey his instructions.

In verse 1, Joshua gives commands to the two men: "Go (hlk), see (r'h) the land and Jericho."[10] The text immediately relays that they go (hlk) to Jericho as instructed, but instead of seeing (r'h), they go in (bw') to a house and lie down (skb). Both of the latter two verbs have sexual connotations in idiomatic usage. Such undertones might

---

[8] See, for example, L. Daniel Hawk, *Joshua. Berit Olam: Studies in Hebrew Narrative and Poetry* (Collegville, Minn.: Liturgical Press, 2000), which emphasizes this point from the very first page of the introduction.

[9] Robert Alter, *The Art of Biblical Narrative* (New York: Basic Books, 1981), 63–87.

[10] Translations are my own where not otherwise indicated.

go unremarked if not for the narrative's specification that the woman living in this house is a *zonah*, a sex worker. Moreover, Rahab's own name means "broad," "wide," or "spacious," invoking not only the openness of the land, which is regularly described as *rahab*, but also the "openness" of Rahab's own body.[11] While the text does not explicitly say that the spies had sex with Rahab – she is never the object of their verbs – the confluence of vocabulary here raises that possibility with a wink to the reader.

When word is relayed to the king of Jericho that the spies are in Rahab's house, he demands Rahab bring them out. They have come (*bw'*), he tells her, to spy out *all* the land– implying that they are not there just to go (*bw'*) into her house. Curiously, the king does not go into her house to get them, nor does he send in forces to extract them. Instead, he relies on Rahab's testimony that she was ignorant of the men's nationality and that they left at dark (verse 5). In her response to the king, Rahab twice says, "I did not know." She claims to know neither where the men came from nor where they have gone. Yet the verb "to know" (*yd'*) again carries a double entendre, since it is a verb that also refers to sexual intercourse.[12] Rahab acknowledges that the men did come (*bw'*) to her, but claims she does not know (*yd'*) anything about them.

The king follows Rahab's instructions to set pursuers upon the Israelite men with the expectation that they could still catch up to them (verse 5). Meanwhile, Rahab has acted upon the spies, who are the objects of her verbs: she *sent* them and *hid* them (verse 6). Even the flax, though described in the passive voice, has been laid out "*by her* upon the roof" (verse 6). The king of Jericho and the spies of Israel are all at Rahab's mercy; she, the primary actor in the passage, is in control.

With the pursuers safely on the other side of the gate from the Israelites, Rahab returns to the roof to address the two men. The closed gate means that the spies are protected from the king's agents, but they are also now captives in Rahab's home, vulnerable and indebted.[13] Just as she has been the subject of most of the action in the story so far, Rahab will also do most of the talking. Addressing the spies, she gives extended testimony proclaiming that the battle for the land has already

---

11   Van Wijk-Bos, *The End of the Beginning*, 61–63; Hawk, *Joshua*, 41.
12   Perhaps the most famous usage of *yd'* for sexual intercourse refers to Adam and Eve at Genesis 4:1: "And the man *knew* Eve, his wife, and she conceived."
13   Hawk, *Joshua*, 43.

been won, thanks to YHWH's favor over Israel. Rahab's speech begins, "I know ..." The three relative clauses under that verb, each introduced by *ki*, emphasize the breadth of Rahab's knowledge:

- "... that YHWH has given you the land" – Rahab's first datum is a theological claim. She has knowledge of Israel's God, of that God's power, and of that God's actions.
- "... that your terror has fallen upon us" – Rahab's second piece of knowledge points to the relationship between Israel and the Canaanites. Dread of Israel blankets Rahab's land, even before Israel's forces enter it.
- "... that all the inhabitants of the land melt before you" – Rahab's third claim to knowledge describes the reaction of active despair that her people exhibit in the face of Israel's impending invasion. Along with the preceding claim, Rahab's language here echoes the Song of the Sea sung after the Israelites escape from Egypt in the exodus, further linking Rahab to Israelite tradition and connecting the exodus event with the impending conquest: "all the inhabitants of Canaan melted away. Terror and dread fell upon them" (Exod. 15:15c–16a).

Rahab knows the actions of all the major players in this drama: her own people, their enemies (the Israelites), and even the Israelites' God. This surfeit of knowledge contrasts significantly with her feigned ignorance in verses 4–5, when she told the king that she knew neither where the men were from nor where they had gone.

In verse 10, Rahab elaborates on what she knows, introducing the next set of information with "we have heard," and following the same pattern of actors: what YHWH has done (dried the sea), what Israel has done (annihilated Sihon and Og), and what the Canaanites have done in response (melted and became breathless). Having established her thorough command of the situation, Rahab leverages her knowledge – along with the fact she has hidden the spies – in order to secure a pledge for her family's safety, using the spies' own God as witness to the oath.

Only now, having been directed by Rahab's imperative to "give me a sign of fidelity" (verse 12), do the two spies find their voice. They agree to her proposal and offer their own lives as collateral in their oath. As Hawk points out, the spies are in quite a predicament. If they refuse her, she may give them over to the king of Jericho. However, if they accept, they are violating the law of Moses that Joshua has just exhorted them to continue to obey (Josh. 1:7–8), since it "explicitly forbids agreements with any of the peoples of the land (Exod. 23:32–33;

Deut. 7:2–15)."[14] Now the reader familiar with those laws begins to wonder: is Rahab a hero or a villain? Does she save or does she entrap?

It is also at this juncture in the story that the narrator reveals that Rahab's house is in the outer wall of the city.[15] We now realize the spies have only made it as far into Jericho as the city's outer wall! Rather than seeing all the land, they have seen only the inside of Rahab's home and the underside of her rows of flax. Like the near-sighted spies, the reader has had only a limited view of the scene of this story. True to Alter's observations, additional details are provided only when necessary to move the plot.

Ostensibly the detail about the location of Rahab's house simply clarifies how she is able to help the men escape when the city gates are shut. Yet her location also draws the reader's attention to theme of border-crossing that features so prominently throughout Joshua. Rahab dwells right at the point of contact between Israel and Canaan. These in-between spaces – both literal and metaphorical – that Rahab inhabits create drama in the narrative and thus anxiety for the reader. Rahab's own characterization is part of that drama. To whom will she be loyal? She is a Canaanite, and yet she forges fidelity – *chesed* – with the Israelite spies. Does she speak truthfully? She can testify uncannily to the power of Israel's God, but she can also lie convincingly, as her successful redirection of the king suggests. She is a woman, a foreigner, and a prostitute – all identity markers associated very negatively with apostasy in the Deuteronomistic History – and yet her allegiance to Israel is necessary for Israel's success in Canaan.

Having shimmied down the rope from Rahab's window, the two men suddenly become loquacious. They outline arrangements for Rahab's family to be saved during the coming invasion, framing their speech with reiterations that Rahab's failure to abide by the stipulations would release them from their oath. For all of Rahab's power and agency the text has acknowledged so far, the men's speech here highlights her profound vulnerability. As a member of the enemy people the Israelites have come to annihilate, what can set her apart? No one will be stopping to hear her confession of Yahwistic faith in the fog of war.

The two spies introduce the red cord as a signal for Rahab's safety. This detail immediately evokes comparisons with the red blood smeared over Hebrew doorposts in Egypt at the first Passover (Exod. 12);

[14] Hawk, *Joshua*, 46.
[15] This specificity is unique to the Masoretic Text; the Septuagint does not include the detail about the outer wall. Cf. Sharp, *Joshua*, 116, 121.

the red sign spares the family within from death.[16] For the reader familiar with the book of Genesis, Rahab's red thread also recalls the story of another Canaanite woman, Tamar, who gives birth to twins after posing as a prostitute to lure her father-in-law Judah into fulfilling his family's levirate marriage duties (Gen. 38). The midwife ties a crimson cord around the first infant hand to appear, but the second twin – the one without the cord – emerges first out of the womb. The story makes clear that Tamar shows more fidelity to the traditions of Israel than do the Israelite men she married, something Judah himself acknowledges (Gen. 38:26).

Like Tamar, Rahab exhibits a righteousness that the Israelite men in the story do not muster. After all, the two men did not immediately follow Joshua's order to spy out the land and Jericho, and they would have had nothing to report to Joshua – nor would they have survived to attempt a report – if not for Rahab's intervention. Thus the red thread serves as a signal not only for the invading army, but also for the reader, connecting Rahab's fidelity to that of Tamar, and her survival to that of the Hebrews in Egypt.

After hiding out in the hill country for three days as Rahab instructed them, the men return to Joshua and make their report. The content of the spies' statement consists only of observations Rahab herself relayed to them in verse 9: "Surely the LORD has given into our hand all the land! For thus all the inhabitants of the land melt before us" (Josh. 2:24). The whole story of Joshua 2 is framed by conversations between the two spies and Joshua, but as we have already noted, Rahab does most of the talking in the middle. By constituting the language of the spies' report, Rahab's voice seeps out of the text's own structural boundaries, and another border is crossed.

Inner-Biblical Allusion

I noted earlier that Joshua 2 evokes connections to Genesis 38, Exodus 12, and Exodus 15. Daniel Hawk also maps significant similarities between Rahab's story and the story of the destruction of Sodom and Gomorrah in Genesis 19:1–29.[17] He divides each story into five parallel episodes that begin with two male strangers entering a city and seeking lodging with a host (Lot or Rahab). People demand access to the strangers, and the host protects them. When those who sought the strangers have been sent away, the coming destruction of the city is announced.

---

[16] Hawk, *Joshua*, 49.
[17] Hawk, *Joshua*, 36–40.

Lot and the spies are both instructed to flee to the hills, and negotiations ensue. At the end of the stories, each city is destroyed but the host and his or her family survive (with the exception of Lot's wife).

The commonalities between the narratives are striking, so much so that Hawk proposes the Rahab account was deliberately structured on analogy with the Sodom and Gomorrah story. While the spies parallel the angelic visitors in Genesis, and Rahab the host corresponds to Lot, Hawk notes that "the traits of the two characters in the two stories are reversed."[18] He explains:

> By shaping this story along the lines of the other, the narrator accomplishes two things. First, the dark mood rendered by the association suggests that something is seriously wrong at Jericho. Second, the reversal of character traits confuses issues of guilt and punishment. Like the people of Sodom, the Canaanite inhabitants of Jericho are wicked (Deut 9:4–5) and therefore subject to extermination. Yet Rahab displays the heroic traits attributed to the angels in the Genesis story, while the spies display the fluctuation of Lot … This Canaanite prostitute acts, in short, like an angel of God and succeeds, like Sodom's visitors, in rescuing an entire family from death.[19]

Regardless of whether these and other connections with biblical texts outside Joshua were intentional or accidental, it is clear that the narrative boundaries of the story are porous, allowing vocabulary and motifs from other stories to color and be colored by the story of Rahab and the spies. The effect of these inner-biblical resonances is simultaneously to enrich and to destabilize characterization, both for the Joshua narrative in general and for the reader's understanding of Rahab in particular.

In the way that she forces the spies to make a forbidden arrangement with her, a Canaanite woman, Rahab confirms the polemical fears against foreign women in the Deuteronomistic History. And yet her confession of the power of Israel's God, her alignment with the angels who visit Sodom, and her facilitation of the survival and success of the men who visit provide a countertestimony to those fears. Is she a savior of the Israelite spies and their cause, or does she trap them into disobedience of the law of Moses? This ambiguity remains unresolved. The aesthetics of characterization are not the only thing at stake in such ambiguity. As Sharp notes, "In the artful storytelling of Joshua 2, Rahab has been rendered as fully human, one who protects others and engages

---

[18] Hawk, *Joshua*, 39.
[19] Hawk, *Joshua*, 39–40.

in spirited dialogue and theological reasoning. She, and by extension the other Canaanites of Jericho, can no longer be treated as the faceless and dehumanized Other."[20] Polemics have been destabilized, and conquest has been problematized.

JUDGES

The stories of the Israelite "heroes" in the book of Judges are diverse and wide-ranging, but they have been corralled into a narrative pattern regularly noted by commentators and acknowledged in a theological reckoning within the narrative itself (Judg. 2:16–19). The Israelites do evil in the eyes of the LORD, who hands them over to their enemies for a time. The Israelites then cry out to God, who raises up a deliverer in the form of a judge – that is, a charismatic military leader. The judge dies, and the cycle begins again. More than a cycle, though, the pattern resembles a downward spiral, or perhaps an utter breakdown of structure, what Cheryl Exum refers to as "dissolution." Exum notes, "The political and moral instability depicted in Judges is reflected in the textual instability. The framework deconstructs itself, so to speak, and the cycle of apostasy and deliverance becomes increasingly murky."[21] The progressively more shocking incidents, particularly with regard to violence against women, mirror a disintegration of the narrative's structure. The narrator pronounces judgment on these events by pointing to the lack of monarchic rule, repeating this refrain four times in the last five chapters of the book: "In those days there was no king in Israel; each man did what was right in his own eyes" (Judg. 17:6; 18:1; 19:1; 21:25).

Samson

To get to the characterization of Delilah, we must first make a few brief notes about Samson, because her story is intimately wrapped up in his. The saga of Samson occurs in the second half of the book of Judges, marking the point where, as Exum puts it, "the Deuteronomistic framework breaks down altogether."[22] Samson's characterization commences in the narrative before he is even born. A messenger of YHWH appears to Samson's mother and announces that she will bear a child who "shall be a nazirite of God from the womb. And he shall begin to rescue Israel from

---

[20] Sharp, *Joshua*, 116.

[21] J. Cheryl Exum, "The Centre Cannot Hold: Thematic and Textual Instabilities in Judges," *CBQ* 52 (1990): 410–34.

[22] Exum, "The Centre Cannot Hold," 423.

the hand of the Philistines" (13:5 Alter). After Samson is born and grows up, YHWH blesses him, and he is visited by God's spirit (Judg. 13:25).

At first glance Samson seems well positioned to be another victorious, if also complicated, hero. Yet there are early indications of trouble: "The spirit of YHWH began to throb [in] him" (Judg. 13:25). The verb I have translated here as "throb" is *p'm*, an unusual verb that appears only five times in the Hebrew Bible. All other occurrences refer to the disruption of sleep by dreams or restlessness (Gen. 41:8; Ps. 77:4 [77:5 in the Hebrew]; Dan. 2:1, 3), and its root is related to pacing or keeping time. Van Wijk-Bos suggests "to trouble him" as the translation, while Alter uses "to drive him," reflecting that the word "neatly adumbrates his career of intermittent violent action."[23] The unique choice of verb foreshadows the impulses that will propel Samson's life and immediately casts doubt on the possibility that Samson could follow the disciplines of a Nazirite. Samson's characterization continues down this dubious path at the beginning of chapter 14, when, despite the fact that the Philistines are ruling over Israel and Samson is meant to be a warrior against them, he nonetheless insists on marrying a Philistine woman.

Exum describes Samson as a liminal figure: "He is always crossing boundaries. He does not keep the Nazirite regulations, thus violating the distinction between clean and unclean; he marries a Philistine woman, entering an exogamous relationship; and he prefers foreigners to his own kind."[24] The theme of boundary-crossing observed in Joshua crops up again here in Judges, where the well-ordered divisions of tribes and peoples previously established are now beset by anxiety about military and ethical leadership. A descent toward chaos prompts nervousness about maintaining boundaries. Onto this stage enters Delilah, a character whose identity markers are sparse and whose presence is disorienting.

Delilah

The most immediate ambiguity regarding Delilah is her nationality: is she an Israelite, is she Philistine, or does she belong to another ethnic group? The text never specifies. Samson has shown a proclivity for Philistine women, first by pursuing a Philistine wife (14:2–3) and then

23 Van Wijk-Bos, *The End of the Beginning*, 272; Robert Alter, *Ancient Israel: The Former Prophets: Joshua, Judges, Samuel, and Kings. A Translation with Commentary* (New York: W. W. Norton), 178.

24 Cheryl Exum, *Fragmented Women: Feminist (Sub)versions of Biblical Narratives*, 2nd edition, Cornerstones (London: T&T Clark, 2015), Kindle edition, loc. 1658. See also Gregory Mobley, *Samson and the Liminal Hero in the Ancient Near East*, LHBOTS 453 (London: T&T Clark, 2006).

by visiting a sex worker in the Philistine city of Gaza (16:1). Though the text does not stipulate the prostitute's nationality, her unambiguously Philistine location suggests it. Thus, these first two of Samson's lovers may also point the reader toward a Philistine identity for Delilah; at the same time, her Hebrew-sounding name suggests she is an Israelite. Like Samson, Delilah is a liminal figure. Like Rahab, Delilah lives in a border space, specifically Nahal Sorek, a region where Philistine territory meets the Israelite territory of Dan, Samson's own ancestral tribe.[25] Delilah crosses easily between Israelite and Philistine spaces; there is no suggestion, for example, that there are any language barriers as she communicates with both Samson and the Philistine leaders. There are few ready stereotypes to bring to her characterization at the outset of the story; readers must wait for the action to unfold.

Delilah is approached by Philistine overlords to spy out the secrets of Samson's strength in exchange for a very substantial amount of money. The fact that they use bribery rather than threats may further suggest Delilah is herself a Philistine, rather than a vulnerable Israelite subject. The narrative provides almost no details about her backstory, her means, her work, her station in life, or anything else. Wil Gafney posits that "her unexplained life is presented to evoke suspicion;" since other places in the Samson saga are eager to label women as Philistines or sex workers, it is more likely she is an Israelite, and except for the story's proximity to Samson's excursion in Gaza, there is nothing to support the common assumption that she is a prostitute.[26]

Delilah accepts money from the Philistine leaders to carry out their scheme. Again, the narrative provides no comment on this exchange, which can be read as treachery, as another kind of prostitution, or, as Gafney notes, as a mark of self-sufficiency: "Delilah appears to be the rare woman who has escaped biblical patriarchy with her body weight in bling, silver, to boot."[27] The very high price offered points to the depth of the Philistine leaders' desire to bring down Samson.

[25] Royce M. Victor, "Delilah – A Forgotten Hero (Judges 16:4–21): A Cross-Cultural Narrative Reading," in *Joshua and Judges*, Texts @ contexts, eds. Athalya Brenner and Gale A. Yee (Minneapolis: Fortress, 2013), 235–55.

[26] Wil Gafney, "A Womanist Midrash of Delilah: Don't Hate the Playa Hate the Game," in *Womanist Interpretations of the Bible: Expanding the Discourse*, eds. Gay L. Byron and Vanessa Lovelace, SemeiaSt 85 (Atlanta: SBL Press, 2016), 49–72. Cf. Tammi Schneider, *Judges. Berit Olam: Studies in Hebrew Narrative and Poetry* (Collegeville: Liturgical Press, 2000), 221, describes one of Delilah's liminal positions as between wife and prostitute, as she is neither like the woman from Timnah nor the sex worker from Gaza.

[27] Gafney, "A Womanist Midrash of Delilah," 70.

In the discussion of Rahab earlier, I noted that the action and dialogue in Joshua 2 are remarkably one-sided, particularly in the first half of the story, when Rahab is the primary speaker as well as actor. By contrast, the interactions between Samson and Delilah are much more balanced; the two are very much in this drama together. Notably, however, the narrator's comment that Samson loved Delilah (16:4) is not matched by any note about Delilah's inner feelings. Is she in this relationship for love of Samson, for love of money, for love of country, for fear, for spite, for self-preservation? Her motivations remain mysterious.

Delilah's attempts to discover the source of Samson's strength begin with a very close repetition of the elements the Philistine overlords have asked Delilah to "see" (i.e., to find out): "Tell me how your strength is so great, and how you could be bound for someone to subdue you" (16:6). Three times Delilah asks this question, and three times Samson gives her a different answer, each suggesting a different material: seven moist and undried bowstrings (verse 7), unused ropes (verse 11), and his seven locks of hair woven into a loom and secured with its pin (verse 13). Each time after she has bound him, Delilah shouts, "The Philistines are upon you, Samson!" Propelled into fighting mode, Samson successfully throws off the bindings. It is unclear whether Samson suspects there is danger to him in this drama, or if he is simply enjoying the game.

In the fourth and final iteration of this pattern, Delilah finally presses Samson to reveal the truth: his power is linked to his unshaven hair, part of his Nazirite identity. It is curious that Samson does not seem to suspect that Delilah will act on this new information, since she has done so according to his words three times before. Or perhaps her pestering (verse 16) has led him to seek relief rather than good sense. In any case, Delilah has no trouble putting him to sleep on her knees, where she can shave and thus subdue him (verse 19). Upon waking, Samson is unable to throw off the binding as before, something the narrator attributes not primarily to the agency of Delilah or the Philistine leaders, but because, translated woodenly, "YHWH had left from upon him" (verse 20). This awkward rendering of the prepositional phrase helps to illustrate its parallel with Delilah's refrain, "The Philistines are upon you!" Once YHWH is no longer "upon" ('al) Samson, the Philistines will be "upon" ('al) him instead.

The word I have rendered as "subdue" in verses 6 and 19 is 'nh, which can also be translated as "rape," as in the rape of the Levite's concubine at Judges 19. Indeed, the whole exchange between Samson and Delilah carries undertones of both sex and sexual violence. Alter, who

translates 'nh as "torture," remarks that "the talk of binding and torture also makes this sound like a perverse sex game they are playing."[28]
Delilah herself ties up Samson each time, and he frees himself from her
restraints with a great outburst of power, all while the Philistines watch
from their hiding place. Once Samson is sleeping on her knees and she
is shaving his head, Delilah "began to subdue ['nh] him" (16:19); the
text again invokes the language of sexual violence. Even when Samson
has been carried away to prison, he is "set to grinding," a phrase laden
with innuendo, as in this passage from the book of Job: "If my heart
has been enticed by a woman, and I have lain in wait at my neighbor's
door, then let my wife grind for another, and let other men kneel over
her" (Job 31:9–10 NRSV). Then, when the Philistines ask for Samson to
"play" for them (16:25), the verb there is a Piel-stem form of tshq/shq,
which can mean either playing, mocking, or fondling/sexual play. It is
the same form that indicates Rebekah is Isaac's wife rather than his
sister at Genesis 26:8. Given the sexual violence against women that
pervades the book of Judges, Delilah's control and Samson's subjugation
appear as a stark reversal.

Besides the frequent repetition of sexually suggestive language, the
verb r'h, "to see," also functions as a significant *leitwort* in the Samson
saga.[29] Samson *sees* a Philistine woman in Timnah and wants to marry
her (14:1–3). Samson *sees* a prostitute in Gaza and sleeps with her (16:1).
But Samson *loves* Delilah, a feeling that has apparently obscured his
vision, breaking the pattern through which he became involved with
the first two women (16:4). Delilah never utters any statement of recip-
rocal affection, instead using his feelings to taunt him: "How can you
say 'I love you' when your heart is not with me?" (16:15) She continues
to harass him almost "to death" (16:16), so that once he finally spills
his guts, Delilah *sees* that Samson has "told all his heart to her" (16:18).
In an ironic twist, Delilah's relationship with Samson leads to the loss
of his eyes and eventually to his actual death. Samson's vision has been
about appetite, while Delilah's vision produces insight.

Assuming the reader takes the side of the Israelites in these tales, then
Delilah as Philistine is yet another manifestation of the Deuteronomistic
seductive and apostate foreign woman, while Delilah as Israelite is a
traitor. Regardless of her identity, her character from an Israelite point
of view is maligned. But should the reader be expected automatically to
sympathize with Samson or his people? Samson has boorishly stomped

---

[28]   Alter, *Ancient Israel*, 189.
[29]   Cf. Lackowski, "Victim, Victor, or Villain," 211–12.

his way through chapters 14–15, propelled by his urges and whims, prone to outbursts of violence and vulgarity. He is a leader of Israel, and the spirit of the LORD is – at least on some occasions – with him. At the same time, the Samson cycle of stories is on the downward slope of the book of Judges, when the actions of Israel's leaders are regarded with disdain by the narrator. Is Samson, then, the "hero" in his encounter with Delilah? Is he, like Tony Soprano in HBO's *The Sopranos*, an anti-hero whom the reader roots for but also finds morally objectionable? Or is Samson no kind of hero at all, in a text that emphasizes pre-monarchic Israel's slide into chaos? Each of these possibilities, along with many more, inheres in the laconic prose of the book of Judges.

Royce M. Victor reads Delilah as the real hero of this story. Working from a Philistine perspective and reading Delilah's identity as Philistine, Victor understands Delilah as a "forgotten hero," "a Philistine woman who is ready to sacrifice her life for the defense of her land and people."[30] In this reading it follows that Delilah is more noble than Samson, for he acts always on behalf of himself, whereas she takes on risk for the group.[31] In a variation on the theme of Delilah's heroism, Gafney points to Delilah's independence: she is her own hero. Gafney writes, "She is not punished in the text for her role in Samson's death. She is not subjected to the authority of any man. She leaves the text, wealthy and free."[32] What readers might describe as a dearth of identity markers for Delilah turns out to be space for possibility rather than lack. Of course, Delilah can also still be read as a stumbling block for Israel and an enemy of its people for her trickery and treachery toward Samson; that possibility also inheres in the text. As Lackowski observes, "Delilah bears the marks of a complex, unfinalized character who is not easily defined, known or understood."[33] Such "unfinalizability" is also characteristic of Rahab, who, with Delilah, crosses borders and blurs boundaries.

Perhaps the author(s) of Joshua and Judges intended such ambiguity when they fashioned their words into these stories, or perhaps not. We cannot know who the authors of the books were, much less what was in their minds as they wrote. To be sure, the historical and cultural contexts of the implied authors offer important insights into possibilities for interpretation. But the literary artistry exhibited in these texts

---

[30] Victor, "Delilah – A Forgotten Hero," 235.
[31] Victor, "Delilah – A Forgotten Hero," 241.
[32] Gafney, "A Womanist Midrash of Delilah," 71.
[33] Lackowski, "Victim, Victor, or Villain," 217.

also creates room for interpretation that surpasses the imaginations of the authors who first wrote them down. In their fractures, fissures, and ambiguities, meaning continues to bubble up through these ancient texts in new and surprising ways.

SELECTED FURTHER READING

Alter, Robert. *The Art of Biblical Narrative*. New York: Basic Books, 1981.

Alter, Robert. *Ancient Israel: The Former Prophets: Joshua, Judges, Samuel, and Kings. A Translation with Commentary*. New York: W. W. Norton, 2013.

Bal, Mieke. *Death & Dissymmetry: The Politics of Coherence in the Book of Judges*. Chicago Studies in the History of Judaism. Chicago: University of Chicago Press, 1988.

Exum, J. Cheryl. "The Centre Cannot Hold: Thematic and Textual Instabilities in Judges." *Catholic Biblical Quarterly* 52 (1990): 410–443.

Exum, J. Cheryl. *Fragmented Women: Feminist (Sub)versions of Biblical Narratives*. 2nd edition, Cornerstones. London: T&T Clark, 2015. Kindle edition.

Gafney, Wil. "A Womanist Midrash of Delilah: Don't Hate the Playa Hate the Game." Pages 49–72 in *Womanist Interpretations of the Bible: Expanding the Discourse*. Edited by Gay L. Byron and Vanessa Lovelace. Semeia Studies 85. Atlanta: SBL Press, 2016.

Hawk, L. Daniel. *Joshua. Berit Olam: Studies in Hebrew Narrative and Poetry*. Collegeville, MN. Liturgical Press, 2000.

Lackowski, Mark. "Victim, Victor, or Villain? The Unfinalizability of Delilah." *Journal of the Bible and Its Reception* 6.2 (2019): 197–225.

Mobley, Gregory. *Samson and the Liminal Hero in the Ancient Near East*. Library of Hebrew Bible / Old Testament Studies 453. London: T&T Clark, 2006.

Römer, Thomas. *The So-Called Deuteronomistic History: A Sociological, Historical and Literary Introduction*. London: T&T Clark, 2007.

Schneider, Tammi J. *Judges. Berit Olam: Studies in Hebrew Narrative and Poetry*. Collegeville, MN: Liturgical Press, 2000.

Sharp, Carolyn J. *Joshua. Smyth & Helwys Bible Commentary*. Macon, Georgia: Smyth & Helwys, 2019.

Van Wijk-Bos, Johanna. *The End of the Beginning: Joshua & Judges*. Volume 1 of A People and a Land. Grand Rapids: Eerdmans, 2019.

Victor, Royce M. "Delilah – A Forgotten Hero (Judges 16:4–21)." Pages 235–255 in *Joshua and Judges. Texts @ Contexts*. Edited by Athalya Brenner and Gale A. Yee. Minneapolis; Fortress, 2013.

5 Saul the Undead and David the Bringer of Life

STEPHEN B. CHAPMAN

The Samuel narrative is one of the Bible's greatest literary achievements, a cornerstone of Western civilization, and a crucial scriptural text for the Christian tradition.

The narrative is now found in two biblical books: 1 and 2 Samuel. Internal and external evidence indicates that these books constituted a single narrative prior to their division. Internally, 2 Samuel continues the action of 1 Samuel. The beginning of 2 Samuel (2 Sam 1) relies on the end of 1 Samuel (1 Sam 31) in order to offer a new perspective on the event just related. Moreover, the concluding section of the Samuel narrative in 2 Samuel 21–24 looks back to the time of 1 Samuel as well as the time of 2 Samuel. The initial poetry appearing in 1 Samuel 2:1–11 enjoys verbal and thematic links with the concluding poetry in 2 Samuel 22–23, bracketing the entire narrative with psalm-like material.[1] Externally, Hebrew manuscript evidence points to routine division of the Samuel narrative only beginning in the late medieval period, although the books had already been divided in Greek Bibles since antiquity – not always, however, in the same place.[2]

The biblical books of 1 and 2 Samuel appear among the narrative books that follow the Bible's first five books, or Pentateuch (Genesis–Exodus–Leviticus–Numbers–Deuteronomy). These post-pentateuchal narrative books (Joshua–Judges–Samuel–Kings) continue the story of Israel and provide a bridge to the books of the Prophets.[3] Accordingly,

---

[1] Brevard S. Childs, *Introduction to the Old Testament as Scripture* (Philadelphia: Fortress, 1979), 273–78.

[2] P. Kyle McCarter, Jr., *1 Samuel*, AB 3 (Garden City, NJ: Doubleday, 1980), 3; Julio Trebolle Barrera, "Samuel/Kings and Chronicles: Book Divisions and Textual Composition," in *Studies in the Hebrew Bible, Qumran, and the Septuagint Presented to Eugene Ulrich*, eds. Peter W. Flint, Emanuel Tov, and James C. VanderKam, VTSup 101 (Boston: Brill, 2006), 96–108. The midpoint of the Hebrew text of Samuel is designated in the Masoretic tradition as 1 Sam 28:23.

[3] The book of Ruth appears between Judges and Samuel in Greek Bibles but not in Hebrew Bibles. In Hebrew Bibles, Ruth instead appears in the Writings, the third section of the biblical canon used in Rabbinic Judaism.

this narrative subcollection is sometimes known as the Historical Books and sometimes as the Former Prophets. Its thematic unity as a subcollection is disputed.

Martin Noth (1902–68) influentially reconstructed a precanonical "Deuteronomistic History" (DtrH), consisting of the books of Deuteronomy through 2 Kings.[4] For Noth, this earlier literary collection was severed from its taproot when Deuteronomy was detached and repositioned as the conclusion to the Pentateuch rather than continuing to serve as the introduction to the DtrH. Noth viewed some of the contents of the DtrH as having originated prior to their combination, but he sought to trace how it was their eventual compilation and editing that determined the literary shape and present coherence of the entire narrative. This activity was attributed by Noth's followers to a Jerusalem-based reform group in the seventh and sixth centuries BCE ("the deuteronomists"). The purpose of this group's literary work was to provide an explanation for Israel's eventual destruction and exile, and to offer a theological defense of God's justice in response to Israel's disobedience.

Noth's proposal, which was once widely accepted, has been treated more skeptically in recent scholarship. Moreover, the deuteronomistic elements of the Samuel narrative appear rather slight to some contemporary researchers.[5] Gerhard von Rad (1901–71) had already pointed out the high confidence in the Davidic line evident at places within the DtrH, particularly in Samuel (e.g., God's *eternal* promise to David in 2 Sam 7:16). For von Rad, the DtrH not only justified Israel's destruction, but it also expressed hope for Israel's future. It identified abiding features of Israel's heritage that could be employed to revive Israel's common life on the far side of divine judgment.[6] So the extent to which the Samuel narrative should be read on its own apart from the other Historical Books or together with them as part of a single DtrH remains an open question, as does the main theme or purpose of the DtrH, if such a history did in fact exist.

---

[4]   Martin Noth, *The Deuteronomistic History*, 2nd edition, JSOTSup 15 (Sheffield: Sheffield Academic, 1991).

[5]   See Christa Schäfer-Lichtenberger, ed., *Die Samuelbücher und die Deuteronomisten*, BWANT 188 (Stuttgart: Kohlhammer, 2010); Cynthia Edenburg and Juha Pakkala eds., *Is Samuel among the Deuteronomists? Currents Views on the Place of Samuel in a Deuteronomistic History*, AIL 16 (Atlanta: Society of Biblical Literature, 2013).

[6]   Gerhard von Rad, "The Deuteronomistic Theology of History in the Books of Kings," in *Studies in Deuteronomy*, trans. David Stalker, SBT 9 (London: SCM, 1953), 74–91.

THE SUBSTANCE AND STYLE OF THE SAMUEL NARRATIVE

The narrative is broadly organized around three central figures: Samuel, Saul, and David. The outset of the narrative (1 Sam 1–8) focuses on Samuel, who is a transitional figure with similarities to the judges who came before him and the priests and prophets who follow him.[7] However, Samuel is also presented as an exemplary figure within these leadership traditions, and not merely a bridge from one to the next. A momentous development occurs in 1 Samuel 8, when God reluctantly decides to grant the request of the people for a king, a type of leadership that Israel previously lacked and actively resisted (Judg 8:22–23; 9:6–21; 17:6; 18:1; 19:1; 21:25).[8]

Beginning in 1 Samuel 9, the primary focus shifts to Saul, who regularly appears in the narrative until his death in 1 Samuel 31. Saul is introduced as the figure chosen by God to be Israel's first king, and yet – shockingly – Saul turns out to be an unsuccessful monarch. Saul does a lot that seems heroic and right. He defends Israel from hostile forces (1 Sam 11:1–11; 14:20–23, 47–48). He is conventionally religious (1 Sam 9:7; 10:13; 11:6; 13:9, 12; 14:18–19; 15:24–31). He respects the authority of Samuel (1 Sam 13:8; 15:24–25). He receives God's support at first (1 Sam 9:17; 10:1, 10, 24; 11:6). God is even said to change Saul's heart (1 Sam 10:6, 9), so as to make him fully suited for his royal role. But the narrative also repeatedly employs motifs relating to physical size and appearance in order to sow doubt about Saul's long-term success.[9] Introduced as head-and-shoulders taller than other Israelites (1 Sam 10:23), Saul looks every bit a king. Yet there is something hollow about him. He seeks to draw other big men into his service (1 Sam 13:2; 14:52) and he esteems weapons (1 Sam 13:22). These are classic symptoms of human self-reliance in the Bible, which worries about how such things undermine faith in God (e.g., Deut 1:41–44; 1 Sam 2:9; 15:12; 16:7; 17:45; Pss 20:7; 33:16–17; 147:10–11; Isa 31:1; Zech 4:6; 2

---

[7] The Samuel narrative begins by describing how Samuel becomes a priestly apprentice to Eli (1 Sam 1:24–28; 2:11). It goes on to refer to him as a "prophet" (1 Sam 3:20) and a "judge" (1 Sam 7:6, 15–17).

[8] Here I am describing the narrative's presentation. There are many questions about the relationship between its presentation and the actual course of history, but these are not my present concern. For an exploration of the relationship between the historical rise of the monarchy in Israel and the portrayal of that rise in the Samuel narrative, see Walter Dietrich *The Early Monarchy in Israel: The Tenth Century B.C.E.*, BE 3, transl. Joachim Vette (Atlanta: Society of Biblical Literature, 2007).

[9] Keith Bodner, *1 Samuel: A Narrative Commentary*, HBM 19 (Sheffield: Sheffield Phoenix, 2008), 28.

Chr 32:7–8). A repeating motif in the Saul stories is thus how Saul's ritual activities consistently misfire (e.g., 1 Sam 14:37, 41). Something about Saul does not work (1 Sam 28:6).

The narrative in 1 Samuel 9–15 not only reports these events; it also probes the theologically fraught conundrum of how a leader chosen by God could possibly fail a divine commission. But fail Saul does. So God raises up another king-candidate beginning in 1 Samuel 16, namely David. The second half of 1 Samuel depicts a fascinating state of affairs in which Saul has been rejected by God (1 Sam 15:29, 35) but still is king, while David has been chosen by God to be king and nevertheless is not yet recognized as one. Here again, powerful theological questions are aired. If God has rejected Saul as king, why does God not depose him? If God has chosen David, why does God not install him as king? Such questions reveal how the narrative compels the reader to reflect on the nature of divine action and the character of God. Why is there such restraint on God's part? Why does God seemingly want these human figures to work out for themselves their divinely ordained destinies?

A related narrative motif is that of secrecy. When Samuel anoints David at God's instruction (1 Sam 16:13), the act is private. Although the narrative does not call attention to the significance of the fact, God's choice of David is known at the time only to God, Samuel, David, and David's immediate family (1 Sam 16:13). So while 1 Samuel 16–31 generally portrays Saul and David as they jockey against each other for power, it turns specifically on the nature of David's true identity and whether other characters in the narrative eventually perceive David rightly or not (e.g., Jonathan in 1 Sam 23:17 and Saul in 1 Sam 24:20).[10] This motif is mirrored by the "messianic secret" in the New Testament's Gospel of Mark.[11] Like Peter, who comes to acknowledge Jesus' true messianic identity (Mark 8:27–30), it is Abigail who fully acknowledges David as Israel's true king and messiah (1 Sam 25:28–31). Although both Jonathan and Saul do recognize David as the future king, it is only Abigail who understands how David has a pivotal role within God's program to promote life and therefore must refrain from shedding innocent blood (1 Sam 25:26–31).

Secrecy and discovery operate not only with regard to the narrative's characters. One of the narrative's most brilliant stylistic features is to

---

[10] Karl Barth, *Church Dogmatics, II/2: The Doctrine of God* (Edinburgh: T&T Clark, 1957), 374.

[11] For the classic critical presentation of this aspect of Mark, see William Wrede, *The Messianic Secret*, transl. J. C. G. Greig (Cambridge: J. Clarke, 1971).

include its implied reader as essentially another character within its discourse, but implicitly rather than explicitly. Unlike some nineteenth-century novels, the biblical narrator never introduces phrases such as "Dear Reader ..."[12] However, the Samuel narrative is constructed in such a way as to present the reader with multiple interpretive possibilities, either by omitting or presenting choice tidbits of information. Just as the narrative's characters attempt to discern David's identity, the narrative's reader becomes engaged in the same interpretive task. Who is David really? What is his exact status? If he has indeed been chosen by God, why is he not yet King? Moreover, does David truly act like or deserve to be God's chosen one?

These questions multiply and intensify as the narrative moves into what is now the book of 2 Samuel. With the death of Saul, David is publicly acknowledged and crowned, first by people of Judah (2 Sam 2:4) and then by all Israel (2 Sam 5:3). This turning point resolves the issue about David's royal status, which is no longer a secret, but not the questions about his character and role within God's plan. The bloody events arising from David's concentration of power (2 Sam 2–5) raise concerns for the reader about his administration of justice. Even within the narrative, David is eventually known as a "man of blood" (2 Sam 16:8), and apparently for that reason is forbidden by God to build a temple (2 Sam 7:5, 12–13; cf. 1 Chr 22:8; 28:3). David's opportunistic, abusive treatment of Bathsheba and Uriah (2 Sam 11) suggests that he has become a jaded, cynical ruler interested only in leisure, pleasure, and self-advantage. He reaches his lowest point when his son Absalom raises a rebellion against him from within his own family (2 Sam 15:1–12). Although he defeats Absalom and regains the throne, David later appears emotionally and physically shattered because of what has occurred (1 Kgs 1:1–27). Yet God maintains an unwavering commitment to David throughout these messy, troubling episodes. Indeed, God considers that commitment to include David's descendants, having promised David a secure royal line for ever (2 Sam 7:12–16; cf. 2 Sam 23:5).

The rationale for God's favor to David is just as challenging to understand as the rationale for God's disfavor concerning Saul. The narrative characteristically does not offer the reader much in the way of reasons or explanations for the events it relates. But the divine security of David and the Davidic house is stubbornly upheld. The reader is confronted again and again with the dilemma of a David who sometimes

---

[12]   The most famous instance of this device is the final line of Charlotte Brontë's 1847 novel *Jane Eyre*: "Reader, I married him."

does terrible things but nonetheless enjoys God's firm support. How can this be? David himself does not provide much help to the reader because he is sparing of speech (1 Sam 16:18), and the narrator declines to reveal David's inner thoughts. With other characters in the narrative, especially Saul, the narrator offers occasional information about their private perspectives or motivations (e.g., 1 Sam 18:8–9, 11–12, 17, 29; 20:26). With David, this occurs only rarely (1 Sam 27:1 is one instance). The result is not a two-dimensional David – as a character, he seems fully realized – but rather a strategic, calculating David: a David who knows the difference between public and private speech, a David who is able to dissemble (1 Sam 21:12–13), a David who plays things close to the vest. In the narrative's telling, David is an elusive character whose interior life is always just out of reach.

So it is a genuine surprise to reach the last four chapters of 2 Samuel and encounter a David who all of a sudden pours forth speech. These final chapters have been artfully designed. They are set within a classic A–B–B'–A' pattern. The last one (2 Sam 24) depicts a second ritual threat to Israel's well-being, just as in the first one (2 Sam 21), even using the Hebrew verb for "adding" or "doing again" (y-s-p Hiph., 2 Sam 24:1), in order to draw attention to the relationship between the two accounts. The middle two chapters both contain poetry, with David as the speaker each time. The poetry in 2 Samuel 22 is largely identical to Psalm 18, whereas the poem in 2 Samuel 23:1–7 stands on its own and is introduced as "David's last words." Striking is not only how much David now says, after substantially refraining from speech throughout the prior narrative,[13] but also the nature of his speech. If the poetry in 2 Samuel 22–23 represents David's native, internal discourse, a reflection of his own perception of himself and the world around him, then it is deeply and unwaveringly pious. David often earlier appeared to be pragmatic and worldly. Yet that same David has somehow had the God-drenched language of the Psalms "inside" him all along.

This literary disclosure therefore does on a large scale what the Samuel narrative has consistently done on a small scale along the way. The narrative has not only ambiguated David by presenting him as a cipher and raising all sorts of competing questions about his character and motivation, but it has slowly provided guidance to the reader so as to clarify these points retrospectively. Both the ambiguation and disambiguation of David are mostly subtle and incremental, a style of

---

[13]   See also 2 Sam 1:17–27, David's moving lament over Saul and Jonathan. In this case, however, David's words seem gauged for a public audience.

storytelling offering many opportunities for artistry and irony. Then, with a grand flourish, the narrative's conclusion stages a major disclosure and resolves lingering uncertainties.[14] The retrospective disambiguation of the Samuel narrative is another of its most impressive literary features. It gives the narrative its distinctive drama and results in a high level of existential involvement on the part of the reader. To read the Samuel narrative attentively is to be drawn into its world, to want to understand its characters, particularly David, and learn more about the kind of God who would do things this way.

The other noteworthy feature of the conclusion to the Samuel narrative is that these chapters do not continue the sequential unfolding of the main storyline, as has occurred since the beginning of 1 Samuel. Instead, 2 Samuel 21–24 interrupts that storyline, which is picked back up again in 1 Kings 1. Moreover, the individual elements within 2 Samuel 21–24 are items "out of time." The ritual threat narratives in 2 Samuel 21 and 24 do not receive firm historical settings. The poems in 2 Samuel 22 and 23 extend beyond single settings too, even though 2 Samuel 22:1 is introduced with a vague allusion to a particular day and 23:1–7 is presented as David's final discourse.[15] Also significant is how some of the shorter narrative units found in these final chapters refer to characters and events during Saul's reign (e.g., 2 Sam 21:1–14), giving the material a chockablock, mopping-up feel. This use of non-narrative material and broken narrative fragments pauses the forward motion of the larger story in order to offer a summary statement of what has occurred thus far. It is another way in which the final chapters of 2 Samuel function as a formal literary subunit and a self-conscious conclusion to the Samuel narrative as a whole.

THE SAMUEL NARRATIVE IN WESTERN CIVILIZATION

Because of the Samuel narrative's focus on leadership and kings, it has always held an important place in Western political thought. Within the West's traditional Christian culture, ideas about political organization after the fall of Rome took on something of their texture and shape through consultation with the stories of Saul and David. Moses was also an important figure for political theory and some evidence suggests

[14]   A similar storytelling technique is used to great effect in James Clavell's 1975 novel *Shōgun*, right down to the concluding inner monologue of its main character Toranaga.

[15]   Yet David remains alive in 1 Kings 1 and he offers a dying charge to Solomon in 1 Kings 2:1–9.

that he was a more common biblical touchstone in Christianity's first few centuries.[16] But already with Ambrose of Milan's *Defense of the Prophet David to the Emperor Theodosius* (ca. 390 CE), a Davidic typology was applied to temporal rulers.[17] Further use of this Davidic typology in the Byzantine Empire suggests the inclusion of David alongside Moses as two biblical figures with particular relevance for the conduct of Christian rulers.[18] Byzantine emperors were sometimes styled as second Davids.[19] However, a new concentration on David and the Davidic line came about with the rise of the Carolingian dynasty in medieval Europe.

Beginning with Pepin the Short in the mid-eighth century CE, the Carolingian monarch began to be known as a "new David" (*novus david*) and was anointed with holy oil in keeping with the biblical practice. While there may have been earlier instances of royal anointing, only with the Carolingian kings did it become a standard coronation practice.[20] Throughout the latter half of the eighth century and into the ninth, the self-identity of the Frankish people was increasingly shaped by the idea of being the "new Israel."[21] Charlemagne's state seal bore the legend: "Samuel renewed the empire" (cf. 1 Sam 11:14). Charlemagne's personal nickname among members of the royal court was "David."[22] His throne at Aachen was built with six steps, in keeping with Solomon's (1 Kgs 10:19). Although there were also differences from the biblical practices and symbols of royalty (Charlemagne's throne apparently did not have a rounded back like Solomon's),[23] the association between Carolingian royal culture and biblical Israel was

---

[16] Averil Cameron, *Christianity and the Rhetoric of Empire: The Development of Christian Discourse* (Berkeley: University of California Press, 1994), 53–6; Claudia Rapp, "Comparison, Paradigm and the Case of Moses in Panegyric and Hagiography," in *The Propaganda of Power: The Role of Panegyric in Late Antiquity*, ed. Mary Whitby, MnemosyneSup 183 (Leiden: Brill, 1998), 277–98.

[17] St. Ambrose, *Treatises on Noah and David*, FOC 140, transl. Brian P. Dunkle (Washington, DC: Catholic University of America, 2020).

[18] Claudia Rapp, "Old Testament Models for Emperors in Early Byzantium," in *The Old Testament in Byzantium*, eds. Paul Magdalino and Robert Nelson (Washington, DC: Dumbarton Oaks Research Library, 2010), 175–97.

[19] Heinrich Fichtenau, *Byzanz und die Pfalz zu Aachen* (Graz: H. Böhlaus, 1951), 30.

[20] Michael J. Enright, *Iona, Tara, and Soissons: The Origin of the Royal Anointing Ritual*, Arbeiten zur Frühmittelalterforschung 17 (Berlin: de Gruyter, 1985).

[21] Mary Garrison, "The Franks as the New Israel? Education for an Identity from Pippin to Charlemagne," in *The Uses of the Past in the Early Middle Ages*, eds. Yitzhak Hen and Matthew Innes (New York: Cambridge University Press, 2000), 114–61.

[22] Henry Mayr-Harting, "Charlemagne, the Saxons, and the Imperial Coronation of 800," *The English Historical Review* 111.444 (1996): 1113–33.

[23] Garrison, "Franks," 155.

widely recognized at the time. The strength of this association has recently been reinforced by renewed appreciation for the vitality of biblical scholarship during the Carolingian period.[24]

Because of the Carolingian dynasty, an Israel typology became a customary reflex within the Holy Roman Empire, especially on the part of its ruling monarchs and educated elites. This reflex is enshrined in the imperial crown of Otto I (936–61 CE), with its portrait panels depicting Christ, Hezekiah (alongside Isaiah), Solomon, and David, and with its twelve stones in the front for the twelve apostles and twelve stones in the back for the twelve tribes of Israel. Used in the coronation of the "King of the Romans" for centuries until the dissolution of the Holy Roman Empire in 1806, the crown can still be viewed today in Vienna's Imperial Treasury.[25] The Israel typology, often centering on David, also surfaces in works written to offer advice for ruling monarchs and would-be monarchs, works known collectively as the *Fürstenspiegel* or "mirrors for princes" literature.[26]

The Davidic typology in particular received an egalitarian expansion by Nicholas of Lyra (1270–1349 CE), who described David's character as worthy of emulation by all Christians.[27] Nicholas went so far as to urge the "imitation of David" (*imitatio davidis*) as a prime means of conducting the Christian life, an idea that would become widely compelling in the Renaissance and Reformation.[28] In the early

---

[24]   Celia Chazelle and Burton Van Name Edwards, eds., *The Study of the Bible in the Carolingian Era* (Turnhout: Brepols, 2003).

[25]   For a description and photos of the crown, see Manfred Jasper-Leithe, *The Kunsthistorisches Museum Vienna: The Imperial and Ecclesiastical Treasury* (New York: Scala, 2005). For an account of its significance in European history, see Reinhart Staats, *Die Reichskrone: Geschichte und Bedeutung eines europäischen Symbols* (Kiel: Ludwig, 2006).

[26]   Hugo Steger, *David Rex et Propheta: König David als vorbildliche Verkörperung des Herrschers und Dichters im Mittelalter, nach Bilddarstellungen des achten bis zwölften Jahrhunderts* (Nurnberg: H. Carl, 1961).

[27]   Nicholas of Lyra, *Postilla super psalmos*, on Psalm 88. See Edward A. Gosselin, *The King's Progress to Jerusalem: Some Interpretations of David during the Reformation Period and their Patristic and Medieval Background* (Malibu, CA: Undena, 1976), 32–5; 40–1. This interpretive tradition lives on in modern devotional works such as Eugene H. Peterson, *Leap Over a Wall: Earthy Spirituality for Everyday Christians* (New York: HarperCollins, 1998).

[28]   Barbara Pitkin, "Imitation of David: David as a Paradigm for Faith in Calvin's Exegesis of the Psalms," *The Sixteenth Century Journal* 24.4 (1993): 843–63; Andrew Butterfield, "New Evidence for the Iconography of David in Quattrocentro Florence," *I Tatti: Studies in the Italian Renaissance* 6 (1995): 115–33; R. Gerald Hobbs, "Bucer's Use of King David as Mirror of the Christian Prince," *Reformation & Renaissance Review* 5.1 (2003): 102–28; Élise Boillet, Sonia Cavicchiolo, and Paul-Alexis Mellet, eds., *Les figures de David à la Renaissance* (Geneva: Droz, 2015).

modern era, both royalists and anti-royalists appealed to the Samuel narrative as a warrant for their political convictions, resulting in intriguingly differing interpretations of it.[29] The narrative was simultaneously cited both in support of the divine right of kings to rule and in favor of the duty of citizens to resist tyrants. Jewish and Christian readings today still look to the Samuel narrative as a basis of Western political ideas.[30]

The Samuel narrative has also inspired artists, musicians, and writers. The earliest visual representations of the narrative are likely those from the synagogue in Dura-Europos, dating to the mid-third century CE.[31] One tableau depicts Samuel anointing David (who is identifiable because the figure being anointed is one of seven, the sons of Jesse). Already a source of characters and scenes in illuminated Bibles, stained glass, and statuary, the Samuel narrative continued to prompt the best work of painters and sculptors in the high Middle Ages and Renaissance. Michelangelo's David (1501–04) is probably the best known of the David statues, with those of Donatello (1440) and Verrocchio (1473–75) close behind. Titian's "David and Goliath" (1542) and Veronese's "The Anointing of King David" (1555–60) are celebrated paintings from the sixteenth century.

Modern painters and visual artists from Rembrandt to Marc Chagall have found inspiration in the Samuel narrative as well. In Rembrandt's painting "David Plays the Lyre for King Saul" (1629), he places the focus on Saul's face, which is suffused with suspicion and uncertainty. In the later "Saul and David" (1651–8), Rembrandt offers an even more psychologically penetrating perspective on the introduction of David to Saul (1 Sam 16) by shrouding the characters in darkness and communicating an ominous sense of foreboding. Chagall's dreamlike, mythic "King David" (1962) is a twentieth-century masterpiece. Other narrative figures that have attracted the interest of painters include Hannah, Eli, Samuel, Jonathan, Michal, Bathsheba, Nathan, Tamar, and Absalom. Narrative episodes receiving particular attention include young Samuel

---

[29] Nevada Levi DeLapp, *The Reformed David(s) and the Question of Resistance to Tyranny: Reading the Bible in the 16th and 17th Centuries*, LHBOTS 601 (London: Bloomsbury T&T Clark, 2014).

[30] For example, Paul R. Abramson, *David's Politics: Servant, Rebel, King* (Lanham, MD: Lexington Books, 2016); Moshe Halbertal and Stephen Holmes, *The Beginning of Politics: Power in the Biblical Book of Samuel* (Princeton, NJ: Princeton University Press, 2017).

[31] Géza G. Xeravits, "David in the Dura Synagogue," in *David in Cultural Memory*, ed. Ida Fröhlich, CBET 93 (Leuven: Peeters, 2019), 163–70.

in the temple (1 Sam 3), the Ark's Philistine sojourn (1 Sam 4–6), David and Goliath (1 Sam 17), Saul's visit to the Witch of Endor (1 Sam 28), David dancing before the ark (2 Sam 6), David and Bathsheba (2 Sam 11), and Nathan's dramatic indictment of David (2 Sam 12).

Musical settings have been a natural outgrowth of the Samuel narrative, given that David himself is presented as a musician (1 Sam 16) and an ecstatic performance artist (2 Sam 6). Choral compositions based on the poems in 2 Samuel 1:17–27, 2 Samuel 22:2–51, and 2 Samuel 23:1–7, as well as the numerous biblical psalms attributed to David, are plentiful and characteristically powerful. The poetry evokes strong emotions. Operas and oratorios based on the Samuel narrative are also numerous and well known,[32] ranging from Marc-Antoine Charpentier's *David et Jonathas* (1699, H 490), to George Frederic Handel's *Saul* (1739, HWV 53), to Carl Nielsen's *Saul og David* (1901), and to Arthur Honegger's *Le Roi David* (1921). The Samuel story features in contemporary popular songs too. The best known is Leonard Cohen's "Hallelujah," with its moving meditation on David's musicianship.[33]

With regard to drama, poetry, and literature,[34] there is a prominent tradition of alluding to the Samuel narrative and of retelling it. Several classic twentieth-century novels offer modern recastings of the Samuel narrative: William Faulkner's masterwork *Absalom, Absalom*,[35] Stefan Heym's subversive *The King David Report*,[36] Joseph Heller's humorous *God Knows*,[37] and Madeleine L'Engle's family saga *Certain Women*.[38] A recent novel based on the life of David is Geraldine Brooks's *The Secret Chord*,[39] a reframing of the biblical story from Nathan's perspective, with a title taken from the Cohen song.

The Samuel narrative now finds itself at the forefront of current debates about gender, with many interpreters calling attention to the presence of heroic women in the narrative (e.g., Hannah, Abigail) as well as disadvantaged and abused women (e.g., Michal, Bathsheba, Tamar,

32   See further Walter Salmen, *König David, eine Symbolfigur in der Musik* (Freiburg [Schweiz]: Universitätsverlag, 1995).

33   Alan Light, *The Holy or the Broken: Leonard Cohen, Jeff Buckley, and the Unlikely Ascent of "Hallelujah"* (New York: Atria/Simon and Schuster, 2012).

34   See Raymond-Jean Frontain and Jan Wojcik, eds., *The David Myth in Western Literature* (West Lafayette, IN: Purdue University Press, 1980).

35   William Faulkner, *Absalom, Absalom* (New York: Random House, 1936).

36   Stefan Heym, *The King David Report* (New York: Putnam, 1973).

37   Joseph Heller, *God Knows* (New York: Dell, 1985).

38   Madeleine L'Engle, *Certain Women* (New York: Farrar, Straus, Giroux, 1992).

39   Geraldine Brooks, *The Secret Chord* (New York: Viking, 2015).

Rizpah), with some or all of the women arguably fitting both categories.[40] Studies of masculinity in the Bible are also taking cognizance of
the Samuel narrative.[41] To contemporary eyes, Saul emerges as a representative of "toxic masculinity."[42] Advocates for gay rights likewise
point to the Samuel narrative, particularly to the friendship between
David and Jonathan, as a biblical warrant for same-sex unions. Although
the biblical narrative does not say explicitly that their friendship was
sexual in nature, a number of recent interpreters have argued that a sexual dimension is either implied in the text or can be reconstructed on
the basis of the text for the historical relationship behind it.[43] Advocates
for persons with special needs have similarly identified Mephibosheth as
a productive symbol for reflection on those who are differently abled.[44]
Finally, following in a long line of political application, business experts
still consult the Samuel narrative for the lessons it may offer to those in
corporate leadership.[45]

So the answer to the question, "Where can we see any influence
from the Samuel narrative on the today's world?" is apparently,
"Everywhere we look."

THE SAMUEL NARRATIVE AND THE CHRISTIAN
TRADITION

Within Christian theology there exists an ancient tradition of typolog-
ical comparison between David and Christ. In this tradition, Christ is

[40]   See further JoAnn Hackett, "1 and 2 Samuel," in *Women's Bible Commentary*, eds.
       Carol A. Newsom, Sharon H. Ringe, and Jacqueline E. Lapsley, 3rd edition (Louisville:
       Westminster Johns Knox, 2012), 232–49; Athalya Brenner-Idan, *The Israelite Woman:
       Social Role and Literary Type in Biblical Narrative*, 2nd edition (London: Bloomsbury,
       2015).

[41]   See Stephen M. Wilson, *Making Men: The Male Coming-of-Age Theme in the
       Hebrew Bible* (New York: Oxford University Press, 2015); Ruth Mazo Karras, *Thou
       Art the Man: The Masculinity of David in the Christian and Jewish Middle Ages*
       (Philadelphia: University of Pennsylvania Press, 2021).

[42]   See further Andrew Smiler, *Is Masculinity Toxic? A Primer for the 21st Century* (New
       York: Thames and Hudson, 2019); Esther De Dauw and Daniel James Connell, eds.,
       Toxic Masculinity: Mapping the Monstrous in Our Heroes (Jackson, MS: University
       Press of Mississippi, 2020).

[43]   James E. Harding, *The Love of David and Jonathan: Ideology, Text, Reception*
       (Oakville, CT: Equinox, 2013); Anthony Heacock, *Jonathan Loved David: Manly
       Love in the Bible and the Hermeneutics of Sex* (Sheffield: Sheffield Phoenix, 2011).

[44]   Jeremy Schipper, *Disability Studies and the Hebrew Bible: Figuring Mephibosheth in
       the David Story*, LHBOTS 441 (New York: T&T Clark, 2006).

[45]   For example, Richard D. Phillips, *The Heart of an Executive: Lessons on Leadership
       from the Life of King David* (New York: Doubleday, 1999).

regarded, on analogy with David, as the Messiah, the Good Shepherd, and the King of the Jews.[46]

The title "Son of David" is applied to Jesus in the New Testament (e.g., Matt 1:1; cf. Rom 1:3), although less often than is frequently supposed.[47] Most of the instances of the title appear in the Gospel of Matthew, primarily in its healing stories.[48] Otherwise, the title is sometimes conspicuous by its absence, leading to the inference that early Christians may have been somewhat ambivalent about it. On the one hand, the ascription "Son of David" would have made an important point for them about the culmination of God's story of Israel in Jesus. On the other hand, "Son of David" may have suggested more of a military messiah-figure, one who would liberate Israel by force rather than following the path of peace modeled by Jesus.[49] Nevertheless, the David typology soon became one of the most important ways that the Christian church understood the person and offices of Jesus Christ, especially after Christianity became the state religion of the late Roman Empire.[50]

The elevation of David within the Christian imagination has been accompanied by a demonization of Saul. Christian interpreters have typically downplayed or ignored the positive aspects of Saul's characterization and sought to identify his flaws, justifying God's rejection of him.[51] The goal of these interpretations then becomes showing how Saul deserved what he got. But not only is Saul portrayed in the biblical narrative as possibly undeserving of his fate (1 Sam 15:24–25, 30–31, 35), interpretations of this sort have trouble explaining why Saul is not

[46] Ernst-Joachim Waschke, "The Significance of the David Tradition for the Emergence of Messianic Beliefs in the Old Testament," *WW* 23.4 (2003): 413–20.

[47] See further Max Botner, *Jesus Christ as the Son of David in the Gospel of Mark*, SNTSMS 174 (New York: Cambridge University Press, 2019); Margaret M. Daly-Denton, "David in the Gospels," *WW* 23.4 (2003): 421–9.

[48] Lidija Novakovic, *Messiah, the Healer of the Sick: A Study of Jesus as the Son of David in the Gospel of Matthew*, WUNT 2/170 (Tübingen: Mohr Siebeck, 2003); Jiří Dvořáček, *The Son of David in Matthew's Gospel in the Light of the Solomon as Exorcist Tradition*, WUNT 2/415 (Tübingen: Mohr Siebeck, 2016); H. Daniel Zacharias, *Matthew's Presentation of the Son of David: Davidic Traditions and Typology in the Gospel of Matthew* (London: T&T Clark, 2016).

[49] Stephen H. Smith, "The Function of the Son of David Tradition in Mark's Gospel," *NTS* 42.4 (1996): 523–39; Nathan C. Johnson, "The Passion according to David: Matthew's Arrest Narrative, the Absalom Revolt, and Militant Messianism," *CBQ* 80.2 (2018): 247–72.

[50] Per Beskow, *Rex Gloriae: The Kingship of Christ in the Early Church*, transl. Eric J. Sharpe (Stockholm: Almquist & Wiksell, 1962).

[51] As detailed in David M. Gunn, *The Fate of King Saul: An Interpretation of a Biblical Story*, JSOTSup 14 (Sheffield: JSOT Press, 1980), 23–31.

deposed from the kingship but left to carry on with his royal duties after his rejection. Such interpretations also tend to minimize God's initially unreserved approval of Saul (1 Sam 9:15–17; 10:9).

Emily Wilson offers this interpretive discussion a fruitful insight with her identification of a tragic subtradition in which a character "overlives" rather than dying at an expected time.[52] Wilson does not explore this subtradition with reference to the Samuel narrative, taking her cue instead from Adam's plaintive remark in Milton's "Paradise Lost": "Why do I overlive, / Why am I mocked with death, and lengthened out / To deathless pain?"[53] She then locates this subtradition in Greek drama (Sophocles' *Oedipus* plays, Euripides' *Heracles*), Seneca, and Shakespeare (*King Lear, Macbeth*), as well as Milton (*Samson Agonistes, Paradise Lost*), arguing for "a central thread in the tragic tradition that is concerned not with dying too early but with living too long."[54] In her account, this type of tragedy "presents a character who experiences an apparently intolerable sense of suffering and loss, and feels that he has lived too long but, nevertheless, decides to resist suicide."[55]

Typically, a particular crisis arises in which the termination of a character's life appears to be the appropriate outcome and yet the character, puzzlingly, does not die. The result is not only the personal disintegration of that character, with tropes of blindness or obscured vision, disguises, hiding, difficulties in perception, and mental confusion,[56] but also disruption in the story's temporal contours. The sequential order of the narrative becomes disjointed, with duplicated entries of several episodes appearing at key points. Time itself no longer seems clear or certain. The events of the narrative create conflict among its characters with regard to dates and schedules. Timing is all, but time is out of joint. The "undead" character usually goes mad. This mental sickness is a symbolic substitution for death, which sometimes finally does come in the form of a belated suicide. But even the eventual suicide falls short of a full resolution, with the characters themselves often debating its merits. As Wilson notes, "Suicide is never presented as a wholly satisfactory solution to the problem of overliving because once a character has lived too long, any death must come too late."[57]

---

[52] Emily R. Wilson, *Mocked with Death: Tragic Overliving from Sophocles to Milton* (Baltimore, MD: Johns Hopkins University Press, 2004).

[53] John Milton, *Paradise Lost*, 10.733–75.

[54] Wilson, *Mocked*, 1.

[55] Wilson, *Mocked*, 1.

[56] Wilson, *Mocked*, 4.

[57] Wilson, *Mocked*, 6.

Admittedly, there is a risk of anachronism in viewing the Samuel narrative in relation to largely later literary works, but the features of this tragic subtradition offer an illuminating comparison. In particular, the psychological deterioration of Saul – one of the narrative's features that seemed so modern to twentieth-century interpreters – falls perfectly into place as Saul's response to his own failure to die. He sometimes appears lucid and sometimes lost. He is at the center of disagreements about time (e.g., how long to wait before offering the sacrifice in 1 Samuel 13) and death (e.g., whether to kill Agag in 1 Samuel 15). Saul is rejected from the kingship but neither deposed nor killed, as might be expected. This circumstance provides the drama for the second half of 1 Samuel, in which Saul enters into a period of competition with David, not only for political dominance but also for his own sanity, a tug-of-war concluded by Saul's eventual death in 1 Samuel 31. Saul's death both is (i.e., he dies by his own hand) and is not (i.e., he kills himself to prevent being misused by captors, not because he wants to die) a suicide. Even prior to his physical death, Saul is in certain respects not unlike the modern notion of a zombie, a being not yet fully dead but no longer fully alive either.

Reading the second half of 1 Samuel in light of zombie theory[58] is not quite as fanciful as it first might seem, particularly since Saul – who represents a failure to die – will in the end pay a nighttime visit to a witch (more properly, a "medium") in order to conjure up the spirit of Samuel, who has since died (1 Sam 28). Horror elements, witchcraft, and magic lurk at the dark outskirts of the Samuel narrative. After his heterodox seance, Saul suffers a symbolic death by losing his physical strength, falling down "to the fullness of his height,"[59] and becoming barely able to function (1 Sam 28:20). Early Christian theologians worried about this biblical passage, because they recognized that if the witch really did raise Samuel, then the Bible could be understood as affirming the efficacy of witchcraft. So some Christian writers instead interpreted the passage as a witch's trick, in which she only appeared to raise Samuel from the dead.[60] Regardless of how this episode is finally read, the key factor for the wider narrative is how it underscores Saul's

---

[58] See further Sarah Juliet Lauro, ed., *Zombie Theory: A Reader* (Minneapolis: University of Minnesota Press, 2017).

[59] For this translation, Bodner, *1 Samuel*, 301.

[60] See further Rowan A. Greet and Margaret M. Mitchell, eds., *The "Belly-Myther" of Endor: Interpretations of 1 Kingdoms 28 in the Early Church*, SBLGRW 16 (Atlanta: Society of Biblical Literature, 2006).

status as someone "undead." Like a zombie, he is neither entirely of this world nor of the next.[61]

Understanding Saul as an undead figure in the second half of 1 Samuel illuminates how David is by contrast a figure of life. At the outset of the Samuel narrative, Hannah sings of God as the one who controls death and life (1 Sam 2:6). In his first act of deliverance, David refers to God as "the living God" (1 Sam 17:26). Traditionally, Christian interpreters have seen correspondences between the Samuel narrative's account of the rise, fall, and return of David to the throne[62] and the incarnation, crucifixion, and resurrection of Jesus.[63] Significantly, the nadir of David's kingly rule comes when he and his retinue flee Jerusalem, cross the Kidron brook (2 Sam 15:23), and arrive at the slope of the Mount of Olives (2 Sam 15:30),[64] the traditional location of the Garden of Gethsemane (Matt 26:30, 36; Mark 14:26, 32; Luke 22:39-40).[65] The only New Testament reference to the Kidron likewise appears in the Gethsemane narrative of John's Gospel (John 18:1).[66] David's "evangelical spirit"[67] in refusing to requite Shimei for cursing him (2 Sam 16:5-14; cf. 19:16-23) parallels the non-retaliation of Jesus: his humiliation, refusal to condemn his persecutors, and endurance of suffering.[68] Ahithophel's betrayal of David (2 Sam 17) foreshadows Judas' betrayal of

[61] Of course, Saul is not completely like a zombie in the modern sense. He remains human and ultimately in control of his mind and body, although that control is depicted as shaky at times.

[62] For a historical–critical reading sensitive to such contours in the narrative, see R. A. Carlson, *David, the Chosen King: A Traditio-Historical Approach to the Second Book of Samuel*, transl. Eric J. Shape and Stanley Rudman (Stockholm: Almqvist & Wiksell, 1964).

[63] For example, James A. Wharton, "A Plausible Tale: Story and Theology in II Samuel 9–20, I Kings 1-2," *Int* 35.4 (1981): 341-54 (353). For a modern commentary interested in these correspondences, see John Woodhouse, *2 Samuel: Your Kingdom Come*, Preaching the Word (Wheaton, IL: Crossway, 2015), 387-8. For traditional examples of such Christian readings, see Gosselin, *King's Progress*; Theresia Heither, *David*, Biblische Gestalten bei den Kirchenvätern (Munster: Aschendorff, 2012).

[64] Dietrich Bonhoeffer, *Theological Education at Finkenwalde: 1935-1937*, eds. H. Gaylon Barker and Mark S. Brocker, Dietrich Bonhoeffer Works 14, transl. Douglas W. Stott (Minneapolis: Augsburg Fortress, 2013): 918-9.

[65] And the site of Christ's ascension as well (Acts 1:9-12). See Cyril of Jerusalem, *Catechetical Lectures*, 2.12, 10, as found in John R. Franke, *Joshua, Judges, Ruth, 1-2 Samuel*, ACCS 4 (Downers Grove, IL: InterVarsity, 2005), 372.

[66] Woodhouse, *2 Samuel*, 393. However, John 18 does not use the term "Gethsemane."

[67] Thus, Ambrose, *Duties of the Clergy*, 1.48. 245-47, as found in Franke, *1-2 Samuel*, 376.

[68] Woodhouse, *2 Samuel*, 407. But note that there are apparently limitations to David's forbearance, since he gives Solomon instructions to kill Shimei after his death (1 Kgs 2:8-9).

Jesus, especially because both commit suicide by hanging (2 Sam 17:23; cf Matt 27:5).[69] The return of King David to Jerusalem (2 Sam 19:9–43) becomes a type of "resurrection" anticipating the resurrection of Christ.

One modern study has sought to uncover hints and allusions to resurrection even in the Hebrew terminology used within the Samuel narrative. Phillip Lefebvre's 2004 volume in this way attempts to offer a bridge between historical–critical analysis and traditional Christian typology.[70] His linguistic arguments are strained, however, and by focusing so intently on individual words and phrases he neglects to attend to the larger logic of the narrative. He initially asks the right question: how can it be that the early Christians understood *everything* in the Law and the Prophets as foretelling the resurrection of Christ (Luke 24:25–27; 1 Cor 15:3–4)? But the answer to this question has to do with broader narrative trajectories and patterns of discourse within the Old Testament (and not so much the possible nuances of individual Hebrew terms).[71]

It remains important not to force a later Christian understanding of resurrection on the Old Testament. Historical–critical scholars used to hold the view that a belief in resurrection was mostly absent from the Old Testament and a genuine innovation in the New Testament. More typical in the Old Testament, scholars routinely affirmed, was the conception of death as an entrance into the underworld of the shades, or Sheol (e.g., Ezek 32:17–32; cf. Luke 16:19–31).[72] The only Old Testament testimonies to resurrection widely accepted by critical scholars were in Daniel 12 and Isaiah 25–26, passages both thought to be quite late. However, this appraisal has recently begun to shift, largely in response to Jon Levenson's brilliant reevaluation of the biblical evidence and his comparison with afterlife traditions in early Judaism.[73] Although there was likely no single conception of resurrection in ancient Israel, it does seem as if there was probably more openness to the idea (and greater uncertainty about what happens after death) than previous biblical

---

69   Woodhouse, 2 *Samuel*, 432. As Woodhouse also observes (641–2 n1), this association was traditionally amplified by viewing the Psalm verse, "Even my bosom friend in whom I trusted, who ate of my bread, has lifted the heel against me" (Ps 41:9; Heb 10, NRSV), as a Davidic prediction of Jesus' betrayal by Judas.

70   Philippe Lefebvre, *Livres de Samuel et Récits de Résurrection: le Messie Ressuscité "Selon les Écritures,"* LD 196 (Paris: Cerf, 2004).

71   Compare the review by Vincent P. Branick in *CBQ* 67.2 (2005): 352–3.

72   See further Philip S. Johnson, *Shades of Sheol: Death and Afterlife in the Old Testament* (Downers Grove, IL: InterVarsity, 2002).

73   Jon Levenson, *Resurrection and the Restoration of Israel: The Ultimate Victory of the God of Life* (New Haven: Yale University Press, 2006).

scholarship was willing to entertain. The very character of Israel's God as the creator of the universe and giver of life pushes against the notion that death is absolute. For if God is all-powerful, promotes life, and generates fruitfulness, how can death have the final say?

This same logic is evident within the first half of the Samuel narrative (1 Sam 1–31), which dramatizes the extended encounter between Saul, who is learning to die, and David, who is learning to live.[74] The fullness of David's transformation only transpires in the Samuel narrative's second half (2 Sam 1–24), in which he undergoes tremendous suffering and even a symbolic death of his own on the Mount of Olives, before he can return to the throne in Jerusalem and resume his rule. Saul lives to die; David dies to live. As Hannah's song announces in advance, the Samuel narrative as a whole will turn on the identification of Israel's messiah as bringer of the life that comes from God alone (1 Sam 2:1–10).

At the conclusion of the Samuel narrative, David confirms his messianic status as anointed servant of the living God (2 Sam 22:51; 23:1).[75] As he does so, he is simultaneously portrayed as an energetic and boyish figure, a portrait at odds with the larger narrative. A reader expects David to be half-dead and elderly at this point, given his stage of life and the trauma he has undergone in Absalom's rebellion. Encountering his "final words" in 2 Samuel 23 underscores this chronological aspect of the narrative's presentation. Yet the lengthy psalm-like expostulation in 2 Samuel 22 presents a David who is physically fit, still young, and brimming with infectious enthusiasm: "By you I can crush a troop, and by my God I can leap over a wall" (2 Sam 22:30, NRSV). The messiah figure of the Samuel narrative is a renewed David, a resurrected king, who not only experiences but also *offers* new life in God. In keeping with this perspective, the New Testament book of Acts names David as a witness to Christ's resurrection (Acts 2:31; cf. 13:34–35).

For modern readers, the idea of an inner-biblical correspondence between the Samuel narrative and the New Testament seems like an inappropriate reach because of concern for the integrity of historical sources. Biblical books are no longer as well known as they were for earlier Jewish and Christian readers either, making canonical modes of reading seem obscure and confusing. For traditional readers, however,

---

[74] See Philip R. Davies, "Son of David and Son of Saul," in *The Fate of King David: The Past and Present of a Biblical Icon*, eds. Tod Linafelt, Claudia V. Camp, and Timothy Beal, LHBOTS 500 (New York, 2010), 123–32; James M. Hamilton, "The Typology of David's Rise to Power: Messianic Patterns in the Book of Samuel," *SBJT* 16.2 (2012): 4–25.

[75] "The LORD lives!" he also exclaims in 2 Sam 22:47.

the Bible was something like a narrative palace, which not only contained a multitude of individual rooms but also possessed a multidimensional floor plan allowing immediate access from each room to every other room. In this kind of traditional understanding, reading the Bible well is more than visiting one of its rooms. It is making an entire tour of the palace, a journey of inner-biblical allusion and correspondence in which each room directs the gaze of the attentive visitor to the riches of all the other rooms, all at the same time.

SELECTED FURTHER READING

Bodner, Keith. *1 Samuel: A Narrative Commentary.* HBM 19. Sheffield: Sheffield Phoenix, 2008.

Brenner-Idan, Athalya. *The Israelite Woman: Social Role and Literary Type in Biblical Narrative.* 2nd edition. London: Bloomsbury, 2015.

Chapman, Stephen B. *1 Samuel as Christian Scripture: A Theological Commentary.* Grand Rapids: Eerdmans, 2016.

Frontain, Raymond-Jean, and Jan Wojcik, eds. *The David Myth in Western Literature.* West Lafayette, IN: Purdue University Press, 1980.

Gosselin, Edward A. *The King's Progress to Jerusalem: Some Interpretations of David during the Reformation Period and their Patristic and Medieval Background.* Malibu, CA: Undena, 1976.

Halbertal, Moshe, and Stephen Holmes. *The Beginning of Politics: Power in the Biblical Book of Samuel.* Princeton, NJ: Princeton University Press, 2017.

Lauro, Sarah Juliet, ed. *Zombie Theory: A Reader.* Minneapolis: University of Minnesota Press, 2017.

Levenson, Jon. *Resurrection and the Restoration of Israel: The Ultimate Victory of the God of Life.* New Haven: Yale University Press, 2006.

Wilson, Emily R. *Mocked with Death: Tragic Overliving from Sophocles to Milton.* Baltimore, MD: Johns Hopkins University Press, 2004.

6 Monarchic Collapse

From Solomon to Jehoiachin in the Book of Kings

RACHELLE GILMOUR

The contrast between the glory and splendour of King Solomon's succession and reign at the beginning of the book of Kings and the "exile" or captivity of King Jehoiachin by the Babylonians at the end points to one of the central themes of the book: the collapse of the monarchy descended from the line of David. This theme is calculated towards an audience living in the period of the exile, or shortly afterwards, who seek to understand the collapse and determine how to live in its shadow.

The account of the Davidic line of kings begins prior to the book of Kings, in the book of Samuel. In this backstory, David becomes king over a united kingdom of Israel, which includes ten northern tribes and David's own southern tribe, Judah. The drama of David's succession to the first king, Saul, the demise of dynastic contenders from Saul's house, and God's continued commitment to David with the promise of an eternal dynasty introduce themes and literary motifs that recur throughout the book of Kings, to produce parallels, irony and contrast between the reign of David and the reigns of his successors.

FROM SOLOMON TO JEHOIACHIN

The book of Kings begins with the succession of Solomon as king after the death of his father David. The succession is not without complications, when Solomon's older brother Adonijah initially vies for the throne and is defeated only through the political negotiations of the prophet Nathan and Solomon's mother, Bathsheba. The struggle for the throne within the house of David is reminiscent of the conflict between Amnon and Absalom, then Absalom and David, for the throne in 2 Samuel. Yet, in 2 Samuel 12:24–25, the narrator gives assurance that God loves Solomon, setting up the expectation that Solomon's claim to the throne will be successful and he will be the son promised in 2 Samuel 7:13, that David's son will build a house for the LORD and his throne will be established forever. Accordingly, in 1 Kings 3–10,

Solomon establishes his kingdom, aided by divinely endowed wisdom, building palace, wealth, land holdings, and the temple, the house for the LORD.

A well-known story from Solomon's reign in 1 Kings 3:16–28 epitomises the glory of his reign and height of his kingdom. In the previous pericope, in 1 Kings 3:1–15, God shows favour to Solomon in a dream where he says to Solomon, "Ask what I should give you" (1 Kgs 3:5). Solomon does not ask for riches or long life, but for "an understanding mind to govern your people, able to discern between good and evil" (1 Kgs 3:9). This dream is not simply a figment of Solomon's sleepy imagination one night, and the proof that God has indeed granted this request is demonstrated in the following vignette.

Two women who work in prostitution come before the king in verse 16 with a case. As Jerome Walsh points out, the naming of their occupation is not to label them as sinful women, in an ancient Israelite context where prostitution was largely understood as a fact more than a moral evil.[1] Rather, their occupation highlights that these women are unprotected by family, are among the most disadvantaged in society, and that the king attends to issues of justice even for the lowest ranks of the community. Furthermore, their occupation provides the background to the case brought before the king: the women live together in one house and have given birth within three days of one another. One woman awakes to find her child lying before her dead, and claims that the other woman exchanged the children when her own child died.

Both women remain unnamed throughout the story and there is a remarkable symmetry between their speech and their claims to the king, highlighting the difficulty and undecidability of the case.[2] In verse 22, one woman says, "No, the living son is mine, and the dead son is yours;" And the other woman replies, "No, the dead son is yours, and the living son is mine." A similar repetition recurs in verse 23, when the king sums up the case: "The one says, 'This is my son that is alive, and your son is dead'; while the other says, 'Not so! Your son is dead, and my son is the living one.'" It is one woman's word against another, providing little grounds for the king to evaluate truth and give a fair judgement.

Yet, Solomon, with divinely endowed wisdom, finds an answer to this conundrum. He asks for a sword and proposes to divide the child.

---

[1]   Jerome T. Walsh, *1 Kings. Berit Olam* (Collegeville: Liturgical Press, 1996), 79–80.
[2]   Robert Alter, *The Hebrew Bible. Vol 2 Prophets Nevi'im. A Translation with Commentary* (New York: Norton, 2019), 451.

The child's mother instantly begs Solomon not to do so, relinquishing her claim to the child. The cleverness of Solomon's response is revealed in a wordplay, as the woman's "compassion" grew warm (verse 26). "Compassion" is etymologically related to the word for "womb,"[3] pointing to the logic that the woman who has truly given birth to the child would capitulate at the threat of danger to the child. Nevertheless, the story remains ambiguous regarding which woman – the first who brings the claim or the second who disputes it – is truly the mother. The solution provided by Solomon's extraordinary wisdom and judgement is shrouded in mystery for the reader, at the same time as revealing Solomon's wisdom to all Israel (verse 28).

The contrasts between Solomon and Jehoiachin, and the corresponding position of their kingdoms, are palpable. Whereas Solomon overcomes his older brothers to succeed David through the political machinations of those closest to him, Jehoiachin is imprisoned and replaced as king by his uncle Zedekiah (Mattaniah) in 2 Kings 24:17, through the imposition of foreign Babylonian imperial rule. Solomon's narrative is characterised by the theme of building projects; filling the temple with riches; and being honoured by foreign monarchs, visited by the queen of Sheba, and sent gifts by King Hiram. In contrast, Jehoiachin's treasures and the treasures of the temple are plundered by the Babylonians led by the foreign king Nebuchadnezzar.

Jehoiachin is eventually released from prison in Babylon and given a seat at the table of the Babylonian king. This fate for a Davidic king is an ironic twist on David's own succession to Saul as king. Throughout David's reign, all dynastic possibilities of Saul are gradually wiped out: Jonathan, Saul's son, dies in battle with Saul; Saul's son Ishbosheth is assassinated after he has taken kingship over the northern tribes; Michal, Saul's daughter who is married to David, is denied children; and the final sons and grandsons of Saul are slaughtered to release Israel from a famine for Saul's violation of a curse against the Gibeonites. The only exception from the house of Saul is Mephibosheth, Saul's grandson through Jonathan, whose feet are crippled. David brings Mephibosheth to sit at the king's table, giving him a portion of the king's food (2 Sam 9:13). Although the release of Jehoiachin initially appears to be a source of hope, the parallel to Mephibosheth, as the final, impotent, member of Saul's house, is foreboding. The parallel resonates as a tragic sign that Jehoiachin may be the last of the house of David as Mephibosheth is the last of the house of Saul. Whereas the

---

[3]   Lissa M. Wray Beal, _1 & 2 Kings_. AOTC 9 (Downers Grove: IVP, 2014), 88.

house of Saul was replaced by David, the house of David is replaced by a foreign imperial power.

For an audience during or after the exile, the descent from Solomon to Jehoiachin raises questions: What brings about this dramatic collapse of the house of David? Has God ceased unfailing support for the Davidic kings and kingdom? What does the loss of the monarchy, and the temple, mean for the people who constitute this kingdom? And is the message of the book of Kings only nationalistic in scope?

The fall from Solomon's reign to Jehoiachin's captivity is charted throughout the book of Kings, answering these questions and others. However, while a reader might expect the course of this collapse to focus only on the reigns and fates of the kings descended from David, the body of the book of Kings traverses another dominant subject: the kings, prophets, and people of the northern kingdom of Israel, who split away from the Davidic southern kingdom of Judah after the reign of Solomon.

A structure for the book of Kings, modified here from Jerome Walsh,[4] highlights the centrality of narratives concerning the northern kingdom within the frame of the collapse of the Davidic monarchy from Solomon to Jehoiachin:

A. Solomon and the construction of the temple (1 Kgs 1–11)
   B. The separation of the northern kingdom – Jeroboam and Rehoboam (1 Kgs 12)
      C. Alternating accounts of the northern and southern kings (1 Kgs 13–16)
         D. The Omride dynasty and the prophetic ministry of Elijah and Elisha in the north (1 Kgs 17–2 Kgs 11)
      C'. Alternating accounts of northern and southern kings (2 Kgs 12–16)
   B'. The fall of the northern kingdom (2 Kgs 17)
A'. The southern kingdom ending in exile with Jehoiachin and looting of the temple (2 Kgs 18–25)

At the heart of this concentric structure is a concentration of material concerned almost exclusively with the northern kingdom of Israel and, in turn, much of this material concerns prophets, not just kings. Much of the other intervening material also focuses on the fate of the north as much as the south, with the exception of the final chapters in 2 Kings 18–25.

---

4   Walsh, *1 Kings*, 373.

These different sections of the book, including sections devoted to northern or southern kings, are bound together by a number of narrative means. For example, the regnal accession formulae, announcing the reign, genealogy, and length of reign of each king, give a linear chronological structure to the book; the series of prophecies and fulfilments within the central prophetic material of Kings and between the outer monarchic accounts bind the book with inner and outer sections;[5] and the frequent intertextual connections and analogies to the story of David gesture towards the overall concern of the book towards the fall of the Davidic monarchy.[6]

Another important narrative means for binding the northern narratives to the collapse of the monarchy, which will be the focus of this essay, is character analogies that compare and contrast different figures throughout the book.[7] Solomon and Jehoiachin are one such character pair placed in analogy with one another. There are also analogies between northern and southern kings Ahab and Manasseh, and Jeroboam and Josiah, and between the Jerusalem temple (despite not being a character) and the prophets Elijah and Elisha. Within the northern material, there is analogy between two foreign women who are from neither north nor south, and whose stories suggest that a dimension of the book looks beyond the insiders of Israel and Judah. These analogies give expression to a portrait of foreboding, significance, and hope concerning the collapse of the Davidic monarchy, the kingdom of Judah, and the temple in Jerusalem.

LOSING KINGDOMS

Before turning to these character analogies, another analogy between the fates of the northern and southern kingdoms sets the scene. Although contrast dominates the narratives of Solomon and Jehoiachin in the frame of the book of Kings, one aspect of their reigns is identical: they do "evil in the sight of the LORD" (1 Kgs 11:6; 2 Kgs 24:9). Solomon's sin is to follow other gods introduced to him by his foreign wives. God's punishment to Solomon is that "I will surely tear the kingdom from you and give it to your servant" (1 Kgs 11:11) in the reign of Solomon's son, an eerie repetition of God's punishment to Saul: "The LORD has torn the kingdom of Israel from you this very day, and has given it to

---

[5]   Nathan Lovell, *The Book of Kings and Exilic Identity: 1 and 2 Kings as a Work of Political Historiography*, LHBOTS 708 (London: T&T Clark, 2021), 50–73.

[6]   See Peter Leithart, "Counterfeit Davids: Davidic Restoration and the Architecture of 1–2 Kings," *TynB* 56 (2005): 19–33.

[7]   See Moshe Garsiel, *The First Book of Samuel: A Literary Study of Comparative Structures, Analogies and Parallels* (Ramat Gan: Revivim, 1985).

a neighbour of yours, who is better than you" (1 Sam 15:28). However, Solomon's son Rehoboam does not lose the whole kingdom; he loses the northern tribes to a general, Jeroboam, who becomes king over this northern kingdom, Israel. Rehoboam remains king over the tribe of Judah, the southern kingdom. Therefore, through Solomon's sin, the northern kingdom is lost by the Davidic kings to a series of northern dynasties who reign alongside Davidic rule maintained in the south.

A second loss of the northern kingdom is narrated in 2 Kings 17, when the northern kingdom is taken into exile by the Assyrians, reportedly for the kings' sins of worshipping other gods, worshipping at high places, and leading the people to other gods. Although the description of the northern kingdom's worship of other gods is significantly more detailed and extensive than the offences of Solomon, there is nevertheless overlap: Solomon built high places and he did not follow "my covenant and my statutes that I have commanded you" (1 Kgs 11:11); so also the people of Israel, according to 2 Kings 17, built high places and disobeyed the demand to "keep my commandments and my statutes" (verse 13).

The loss of the northern kingdom through Solomon's sin, then the northern kings' and peoples' sins, suggests that Jehoiachin's sin is responsible for the loss of the southern kingdom. However, little is said of Jehoiachin's sin, and much precedes this story that points to the possibility of the exile as delayed punishment for the sins of earlier kings. Judah's kings do evil over and again, and there are acute warnings to Judah of the consequences of turning to other gods through the example of the northern kingdom taken into exile. The extensive narrative focus on the northern kingdom throughout the book of Kings conveys as much about the collapse of the southern monarchy as it does about the failure of the northern kings.

That the collapse of the Davidic monarchy should be interpreted in analogy to the northern kingdom is suggested through markers in the narrative: an alternating structure of narratives about the north and south in 1 Kings 13–16 and 2 Kings 12–16, where the northern kings consistently do "evil in the sight of the LORD" as many southern kings will do; and in 2 Kings, the analogy is made directly between the fall of the northern kingdom and the sins of Judah in 2 Kings 17:19. Yet there is also hope for the southern kingdom of Judah through a contrast: the long narrative of Hezekiah king of Judah during this Assyrian crisis (2 Kgs 18–20) shows him to be a faithful king:

> He trusted in the LORD the God of Israel; so that there was no one
> like him among all the kings of Judah after him, or among those

who were before him. For he held fast to the LORD; he did not depart from following him but kept the commandments that the LORD commanded Moses. (2 Kgs 18:5–6)

The important role of the northern kingdom in making sense of the collapse of the southern kingdom can be explored further through two deeply embedded comparative character structures in Kings: between Ahab and Manasseh, a similarity bringing foreboding; and between Jeroboam and Josiah, a contrast bringing hope. In both of these structures, there continue to be echoes of the reign of David from the book of Samuel, reinforcing the fate of the Davidic dynasty as a central concern for the narrative.

AHAB AND MANASSEH: WHY DOES THE MONARCHY OF JUDAH COLLAPSE?

King Ahab is king over the northern kingdom of Israel, succeeding to the throne from his father Omri in 1 Kings 16:28–29. Like all the kings of the northern kingdom, Ahab did "evil in the sight of the LORD"; but he is given an extra qualification: "more than all who were before him" (1 Kgs 16:30). He marries Jezebel, the daughter of a Sidonian king, and worships the Sidonian god, Baal. At this point of the narrative, Ahab is reminiscent of Solomon, marrying a foreign wife and introducing worship of other gods.[8]

Ahab's sin takes a different direction in 1 Kings 21, where Ahab, aided by Jezebel, has his neighbour Naboth falsely accused and killed in order to possess his vineyard. This story is crafted in such a way that it is worth lingering for a moment on some of its details. Ahab sees the vineyard but has no understanding of its value: according to verse 2, he wants to turn it from a vineyard to a vegetable patch, a trivial gardening project compared to the long-term establishment of viticulture.[9] Moreover, the vine is a common metaphor for Israel (Isa 3:14, 5:1–2; Jer 12:10),[10] suggesting that Ahab's lack of value for the vineyard and desire to reduce it to a garden for his own convenience may be a metaphor for his disastrous kingship over his kingdom Israel. Naboth's speech, by contrast, shows he understands its value and does so with due fear of God-given responsibility: in verse 3 he describes the land as "my ancestral inheritance," and he says, "The LORD forbid" that he should sell it.

---

[8]   Leithart, "Counterfeit Davids," 24–25.
[9]   Wray Beal, *1 & 2 Kings*, 274.
[10] Wray Beal, *1 & 2 Kings*, 274.

Ahab's response to Naboth's refusal further shows his inadequacies for rule. He sulks, in verse 4 lying on his bed and refusing to eat, an irony when he wants to plant a vegetable patch. He is also described as "resentful and sullen," the second time he is reduced to this state: identical words are used to describe him at the conclusion to the previous story in 1 Kings 20:43. When he repeats his complaint to his wife Jezebel, Ahab pointedly omits Naboth's pious interjection, "the LORD forbid." At this point, Ahab ceases acting altogether and Jezebel takes charge. She demonstrates her far superior competence, but with a result that magnifies Ahab's disregard for good governance over the people Israel. She, not very secretly, writes letters to elders and nobles with a plot to falsely accuse Naboth and have him killed.

Here, parallels are drawn to David in 2 Samuel 11–12, when he takes Bathsheba and has Uriah killed.[11] Just as David sees Bathsheba bathing from the palace, Ahab wants the vineyard that is near the palace; David sends a letter to Joab to have Uriah killed in battle, avoiding a direct charge of murder, and Jezebel sends letters on Ahab's behalf to use scoundrels to falsely accuse Naboth and have him killed; David takes Bathsheba as his wife and Ahab takes possession of Naboth's vineyard; and finally, both acts are harshly condemned through a prophet, Nathan in 2 Samuel 12:1–15 and Elijah in 1 Kings 21:17–29, bringing about the offender's display of repentance behaviours and God's mitigation of the kings' punishment. These parallels set in place an analogy between Ahab king of Israel and the Davidic line.

However, the full significance of this analogy is only revealed in the narrative of Kings a number of chapters later, in the account of King Manasseh of Judah. Manasseh is given only a short account in 2 Kings 21:1–18, and yet his reign is key to the collapse of the Davidic monarchy. According to 2 Kings 21:12–15, Manasseh's sins are the primary cause of the monarchic downfall, of the destruction of Jerusalem and all of Judah. This claim is repeated in 2 Kings 24:3, that Judah is destroyed "for the sins of Manasseh, for all that he had committed." Crucially, Manasseh's sins are paralleled to those of Ahab, when he worships Baal "as King Ahab of Israel had done" (2 Kgs 21:3). Manasseh's account echoes other accounts of northern sins, especially 2 Kings 17 including making his son walk through fire, and practising soothsaying, augury mediums, and wizards (2 Kgs 17:17; 2 Kgs 21:6). Both Ahab and Manasseh cause the people to sin along with them (1 Kgs 16:26; 2 Kgs

11   Mark J. Boda, *A Severe Mercy: Sin and Its Remedy in the Old Testament*, Siphrut 1. (Winona Lake: Eisenbrauns, 2009), 160 n.37.

21:11, 16), an important justification in the book for the destruction of
the whole kingdoms, not just the line of kings. Manasseh has a northern name, named after one of the northern tribes of Israel.[12] Finally,
Manasseh has blood from the line of Ahab, through the intermarriage of
Athaliah, King Omri's granddaughter, into the Davidic line of kings (2
Kgs 8:26). The exile is blamed on Manasseh and, in turn, Manasseh is a
king like Ahab king of Israel. The end of the northern kings in Assyrian
exile is a foreboding warning in the narrative for the fate of the southern kings.

These parallels between Manasseh and Ahab bring another layer
of clarification to the collapse, explaining why blame for the exile is
foisted upon Manasseh and not just Jehoiachin. When Ahab is punished
for murdering Naboth and taking his vineyard, God says, "I will not
bring the disaster in his days; but in his son's days I will bring the disaster on his house" (1 Kgs 21:29). Disaster is delayed for a generation, and
despite Ahab's premature death in battle (1 Kgs 22:29–40), his sons rule
after him and his dynasty continues until the arrival of the usurper Jehu
(2 Kgs 10). During this delay of Ahab's punishment, there is a period of
prosperity in Israel and return to worship of God, not Baals, particularly
through the ministry of the prophet Elisha who brings food, healing,
and deliverance from enemies (2 Kgs 2–8).[13]

So also there is a delay in the punishment of Manasseh for the
southern kingdom. Jehoiachin is four generations after Manasseh, and
the reign of King Josiah takes place in the intervening period, a king
who brings repentance and restoration of the temple. Josiah's reign does
not annul the punishment for Manasseh's sins but brings about a period
of renewed right worship for Judah. The repetition of the number four
in the execution of these punishments, albeit used in different ways,
suggests a framework for transgenerational punishment (cf. Deut 5:9;
Jehu's line in 2 Kgs 10:30).[14] Four rulers will sit on the throne from
Ahab's house: Ahab, Ahaziah, Joram, and Athaliah; Manasseh is four
generations prior to the exile: after him come Amon, Josiah, Jehoahaz,
and Jehoiakim who are brothers and one generation, and Jehoiachin.

[12]   Francesca Stavrakopoulou, "Blackballing of Manasseh," pages 248–63 in *Good Kings
       and Bad Kings*, edited by Lester L. Grabbe, LHBOTS 393 (London: T&T Clark, 2005).
[13]   Rachelle Gilmour, *Juxtaposition and the Elisha Cycle*, LHBOTS 594 (London: T&T
       Clark, 2014), 220–222.
[14]   Jeremy Schipper, "Hezekiah, Manasseh, and Dynastic or Transgenerational
       Punishment," pages 81–105 in *Soundings in Kings: Perspectives and Methods
       in Contemporary Scholarship*, edited by Mark Leuchter and Klaus Peter Adam
       (Minneapolis: Fortress Press, 2010).

Once again there is an intriguing parallel to the punishment of David, that will be "fourfold" (2 Sam 12:6). Punishment is delayed for sin in God's treatment of the northern kingdom and in God's treatment of the southern kingdom. In this way, the cause of exile and collapse of Judah can be attributed to Manasseh many generations before Jehoiachin.

JEROBOAM AND JOSIAH: HAS GOD FORSAKEN THE PROMISES TO DAVID?

Another delay in punishment of the northern kingdom spans a greater stretch of narrative in the book of Kings, in this case initiated by the sin of Jeroboam. Jeroboam, the first king of the northern kingdom, who wrests the northern tribes from the rule of Rehoboam, Solomon's son, begins his reign well. An intriguing promise is given to Jeroboam, one that echoes the promise of an eternal dynasty made to David, but is made conditional upon obedience:

> If you will listen to all that I command you, walk in my ways, and do what is right in my sight by keeping my statutes and my commandments, as David my servant did, I will be with you, and will build you an enduring house, as I built for David, and I will give Israel to you. (1 Kgs 11:38)

Jeroboam stands on the side of justice when he opposes Rehoboam, who follows in the footsteps of his father Solomon using forced labour (1 Kgs 12:1–19) and acts as a foil to Jeroboam.[15] But as quickly as Jeroboam is promised the possibility of an eternal house, Jeroboam is condemned for setting up golden calves in Bethel and Dan, so that the northern tribes worship in a place outside the temple at Jerusalem (1 Kgs 12:25–33). A prophet from Judah tells Jeroboam that a Davidic king, Josiah, will destroy the altar at Bethel (1 Kgs 13:2–3), and that the people of the northern kingdom will be swept away:

> The LORD will strike Israel, as a reed is shaken in the water; he will root up Israel out of this good land that he gave to their ancestors, and scatter them beyond the Euphrates, because they have made their sacred poles, provoking the LORD to anger. He will give Israel up because of the sins of Jeroboam, which he sinned and which he caused Israel to commit. (1 Kgs 14:15–16)

---

[15] Keith Bodner, *Jeroboam's Royal Drama*. Biblical Refigurations (Oxford: Oxford University Press, 2012), 59.

Therefore, there are two unresolved punishments looming over the northern kingdom awaiting fulfilment: the uprooting of the people in 2 Kings 17, and the reign of Josiah, destroying the temple at Bethel, which will take place in 2 Kings 22–23. In this way a character contrast is drawn: Jeroboam, king of the northern kingdom, who builds the altar, and Josiah, king of the southern kingdom, who will tear down the altar.

The contrast between Jeroboam and Josiah is highlighted through the contrasts between Jeroboam and David also found throughout the book of Kings. David is repetitively held as the paradigm of a good king in the regnal formulae, although not necessarily the narrative structures,[16] against whom other good kings are measured. Jeroboam becomes the paradigm for evil kings, used as a point of reference for the sins of future northern kings. Hezekiah, for example, will be described, "He did what was right in the eyes of the LORD just as his ancestor David had done" (2 Kgs 18:3); but Ahab, for example, will be described, "For he walked in all the way of Jeroboam son of Nebat" (1 Kgs 16:26). Josiah is measured according to the paradigm of David: "He did what was right in the sight of the LORD, and walked in all the way of his father David" (2 Kgs 22:2), generating paradigmatic opposition between Josiah and Jeroboam.

On the one hand, the potential for Jeroboam's eternal house, snatched away before it is even granted, may suggest that the promise to David of an eternal house has been annulled through the sins of that house. The rephrasing of the dynastic promise to David in the narrative of Solomon, now adding a condition of obedience in 1 Kings 9:3–4, suggests this modification. On the other hand, there remain fundamental differences between the northern and southern kings, highlighted through the contrast between Jeroboam and Josiah. Northern kings make some attempt to undo the worship of other gods (for example Jehu in 2 Kgs 10), but none restores worship to Jerusalem. Josiah brings about the full repentance of Judah from worship at high places and idols, augury, mediums, and passing children through fire. In this way, Josiah undoes what Manasseh has done. By destroying the altar at Bethel, Josiah has also undone what Jeroboam has done.

Josiah's repentance does not remove the punishment foretold against Judah; however, the repentance delays the punishment. Moreover, Josiah is able to erase his own past sins, these reforms removing wrong worship practices not taking place until ten years into his reign. This point of difference from the northern kings brings hope

---

16   See Alison L. Joseph, *Portrait of the Kings: The Davidic Prototype in Deuteronomistic Poetics* (Minneapolis: Fortress Press, 2015), 77–105.

when Jehoiachin is left alive at the conclusion of the book. The repentance of Josiah functions as one of several "lessons for Jehoiachin," as David Janzen has described the final chapters of the book of 2 Kings.[17] 2 Kings 18–25 shows that past sins of Josiah and Hezekiah can be "simply erased" through repentance when these kings are evaluated as doing right in the eyes of the LORD. To the extent that Jehoiachin's evil sits alongside Manasseh's evil, contributing to the collapse of the monarchy, there is hope that Jehoiachin may still repent, and the punishment of exile may come to an end.

ELIJAH, ELISHA, AND LIFE AFTER THE TEMPLE

Some of the most intricate detail and narrative description in the book of Kings is devoted to the building of the temple in Jerusalem. The focus upon the temple provides the basis for the sin of the kings that follow: alongside worship of other gods, the sin of worshipping in places outside the temple of Jerusalem is a recurring motif in the litanies of offences. Moreover, the temple is God's presence in Israel and, alongside the monarchy, the locus for God's promises of protection and blessing upon the people. The details relating to the building of the temple, and especially the long account of its dedication (1 Kgs 7–8), increase the pathos of the destruction of Jerusalem and pillaging of the temple at the conclusion of the book. Once again, however, another layer of significance is revealed through a narrative analogy, this time not between two kings, but between the temple and the prophets Elijah and Elisha.

As Nathan Lovell has demonstrated, there is a striking parallel between the role of the temple described in Solomon's prayer in 1 Kings 8:22–53 and prophetic ministry in the northern kingdom of Israel at the core of the book in 1 Kings 17–2 Kings 11, especially the ministry of Elijah and Elisha.[18] For each of Solomon's prayer requests regarding the temple, Elijah or Elisha bring a corresponding blessing on Israel:

- The temple will be a centre for prayer: Elijah repeatedly prays to God when he performs miracles, brings the son of the woman of Zarephath back to life (1 Kgs 17), and lights the water-soaked altar in his contest with the prophets of Baal (1 Kgs 18).

---

[17] David Janzen, "The Sins of Josiah and Hezekiah: A Synchronic Reading of the Final Chapters of Kings," *JSOT* 37 (2013): 349–70.

[18] Lovell, *The Book of Kings*, 193–195. See also Nicholas P. Lunn, "Prophetic Representation of the Divine Presence: The Theological Interpretation of the Elijah-Elisha Cycles." *JTI* 9 (2015): 49–63.

- An oath in the temple will ensure justice: Elijah rebukes Ahab for his mistreatment of Naboth (1 Kgs 21), and a woman from Shunem has her land restored to her because of her association with the name of the prophet Elisha (2 Kgs 8).
- Prayer in the temple will bring restoration after military defeat: Elisha intervenes to bring restoration when King Ben-Hadad of Aram sieges the Israelite city of Samaria (2 Kgs 6–7).
- Prayer towards the temple will end drought with rain: Elijah's contest with the prophets of Baal restores rain (1 Kgs 18), Elisha provides clean water to Jericho (2 Kgs 2), and a flood in battle against the Moabites (2 Kgs 3).
- Prayer towards the temple will provide relief to other calamities such as famine and plague: Elijah provides food to the widow of Zarephath (1 Kgs 17) and Elisha provides food and relief to his followers (2 Kgs 4).
- The temple will allow access to God's presence for foreigners: the foreign commander Naaman applies to Elisha for healing from leprosy (2 Kgs 5).
- Prayer towards the temple will ensure victory in war: Elisha is called upon to assist the Israelite king in war against the Moabites (2 Kgs 3).

Moreover, as Lovell points out, Elijah and Elisha are more effective in these roles than the temple is elsewhere in the book of Kings.

One vignette captures some of these dynamics in the ministry of the prophet Elisha: his provision of relief from calamity and offer of God's presence for foreigners. In 2 Kings 5, an Aramean commander called Naaman suffers from leprosy. Just as 1 Kings 8:41 describes a foreigner from "a distant land" who may hear of God's great name, mighty hand, and outstretched arm, so Naaman hears of the prophet Elisha far away in his own land, from a young Israelite girl who is a servant in Naaman's house (verses 2–3). Keith Bodner points out that a servant voice knowing of Elisha's capacity beyond the borders of Israel would have been an important point of reflection for an audience after the Babylonian exile, also living beyond the borders of Israel.[19]

Naaman first approaches the Israelite king for help, an act that initially causes great distress to the king: as a northern king, without temple, he has no means to pray for healing for the sick Naaman. But there

---

[19] Keith Bodner, *Elisha's Profile in the Book of Kings: The Double Agent* (Oxford: Oxford University Press, 2013), 86.

is another locus for God's presence in the north, and the prophet Elisha hears of the king's distress and intervenes with instructions for Naaman to be healed. Naaman is initially indignant that he is told to wash in the River Jordan, but again the voices of wise servants intervene in verse 13 to convince Naaman to follow Elisha's command.

When Naaman is miraculously healed, his response to Elisha takes an about-turn, and Naaman declares before him in verse 15, "Now I know that there is no God in all the earth except in Israel." Again there is an echo of Solomon's prayer in 1 Kings 8:43, that prayers towards the temple might be answered "so that all the peoples of the earth may know your name and fear you." Naaman's new commitment to worshipping the God of Israel even goes so far as requesting "two mule-loads of earth" (verse 17) from Israel to take back to Aram, so that he can continue to worship the God of Israel on the land of Israel from a distance.

Jeroboam has built places of worship in Bethel and Dan as alternatives to the temple in Jerusalem, leading to exile; but the prophets Elijah and Elisha in the north represent a different alternative, one that brings blessing to the people and restores worship of God even when the temple is not available. Such a formulation for the prophets promises something of hope for Judah (and Israel) after the destruction of the temple at the conclusion of the book of Kings: even without the temple, God may continue to bring blessing and relief to the people through prophetic ministry. The exile is not the end of God's commitment to the people of Judah.

JEZEBEL AND THE WOMAN OF ZAREPHATH: THE OUTSIDER IN THE BOOK OF KINGS

Male characters dominate the book of Kings, but some exceptions emerge: negatively, Athaliah is portrayed as a usurping queen (2 Kgs 11), without prophetic backing like corresponding usurping kings, Jehu and Jehoiada;[20] and positively, Huldah is a faithful prophet at a key moment of Josiah's reforms (2 Kgs 22:14–20). Jezebel, the wife of Ahab at the centre of the book of Kings, is treated in the narrative as a profoundly negative character. The introduction of Baal worship to Israel is traced to Ahab's marriage to Jezebel; Jezebel is an active agent, spurring Ahab to take Naboth's field and killing prophets of God; and

---

[20] Patricia Dutcher-Walls, "Athaliah: The Queen Who Was Not," pages 182–198 in *Characters and Characterization in the Book of Kings*, edited by Keith Bodner and Benjamin J. M. Johnson, LHBOTS 670 (London: T&T Clark, 2020), 188.

she is posed as Elijah's opponent. The prophecy and fulfilment of her
death in the narrative relishes in the detail of her grisly end, her blood
spattered, her body trampled by horses, and her flesh eaten by dogs (1
Kgs 21:23; 2 Kgs 9:30–37). In contrast to Athaliah and Huldah, Jezebel
is not from the north or south, although married to a northern king.
Jezebel is a foreign woman, the daughter of the king of Sidon (1 Kgs
16:31), making the marriage reminiscent of Solomon's marriage to foreign wives, leading him away from worship of the God of Israel. With
the portrait of Jezebel in isolation, where a foreign woman is equated
with all that goes astray for the kings of Israel and Judah, a nationalistic agenda appears to be in view, blaming the downfall of the kingdoms
on outsiders and the practices of outsiders. One last character analogy,
between Jezebel and the woman of Zarephath, however, challenges
this portrait.[21]

The narration of the woman of Zarephath's story in 1 Kings 17:8–24
captures beautifully the plight of a generous woman in a fragile situation. When Elijah first asks the woman for a drink in verse 10, she does
not hesitate in providing for his need in verse 11. But when Elijah adds
to the request a morsel of bread, the woman's situation is revealed. The
audience already knows she is a widow from verses 9 and 10, but added
to this vulnerability, the woman explains in verse 12, she has only a
little flour, and "I am now gathering a couple of sticks, so that I may go
home and prepare it for myself and my son, that we may eat it, and die."

Elijah appears unaffected by the pathos of the woman's declaration,
telling her in verse 13 not to be afraid and to prepare a cake. He says to
"bring it to me, and afterwards make something for yourself and your
son." As Robert Alter points out, this request demands a lot from the
woman.[22] She has already declared that there is only enough flour for a
last meal for two, and here the prophet asks her to feed three: him first,
herself second, and only lastly her son. Her obedience is rewarded when
the jar of meal is not emptied and the oil is not used up.

This woman's woes are not finished with the provision of food. In
verse 17, her son becomes ill and there is "no breath left in him." Elijah's
power from God is revealed once again when he brings the child back to
life. However, the miracle is not instantaneous, and tension regarding his
success is built up in the story. First, he carries the son out of sight to his
own chamber, perhaps so that the woman cannot see his own distress,

---

21   Stephanie Wyatt, "Jezebel, Elijah, and the Widow of Zarephath: A Ménage Trois That
     Estranges the Holy and Makes the Holy the Strange," *JSOT* 36 (2012): 435–58.
22   Alter, *The Hebrew Bible*, 504.

indicated when Elijah "cried out" to God in verse 20. He then stretches himself over the child not once but three times before once again he "cried out" in verse 21. With the reader's sigh of relief, in verse 22, finally "the LORD listened" and the child is revived. The miracle may have been performed by Elijah, but the woman of Zarephath has the last, theologically insightful, word: "Now I know that you are a man of God, and that the word of the LORD in your mouth is truth" (verse 24).

The primary parallel between Jezebel and the woman of Zarephath is that they are both Sidonian, as Zarephath is a locality belonging to Sidon (1 Kgs 17:9). Many other points of connection emerge between their stories that contrast rather than parallel these two Sidonian women. Israel is plunged into drought and famine by the word of God, bringing Elijah into the woman of Zarephath's house. This is a direct assault on the domain of Baal, god of rain and fertility;[23] and this famine is only lifted when Jezebel's prophets of Baal are slaughtered (1 Kgs 18:40–41). Whereas Jezebel is associated with famine, the woman of Zarephath provides food for the prophet Elijah, albeit with divine help. Jezebel does not recognise the word of God in Elijah, and instead opposes him; the woman of Zarephath makes the declaration that the word of God is in Elijah. The result of Jezebel's prompting to Ahab to take Naboth's vineyard is that disaster will come upon Ahab's sons and the house will come to an end; the son of the widow of Zarephath is brought to life by the prophet Elijah.

The outsider, in this case a foreign woman, Jezebel, is associated with the collapse of the monarchy, both north and south. But another Sidonian outsider, the woman of Zarephath, is associated with the blessings received through the prophet Elijah and the possibility of life without the temple. In this way, the character analogy promises hope alongside danger for life among outsiders in captivity.

CONCLUSION: THE COLLAPSE OF THE MONARCHY

The similarities and contrasts drawn between Solomon and Jehoiachin in the frame of the narrative of Kings raise a number of questions about the collapse of the Davidic monarchy: What brings about this dramatic collapse of the house of David? Has God ceased unfailing support for the Davidic kings and kingdom? What does the loss of the monarchy and the temple mean for the people who constitute this kingdom? And is the message of the book of Kings only nationalistic in scope?

[23]   See Wray Beal, *1 & 2 Kings*, 230.

Just as the book of Kings is framed by a character analogy, so also these questions are answered by a series of character parallels and contrasts. There is no simple dichotomy of the evil north and the good south; instead, southern kings are shown to have much in common with the north, bringing warning and explanation for the collapse. The south is also set apart by God's promise to David, and the repentance of the Davidic king Josiah offers a model for the lingering Jehoiachin. Finally, in the north, life without the temple is envisioned, where the word and blessing of God come through prophetic presence, and where outsiders can be associated with both danger and blessing. This vision of life in the north brings hope to the narrative of the south, that the people of Judah may too continue to receive God's blessing through prophets and life among foreign peoples in exile.

SELECTED FURTHER READING

Alter, Robert. *The Hebrew Bible. Vol 2 Prophets Nevi'im. A Translation with Commentary*. New York: Norton, 2019.

Boda, Mark J. *A Severe Mercy: Sin and Its Remedy in the Old Testament*. Siphrut 1. Winona Lake: Eisenbrauns, 2009.

Bodner, Keith. *Jeroboam's Royal Drama*. Biblical Refigurations. Oxford: Oxford University Press, 2012.

Bodner, Keith. *Elisha's Profile in the Book of Kings: The Double Agent*. Oxford: Oxford University Press, 2013.

Dutcher-Walls, Patricia. "Athaliah: The Queen Who Was Not," pages 182–198 in *Characters and Characterization in the Book of Kings*, edited by Keith Bodner and Benjamin J. M. Johnson. LHBOTS 670. London: T&T Clark, 2020.

Garsiel, Moshe. *The First Book of Samuel: A Literary Study of Comparative Structures, Analogies and Parallels*. Ramat Gan: Revivim, 1985.

Gilmour, Rachelle. *Juxtaposition and the Elisha Cycle*. LHBOTS 594. London: T&T Clark, 2014.

Janzen, David. "The Sins of Josiah and Hezekiah: A Synchronic Reading of the Final Chapters of Kings." *JSOT* 37 (2013): 349–70.

Joseph, Alison L. *Portrait of the Kings: The Davidic Prototype in Deuteronomistic Poetics*. Minneapolis: Fortress Press, 2015.

Leithart, Peter. "Counterfeit Davids: Davidic Restoration and the Architecture of 1–2 Kings." *TynB* 56 (2005): 19–33.

Lovell, Nathan. *The Book of Kings and Exilic Identity: 1 and 2 Kings as a Work of Political Historiography*. LHBOTS 708. London: T&T Clark, 2021.

Lunn, Nicholas P. "Prophetic Representation of the Divine Presence: The Theological Interpretation of the Elijah-Elisha Cycles." *JTI* 9 (2015): 49–63.

Schipper, Jeremy. "Hezekiah, Manasseh, and Dynastic or Transgenerational Punishment," pages 81–105 in *Soundings in Kings: Perspectives and Methods in Contemporary Scholarship*, edited by Mark Leuchter and Klaus Peter Adam. Minneapolis: Fortress Press, 2010.

Stavrakopoulou, Francesca. "Blackballing of Manasseh," pages 248–63 in *Good Kings and Bad Kings*, edited by Lester L. Grabbe. LHBOTS 393. London: T&T Clark, 2005.

Walsh, Jerome T. *1 Kings. Berit Olam*. Collegeville: Liturgical Press, 1996.

Wyatt, Stephanie. "Jezebel, Elijah, and the Widow of Zarephath: A Ménage Trois That Estranges the Holy and Makes the Holy the Strange." *JSOT* 36 (2012): 435–58.

Wray Beal, Lissa M. *1 & 2 Kings*. AOTC 9. Downers Grove: IVP, 2014.

7 Ruth and Jonah

Inner-Biblical Explorations of the Patriarchs and Prophets

MARIAN KELSEY

INTRODUCTION

The books of Ruth and Jonah are both short, vivid stories from the late Second Temple period that reuse and play with other biblical texts to add depth to characters, to critique traditions and to dramatise theological arguments. The book of Ruth interacts with the patriarchal stories to show a Moabite woman in positive contrast to the ancestors of Israel. The book of Jonah evokes various prophetic traditions to explore the limits of prophecy and the absolute autonomy of God.

In both texts, the allusions to biblical literature weave together several narratives with shared themes. An allusion normally creates a relationship between two texts: the alluding text and the source text. Allusions in the books of Ruth and Jonah frequently go beyond such a one-to-one relationship. Instead, aspects of each book simultaneously evoke multiple texts, all of which share common features that are also shared with Ruth or Jonah.[1] The broader intertextual patterns created by the allusions thus encompass a set of texts to which Ruth or Jonah belong. I call these interlocking allusions. The evocation of the set of texts – the interlocking allusion – prompts a richer interpretation to emerge from the whole than if each allusion were treated as a one-to-one relationship.

The interlocking allusions of the books of Ruth and Jonah imitate, vary and invert patterns within biblical literature. The implications of the traditional patterns are thereby explored, especially when applied to new situations that do not otherwise occur in the biblical literature. This in turn influences how one returns to and understands the earlier

---

[1] Due to the similarity in the evoked texts, it is not uncommon to find that some of them already allude to each other, before both are taken up into the interlocking allusion.

biblical literature. Through this process, the books of Ruth and Jonah engage with and reflect on the traditions that they inherited.

GIVE YOUR STRENGTH TO WOMEN

The book of Ruth is concerned with matters of inheritance, family security and lineage. Naomi and her daughters-in-law are left vulnerable at the death of all the men in their family. The rest of the narrative concerns their efforts to secure a husband and, ultimately, a son to support them. They not only succeed in their efforts, but Ruth's son also becomes the grandfather of the future greatest king of Israel.

Threats to safety and lineage are common within the patriarchal stories, several of which are woven into the narrative of Ruth. The evocation of the patriarchal stories serves to characterise the two main characters in the story, Naomi and Ruth. Naomi fares badly from the comparison. It indicates that she follows in the footsteps of her forefathers (and her foremother Rebekah), by risking the safety of somebody in her care for the sake of her own interests. The foreigner Ruth, by contrast, is shown to act with greater judgement than her Hebrew ancestors-in-law and is rewarded for it.

The Wife-Sister Stories

The beginning of the book of Ruth includes the words ויהי רעב בארץ, 'there was a famine in the land'. The same words open two other stories in the Hebrew Bible, Genesis 12:10–20 and Genesis 26:1–16.[2] These are two of the three related wife-sister stories. It seems that the book of Ruth is deliberately referencing – and inverting – the expectations that readers familiar with those stories might have when they begin reading Ruth.

In each of the wife-sister stories, a patriarch travels to a foreign land: Abraham in Genesis 12 and Genesis 20, and Isaac in Genesis 26. In each story, the patriarch persuades his wife to present herself as his sister in order to protect his life (Gen 12:13, 20:2, 26:7). Doing so presents a danger to the patriarch's line of descendants, not to mention his wife, because the wife is then seen as potential marriage material by the foreign king involved. Nevertheless, it works out very conveniently for each patriarch, who finds himself well rewarded by the foreign king on account of his 'sister'. After the wife's true identity is revealed, the

---

[2] The exact phrase appears nowhere else in biblical literature outside these three stories, but compare Gen 41 in the Joseph cycle.

foreign king justly rebukes the patriarch for his duplicitous behaviour, but the patriarch nevertheless returns home enriched by his trickery.

The book of Ruth, too, opens with a famine, which drives an Israelite and his wife to a foreign land. Readers may think they know what to expect: the Israelite and his wife will act with cunning to return later laden with foreign wealth. The name of the Israelite even adds to this expectation. In Genesis 20 and 26 the foreign king was called Abimelech, 'my father is king'. In Ruth, the name of the Israelite is Elimelech, 'my God is king', a distinctly more pious beginning, perhaps even hinting that Elimelech will surpass the behaviour of the foreign king(s) Abimelech. The reader's expectations, however, are swiftly overturned. Elimelech dies. His sons take wives, and perhaps for a moment there is hope that a second generation might fare better. The chief crisis that required resolution in the wife-sister stories – the danger to the line of descendants – might be resolved through Elimelech's sons. But, as bringing Sarah into the house of Abimelech resulted in barrenness all round (Gen 20:18), so in the book of Ruth the union of Israelites and foreigners fails to result in offspring for ten years. Within five verses of the book's opening, Elimelech's sons too die, and Naomi is left to return to her homeland, not laden with wealth, but bereaved and ריקם, empty (Ruth 1:21).[3] The threat to the line of descendants has come to pass: as Naomi puts it, she no longer even has sons in her womb who could continue Elimelech's line through his daughters-in-law (1:11).

The evocation of the wife-sister stories is brief and confined largely to the first chapter of the book of Ruth. The effect, however, is to magnify the calamity experienced by Naomi.[4] There is a pattern in God's dealing with his people:[5] when they are forced into a foreign land, God protects them, God ensures that they prosper and God brings them home. Naomi's sense of God's betrayal at the end of the first chapter is not surprising. By all biblical accounts, this is not how things are supposed to be.

[3]   The death of Elimelech and his sons has sometimes been considered implied divine punishment for lingering in Moab (see, for example, Joshua A. Berman, "Ancient Hermeneutics and the Legal Structure of the Book of Ruth," *Zeitschrift Für Die Alttestamentliche Wissenschaft* 119 (2007): 22–38). Given that (in)fertility was also the province of God, it would likely follow that Ruth's and Orpah's failure to bear children is designed to be read as some sort of divine penalty, presumably for the forbidden nature of the Israelite–Moabite marriage.

[4]   Yitzhak Berger, "Ruth and Inner-Biblical Allusion: The Case of 1 Samuel 25,"*Journal of Biblical Literature* 128 (2009): 253–72.

[5]   A pattern not confined to the wife-sister stories; see, for example, the exodus.

One more episode from the book of Ruth recalls the wife-sister stories. In each wife-sister story, the patriarch takes the ethically dubious decision to conceal his wife's identity to protect himself, even though it endangers her and exposes her to sexual advances by the foreign king. Similarly, in chapter 3, Naomi urges Ruth to go under cover of darkness to Boaz, and in effect to make a sexual advance towards him (3:2–4). While Naomi dresses the plan in language suggesting it is for Ruth's good, it is clearly for Naomi's future security too, although it places Ruth in no little danger.[6] In her treatment of Ruth, Naomi behaves as her forefathers did in their treatment of their wives. However, just as the foreign kings in the wife-sister stories seemed to have better moral sensibilities than the patriarchs, so in the book of Ruth, the Moabite will find a better way of achieving her aims.

Jacob, Leah and Rachel

Moving from the opening lines of the book of Ruth to the conclusion, in 4:11 the people of Bethlehem compare Ruth to Leah and Rachel, Jacob's wives: 'May the Lord make the woman, who is coming into your house, like Rachel and Leah, who together built up the house of Israel.' As with the wife-sister stories, the book of Ruth references and echoes elements of the third patriarch's story. Jacob, too, leaves his home to travel to a foreign land and, like his fathers, he returns enriched. The contrast between Jacob and Ruth is particularly stark: Jacob returns with two wives, multiple children and numerous flocks (Gen 31:17–18). Naomi returns from Moab with, initially, two foreign daughters-in-law, no children and no means of support.

Unlike his fathers, Jacob does not play the wife-sister trick, but has it played upon him.[7] His fathers each presented his wife as his sister; Jacob is given the wrong sister as his wife. Naomi's actions here, then, recall those of Laban. Naomi sends her daughter-in-law Ruth incognito into Boaz's bed, as Laban secretly sent his daughter Leah instead of Rachel to Jacob's bed (Ruth 3/Gen 29). Laban sought to gain by the trick seven more years of service from his son-in-law. Naomi seeks a son and thereby security for her and her daughter-in-law. Naomi's plan is that Ruth too should conceal her identity and אל־תודעי לאיש 'not make [herself] known to the man' while he eats and drinks and finally retires (3:3).

---

6 Danna Nolan Fewell, "Feminist Reading of the Hebrew Bible: Affirmation, Resistance and Transformation," *Journal for the Study of the Old Testament* 12 (1987): 82.

7 Marian Kelsey, "Jacob and the Wife-Sister Stories," *Jewish Bible Quarterly* 46 (2018): 226–30.

Only in the night is she to creep to where Boaz is sleeping and lie beside him. While Naomi does not make it explicit, her plan seems to be that Ruth will simply sleep with Boaz and conceive by him, as did Lot's daughters and Tamar, so securing progeny for herself by a kinsman.[8]

There is, however, a crucial difference between the two stories. Leah seemingly goes along with her father's deception, concealing her identity from Jacob until the morning (Gen 29:23–25). The cost of the decision seems to be her relationship with her sister: she envies Rachel as the wife Jacob truly loves (Gen 29:31–35), whereas Rachel covets her sister's fertility (Gen 30:1–8). Yet unlike Leah, Ruth decides not to follow her parent's plan to the letter. When Boaz wakes and asks who she is, she proclaims rather than conceals her identity (Ruth 3:9). Her openness appears to work in her favour. Naomi had told her that '[Boaz] will tell you what to do' (3:4). But in fact, on learning Ruth's identity and hearing her request, Boaz declares to Ruth, 'I will do for you all that you ask' (3:11).

The question of Ruth's identity in the gloom of the threshing floor evokes another element of Jacob's story. That Jacob was the victim, rather than the perpetrator, of his ancestor's wife-sister trick is usually connected to his own identity deception in his early life (Gen 27). Jacob's mother urges him to conceal his identity, go to Isaac and receive a blessing. Jacob obeys, and when Isaac asks מי אתה בני, 'Who are you, my son?', Jacob responds with Esau's name (Gen 27:19). When Esau returns, Isaac asks מי אתה, 'Who are you?', and trembles, ויחרד at realising the deception (Gen 27:32–33). The result of the deception is that Jacob must flee for his life. As identified by Edward Allen Jones, the Hebrew elements are reversed in Ruth's story.[9] Ruth's mother-in-law urges her to conceal her identity, go to Boaz and, in effect, conceive a child. Ruth seems at first to obey, but when Boaz trembles, ויחרד, on waking and asks מי את, 'Who are you?', Ruth responds by identifying herself honestly (3:8–9). On returning to Naomi afterwards, her mother-in-law asks מי את בתי, 'Who are you, my daughter?' (3:16). The result of Ruth's actions is that she has accomplished safety and security for the two women. The honesty of Ruth compared to the deception of Jacob evidently works out better for Ruth than it did in the short term for Jacob. Later, as discussed Jacob is the

---

8 The story of Lot's daughters in Gen 19 also has many parallels with those discussed here; there is simply not space enough to discuss them all.
9 Edward Allen Jones III, "'Who Are You, My Daughter?' A Reassessment of Ruth and Naomi in Ruth 3," *The Catholic Biblical Quarterly* 76 (2014): 653–64.

victim of a parentally contrived identity deception at his wedding, which also resembles Ruth's experience.

Naomi fares badly in these comparisons to her forefather Jacob's life. She stands in the place of both Rebekah and Laban, both of whom urge those in their care to engage in a risky deceit, as do Abraham and Isaac in the wife-sister stories. Whereas in the wife-sister stories the patriarchs seem to suffer no harm from the deception, this is not the case for Rebekah and Laban. Rebekah ultimately loses her favoured son, as he must flee the wrath of his brother (Gen 27:41–45). The Bible records no reunion between mother and son. Laban, too, loses his daughters and grandchildren, an event that causes him evident anguish (Gen 31:43, 50). Having already lost husband, sons and one daughter-in-law, one might expect Naomi to be a little more careful of the one near relation she has left, particularly given the examples of her ancestors. She is not.

On the other hand, Ruth contrasts well with Jacob and Leah by refusing to become complicit. The explicit comparison of Ruth to both Rachel and Leah at the end of the book highlights the ultimate outcome of each night-time escapade. Together, Rachel and Leah 'built up the house of Israel' (4:11). Ruth becomes the ancestor of the house of David (4:18–22). Moreover, although the prompting into a husband's bed came from a parent, the significant consequences arguably came from the women themselves. It was Leah's and Rachel's own efforts (albeit in rivalry) that made Jacob the father of thirteen children, including twelve sons. Likewise, the reader might wonder whether it was Ruth's adaptation of Naomi's plan that led to its great success.

Bringing together the book of Ruth, the wife-sister stories and the Jacob cycle's identity-deception stories, all share certain elements. In each case, a Hebrew husband or parent urges one whom they should protect to engage in a risky identity deception. Excluding Rebekah, all intend a kind of 'bed-trick', namely to expose their charge to the sexual advances of another, that they might benefit from it. Abraham and Isaac seem to benefit from their cunning, leaving the foreign lands enriched. Rebekah and Laban, by contrast, ultimately lose their children to the deceit. Naomi seems to have lost everything before she even initiates the deceit: unlike Abraham and Isaac, she returns from abroad impoverished; like Rebekah and Laban, she has lost her children. While Naomi may believe she therefore has little to lose in playing the trick of her ancestors, it will not work as she expects. The narrative will end with Naomi restored to security and family, but thanks to Ruth's strategy rather than her own.

Tamar

Among the sons born to Jacob by Leah is Judah, and with him we have the third patriarchal story evoked by the book of Ruth. As with Rachel and Leah, the connection is made explicit within the book of Ruth: Ruth, Boaz and their child are compared to Tamar, Judah and Perez: 'Through the children that the Lord will give you by this young woman, may your house be like the house of Perez, whom Tamar bore to Judah' (4:12). The parallels between the Ruth and Tamar stories are extensive, as demonstrated by Ellen Van Wolde.[10] Certain central elements to the analogy also overlap with the wife-sister stories and the episodes from Jacob's life discussed earlier.

Once again, the narrative starts with Hebrew man leaving home. Judah (notably, the ancestor of Elimelech's tribe) leaves without a wife, but soon marries a woman from his new home. He fathers three sons and, like Elimelech, finds a foreign wife, Tamar, for the eldest. But, as with Naomi in the book of Ruth, in the space of a few verses he loses two sons and his spouse and is left with a foreign daughter-in-law but no grandchildren (Gen 38:1–12). Unlike Naomi, Judah succeeds in sending away his daughter-in-law. He tells her to return to the house of her father, as Naomi urged Ruth and Orpah each to return to the house of her mother. Judah's success seems to lie in promising Tamar his third son – a possibility bitterly contrasted with Naomi's declaration that her womb is empty of sons to offer Ruth and Orpah (Gen 38:11/Ruth 1:11). The promise, however, is duplicitous – Judah does not intend to give Tamar to his third son, as he blames her for the deaths of his first two. Similarly, perhaps Naomi's insistence on Ruth and Orpah returning is prompted by a suspicion that these foreign wives may somehow be responsible for Naomi's bad luck.[11] Tamar learns that Judah has not kept his promise, leaving Ruth and Tamar in very similar situations: widowed, childless and in need of securing their future and their husbands' lineage through conceiving a child by a kinsman of their late foreign husbands.

Tamar's plan follows the same lines as those of Abraham, Isaac and Laban (and, for that matter, Naomi). She decides to conceal her identity and allow the sexual advances of another, that she might gain by it. Tamar does not present herself as a potential wife, but as a prostitute. So

---

[10]   Ellen Van Wolde, "Texts in Dialogue With Texts: Intertextuality in the Ruth and Tamar Narratives," *Biblical Interpretation* 5 (1997): 1–28.

[11]   Danna Nolan Fewell and David M. Gunn, "'A Son Is Born to Naomi!': Literary Allusions and Interpretation in the Book of Ruth," *Journal for the Study of the Old Testament* 40 (1988): 103–04.

may be Naomi's intention for Ruth.[12] In contrast to her husband's fore-fathers, and in contrast to Naomi in the book of Ruth, Tamar does not urge a wife or daughter to take such a risk. She must take the risk herself, forced by the circumstances imposed upon her by her father-in-law.

The comparison between the Tamar story and the book of Ruth highlights a crucial similarity between the actions of the foreign women. Tamar, without any elder relative to urge her on, acts on her own initiative throughout. Ruth seems at first to be submitting to Naomi's plan, but later, like Tamar, pursues her own plan to resolve her situation. Tamar's approach to conceiving a child succeeds, but due to the necessity of doing so through concealing her identity, she is endangered. Judah is ready to have her burned for adultery. Only once she confronts him with his own role in the matter does he finally acknowledge his failure to fulfil his obligations. Unlike Tamar, Ruth's plan involves openly identifying herself and confronting Boaz with his obligations. The strategy may be riskier in the short term, as she has identified herself as creeping into a man's bed at night. Nevertheless, it also carries the possibility of greater reward: the security of marriage and offspring, rather than only a child.

The comparisons to the wife-sister and Jacob stories highlight another similarity: Abraham and Isaac act out of fears for their own safety, and Laban seemingly for the extra years of work he might thereby get out of Jacob. Tamar, however, acts simply to get what is owed to her after her kinsman failed in his obligations. Likewise, Ruth reminds Boaz of his obligations, as she and Naomi see them.[13] Indeed, Ruth goes beyond Tamar in that while Tamar acts to get what is due to her, Ruth prompts Boaz about his responsibility as גאל, kinsman-redeemer. Such a responsibility is to Naomi at least as much as, or more than, to Ruth.[14] In all cases, the foreign women act in sharp moral contrast to the ethically dubious actions of the Hebrew men, and occasionally women.

Comparisons and Consequences

In each generation of patriarchs, from Abraham to his great-grandson Judah, the Bible recounts the men behaving in morally dubious ways

---

[12] Compare Hos 9:1: 'You have loved a prostitute's pay on all threshing-floors.' Fewell and Gunn, 105.

[13] As Van Wolde points out, technically neither Boaz nor Judah have levirate obligations; rather it is the women's 'creative interpretation of these laws' that drives the action: Van Wolde, "Texts in Dialogue With Texts," 18.

[14] Jack M. Sasson, "The Issue of Ge'Ullah in Ruth," *Journal for the Study of the Old Testament* 3 (1978): 52–64.

concerning the women under their protection. Abraham and Isaac each presents his wife as his sister, exposing her to the sexual advances of foreign rulers, out of fear for his own safety. Their kinsman Laban similarly presents the wrong sister as a wife to wring seven more years of service from Jacob. This in turn is narrative comeuppance for Jacob's own complicity in his mother's variation on the identity-deception trick, putting her favoured son in the place of her elder. Finally, Judah too finds himself on the receiving end of such a trick, because he has failed in his duties to his daughter-in-law.

The wife of Judah's descendant Elimelech seems to have learned well the tricks of her ancestors. Her daughter-in-law Ruth is in her care, but she persuades the woman to conceal her identity and open herself up to sexual advances – if not directly to play the prostitute – in order to secure a future for Naomi. That this future security is also for Ruth does not obscure the fact that it is Ruth who is urged into the dangerous role of seducer. The other stories are evoked through direct references at the end of the book and exact phrase-borrowings at the start, together with the pattern of identity deception at the heart of each tale. The evocations do not reflect well on Naomi. She is put in the place of Abraham and Isaac, Laban and Rebekah, and even Judah, in her treatment of Ruth. While Abraham and Isaac seemed to escape the consequences of their actions, the other figures all face narrative rebuke for their behaviour. That it all works out well for Naomi seemingly has more to do with her daughter-in-law's devotion and adaptation of the plan than Naomi's own scheming.

By contrast, the allusions to the other stories show Ruth in positive distinction to the other characters. Like Leah and Rachel, she becomes the mother of a great house – but without the cost of her relationship to her existing family. She gains security and offspring for herself and Naomi, safeguarding their future and lineage. Furthermore, she gains for herself a husband and a position, and is acknowledged as a worthy woman, אשת חיל and better than seven sons (3:11; 4:15). Her success in this seems due to two factors.

First, like Tamar, she takes events into her own hands. The two foreign women act to confront the Hebrew men with their responsibilities to the women as members of their clan.

Second, Ruth goes beyond Tamar – and beyond all her Hebrew ancestors-in-law – in her execution of the plan. Though urged into an identity deception, Ruth refuses to be complicit. Honesty may be the riskier strategy but, as Ruth demonstrates, it has the greater rewards. Her moral judgement and her actions through the story set her on a par with, and even above, the patriarchs of the nation.[15] While they urge deception, Ruth acts with honesty and truth. While they exploit those in their protection, Ruth demonstrates חסד, loyalty (3:10). The narrative positioning of the Moabite woman both elevates Ruth and serves as a critique of the more dubious moments in the lives of the patriarchs.

IS JONAH ALSO AMONG THE PROPHETS?

The book of Jonah is shaped by questions about the role of prophets and the function of prophecy. A prophet and his actions are the driving force of the plot, and several times the book alludes to narratives in which other prophets play a leading role. The allusions function together to illustrate Jonah's failure to assume the normal roles of a prophet, especially the roles of intercession and warning. In turn, the use of the allusions in Jonah creates a lens through which the reader then views the earlier stories: the reader understands the earlier stories differently in light of the book of Jonah. By creating such an effect, the book casts doubt on the true efficacy of prophets even when they appear to succeed in other biblical narratives.

Sodom and Gomorrah

The first allusion to explore is to the Sodom and Gomorrah narrative in Genesis 18–19. When the prophet Jonah finally reaches Nineveh, he announces that in forty days Nineveh will be overthrown (3:4). The root used for 'overthrown', הפך, is particularly evocative of the fate of Sodom and Gomorrah. Throughout the Bible, whenever the root is used to refer to a city, Sodom and Gomorrah are almost always named or implied.[16]

---

[15] See Zakovitch for how an allusion from Ruth to Gen 12 also makes this point by directly contrasting Ruth and Abraham: Yair Zakovitch, "Through the Looking Glass: Reflections/Inversions of Genesis Stories in the Bible," *Biblical Interpretation* 1 (1993): 139–52.

[16] The explicit references to the overturning of these cities, using the root as either verb or noun, occur in Deut 29:23; Isa 1:7; 13:19; Jer 49:18; 50:40; Lam 4:6; Amos 4:11. In Jer 20:16 the cities are not named but seem implied. See Abraham Z. Ephros, "Nineveh and Sodom Juxtaposed: Contrasts and Parallels," *Jewish Bible Quarterly* 30 (2002): 244; Jonathan Magonet, *Form and Meaning: Studies in Literary Techniques in the Book of Jonah*, 2nd edition, Bible and Literature Series 8 (Sheffield: Almond, 1983), 65. Exceptions occur in 2 Kgs 21:13 (where in the context the verb refers to a dish, as metaphor for a city) and 2 Sam 10:3/1 Chron 19:3 (which might also be intended to allude to Sodom: Nathan MacDonald, "Hospitality and Hostility: Reading Genesis 19 in Light of 2 Samuel 10 (and Vice Versa)," in *Universalism and Particularism at Sodom and Gomorrah: Essays in Memory of Ron Pirson*, ed. Diana Lipton (Atlanta: Society of Biblical Literature, 2012), 179–90. See also Zakovitch, "Through the Looking Glass," 148 n18.)

The use of the root therefore immediately draws attention to the story of Sodom and Gomorrah and the enduring memory of the cities throughout biblical literature. The connection is reinforced by plot similarities between Jonah and Genesis 18–19. In each case, some account of a gentile city's wickedness becomes known to God. God sends, in the one case angels, in the other the prophet Jonah. The cities' inhabitants respond in very different ways, and the difference is then matched by the contrasted outcomes.

The most noticeable comparison between the stories is that each account reports a discussion between God and his prophet concerning the fate of the wicked city. Abraham and Jonah are starkly and obviously contrasted in both their attitudes and the roles that they take upon themselves. Abraham fulfils his role as a prophet in interceding with God on behalf of Sodom. Jonah, however, is silent before God when he first hears of Nineveh's wickedness, and later angry when Nineveh is spared. Abraham asks, 'Shall not the Judge of all the earth do what is just?' (Gen 18:25), whereas Jonah complains, 'Is not this what I said while I was still in my own country? ... for I knew that you are a gracious God and merciful' (Jonah 4:2). Abraham wishes to know if the wholesale destruction of Sodom is just, whereas Jonah laments the mercy shown to Nineveh. There is a complicated interplay of wording and intent. Abraham speaks of justice, but beneath his words he seems to be questioning God's mercy. Jonah speaks of mercy but is apparently questioning God's justice. Jonah's complaint is made as he sits outside the city and sees to his chagrin that it is still standing: his complaint does not change God's mind. Notably, though, Abraham is no more successful than Jonah. His intercession fails. Nonetheless, matching the obliqueness of Abraham's and Jonah's words, both got exactly that of which they spoke, though perhaps it was not what they wanted. God agreed to every proposition Abraham put to him, so was indeed just by the definition Abraham thereby presented. In fact, God went beyond the point at which Abraham ceased his intercession, proceeding with the destruction of Nineveh because 'all the people to the last man' (Gen 19:4) proved wicked, never mind all but ten. Similarly, Jonah's 'complaint' about God's habit of relenting was resolved in that Nineveh was eventually destroyed. It was not, though, in the time span Jonah might have wished, and he did not get to stand like Abraham over the city's smoking ruin.

The allusion to Genesis 18–19 leads to a well-developed contrast between Abraham and Jonah. A major part of the contrast is that Abraham does his job as a prophet by interceding on behalf of the wicked foreign city, whereas Jonah conspicuously fails to do so. But alongside that important contrast is a certain similarity. Both challenge the divine character, especially in relation to the balance between justice and mercy, but each fails to get the outcome he seeks. While God engages with them in their probing of God's actions, ultimately it is immaterial to the outworking of God's intended purpose.

Israel at Sinai

A second allusion in the book of Jonah is to Israel's and Moses' experiences at Sinai. Though Abraham was unsuccessful in interceding on behalf of Sodom, the book of Jonah also alludes to another, far more successful example of prophetic intercession. The king of Nineveh tells his people, 'Who knows? God may turn and relent, and turn from his fierce anger, so that we do not perish' (3:9). The words he uses are close to those of Moses on Mount Sinai, when he pleads with God, 'Turn from your fierce anger and relent concerning the evil [you plan to do] to your people' (Exod 32:12). The Exodus and Jonah passages are uniquely related in that the phrase 'turning from fierce anger' (אף + חרון + שׁוב) and the concept of God relenting, נחם, are combined nowhere in biblical literature except in Exodus 32:12 and Jonah 3:9.[17]

The result of the king of Nineveh's warnings is also recounted in a phrase borrowed from Exodus 32, with only the very slightest variation. In both Exodus and Jonah, we read that 'God/the Lord relented concerning the evil that he said he would do to them/his people' (Jonah 3:10; Exod 32:14). The shared phrases are strengthened in allusive force by the broader context of each passage. In each case, God has threatened an entire people with complete destruction, but upon the intervention of a human figure, God changes his mind and the people are spared.

What is noticeable about the comparison created by these texts is that Moses' words of intercession are not spoken by Jonah. They are in the mouth of the king of Nineveh. Not only does Jonah fail to intercede, but the nearest approximation of the intercessory role is assumed by another (an approximation only, because the relevant words are spoken to the Ninevites, not to God). Yet the king of Nineveh shares the success of Moses in preserving his people from God's immediate anger.

Drawing together the three stories of Sodom, Nineveh and Sinai, in each case the wickedness of a group of people comes before God. God becomes aware of the fact and determines to destroy them. The intervention of a human figure is crucial. Abraham and Moses both argue with

---

[17]   For similar discussion, see Magonet, *Form and Meaning*, 71.

God in an attempt to protect the people. The king of Nineveh takes up Moses' words in speaking to his own people. The three-way comparison has two implications. First, Abraham and Moses alike stand in contrast to Jonah. They intercede; Jonah conspicuously does not. Each allusion, and especially the combination of the two, emphasises Jonah's failure to take up the prophetic task of intercession. Second, the juxtaposition of the Sodom and Sinai narratives denies the reader any assumption that intercession guarantees God's relenting. Moses was successful, but Abraham was not. Jonah failed in his role by not interceding, but we are not to assume that, had he interceded, it would necessarily have saved Nineveh.

Jeremiah

Shifting from the intercessory to the warning role of prophets, the book of Jonah in several places uses language particularly reminiscent of Jeremiah. Variations on the phrase discussed earlier, 'relenting concerning the evil he said he would do', appear throughout Jeremiah, five times in all, three of which are in Jeremiah 26.[18] A second expression in Jonah, '[each] man shall turn from his evil way' (3:8, 10), also appears throughout the book of Jeremiah, including in Jeremiah 26:3, but nowhere else in the Hebrew Bible (in that form).[19] The two expressions are therefore particularly evocative of Jeremiah, and especially Jeremiah 26. Moreover, Jonah and Jeremiah 26 both combine the two phrases, or versions of them, in an apparent cause and effect relationship. In Jeremiah 26:3 God says, 'Perhaps ... they will turn each man from his evil way and I will relent concerning the evil which I planned to do to them.' In Jonah 3:10 God sees 'that they turned from their evil way and God relented concerning the evil which he had said he would do to them'.

In Jeremiah 26, the phrases are used in the context of God's message to and hope for his people, communicated via the prophet.[20] Jeremiah

---

[18]   Similar expressions occur in Jer 18:8; 26:3, 13, 19; 42:10.

[19]   The expression appears (with only contextual interference) in Jer 18:11; 25:5; 26:3; 35:15; 36:3, 7, and nowhere else in the Hebrew Bible. A similar phrase, lacking the איש, appears in 1 Kgs 13:33; 2 Kgs 17:13; 2 Chr 7:14; Jer 23:22, Ezek 13.22; 33:11; Zech 1:4.

[20]   Every instance of the phrase 'turn each from their evil way' in Jeremiah is spoken by or through a prophet, and every instance of the phrase minus the איש in the wider biblical corpus is also spoken by a prophet, or a prophet is being criticised for not speaking it. When the king of Nineveh uses the phrase as a command to his people, it is thus the only place in the Hebrew Bible where the words are placed in the mouth of a person other than a prophet.

is sent to speak out against the wickedness of Judah. He calls on them to amend their ways and obey the Lord, so that God will relent from the planned disaster. The people and the officials in Jerusalem initially react with hostility, though they later accept that Jeremiah's words are a message from God. But one element is missing – there is no account of people repenting, even when they accept the veracity of Jeremiah's message. Jeremiah 26 does not relate the eventual outcome for Jerusalem, but we of course know it from the rest of the book.

In Jeremiah 26, Jeremiah acts in his prophetic role of warning the people to change their ways. In the book of Jonah, however, the prophet does not warn any more than he intercedes. Jonah's bald announcement that Nineveh will be overthrown gives no hint of a remedy to or reversibility of that outcome. Once more, it is left to the king of Nineveh to take up the prophetic mantle and call upon his people to change their ways and to hold out the possibility that God may relent. Once more, he experiences remarkable success in the task. Jonah 3:10 records that the Ninevites turn from their evil way. In fact, it is the only time in the entire Hebrew Bible in which any variation on רע + דרך + שוב is a *description* of a reversal of behaviour, rather than an imperative, a conditional, a plea, negated or the like.[21] Of the many uses of the phrase in Jeremiah, all are warnings that are ultimately ignored, or occasionally a warning that the prophets fail to give.[22] The king of Nineveh has not only replaced Jonah in performing the prophetic task but has also bested Jeremiah (and all other biblical prophets) in his success at it.

The allusion to Jeremiah 26, as with the allusions to the Sodom and Sinai narratives, has two implications. First, it continues the development of Jonah's character as a contrast to the prophetic norm. Having failed to intercede, Jonah also fails to properly warn. Second, warning the people is no more a guarantee of success than interceding with God. Jeremiah's warnings to the people, unlike those of the king of Nineveh, are disregarded, and the consequences for Jerusalem are described elsewhere in the book.

---

[21] Gottfried Vanoni, *Das Buch Jona: literar- und formkritische Untersuchung* (St. Ottilien: EOS-Verlag, 1978), 136. Other uses include 1 Kgs 13:33, which describes Jeroboam not turning despite being warned; 2 Kgs 17:13, in which Israel and Judah did not turn despite being warned; and Zech 1:4, which warns readers not to be like their ancestors who did not turn when warned. In Ezek 13:22, the combination רע + דרך + שוב appears in a narrative segment in which prophets are criticised for not encouraging the wicked to turn from their evil way.

[22] See Jer 18:11; 23:22; 25:5; 26:3; 35:15; 36:3, 7.

Comparisons and Consequences

The three evoked texts, Jeremiah 26, Exodus 32 and Genesis 18–19, all involve the wickedness of a people coming before God, threatened punishment and the intervention of a prophet or prophet-like figure to intercede or to warn. By alluding to all of them, the book of Jonah creates a pattern of variation within the similar overall structures of the book itself and the three other texts. Twice the prophet involved intercedes directly with God. Moses is successful; Abraham is not. Twice the prophet, or prophetic figure, warns the people to repent. Jeremiah's warnings go unheeded; the king of Nineveh's warnings to repent are obeyed. Strikingly, however, Jonah attempts neither prophetic task. Although he is the prophet of the story, in that he is the one who has received God's word and mission, he conspicuously fails to perform as such.

By bringing together multiple biblical texts and forcing comparison between them, the book of Jonah also shapes one's reflections on their common themes. Why was Moses successful in intercession but Abraham was not? Was Abraham's voice any less regarded by God than that of Moses? Similarly with Jeremiah: was the gentile king of Nineveh truly better at the prophetic task than one of the greatest prophets of Israel? The divergent outcomes for the wicked people in the various texts suggest that neither approach to the prophetic task, intercession or warning is guaranteed success. Or, optimistically, either has the potential to avert disaster.

It would be tempting to look at the comparison between Jonah 3 and Jeremiah 26 and think Jeremiah ultimately failed because the people did not heed him and did not repent, whereas the Ninevites did repent and that is why they were saved. Curiously, though, the book of Jonah is reluctant to leave its readers with that conclusion. If repentance were the focus, the book could have ended at Jonah 3. Instead, it continues into a fourth chapter. When Jonah protests God's relenting over Nineveh, God does not respond by citing the Ninevites' repentance. Even the language changes, from the relenting of God (נחם), which was associated with the question of whether or not the people would turn (שוב) from their evil ways, to a description of God's mercy, חוס. And it seems God's חוס may be shown as and when God pleases. In fact, the characters of the book are portrayed as knowing this. The ship's captain qualifies his hope for divine deliverance with אולי, 'perhaps', a tentativeness of expectation matched by the king's מי־יודע, 'who knows' if God will relent (1:6, 3:9). The repentance of the Ninevites is, one presumes, appropriate, but it does not inevitably result in the saving of the city. By moving into the fourth chapter and beyond the language of Jonah 3, the author places God's mercy towards

Nineveh in the same category of absolute divine autonomy as the God who destroyed Sodom despite Abraham's intercession but spared Israel after the intercession of Moses. Whatever action the prophet takes (or fails to take), the decision is God's alone.

In the most straightforward sense, then, the book of Jonah describes how God might unexpectedly relent and have mercy even on the wickedest of people. However, when the object of that mercy is a people not one's own, and indeed a people for whom one might have little sympathy, such a conclusion might feel at best abstract, and at worst a little depressing. If the book were merely an illustration of divine sovereignty to relent or not, set in a situation without direct relevance to its readers, one might wonder why it needed to be written at all.

I can only intimate the solution in the space here.[23] Crucially, when the book of Jonah was most likely written, in the Persian period, everyone reading it would have known that Nineveh's reprieve did not last for long. Nineveh was destroyed, as other biblical books record. In fact, it was infamous in cultural tradition for being the paradigmatic example of a city destroyed and never rebuilt. God's absolute freedom to relent, regardless of prophetic action or inaction, includes an absolute freedom to reverse the decision too.

What relevance does that message have for the readers? Several times throughout the book of Jonah, the language and events indicate comparisons between Nineveh and Jerusalem.[24] Perhaps it was the fate of Jerusalem that prompted the author to explore through his book the question with which he ends. Should not God show mercy to Nineveh, despite their wickedness? The question is a genuine one. Should a God who relents of evil have mercy on a wicked people? The biblical precedents give no single answer, demonstrating as they do the freedom of God to decide when and how God relents. But the indeterminacy is not without an encouraging aspect. Nineveh, for all the ending of Jonah, was at the last destroyed and indeed became a byword for such eradication from human history. But if such a reversal in that city's fortunes were possible, then perhaps the same could be hoped for with regard to Jerusalem. God might just as dramatically turn and change that city's fortune.

---

[23]   For a full account, see Marian Kelsey, "Jonah: Co-Texts and Contexts" (St Andrews, 2018).

[24]   Briefly, those hints include the sort of wicked deeds ascribed to Nineveh; the description of Nineveh as עיר גדולה, great city; and the allusion to Jer 26 in the book which records Jerusalem's fall. Such a deliberate ambiguity, or 'double-image', may also be at work in the book of Nahum: K. L. Noll, "Nahum and the Act of Reading," *Proceedings – Eastern Great Lakes and Midwest Biblical Societies* 16 (1996): 107–20.

8 Theaters of Empire and Exile in Daniel and Esther

LAURA CARLSON HASLER

The stories of Esther and Daniel begin and end in exile. While different in style, content, and (arguably) message, both biblical narratives
highlight the mortal dangers and dynamic possibilities of living outside
Judah and within the court of a non-Judean king. To highlight the differences as well as the similarities between Daniel and Esther's dealings
with their imperial hosts, we can approach these stories as two "theaters," with space in Daniel and Esther understood as a stage and the
movements of their primary characters as actors. This analogy reveals
aspects of these narratives that, while set in the midst of "foreign"
empires, do not conform to the binaries of assimilation and resistance
that scholarly approaches to these texts sometimes assume. By looking
closely at narrated space and the actors within it, we can ask more complex questions than simply: who is complicit with imperial power and
who is resisting it? Instead, we can trace the complex varieties of power
that intersect in these stories (their boundaries as well as their possibilities) and compare them among these narrative stages.

Esther and Daniel 1–6 are set in empires and explore the possibilities of outsiders surviving within them. Daniel 1–6 follows its eponymous protagonist and his companions as they are selected by their
Babylonian captors for service in the court of Babylonian and Median-
Persian kings. In this setting, Daniel encounters both opportunity and
peril: various emperors reward Daniel handsomely for his skill in dream
interpretation, but these rulers also attempt to execute him and his
friends for their devotion to their patron deity.

The story of Esther likewise showcases the mortal stakes of living
within the court of a foreign king. Esther, a child of Judean exiles, marries the mercurial Persian king Xerxes after her predecessor is deposed.
When a plot to slaughter all of the Judean inhabitants of Persia is uncovered, Esther and her relative Mordecai work to reverse it. The story
ends with the imperially sanctioned death of thousands of Persians at
the hands of their would-be victims, as Esther and especially Mordecai

amass more power in Xerxes' court. Like Daniel 1–6, the story of Esther envisions the space of empire as one in which the threat of death shadows even the most upwardly mobile Judean exiles.

Esther and Daniel thus exude a particular kind of ambivalence regarding the imperial institutions and authority that govern their narrative frameworks.[1] The term "imperial-exilic theater" invites consideration of imperial space and movement within that space as important to the overall representation of Daniel and Esther.

Movement and space are intimately entangled with empire in antiquity, as they are today.[2] The movement of imperial armies across the Levant in the first millennium BCE shaped the terms and anxieties of Israelite and Judean life well before the Assyrian and Babylonian incursions in the eighth and sixth centuries BCE.[3] While modern uses of the term "travel" typically (if mistakenly) connote voluntary movement and leisure, representations of both involuntary travel and confinement permeate biblical narratives.[4] As early as the Exodus story, imperially instigated travel in biblical stories "take[s] place under conditions of necessity, reluctance, coercion, and deprivation."[5] In narratives set in exilic and postexilic contexts, empires can seem inescapable.[6]

But labeling space in Daniel 1–6 and Esther as "imperial" or movement as "imperially instigated" does not exhaust their significance.[7] Daniel 1–6 and Esther depict imperial spaces and movements into, across, and away from them in ways that demonstrate remarkable

---

[1] The fact that MT Esther is often described as a farce need not discount its moments of "serious" play with concepts of empire, power, and violence (see Robert Alter, *Strong As Death is Love: The Song of Songs, Ruth, Esther, Jonah, and Daniel* [New York: Norton, 2015], 85–86; and Timothy K. Beal, *The Book of Hiding: Gender, Ethnicity, Annihilation, and Esther* [New York: Routledge, 1997], 2).

[2] Robert Clarke, "Towards A Genealogy of Postcolonial Travel Writing," in *The Cambridge Companion to Postcolonial Travel Writing*, ed. R. Clarke (Cambridge: Cambridge University Press, 2018), 1–15.

[3] See, e.g., Amos 1–5; Isa 36–39.

[4] Robert Clarke, "History, Memory, and Trauma in Postcolonial Travel Writing," in Clarke (ed.) *The Cambridge Companion to Postcolonial Travel Writing*, 49–62, 54. My approach is inspired by Musa Dube's methodological focus on travel and space in the colonial encounter. (Musa W. Dube, *Postcolonial Feminist Interpretation* [St. Louis: Chalice, 2000], 57–84, esp. 57–58, 61).

[5] Clarke, "History, Memory, and Trauma," 54. See also Gen 12, 18, 37–50.

[6] There are, of course, many exceptions to this imagined inescapability, e.g., Zech 2:10–17 (Hebrew); Zech 2:6–13 (English).

[7] It is possible to track metaphorical movement (e.g., social mobility) in these stories, as many have (see, e.g., Susan Niditch, "Esther: Folklore, Wisdom, Feminism, and Authority," in *The Feminist Companion to Esther, Judith, and Susanna*, ed. A. Brenner; [Sheffield: Sheffield Academic Press, 1995], 26–46 at 36–37).

patterns as well as critical variations. The complexity of these imperial-exilic narrative stages raises questions: Is there an "outside" of the empire? Who can leave it, and what sorts of transformations unfold at its borders? What does travel within imperially governed space yield? Who must remain at the "center" of imperial authority, to their empowerment or peril? Mapping the answers to these questions yields larger insights about how these narratives stage the dynamic intersection of imperial, Judean, and divine power.

In examining Daniel and Esther, it is important to note that there were not single versions of these narratives circulating in Jewish antiquity. Several versions of both of these stories were passed down from the late first millennium BCE. Here, I will focus first on (presumably older) Hebrew versions of these stories found in the Masoretic Text (MT). One of the Greek versions of Esther, found in the Septuagint (LXX), will serve as a "third term" for comparison, demonstrating a revelatory departure from both of the Masoretic imperial-exilic theaters considered.[8] By reading each of these narratives as an imperial-exilic theater, we see fantasies of empire in their breadth and possibilities, as well as their dangers and limits.

A. MT ESTHER AND DANIEL 1–6: EMPIRE IS EVERYWHERE

Exile, the condition of forced movement away from spaces and structures of political autonomy, is the premise of both Esther and Daniel. Both narratives correspondingly imagine empire as a consumer of those autonomous spaces from an alternative space of power. The movements of the characters of Daniel 1–6 and Esther are the result of a royal

---

[8]   Cf. Jonathan Z. Smith, *Drudgery Divine: On the Comparison of Early Christianities and the Religions of Late Antiquity* (Chicago: University of Chicago Press, 1990), 115. Though there are two extant Greek versions of Esther, the Septuagintal "Old Greek" (OG) version and the "Alpha" text, my comparison will be based on the LXX/OG edition, not because it is (arguably) older but because its relative length affords more narrative fodder for comparison (Karen H. Jobes, "Esther: To the Reader," in *A New English Translation of the Septuagint* [Oxford: Oxford University Press, 2007], 424–25, 424). For detailed discussion of the LXX version of Esther and its relationship to the Masoretic (Hebrew) version, see Meredith J. Stone, *Empire and Gender in LXX Esther* (Atlanta: Society of Biblical Literature Press, 2018), 5–17. The book of Daniel also has two Greek recensions (OG and Theodotian) with multiple additions (including Susanna and the Prayer of Azariah) (see discussion in Carol Newsom, *Daniel: A Commentary* [Louisville: Westminster John Knox Press, 2014], 5–6). While these additions are worthy of analysis as "theaters," space constraints prevent consideration of these more diffuse additions here.

summons to move towards the new centers of power, where actors
(kings, bureaucrats, Judeans) generate fateful imperial decrees. The
comparison of these theaters underscores the dynamic, perilous, and
often gendered variations common to inhabiting *their precarious positions at the heart of the empire.*[9]

No Exit: Defining Imperial Space in MT Esther and Daniel 1–6

The representation of empire is not univocal in these – or any – biblical
narratives.[10] In Daniel 1–6, for example, both Babylonian and Median-
Persian kings articulate the reach of their authority in universal terms.
Nebuchadnezzar and Darius alike articulate the scope of their power
in terms of: "all people, nations, and languages ... all those who live
on the earth" (Dan 4:1; 6:25).[11] Of course, this "universal reach" may
not always be voiced by the author with a straight face.[12] The notion in
Daniel 3, for example, that "all nations" bow down to Nebuchadnezzar's
new statue when they hear certain music must be pragmatically
amended to "all those within earshot" (Dan 3:4–5). Still, the common
phrasing unites Nebuchadnezzar and Darius under a shared conception
(or conceit) of their own spatial authority.[13] They perceive their empires
to be everywhere.[14]

Empire is, in both Esther and Daniel, an overwhelming spatial reality. But an empire's envelopment of space does not mean that empire is
identically imagined or engaged with in these tales. Here is how Daniel
6 describes Persian space and its governance:

> It pleased Darius to appoint over the kingdom one hundred and
> twenty satraps to be in charge of the whole kingdom; over them

---

9   See discussion in Stone, *Empire and Gender*, 50–66.
10   Nor is "empire" itself a term, strictly speaking, emic to Esther or Daniel. The word
     "emperor" or "empire" is not presented as an entity semantically different from
     "king" (*melek*), "queen" (*malkah*), and "kingdom" (*mamlakah, malku* [Aramaic])
     of a more provincial variety. But textualized concepts, though reliant on language,
     are not limited to stand-alone terms. The notion of empire is not constrained by
     terms like "king" and "kingdom," and invites further explorations of its narrated
     dimensions.
11   See also Dan 3:4.
12   See Carolyn J. Sharp, *Irony and Meaning in the Hebrew Bible* (Bloomington, IN:
     Indiana University Press, 2009), 61–64. See also David M. Valeta, "Court or Jester
     Tales? Resistance and Social Reality in Daniel 1–6," *Perspectives in Religious Studies*
     32 (2005): 309–24. NJPS translation here and following, unless otherwise marked.
13   For connections between Dan 3 and Dan 6, see Newsom, *Daniel*, 190–91.
14   For application of this concept in Ezra-Nehemiah, see Laura Carlson Hasler, "Persia
     is Everywhere Where Nothing Happens: Imperial Ubiquity and Its Limits in Ezra-
     Nehemiah," *Bible and Critical Theory* 16 (2020): 140–69.

were three ministers, one of them Daniel, to whom these satraps
reported, in order that the king not be troubled. (Dan 6:2–3)[15]

The Persian empire in the book of Esther, like Babylon and Media-Persia
in Daniel 1–6, covers nearly all narrated space: "Xerxes reigned over
a hundred and twenty-seven provinces from India to Ethiopia" (Esth
1:1). Like Daniel 6, Esther's Persia is marked at the very outset by its
spatial excesses. In Esther, Xerxes' 127 Persian provinces rival Darius'
120 satrapies. Xerxes' kingdom stretches "from India to Ethiopia." Yet
even within this latter notice, there is an acknowledgment that Xerxes'
Persia is vast but not, strictly speaking, everywhere. Naming boundaries, even in the near-unthinkable scope of India to Ethiopia, still
delimits the parameters of this imperial theater. Articulating boundaries makes travel beyond them thinkable, even if barely so. Similarly,
later on, Persian decrees are sent "to all royal provinces, to every province in its own script and to people in their own language" (MT Esth
2:22). This is a circulation that is impressive but does not quite achieve
the boundaryless movement of Darius' letter in Daniel 6, which is sent
to "every dweller on the earth" (Dan 6:25). In this way, even the "every-
whereness" of empire has variation.

At the beginning of each tale, we see travel and movement at work.
This movement is the consequence of Babylon's and Persia's consump-
tive movement *outward* (to exert themselves over other groups and territories), and then of subjugated persons' movement *inwards*, towards
the empire's center: Babylon and Susa. Spatially speaking, MT Esther
begins in the heart of Persian authority. The book of MT Esther begins
not just within the Persian citadel of Susa but at a party thrown by
the king. This party, which eventually welcomes the entire city population, makes a mockery of time, lasting six months and one week
(MT Esth 1:3–5).[16] The book of Daniel begins more soberly, recounting
the Babylonian destruction of Jerusalem as a way of explaining Daniel
and his companions' presence in Nebuchadnezzar's court. Instead of
a wild party, Daniel's story begins with a siege, a deportation, and a
Babylonian cultural education:

> The Lord delivered King Jehoiakim of Judah into [Nebuchadnezzar's]
> power, together with some of the vessels of the House of God, and
> he brought them to the land of Shinar to the house of his god; he
> deposited the vessels in the treasury of his god (Daniel 1:2)

---

[15] Dan 6:2–3 (Hebrew; NJPS translation here); Dan 6:1–2 (English).
[16] Beal, *Book of Hiding*, 16–17.

Jerusalem and its temple are imagined here but only as those sites that the empire has consumed (Dan 1:2).[17] Like Esther, Daniel, Hananiah, Mishael, and Azariah are selected to undergo a cultural conversion at the heart of the empire (Dan 1:1-7).[18]

Mordecai (MT Esth 2:5-6), like the character of Daniel, is introduced in terms of his movement into the empire (having likewise traveled forcibly away from Jerusalem).[19] Unlike Daniel, Mordecai is not brought directly into the imperial court but occupies its margins, lingering outside the royal gate for much of the story (MT Esth 2:11, 21; 3:1-6; 4:1-3). Indeed, various intra-imperial spaces and provisional boundaries serve as critical markers of each major Judean character. Mordecai, Esther, and Daniel each perform risky, circuitous movement within imperial environs as they attempt to negotiate the directives of bureaucrats and kings. Though diverse in their patterns of movement, all three characters ultimately move into the imperial court and never leave.

Movement and Transformation within Imperial Spaces in MT Daniel and Esther

Can actors on such imperial-exilic stages – even theoretically – leave?[20] Masoretic Daniel 1-6 and Esther imagine Babylon and (Media-)Persia as taking up traversable space as the Judean protagonists attempt to find stable footing in the imperial court. But other characters are shown traveling opposite or even "vertical" paths, but generally to their doom: Haman is strung up on impossibly high gallows (MT Esth 7:9-10), while Daniel's rivals are thrown down into the pit of lions to be crushed and devoured (Dan 6:24). Both grisly, involuntary movements are inclusive in their reach: these deadly, vertical "travels" are imposed not only on the perpetrators but also on their families. These longitudinal means of exit from the imperial stage turn out to be different ways of dying.

The stories of Daniel and Esther also include accounts of lengthier and more ambiguous movements from the imperial center outward: Vashti's "banishment" (MT Esth 1:19) and Nebuchadnezzar's "exile"

---

17 Newsom notes, however, that Nebuchadnezzar is not pictured here as "taking" Jerusalem and the temple objects but rather that it is God who bestows it (Newsom, *Daniel*, 41).

18 See Beal, *Book of Hiding*, 37; also discussion of Judean "training" in Newsom, *Daniel*, 42–48.

19 On the elasticity of Mordecai's genealogy in MT Esth 2:5-6, see Carol M. Bechtel, *Esther* (Louisville: Westminster John Knox Press, 2001), 30.

20 On the symmetrical structure of MT Esther, see Jon D. Levenson, *Esther: A Commentary*, OTL (Louisville: Westminster John Knox Press, 1997), 5. For discussion of centers and peripheries in Esther, see Beal, *Book of Hiding*, 18–20.

(Dan 4). Vashti's refusal to appear before Xerxes and his companions is met with his feverish anger but only vague consequences: that "Vashti shall never enter the presence of King Xerxes" (MT Esth 1:19a).[21] But what does this prohibition actually mean? Whether it signals demotion, exile, or death is not clear.[22] Narratively, however, Vashti is banished from the stage and is quickly replaced by Esther. Vashti's brief presence in the story (MT Esth 1:9; 12) and mandated absence from it suggests a path "elsewhere": away from patriarchal-imperial spaces.[23] However, this movement is barely legible and, within the story, barely thinkable.

Nebuchadnezzar's travel away from his own court in Daniel 4 is, by contrast, vividly detailed. His movement away from the central site of his authority occurs because of hubristic speech. Nebuchadnezzar attributes his success to his own work, exclaiming, "There is great Babylon, which I have built by my vast power to be a royal residence for the glory of my majesty!" (Dan 4:27 (4:30 Eng)). For this, his kingdom is temporarily "revoked" (it literally "passed away," or "moved on" from him; Dan 4:28 (4:31 Eng)), along with his humanity. His expulsion from central, male-dominated space results in his eating, feeling, and looking like an animal (Dan 4:30 (4:33 Eng)). Critically, this involuntary travel is not permanent. Nebuchadnezzar's exile ends in a remarkable transformation. After a set time frame, he once again articulates the important truth that Daniel's god is the ultimate sovereign:

> At the end of the days I, Nebuchadnezzar, lifted my eyes to heaven, and my reason was restored to me. I blessed the Most High, and praised and glorified the Ever-Living One, whose dominion is an

---

[21]   NJPS translation here and following (for MT). For the irony within Vashti's "punishment," see Sharp, Irony and Meaning, 72–73 and Beal, Book of Hiding, 23, 39. Susan Niditch describes twentieth-century feminist appeals to Vashti's heroism, arguing that "for the writer of Esther, Vashti's foolishness is the foil for Esther's wisdom" (Niditch, "Esther," 33; italics mine).

[22]   Dorothy Bea Akoto reads Vashti's punishment as an instance of divorce (Dorothy Bea Akoto, "Esther," in The Africana Bible: Reading Israel's Scriptures from Africa and the African Diaspora, ed. H. R. Page [Minneapolis: Fortress Press, 2010], 268–72, 270). See Vashti's departure from the palace depicted in Fillipino Lippi's, "La regina di vasti cacciata" (1480; Florence: Museo Horne).

[23]   Madipoane Masenya draws attention to how readers of Esther tend to "collude with the author of the text" in passing over Vashti as a noteworthy character in this story (Madipoane Masenya [ngwana' Mphahlele], "Their Hermeneutics Was Strange! Ours is a Necessity! Rereading Vashti as African-South African Women," in Her Master's Tools? Feminist and Postcolonial Engagements of Historical-Critical Discourse, eds. C. Vander Stichele and T. Penner [Atlanta: Society of Biblical Literature Press, 2005], 179–90, 180, 186–87). Masenya argues that Vashti's "gender speaks louder than her class" from the narrator's perspective and that her boldness serves as exemplary (Masenya, "Rereading Vashti," 192–3).

> everlasting dominion and whose kingdom endures throughout the generations ... He does as he wishes with the host of heaven and with the inhabitants of the earth. There is none to stay his hand or say to him, "What have you done?" (Dan 4:31–32 (34–35 Eng))

Nebuchadnezzar's temporary exile inspires his acknowledgment that Daniel's god is, in fact, the emperor of emperors.[24] This god's power is all-encompassing and inescapable.

The actions that instigate Vashti and Nebuchadnezzar's banishments are similar: both proffer an affront to formidable authority. However, the results of their involuntary travels are different: Vashti, without the intervention of deity or king, is dismissed from the narrative stage permanently. Nebuchadnezzar's exile is exhaustively foretold, depicted, and then resolved. In both cases, the expulsion is framed in educational terms: Vashti's banishment is meant to *keep* Persian women from learning to scorn their spouses (Esth 1:17–18); Nebuchadnezzar's so he understands where the true source of his power lies. Yet only Nebuchadnezzar has the benefit of learning the lesson himself and implementing it after his restoration. This kind of rehabilitation requires the possibility of a return trip, engineered by divine intervention. By contrast, such "redemptive" travel is not made available to Esther's Vashti.[25] She is consigned permanently to being *elsewhere*.

Yet, in MT Daniel 1–6 and Esther, such travels away from centers of imperial power are relatively rare. Far more common, especially for the Judean protagonists, is the reverse condition: movement towards and stasis within the imperial court. While escape, martyrdom, even stasis at the *margins* of imperial power are all theoretical options that these characters might explore, the imperial court is where Daniel, Esther, and Mordecai are compelled to travel and where they remain.[26]

Stagnation and Transformation in MT Esther and MT Daniel 1–6

For Daniel, Mordecai, and Esther, movement towards the center of imperial power is uneven and risky.[27] Daniel's summons to the Babylonian

---

[24] Newsom, *Daniel*, 146.

[25] Newsom, *Daniel*, 148–49. See discussion in Beal, who identifies Vashti as the (Kristevean) abject "who is neither subject nor object within the present order, and which therefore must be pushed outside its borders" (Beal, *Book of Hiding*, 17; also 26–28).

[26] The character of Daniel does also descend into the den of lions (Dan 6:17), as his friends are cast into the furnace (Dan 3:20). Both of their return travels come at the behest of divine intervention but do not appear to instigate transformation.

[27] Of Esther, Beal writes: "One can map the space of this narrative world as it emerges in terms of concentric circles of power" (Beal, *Book of Hiding*, 18).

court as a dream interpreter is initially laden with physical threat: he intervenes with his miraculous interpretation after his Babylonian colleagues have been sentenced to death (Dan 2:12–13).[28] But even investiture with relative power (Dan 5:29; 6:1–3) cannot keep Daniel from danger – this imperial center has edges from which one can quickly fall. When Daniel's outlawed acts of devotion are discovered by Darius' other advisors, it becomes clear that no space in this capital city is truly private; there is no place, in other words, outside the imperial surveillance. To be visible, moreover, is to be at risk.

Mordecai and Esther's journey to the Persian palace is likewise halting and perilous (MT Esth 2:11, 21–23; 3:1–6; 4:11). After Mordecai urges Esther towards Xerxes' court, he stalks the walls outside, an acknowledgment that he has surrendered control over Esther's fate: "Every single day Mordecai would walk about in front of the court of the harem, to learn how Esther was faring and what was happening to her" (MT Esth 2:11). Esther's own limited movement emerges in the spaces between Xerxes' and Mordecai's spheres of action: the city gate and the Persian court. Esther's travels between Mordecai and Xerxes marks her first as courier (MT Esth 2:21–22), then as front-line negotiator between these two men.[29] By Esther 4, it becomes clear that both Mordecai and Xerxes wield the threat of death over Esther: unbidden entry to Xerxes' court means execution (MT Esth 4:11), while Mordecai warns that remaining silent in the face of Judean peril will dismantle her privilege and cause her and her family to perish:

> Do not imagine that you, of all the Jews, will escape with your life by being in the king's palace. On the contrary, if you keep silent in this crisis, relief and deliverance will come to the Jews from another quarter, while you and your father's house will perish. (MT Esth 4:13b–14a)

Like Daniel in the court of Darius, for Esther in Xerxes' court, the space for any private or free action has dissolved.[30] This becomes clear in Esther's reply to Mordecai:

---

[28] See Daniel Smith-Christopher's characterization of Daniel in Dan 2, in which "dream interpretation is an act of spiritual warfare or 'wisdom warfare'" (Daniel Smith-Christopher, *A Biblical Theology of Exile* [Minneapolis: Fortress Press, 2002], 183). Daniel's subsequent interpretive missions are accompanied by more promise than peril, however (Dan 5:16).

[29] For discussion of possible points of resistance in this episode, see Beal, *Book of Hiding*, 75–79.

[30] "[Esther] is an object that has been exchanged between and circulated among the men" (Beal, *Book of Hiding*, 36).

> Go, assemble all the Jews who live in Shushan, and fast in my behalf; do not eat or drink for three days, night or day. I and my maidens will observe the same fast. Then I shall go to the king, though it is contrary to the law; and if I am to perish, I shall perish! (MT Esth 4:16)

No secure space exists for her "between" the Judean and Persian authorities, making the repetition in Esther's statement, "If I perish, I perish," emphatic rather than tautological.[31]

For Esther, Daniel, and Mordecai, journeys into the site of imperial authority have no parallel, permanent trip away from court. For Daniel and Mordecai, however, eventual stasis within the empire entails investiture with capacious authority. Daniel begins the final story of the Court Tales on the verge of crucial administrative power: "the king considered setting him over the whole kingdom" (Dan 6:3b). In the course of this story, Daniel himself briefly falls out of favor, is cast downward into a pit of lions, then, like Nebuchadnezzar, is restored to court by divine intervention. By the end, Daniel has so effectively secured his hold on spaces of imperial authority that he outlasts kings and kingdoms: "Thus Daniel prospered during the reign of Darius and during the reign of Cyrus the Persian" (Dan 6:28). When compared to Vashti, Haman, or the Median bureaucrats of Darius' court, whose travels "away" from imperial power mean erasure, Daniel's survival requires that he remain visible on an imperially governed stage.

Similarly, Mordecai becomes "powerful in the royal palace, and his fame was spreading through all the provinces; the man Mordecai was growing ever more powerful" (MT Esth 9:4). His authority expands so rapidly that it mirrors the patterns of imperial growth, until he is ensconced in royal writing once again:

> All his mighty and powerful acts, and a full account of his greatness to which the kings advanced Mordecai are recorded in the Annals of the Kings of Media and Persia. (MT Esth 10:2)

While Daniel endures through the rise and fall of multiple kings and empires (Dan 6:28), Mordecai has preserved himself even more effectively: by becoming written about and permanently archived in the imperial center of power.

---

[31]   See Esther Fuchs, "Status and Role of Female Heroines in the Biblical Narrative," in *Women in the Hebrew Bible*, ed. A. Bach (New York: Routledge, 1999), 127–40 at 79–80.

We may compare these ascents and acts of preservation with the figure Esther, who writes but whose acts are not inscribed in the Persian annals. Esther's intermediary positions – as contestant-queen, as courier, as negotiator, and finally as author – can be read as repeated attempts to find space between, within, or alongside the imperial court/yard and its influential occupants. Esther arguably achieves the most prolonged success in this regard in the course of her two-day feast for Xerxes and Haman (MT Esth 5:4–5; 6:14–7:1–2). Between the accepted dinner invitation and the execution of Haman, Esther controls her space and, for a brief moment, suspends the narrative action. In these short verses, Esther claims provisionally secure space through a deferred request. But the progression of narrative action proves inexorable, with Esther herself soon urging it along by pleading for rescue and indicting Haman (MT Esth 7:3–6). In the end, moreover, Esther's own role at the center of violent imperial machinations is overtaken – and overwritten – by Mordecai.[32]

Writing as a Means of Imperial Power in MT Daniel and MT Esther

In both the MT books of Daniel and Esther, mobile forms of writing aid imperial control over spaces.[33] Writing, in the Masoretic edition of Esther, appears as a seamless means of metabolizing imperial will into action, enabling the king – and his rota of advisors, including Esther and Mordecai – to control and to instigate violence, even in the remote sites of his kingdom. Writing – death-dealing, directive, and commemorative – occupies the final chapters of MT Esther (9:1, 20, 29; 10:2).[34] Writing is what activates Xerxes' will in the vast spaces that he governs.[35] The logistics required to circulate the written word around the sprawling Persian empire is described in detail:

> He had them written in the name of King Ahasuerus and sealed with the king's signet. Letters were dispatched by mounted couriers, riding steeds used in the king's service, bred of the royal stud. (MT Esth 8:10)

Nothing is said, however, about the theoretical space between word and action: the words, once circulated, are fulfilled. By contrast, the

---

32   See Fuchs, "Female Heroines," 80–81, 83.
33   Newsom, *Daniel*, 196; James Nati and Laura Carlson Hasler, "Varieties of Writing, Truth, and Power in the Book of Daniel" (paper presented at the annual meeting of the Association for Jewish Studies, 16 December 2020, online).
34   Beal, *Book of Hiding*, 25.
35   Bechtel, *Esther*, 14–16.

distance between writ and behavior is a space that Daniel briefly occupies when he refuses to act in accordance with a signed imperial decree (Dan 6:10–11), a space that is collapsed by his arrest and punishment.[36] "Texts can kill," Carolyn Sharp has observed about Daniel 1–6.[37] In MT Esther, texts not only spur killing, they also commemorate it. At the end of Esther 9, Esther and Mordecai both compose "Purim letters" that ensure that these blood-soaked days will be "recalled and observed in every generation: by every family, every province, and every city" (MT Esth 9:28).

Daniel 1–6 also culminates in a universally circulated imperial letter. It is worth noting the parallels imagined in both Daniel and Esther between circulated writing and imperial power. In both stories, letters traverse imperial space in crucial ways, creating conformity among imperial subjects and enabling monarchical control from the center over the imperial periphery. That said, our three Judean protagonists do not have the same relationship to writing, nor to imperial power: Mordecai writes and his own achievements are archived. At the end of "Esther's" story, we are told that "a full account of the greatness to which the king advanced Mordecai, are recorded in the annals of the Kings of Media and Persia" (MT Esth 10:2; also 9:20–23). Esther writes but, unlike Mordecai, her deeds are not archived in the Persian annals (MT Esth 9:29–32). Daniel interprets and inspires writing but never produces texts himself (Dan 5:13–28; 6:26–28).

In MT Esther and Daniel, writing is a means of collapsing the space between the emperor's will and his subjects, thus reproducing the power of the empire.[38] Yet we also can observe Mordecai, Esther, and Daniel as diversely positioned and unevenly compensated with respect to such writing. Mordecai and Esther reproduce imperial power and violence through writing but are unequally remembered for it. Daniel's interpretation of writing permits him to endure in the halls of Babylonian and Median-Persian power, though not in their archived histories.

---

[36] Donald C. Polaski, "Mene, Mene, Tekel, Parsin: Writing and Resistance in Daniel 5 and 6," *Journal of Biblical Literature* 123 (2004): 649–69 at 658.

[37] Sharp, *Irony and Meaning*, 62, echoing Mieke Bal, *Anti-Covenant: Counter-Reading Women's Lives in the Hebrew Bible* (Sheffield: Sheffield Academic Press, 1989), 14), 14: "The Bible is ... endowed with the power to kill."

[38] Polaski, "Mene, Mene," 662, 668. At the end of Esther, Beal suggests, "[n]either is writing itself so stable as it had appeared [earlier in Esther], despite royal pretenses to the contrary" (Beal, *Book of Hiding*, 84). See also Newsom, *Daniel*, 199–201.

B. "A GOD WHO ALWAYS SEES EVERYTHING": THE
IMPERIAL-EXILIC THEATER OF LXX ESTHER

In the Old Greek (LXX) version of Esther, spatial configurations, depictions of movement, and power relations implied therein surface differently than in either story found in the Masoretic Text. In this edition of Esther, the framework of dreams constricts the imperial stage and provincializes imperial authority, the inner lives of Mordecai and Esther create sites of dissent, and the "vertical" gestures towards divine authority rewrite the imperial-exilic stage as choreographed by divine will and not by Persian power.

Decentering the Space of Empire in LXX Esther

The Greek version of Esther does not begin with a raucous Persian party, hosted by an inebriated king (as in MT Esth 1). It begins in Mordecai's subconscious. Though Mordecai himself is located in exile (LXX Esth Add A 12:4), his dream transports him beyond his imperial-exilic confines. In this dream, Mordecai views, as if from above, the sparring of great dragons, nations preparing for war, a rising flood, the exaltation of the "lowly," and the devouring of the honored (LXX Esth Add A 12:10–11). Here, the ability of empires to wield power is acknowledged: the "whole righteous nation" trembles at the prospect of the approaching battle (LXX Esth Add A 12:9). But this imperial authority is also decentered. Ultimate power – to devour and to save – is sourced *elsewhere*.

In response to the cry of the righteous nation, water and light mete out judgment. In language reminiscent of Amos' eighth-century call that "judgement will roll down like water,"[39] we hear that:

> They cried out to God, and from their cry as though from a small spring, there came a great river, abundant water; light, and the sun rose, and the lowly were exalted and devoured those held in esteem. (LXX Esth Add A 12:9–10)[40]

If Addition A is somewhat vague in identifying the orchestrator of this salvific moment, LXX Esther's conclusion (Addition F) is not. In reflecting upon this dream after the harrowing events of the story unfold, Mordecai is unequivocable: "From God these things have come ... The Lord has saved his people, and the Lord has rescued us from all these

---

[39]   LXX Amos 5:24a (NETS translation).
[40]   NETS translation here and following.

evils" (LXX Esth Add F:1a, 6). Persian authority is decentered by the authority of Mordecai's patron deity.[41]

LXX Esther is not absent depictions of Persian universal rule, however. The Persian king, Artaxerxes, views his own power in comprehensive terms. In his first cited decree, Artaxerxes writes:

> Being ... master of the whole world I have determined (not high-mindedly with presumption of authority but always acting in moderation and with kindness) to secure lasting tranquility in the lives of my subjects and, in order to make my kingdom peaceable and open to travel through all its extent, to restore the peace desired by all people. (LXX Esth Add B:2)

Artaxerxes' self-regard as benevolent global tyrant is ironically gainsaid by his ruthless "peace-enforcement plan."[42] According to Artaxerxes' first letter, "a certain hostile people ... scattered among the tribes of the world" (LXX Esth Add B:4) threaten Persian tranquility and will be met with totalizing slaughter.[43] They will be killed "including women and children – by the daggers of their enemies, without any compassion or restraint" (LXX Esth Add B:6). Artaxerxes' "moderation" and "kindness" is called into question by his plan for such bloodshed. His claims to universal rule are also subject to critique soon thereafter. Still, there may be reason to take seriously at least part of Artaxerxes' understanding of global Persian tranquility. The king's ambition to craft a landscape of unending peace is illustrated by a vision of safe travel throughout his empire: "to make my kingdom peaceable and open to travel throughout all its extent" (LXX Esth Add B:2). Here, free movement *within imperial borders* is a hallmark of imperial peace.

Artaxerxes' vision of travel in a seamlessly controlled empire can be paired with the redoubled threat in his second written edict:

> Every city and country, without exception, that does not do according to this by spear and fire shall be consumed with wrath. It shall be made not only impassable for people, but also most hostile to wild animals and birds for a time. (LXX Esth Add E:24)

Those who do not heed Artaxerxes' Purim mandates will not only be exterminated; their land will also be made impassible. Movement and

---

[41]   See Stone, *Empire and Gender*, 69.
[42]   See Sharp, *Irony and Meaning*, 69.
[43]   See discussion in Stone, *Empire and Gender*, 185–7; Laura Carlson Hasler, "Persia is Everywhere," 148–53.

stagnation are wielded, within Artaxerxes' imperial vision, as tools of promise and threat. Living within peaceful imperial space promises (limited) mobility. Likewise, Esther and Mordecai's own residence within the Persian court are characterized by limited spaces of differentiation and dissent.

Opening Sites of Dissent within the Imperial Courts in LXX Esther

The Judean protagonists of MT Daniel and Esther are compelled to travel to and remain within the imperial court. The same is also true in LXX Esther. Yet in this latter text, the character of Esther carves out more obvious spaces of dissent within the center of Persian power. In this Greek version, Esther is less confined by the constraints of the Persian court, creating sites for being *otherwise*. MT Esther attests that Esther conceals her Jewish origins: "Esther had not made known her kindred or her people, as Mordecai had commanded her" (MT Esth 2:20). The LXX version agrees and adds: "Esther had not changed her way of life" (LXX Esth 2:20). In both versions, by Esther 2, Esther lives within the walls of the Persian palace and never leaves this narrated stage. According to this Greek version, however, this position near the center of Persian power has not entirely impinged on Esther's performance of her "Judeanness." Somehow she has figured out a way *both* to conceal and to play out her identity.

The extent of Esther's repudiation of Persian culture, as well as the compromises this position demands of her, becomes clearer in Addition C. When Esther hears of Haman's genocidal edict, she "fled to the Lord," removing her "garments of glory" and, like Mordecai, put on "garments of distress" (LXX Esth Add C:12–13). In her ensuing prayer, Esther vents about her distaste for her Persian husband, Artaxerxes:

> You have knowledge of everything, and you know that I hate the glory of the lawless and abhor the bed of the uncircumcised or of any foreigner. You know my predicament – that I abhor the sign of my proud position that is upon my head on the days when I appear in public. I abhor it like a menstrual cloth, and do not wear it on the days when I am in private. And your slave has not eaten at Haman's table, and I have not honored the king's banquet nor drunk the wine of libations. Your slave has not rejoiced since the day of my change until now, except in you, O Lord, God of Abraam. (LXX Esth Add C:15b–19)

This passage details the conditions – and compromises – of Esther's cultural dissent, particularly its spatial contours. What Esther can avoid (Persian meals), she does, refusing to "honor the king's feast" in a boundary reminiscent of her predecessor, Vashti. What she cannot avoid (the king's bed, "the sign of [her] proud position") she inhabits but abhors. Addition C, in other words, reveals the scope of Esther's space of independence: it includes meals and (sometimes) clothing. Esther's navigation of Persian culture here is spatially articulated: while she wears the "sign[s]" of her prominent Persian role in public, she refuses to do so in her own "leisurely" spaces that permit private devotion.[44] Un-surveilled (or less-surveilled) space for Esther does exist within this imperial-exilic stage, however narrowly.[45]

It is perhaps ironic, in Esther's subsequent entrance into Artaxerxes' throne-room, that the king reassures Esther that the laws governing his court do not apply to her: "What is it Esther?" Artaxerxes says, "I am your brother. Take courage. You shall not die, for our ordinance is only for the common person. Come here" (LXX Esth Add D: 9–10). From Esther's perspective – articulated in her Add C prayer – her private space of cultural dissent is indeed narrow, but it exists. From Artaxerxes' perspective, however, Esther's political position is even more closely merged with his. Artaxerxes is, after all, her "brother" now and, in Artaxerxes' imagination, she shares his role and thereby *his* space. Persian law only applies to those subjects *below both of them*. From Artaxerxes' vantage point, Esther is completely absorbed by her identity as a Persian queen.

Yet there is reason for the reader of LXX to be suspicious of Artaxerxes' perspective (he has, after all, been wrong before).[46] Recall, moreover, that Esther's prayer, like Mordecai's dream (and unlike the Masoretic version), reorients us to sources of power and identity that are untethered to the Persian monarchy.[47] "You alone are our king," Esther declares to God (LXX Esth Add C:14), beginning her prayer with

---

44   Stone articulates Esther's words in Add C as expressions of agency (Stone, *Empire and Gender*, 213. For a more curtailed account of Esther's agency, see Esther Menn, "Prayer of a Queen: Esther's Religious Self in the Septuagint," in *Religion and the Self in Antiquity*, eds. D. Brakke, M. L. Satlow, and S. Weitzman [Bloomington, IN: Indiana University Press, 2005], 70–90 at 72). While agency is a helpful term, movement and space articulate more precisely the possibilities and constraints with which Esther's performance is represented.

45   For further arguments about the nature of Esther's agency see Stone, *Empire and Gender*, 203–11. See also Menn, "Prayer," 83.

46   See Alter (of MT Esther): "The writer ... introduces a couple of arch hints that may lead us to wonder about [Xerxes'] virility as well as his intelligence" (Alter, *Strong as Death*, 86).

47   See Menn, "Prayer," 70–71.

a denouncement of her husband's rank and any claim it might make to ultimate authority.[48] She then briefly recounts Judean exilic history:

> I have heard from my birth in the tribe of my family that you, O Lord, took Israel out of all the nations and our fathers from among all their forebears, to be an everlasting inheritance. (LXX Esth Add C:16)

Unlike the Masoretic version, in which mention of God and experiences *before* Persia are almost absent, Esther's prayer spatially and temporally relativizes the Persian imperial-exilic space she and her community presently inhabit.[49] While Persia envelopes nearly all of the narrated space in the Masoretic edition of Esther, the edges of this Greek version's theater are situated well beyond Persia, orienting readers to a more spacious *elsewhere*: a site where Israel is chosen from among the nations, a place where "the glory of [the Jerusalem temple] and altar" may be remembered, praised, and perhaps revived (LXX Esth Add C:20–21). In all of these spaces, the god of Esther and Mordecai governs reality.[50] In this way, in LXX Esther, the eponymous protagonist situates herself both within and beyond imperial centers of power. She creates spaces of independent practice beyond (or at the edges of) of Persian surveillance.[51] In her prayer, Esther orients readers to other histories, to other places beyond Persian borders, and to other sources of power.

The Role of God in MT Daniel and LXX Esther

The presence of God is one of the frequently noted differences between the Masoretic and the Septuagintal editions of Esther.[52] As argued earlier, references to the divine transform the theater of LXX Esther. When Mordecai claims that "the universe is in [God's] power" (LXX Esth Add C:2), when Esther avers that only God is their king (LXX Esth Add C:14), and when Artaxerxes himself gives credence to the "most great, living God" (LXX Esth Add E:16), the narrative stage's boundaries

---

[48] See Menn, "Prayer," 74.

[49] See Fuchs, "Female Heroines," 79. For articulation of MT Esther's divinity-invoking parallels with the Joseph story, see Gabriel Hornung, "The Theological Import of MT Esther's Relationship to the Joseph Story," CBQ 82 (2020): 567–581. While we may note an exception in the mention of Mordecai's exilic lineage in MT Esth 2, Levenson notes that "[o]ne surprising aspect of the political thinking in the book of [MT] Esther is its complete lack of interest in the land of Israel" (Levenson, *Esther*, 14).

[50] For comment on God as (triumphant) competitor in LXX Esther's contest of masculinities, see Stone, *Empire and Gender*, 217–19.

[51] See Stone, *Empire and Gender*, 299.

[52] See discussion in Levenson, *Esther*, 17–18.

expand. Thinking and (theoretically) existing beyond the reaches of Persian authority becomes possible.[53]

While these references to God create obvious distinctions between the spatial configurations of LXX and MT Esther, they also provide a site for comparing LXX Esther with MT Daniel 1–6. God is referenced often in Daniel 1–6 (e.g., Dan 2:17–23, 44; 3:17; 4:34–37; 5:23) and frequently intervenes directly: giving knowledge and skill to Daniel and his friends (Dan 1:17), aiding Daniel's interpretation of Nebuchadnezzar's dream (Dan 2:19–23), and – if Nebuchadnezzar's words are to be believed – saving Daniel's friends from the furnace:

> Blessed be the God of Shadrach, Meshach, and Abed-nego, who sent His angel to save His servants who, trusting in Him, flouted the king's decree at the risk of their lives rather than serve or worship any god but their own God. (Dan 3:28).

Likewise, a divine voice speaks Nebuchadnezzar's transformation and madness into reality (Dan 4:31), and an otherworldly hand inscribes a foreboding message to Belshazzar (Dan 5:5). When Daniel escapes from the lion's den unscathed, he attributes it to divine intervention: "My God sent His angel, who shut the mouths of the lions so that they did not injure me" (Dan 6:22). In Daniel 1–6, God is difficult to lose sight of, as both an intervening agent and a persistent talking point.

The Judean, Babylonian, and Median-Persian voices that refer to God in Daniel 1–6 draw comparisons with the Judean and Persian voices that speak of God's power in LXX Esther. In both Daniel and LXX Esther, references to divine authority construct a narrative theater whose boundaries lie *beyond* the empire. While Daniel's residence in the imperial court has no return trip and his experience therein is full of physical threat, the presence of God – wielding power sourced from outside Babylon/Media-Persia – broadens the boundaries of the story's stage. Likewise, LXX Esther's insistence on God's universal kingship extends the borders of what is thinkable beyond Persian boundaries.

The divinely shaped renderings of these spaces are not identical, however. The divine figure intervenes in Daniel 1–6 far more directly and dramatically than God does in LXX Esther. In the latter, God *acts* only once: "God changed the spirit of the king to gentleness" (LXX Esth Add D:8). Though Mordecai's dream discloses God's purposes and Mordecai confirms that "these things have come from God" (LXX Esth Add F:1),

God's discrete agency in the story's events is not clear. God's role and power are more diffuse in LXX Esther than they are in Daniel 1–6.

LXX Esther's constantly referenced but rarely direct divine activity casts God in a distinctive light: God is described by the other actors as governing narrated space and is credited with controlling the story's events, but is rarely seen having a direct hand in the action. By being ever present but less discretely mappable, God's power in LXX Esther is, again, more diffuse in several senses of that term: it is underdetermined and possibly also *everywhere*. God's disseminated presence contrasts with Daniel's god, who performs on the narrative stage more concretely. Though rarely active, the diffusion of the divine presence in LXX Esther reorients its actors to the limits of Persian power and the ubiquity of God's rule.

Writing and Power in LXX Esther: Artaxerxes' Malleable Decrees
As in MT Esther, writing appears in LXX Esther to implement the king's wishes and control over vast imperial landscapes. LXX Esther actually amplifies this connection between writing and control by presenting the reader with "transcripts" of several Persian decrees. Documents are presented here as crucial means of controlling imperial subjects. In the king's initial decree, for example, the purposes of the cited document are articulated at the outset: "I have determined … to secure lasting tranquility in the lives of my subjects" (LXX Esth Add B:2). Again, the irony of the practical means to achieve such stability (killing all Judeans without pity; LXX Esth Add B:6) should not be understated.[54] But it is also important to note that this circulated writing is the crucial means by which Artaxerxes' bid for "peace" – and the grim means of achieving it – is going to unfold. Artaxerxes argues, moreover, that his written decree expresses not only his own desire but also the desire of "all people" for this gruesomely enforced peace (B:2) (though a "certain" group of subject peoples are excluded from this "all").[55] Writing here seamlessly instigates action and reveals collective will.

The second decree of Artaxerxes (LXX Esth Add E) also assumes the efficacy of writing to enact "peace" over the entire empire (LXX Esth Add E:24). However, this decree additionally names various "others" that intimate the limits of Persia's power. Once again, the explicit mention of God in this writ dislocates Persian authority and gestures to sites and sources of power beyond this empire: Artaxerxes admits that he was deceived by

---

54   Sharp, *Irony and Meaning*, 65–81, esp. 65–66.
55   See discussion of Haman's comments in MT Esth 3:8 about the Judeans as a "scattered" people in Beal, *Book of Hiding*, 56–58.

Haman, the justice of God "who *always observes everything*" condemns him (LXX Esth Add E:4), and while Esther's prayer positions God as superior to and *apart from* Persian authority ("you [God] alone are king!"), Artaxerxes pictures God as superior to but also *in league with* his own political aims. According to Artaxerxes, conniving Macedonians like Haman may be able to dupe a Persian king, but such interlopers will never escape "the evil-hating … justice" of Mordecai and Esther's god with his matchless surveillance capacities (LXX Esth Add E:4). Artaxerxes credits God with the rapid execution of Haman, not his own adjudication: "the God who prevails over all things has recompensed him quickly with the deserved judgment" (LXX Esth Add E:18). In this writ, God has been deputized to serve as a kind of Persian secret police force, perhaps leaving the reader to wonder at the reliability of this particular written document.

Even as it claims that God has served Persian purposes, Artaxerxes' second letter nevertheless acknowledges that there is formidable power – divine and "alien" alike – sourced from *elsewhere*. Haman is, in this document, a Macedonian, a thankless "guest," and "an alien to the Persian blood" (LXX Esth Add E:10). His machinations, the king admits, could very well have turned Persian power over to the Macedonians (LXX Esth Add E:14). This view of Haman – as a native of *elsewhere* who gains power among the Persians – exposes a frayed edge of Persian authority: "outside" empire is not only thinkable, but outsiders have also infiltrated the ranks of Persian bureaucracy and effectively threatened it.

This damning view of Haman as powerful outsider in Artaxerxes' second letter reveals another dimension of Persia's vulnerable boundaries. Writing is presented as a means of implementing imperial policy and ensuring wide-ranging "peace." But it is a faulty technology. Artaxerxes' second letter openly retracts the content of the first letter. In the first letter, Haman was proclaimed "our father" (LXX Esth Add B:6). But in the second, Artaxerxes admits, with direct reference to the first letter's naïve description of the Macedonian, that this characterization was a dangerous mistake (LXX Esth Add E:11–13). LXX Esther is, in this way, unabashed in its exposure of the first letter's foolish claims. Persian writing is powerful, and it also can be wrong.

C. CONCLUSION: MAPPING IMPERIAL-EXILIC THEATERS BEYOND BINARIES

Empire is not a univocal concept in ancient Jewish stories, and their characters do not perform identically upon their imperial-exilic stages. The Judean protagonists of MT Daniel 1–6 and Esther diversely negotiate the constraints of their respective theaters, especially the dangers of living within reach of the emperor and his writing. LXX Esther's imperial-exilic theater likewise showcases these constraints, but it also draws the audience's attention more frequently to other centers of power, sources of history, and bases of identity performance *beyond* Persian boundaries. In LXX Esther, God serves as a reference point that reorients the narrative stage: opening spaces, for example, for Esther to perform her Judean identity on the margins of the Persian gaze. MT Daniel shares LXX Esther's explicit theological reference points and discloses horizons of power beyond Persia without as clearly reifying God's diffuse ubiquity. Daniel 1–6, like MT Esther, also highlights the unresolved dangers of living close to the center of imperial authority without a viable escape hatch. MT Esther, in particular, dwells on the absence of spaces ungoverned by death-dealing men.

In all three stories, writing becomes a means of mapping imperial power, as well as the trajectories of its chief Judean actors. The memory of Mordecai is preserved in both Persian and Judean records. Daniel, for his part, interprets writing and succeeds in having his theological claims circulated by means of imperial writ. Like Mordecai, Esther instigates writing but is eventually left out of the Persian imperial record. In LXX Esther, cited documents showcase the limits of Persian authority, naming sites of power beyond Persia and exposing writing's own faultiness.

The complexity of mapping such imperial-exilic theaters may disorient us. It should also move us away from describing the imperial encounter in these stories in simple binaries: "Persian" versus "Judean," "assimilation" versus "resistance," or even "divine" versus "imperial."[56] None of these stories, nor the actors within them, could adequately be described as simply subverting or assimilating with imperial control. Tracing the imperial encounter in terms of boundary, movement, and sites of power yields a more complex record of what it meant to live and survive upon these imperial-exilic stages.[57] Together, these narrative theaters and the actors who populate them disclose diverse choreographies produced by the conditions of exile and the dominance of empires in Jewish antiquity. Indeed, look at any text closely and we may find that such landscapes are "increasingly complex and difficult to map."[58]

---

[56] See Newsom, *Daniel*, 15–18.
[57] Lydia Lee, "Reflections on the Scholarly Imaginations of God and Evil in the Book of Esther," Biblical Interpretation 28 (2020): 273–302 at 301.
[58] Beal, "Book of Hiding," 1.

The stories of Daniel and Esther reward close reading. Such in-depth analysis permits the contemporary reader to see ancient Jewish ideas about authority, space, and the divine in their kaleidoscopic detail. These diverse features prevent us from seeing biblical authors as a monolith, but as producers of texts that reveal distinctive desires, anxieties, and assumptions about power, both imperial and divine. The complexity of these narrative traditions ought to serve as a robust invitation to readers to be a part of the always unfinished task of interpreting ancient literature.[59]

---

[59]   See Lee, "Scholarly Imaginations," 301.

9 Narrative Art in Chronicles

MATTHEW J. LYNCH

The book of Chronicles poses challenges for modern readers, even those who love a good story. The first nine chapters offer an extended genealogy. Its protagonists lack the flaws and tragic moments recorded in books like Samuel and Kings. It focuses on the world of kings and priests in Jerusalem and omits most of the wild and exciting tales about the northern kingdom of Israel – most notably, the stories of Elijah and Elisha. Finally, Chronicles retells many stories told elsewhere in the Old Testament, especially Samuel and Kings. Like Deuteronomy, which recasts laws from other portions of the Pentateuch, Chronicles lacks the kind of pure originality that we sometimes associate with art.

For these reasons, most handbooks on narrative art in the Bible scarcely mention Chronicles. Robert Alter's groundbreaking book *The Art of Biblical Narrative* mentions Chronicles once in passing but gives no attention to specific passages.[1] Scant references to Chronicles also appear in Meir Sternberg's *The Poetics of Biblical Narrative*, Shimon Bar-Efrat's *Narrative Art in the Bible*, Adele Berlin's *Poetics and Interpretation of Biblical Narrative*, and Jan Fokkelman's *Reading Biblical Narrative*.[2] Instead, such works focus their keen literary eye on books like Genesis, Judges, and Samuel, which present readers with more rounded characters, complex plot twists, and moral ambiguity.

My point here is not to criticize these excellent resources for understanding biblical narrative, but instead to acknowledge that

---

[1]   Robert Alter, The Art of Biblical Narrative (New York: Basic Books, 1981).

[2]   Meir Sternberg, *The Poetics of Biblical Narrative: Ideological Literature and the Drama of Reading* (Bloomington: Indiana University Press, 1985); Shimon Bar-Efrat, *Narrative Art in the Bible*, JSOTS 70 (Sheffield: Almond Press, 1989); Adele Berlin, *Poetics and Interpretation of Biblical Narrative*, BL 9 (Sheffield: Almond Press, 1983); Jan Fokkelman, *Reading Biblical Narrative: An Introductory Guide*, trans. Ineke Smit (Louisville: Westminster John Knox Press, 1999).

the renaissance of literary appreciation for the Hebrew Bible that these books heralded was limited to specific kinds of narrative. Appreciation for literary art in other narrative books depended on specialized monographs, edited volumes, or articles that attended to the full breadth and depth of Hebrew narrative art. Accessible introductions to the rich and wonderful world of biblical narrative tend, for the most part, to ignore books like Joshua, Kings, Chronicles, and Ezra-Nehemiah.

This essay explores ways that readers can build a greater appreciation for the unique art and style of Chronicles, and for its theologically rich portrait of history. Fortunately, some more recent scholarship has attended to Chronicles' narrative technique, so we will begin our journey by looking at some of their insights before focusing our attention on three literary features in Chronicles: (1) its well-crafted genealogy; (2) its use of patterns; and (3) its use of Scripture.

DISCOVERING CHRONICLES

Scholars have begun to recognize Chronicles' literary art in recent decades, mostly in books and articles written *for other scholars*. One important treatment of Chronicles' narrative art is the edited volume *The Chronicler as Author: Studies in Text and Texture.*[3] This work attends to the Chronicler as an artist, with his own aims, theology, and perspective.[4] Of course, this recognition carries with it a need to acknowledge the deep dependence on previous material form Samuel, Kings, and elsewhere in the Old Testament. But that dependency does not *reduce* the Chronicler's stature as an artist. It simply allows us as readers to *recognize* the artistic use of sources (where dependency exists) and the many unique contributions where Chronicles goes its own way. Scholars speak of those unique contributions using the German phrase "Das chronistischen Sondergut" (Chronicles' unique material). It's observed, for instance, that Chronicles is, from beginning to end, constructing its narrative to move its audience in particular ways. In other words, it has *persuasive* ends. In one scholar's view, the Chronicler aims "to move his audience to seek Yahweh through the proper forms

---

[3]   M. Patrick Graham and Steven L. McKenzie (eds.), *The Chronicler as Author: Studies in Text and Texture*, JSOTSup 263 (Sheffield: Sheffield Academic Press, 1999).

[4]   A major part of that development was the recognition that Chronicles is literarily and redactionally distinct from Samuel-Kings, on which see Sara Japhet, "The Supposed Common Authorship of Chronicles and Ezra-Nehemiah Investigated Anew," *VT* 18 (1968): 330–71.

of the Jerusalem cult."[5] By "cult," he and other scholars mean the visible aspects of religious life, like sacrifice, sung worship, priestly activity, and so on. This approach attends to the book's **content**, with its repeated use of phrases calling people to "seek" Yahweh,[6] as well as the book's **form**, namely historical narrative that is punctuated with prophetic and royal speeches that encapsulate this concern for "seeking" Yahweh and attending to proper worship at the temple. We can also recognize the specific shape that disloyalty takes in Chronicles: "The opposite of seeking was not so much the commission of a sinful action, but an unfaithfulness demonstrated by failing to turn to Yahweh and by neglecting the temple cultus."[7]

We can also pay attention to the book's **structure**, with its use of "*inclusio*, chiasm, typology, repeated motifs and contrasting motifs."[8] For instance, the genealogy in 1 Chronicles 1–9 begins with Adam (1:1) but gives ample attention to Judah (2:3–4:23), with special attention to the Davidic line (2:3–17; 3:1–24). Chronicles then gives disproportionate attention to the Levites (6:1–81), with specific attention to the Aaronic priests (6:1–15, 50–53) and musicians (6:31–47). In other words, the genealogy of all humanity and all Israel focuses our eyes on the temple servants and the royal line.[9] The next major section (1 Chr 10–2 Chr 9) zeroes in on David and Solomon to persuade readers through their example that pursuing Yahweh required faithfulness in temple worship. The result of such "seeking" was tremendous blessing.[10] The third and last major section (2 Chr 10–36) illustrates the agonies of forsaking worship of Yahweh (exemplified chiefly with Ahaz) and the blessings of seeking him in humility and worship (e.g., during the reign of Jehoshaphat and Hezekiah).[11]

In short, we need to pay attention to content, form, and structure when analyzing Chronicles as a work of narrative art. In the brief

---

[5]   Rodney K. Duke, "A Rhetorical Approach to Appreciating the Books of Chronicles," in *The Chronicler as Author: Studies in Text and Texture*, eds. M. Patrick Graham et al.; JSOTSup 263 (Sheffield: Sheffield Academic Press, 1999), 100–135 [115]; cf. Rodney K. Duke, *The Persuasive Appeal of the Chronicler: A Rhetorical Analysis* JSOTSup 88 (Sheffield: Sheffield Academic Press, 1990).

[6]   E.g., 1 Chr 16:10–11; 22:19; 28:9; 2 Chr 7:14; 11:16; 12:14; 14:4; 15:2, 12–13; 16:12; 18:4; 19:3; 20:4; 30:19; 34:3.

[7]   Duke, "A Rhetorical Approach," 117.

[8]   Duke, "A Rhetorical Approach," 119.

[9]   Duke, "A Rhetorical Approach," 119–120.

[10] Duke, "A Rhetorical Approach," 120–122.

[11] Duke, "A Rhetorical Approach," 122–123.

sections that follow, I'll offer a sampling of the ways that Chronicles deserves its seat at the biblical artists' table, with attention to these three areas along the way.

CHRONICLES' GENEALOGY

I'm convinced that we have it wrong about kids. We're often told that kids just like stories, and if we read Scripture with them, we should focus squarely on narratives like Jacob and Esau, Joseph in Egypt, the exodus, David and Goliath, and so on. Yet when I read through the Bible with my son at the age of seven or eight, I was surprised at the parts he especially enjoyed. He loved the stories, to be sure, but also loved the law. Finding out who gets in trouble for what proved *very* interesting. He also enjoyed the genealogies. It's a good thing, too, since we encounter four genealogies within the first eleven chapters of the Old Testament (Gen 4, 5, 10, and 11). They are also a regular feature in other parts of Scripture, including the New Testament's first chapter. Genealogies and lists of names only gain steam in the post-exilic period (1 Chr 1–9; Ezra 2; 7:1–6; 8:1–14; 10:17–44; Neh 3; 7:6–72; 9:38–10:27; 11:3–36; 12:1–26). One can imagine the importance of these genealogies for communities wrestling with issues of belonging, connection to the past, and bonds to the land. Imagine a public reading of Scripture where you hear your family mentioned out loud. Some might shout out, "That's my family! That's my family!"

What are the characteristics of literary art in Chronicles' genealogies? I'll mention several important features here, drawing especially from the work of Mark Boda. First, *the genealogies establish Israel's connection to nations*. Chapter 1 begins with Adam and ends with the genealogy of Edom (1:38–53), the nation descended from Jacob's brother Esau. The Edomite genealogy is prefaced by a genealogy of Abraham, father of Isaac, who gave birth to Israel and Esau (verse 34), highlighting Israel's intimate sibling relationship with its neighbor. The number of non-Israelites appearing in Israel's genealogy (e.g., sojourners, Canaanites, Edomites, Moabites, Egyptians) reflects a conviction that each group "had a role to play in Judah's development."[12]

---

[12] Mark J. Boda, *1–2 Chronicles* CBC 5a (Carol Stream, IL: Tyndale House Publishers, 2010), 26, quoting Gary N. Knoppers, *1 Chronicles* AB 12 (New York: Doubleday, 2004), 358.

Second, *the genealogies display "narrative movement."*[13] The Chronicler's entire work is framed by an ending-new beginning pattern in 1 Chronicles 1–9 and 2 Chronicles 36. The parallel "endings" (1 Chr 9:1; 2 Chr 36:17–21) involve exile due to "rebellion" (Heb. *ma'al*) before recounting a return to the land (9:2–34; 2 Chr 36:22–23).[14]

Finally, *the genealogies foreshadow the book's themes, characters, and events.*[15] I've already noted the importance of the Davidic line as well as Levites and priests in the genealogies. Both play a major role in the book, and by placing the Levites at the structural center of the gene-alogies, Chronicles highlights the need for kings to remain loyal to the temple and Israel's worship of Yahweh:[16]

A   The peoples of the world (1:1–2:2)
    B   Judah with Simeon (2:3–4:23)
        C   Transjordanian tribes (5:1–26)
           D   Levi (6:1–81)
        C'   The northern tribes (7:1–40)
    B'   Benjamin (8:1–40)
A'   Persian-period inhabitants of Jerusalem (9:2–34).

The Levites, and specifically the Levitical musicians and singers (6:31–48), occupy the center of Israel's life and direct the people toward wor-ship. Placing worship at the center of the genealogies also highlights the world's need for Israel's praise, worship, and joy. As Peter Leithart notes, "To be a priestly nation is, by the Chronicler's lights, to be a cho-ral nation. Israel fulfills its role among the nations through a continuous liturgy of praise."[17]

The genealogy also foregrounds the importance of "all Israel," another major emphasis in the book. As we read through the book, we find that "all Israel" gathered to anoint David (1 Chr 11:1, 10; 12:23–38), followed the ark's procession to Jerusalem (15:3, 28), joined Solomon in worship at the tabernacle (2 Chr 1:2) and at its dedication, and proclaimed the steadfast love of Yahweh (2 Chr 7:3–8). Later kings like Hezekiah (2 Chr 29:24; 30:1–6) and Josiah (2 Chr 35:3) tempo-rarily recovered the unity of God's people by reforming the cult and re-establishing all-Israel worship at the temple. Even at the end of the

---

[13]   Boda, *1–2 Chronicles*, 30, emphasis mine.
[14]   Boda, *1–2 Chronicles*, 30.
[15]   Boda, *1–2 Chronicles*, 30.
[16]   The following chiasm is from Boda, *1–2 Chronicles*, 27.
[17]   Peter J. Leithart, *1 & 2 Chronicles* Brazos Theological Commentary on the Bible (Grand Rapids, MI: Brazos, 2019), 12–13.

book we see Cyrus' summons to "whomever" among "*all* His people" that they should go up to the temple with the knowledge of God's abiding presence (2 Chr 36:23).

THEMATIC PATTERNS

Chronicles also uses repeated patterns to tell its stories. These patterns of repetition reinforce key theological themes and help readers notice the consistent hand of God at work throughout history. Some of these patterns are unique to Chronicles. Here are some examples.

First, *Chronicles portrays good kings as those who reinforce Judah's (and Israel's) cities/fortresses and renew worship at the temple.* The template for this pattern is the reign of David–Solomon (1 Chr 10–2 Chr 9). David and Solomon were master builders who poured their energy into funding, planning, and building God's temple. David led the way by giving generously of his personal wealth for the temple project (1 Chr 29:1–4). When I say he gave generously, I mean *generously.* Based on 1 Chronicles 22, David had given Solomon 100,000 *kikkars* of gold for the temple, or about 2.1 million kilograms (22:14). That's about the weight of five or six Boeing 747 airliners! The number is obviously hyperbolic, and the point is to emphasize David's exceeding generosity and the magnificence of the temple. David then inspired the leaders (29:6–7) and people to follow suit (29:8–9). David also gave the temple plans to Solomon (28:11–13), establishing him as an integral part of the temple project, even though he didn't actually build it. Solomon then built the temple, and David also established the visions of priests and Levites for their duties, which included the sacrifice of offerings, music-making, and gatekeeping (1 Chr 23–26).

Chronicles then tells us that Solomon appointed these priestly and Levitical divisions "in keeping with the ordinance of his father David" (2 Chr 8:14). In this way, the Davidic–Solomonic pattern was set. To engage in priestly renewal or temple worship was to follow the "ordinances" or "law" of David, since David had received specific divine revelation about the plan for the temple (1 Chr 28:11–12, 19). Unlike Samuel–Kings, which focuses exclusively on the law of Moses, Chronicles recognizes the "law" of both (e.g., 2 Chr 23:18; 29:25; 35:4). Moses established the sacrificial laws in the Pentateuch and David established the priestly divisions and orders, especially for music and gatekeeping. Solomon was also a builder of storage and fortification cities. 2 Chronicles 8:2–7 describes a series of fortifications that Solomon built in the north. This is hardly a comprehensive list of the cities Solomon built or reinforced, as we know from 1 Kings 9:15–19, but suffices to establish Solomon as builder of the temple and defensive cities throughout the land. Our composite picture of David–Solomon establishes a pattern where devotion to Yahweh leads toward concern for the temple and its worship system, as well as the defenses throughout the land.

Other Judean kings follow suit when walking with God. Chronicles wants us to notice both when they follow in the footsteps of David and Solomon and when they stray from the pattern of loyalty they established. Solomon's son Rehoboam built fortified cities throughout Judah (2 Chr 11:5–12). While not appointing priestly or Levitical orders (they were already operative), priests and Levites whom Jeroboam fired came to him in Jerusalem (11:14, 16). When Rehoboam strayed from God, however, his fortified cities were captured, and Jerusalem came under threat (2 Chr 12:4).

Judah's king Asa receives high praise from the Chronicler, who gives him far greater attention than the author of Kings (2 Chr 14–16; cf. 1 Kgs 15:9–24). Asa was a religious reformer. He rid the land of illicit altars and high places (2 Chr 14:3) and turned the people toward Yahweh (verse 4).[18] He also built up and reinforced the cities in Judah. The emphasis on military defenses might give the impression that the people's strength was found in cities. However, Asa's words correct this impression:

> "Let us build up these towns," he said to Judah, "and put walls around them, with towers, gates and bars. *The land is still ours, because we have sought the* LORD *our God; we sought him and he has given us rest on every side.*" So they built and prospered. (2 Chr 14:7 NIV)[19]

God's people didn't hold the land in peace because they built towers or walls of protection. Their strength resulted from seeking the LORD. This point becomes abundantly clear in the subsequent narrative, where Asa faced a militarily superior foe, Zerah of Cush, who threatened with a million-man army (2 Chr 14:9). In his desperation, Asa cried out to God and found deliverance (vv. 10–11).

The Chronicler's use of patterning becomes especially clear in the narratives about King Jehoshaphat. Like Asa, Chronicles' account is much longer than the narratives in Kings (2 Chr 17:1–21:1a; cf. 1 Kgs

---

[18] 2 Chr 15:8–15 describe Asa's further reforms.
[19] Emphasis mine. Bible quotations are taken from the NIV unless otherwise stated.

22:1–36, 41–50; 2 Kgs 3:4–27). Note the similarities between Asa and Jehoshaphat in the following chart.[20]

Asa (2 Chr 14–16)	Jehoshaphat (2 Chr 17:1–21:1a
Structure: (a) religious reforms (2 Chr 14:2–8) (b) battle report (2 Chr 14:8–14) (c) reform (2 Chr 15:1–19) (d) battle report (2 Chr 16:1–9) (e) sin and death (2 Chr 16:10–14)	Structure: (a) religious reforms (2 Chr 17:1–19) (b) battle report (2 Chr 18:1–19:3) (c) reform (2 Chr 19:4–11) (d) battle report (2 Chr 20:1–30) (e) sin and death (2 Chr 20:31–21:1a)
Removed high places (2 Chr 14:2–5) *and* is reported as not having done so (2 Chr 15:17)	Removed high places (2 Chr 17:6) *and* is reported as not having done so (2 Chr 20:33)[21]
Built up fortified cities and the land enjoyed peace (2 Chr 14:6)	Stationed troops in fortified cities and garrisons in Judah and Israel (2 Chr 17:1–2) and the land enjoyed peace (2 Chr 20:30)
Cries out to God in battle (14:11)	Cries out to God in battle (2 Chr 20:6)
God's presence with the king (2 Chr 15:9)	God's presence with the king (2 Chr 17:3)
Fear of Yahweh on the nations (2 Chr 14:14)	Fear of Yahweh on the nations (2 Chr 17:10; 20:29)
Prophetic indictment for foreign alliances (2 Chr 16:7–9)	Prophetic indictment for foreign alliances (2 Chr 19:1–3)
Two prophets serve during his reign (Azariah and Hanani)	Two prophets serve during his reign (Jehu and Eliezer)

These striking similarities highlight the extent to which Chronicles takes its practice of narrative patterning.

The pattern of fortifying cities continues in the reign of Uzziah (2 Chr 26:9, 15), though here the pattern shifts. Instead of *reforming* the

---

[20] These parallels are noted in Ralph W. Klein, *2 Chronicles* Hermeneia (Minneapolis: Fortress Press, 2012), 247, and Boda, *1–2 Chronicles*, 323.

[21] For a discussion of these discrepancies regarding the high places, see Ehud Ben Zvi, *History, Literature and Theology in the Book of Chronicles* (London/New York: Routledge, 2006), 50.

cult, he violated it by trying to offer incense (verses 16–18), the job of priests. This violation led to his banishment from the temple and perpetual skin disease (vv. 19–21).

Hezekiah and Josiah are the most significant reformers. Hezekiah's reform included the purification of the temple (2 Chr 29:12–19), the city (2 Chr 30:14), and the land (2 Chr 31:1), with only the latter mentioned in Kings (2 Kgs 18:4). His fortification efforts were extensive, and focused on threat of Assyria (2 Chr 32:2–8). Hezekiah brought water into the city via the Siloam Pool (32:30–31) and dramatically expanded Jerusalem's walls (32:5). Yet like other kings who faced threats from superior powers, such fortifications offered little help against the enemy. Instead, it was only after he and Isaiah cried out to Yahweh that they were delivered (32:20–23).

Josiah also initiated extensive reforms, and like Hezekiah before him he's compared positively to David (2 Chr 29:2; 34:2) and initiated a great Passover celebration (2 Chr 30; 35). His rebuilding efforts focused on the temple itself (2 Chr 34:8–14). In addition to reforming the cult, he reappointed priests and Levites by their divisions to celebrate the Passover (2 Chr 35:4–5).

Even the wicked Manasseh reformed and refortified *after* his exile to Babylon (2 Chr 33:14–17). After returning from his humiliating and humbling exile, he repaired Jerusalem's walls and restored worship at the temple. Though brief, the account of Manasseh offers an illuminating window into the Chronicler's aims. Pursuit of God involved humble prayer, yes, but *also* rebuilding and reform. Long-term loyalty to God required deep reform and physical rebuilding.

All reform and rebuilding efforts cease after Josiah, as Judah began its inexorable slide toward exile. However, the book's last verse combines the reform and rebuild pattern with Cyrus' edict to the Judean exiles, which urged them to go rebuild the temple. Restoration and rebuilding culminated in the post-exilic temple project. It's a royal task indeed!

The example of Manasseh brings us to our second example of narrative patterning in Chronicles: *Chronicles tells the story of a series of mini "exiles" that anticipate the Exile to Babylon.* To anticipate my argument, this reinforces the point that God continually offered his people warnings of the disaster that would come. It also highlights the hope for the land. It's happened in the past and it can happen again. Let's look at several examples of this pattern.

When Israel split from Judah during the reign of Jeroboam, many of the priests were alienated from the temple. In essence, they were exiled from the temple. Chronicles reports (uniquely) that the Levites left their lands to go to Jerusalem, since Jeroboam prohibited them from serving (2 Chr 11:14). Then, people from all Israel's tribes "who set their hearts on seeking the LORD, the God of Israel, followed the Levites to Jerusalem to offer sacrifices to the LORD, the God of their ancestors" (11:16). This remarkable verse highlights the boldness and benefits of "seeking Yahweh." The narrative goes on to tell us that those who came to Judah and Jerusalem "strengthened the kingdom" (11:17). Once again, Judah's strength was not found through military weapons, but by seeking Yahweh in worship.

When King Jehoram rebelled against Yahweh and led Judah astray (2 Chr 21:11), Philistines and Arabs came and carried off the king's possessions, "together with his sons and wives" (21:17). Chronicles leaves us without doubt about the severity of this royal exile: "Not a son was left to him except Ahaziah, the youngest" (21:17). Jehoram's sin almost ended the Davidic line. Similarly, King Amaziah led the people of Judah into idolatry (25:14), setting the LORD against him (25:20). In his folly, he instigated a disastrous war with Israel, where Judah was roundly defeated. King Amaziah was captured, Jerusalem breeched, the temple pillaged, and captives were all brought back to Samaria (vv. 22–24). It isn't entirely clear from the story whether King Joash of Israel *held* Jehoram or released him in exchange for captives when he attacked Jerusalem. Either way, it's clear that his initial capture and Jerusalem's humiliation anticipate the final sack of Jerusalem and exile of its king and people at the end of the book (2 Chr 36).

King Ahaz was the most wicked king in Judah's history, according to Chronicles. He worshipped other deities, sacrificed his son in the fire, and closed the temple's doors (2 Chr 28:1–4, 22–25). Immediately after recounting Ahaz's cultic and moral failures, the narrator reports that the Aramean king Pekah deported "many" Judeans, killed 120,000, and that an Ephraimite killed the king's son Maaseiah along with several other officials (2 Chr 28:5–7). Once again, Judeans were exiled and the Davidic line threatened. The Israelites initially took 200,000 Judeans captive as slaves (2 Chr 28:8–10). Remarkably, Chronicles recounts the opposition to this enslavement plan from within Ephraim. Courageous leadership prevents disaster for the north and leads to a humanitarian response, where the Israelites clothe, feed, anoint them and provide donkeys for their return (28:15). The northern admission of guilt and repatriation prepares the way for a unified Israel under Hezekiah. The provisions for these vulnerable Judean exiles by those from Samaria, as well as the mention of "Jericho" (where they were returned), suggests this story as a backdrop to the Good Samaritan (Luke 10:25–37).

The image of a mini "return" from exile features prominently during the reign of Hezekiah. When appealing to all the people in Judah and Israel, Hezekiah uttered these theologically and historically loaded words:

> Do not be like your parents and your fellow Israelites, who were unfaithful to the LORD, the God of their ancestors ... **submit** to the LORD. **Come** to his sanctuary, which he has consecrated forever. **Serve** the LORD your God, so that his fierce anger will turn away from you. If you *return* to the LORD, then your fellow Israelites and your children will be shown compassion by their *captors* and will *return to* this land, for the LORD your God is gracious and compassionate. He will not turn his face from you if you return to him. (2 Chr 30:7–9)[22]

This speech, which finds no parallel in Kings, could have been given to the Babylonian exiles! The imperative verbs foreground the people's need to serve Yahweh by coming to the temple. Their return would, in turn, prompt compassion upon those still in captivity. For a moment here we glimpse what seems like a direct word to the Babylonian exiles put, anachronistically, in the mouth of Hezekiah (before the exile). As Mark Boda writes, "The community in Hezekiah's time is thus depicted in ways that would have resonated with the community in the time of the Chronicler. ... [R]epentance in worship practice [w]as essential to the experience of the presence of Yahweh, as well as to the safe return of more exiles from captivity."[23]

One more feature of the Chronicler's exile and return pattern deserves attention. In Chronicles, unlike Kings, it seems that every time Judah rebelled against Yahweh by worshipping other gods or sacrificing at illicit sites, worship at the temple ceased. In other words, temple worship was incompatible with non-Yahwistic and unauthorized worship. This is not surprising, since according to Chronicles the temple was supposed to reflect Yahweh's supremacy over the gods of the nations. Solomon puts it this way: "The temple I am going to build will be great, because our God is greater than all other gods" (2 Chr 2:5).[24] The temple was designed to manifest Yahweh's greatness. I include a chart here that demonstrates the ways that Chronicles connects Yahweh's greatness to the temple's greatness:[25]

---

[22] Emphasis mine.

[23] Boda, *1–2 Chronicles*, 391.

[24] I discuss this pattern in Matthew J. Lynch, *Monotheism and Institutions in the Book of Chronicles* FAT 2/64 (Tübingen: Mohr Siebeck, 2014), 75–102.

[25] Matthew J. Lynch, "Divine Supremacy and the Temple: 2 Chronicles 2 and the Fifth Book of Psalms," in *Psalmen und Chronik* FAT 2/107, eds. Friedhelm Hartenstein

	Temple and Divine Greatness
Yahweh – "great"	For *great* is the **Yahweh** and most worthy of praise; he is to be feared above all gods. For all the gods of the nations are idols, but **Yahweh** made the heavens (1 Chr 16:25–26).
Temple – "great"	David said, "The **temple** to be built for **Yahweh** should be of *great* magnificence and fame and splendor in the sight of all the nations." (1 Chr 22:5a)
Temple – "great"	Then King David said to the whole assembly, "… The task is *great*, because this palatial [**temple**] structure is not for humans but for **Yahweh** God." (1 Chr 29:1)
Yahweh – "great"	"Yours, **Yahweh**, is the *greatness* and the power and the glory and majesty and the splendor … Yours, **Yahweh**, is the kingdom; you are exalted as head over all" (1 Chr 29:11)
Temple/ Yahweh – "great"	"The **temple** I am going to build will be *great*, because our **God** is *greater* than all the gods" (2 Chr 2:5)
Temple – "great"	"… because the **temple** I build must be *great* and magnificent" (2 Chr 2:9b)

A byproduct of this emphasis on divine and temple "greatness" is a belief that temple worship to Yahweh and worship of other gods were wholly incompatible. When Israel fell into apostasy or rebellion, Chronicles repeatedly suggests that Yahweh worship ceased. I'll refer to this as the "incompatibility pattern." Yahweh worship and non-Yahwistic worship could not co-exist. Moreover, each "return" to Yahweh involved the resumption or restoration of Yahweh worship at the temple. Let's observe this patterning at work.

During Saul's reign, we're told that Saul sought (Heb. *darash*) a medium and did not seek (*darash*) Yahweh (1 Chr 10:13–14). While this event occurred before the temple's construction, the Chronicler still portrays Saul's disregard in binary terms and focuses on the way Saul forsook the cult. As Chronicles later tells us, failing to seek Yahweh meant that he failed to pursue the *ark's* welfare (1 Chr 13:3), something that sets Saul apart from David.

During Queen Athaliah's tumultuous reign (2 Chr 22), the young Joash hid in the temple. While Chronicles doesn't explicitly state that

and Thomas Willi; (Tübingen: Mohr Siebeck, 2019), 323–42 [331]. Quotations are from the NIV translation with modification and emphasis here.

Yahweh worship *stopped*, the Chronicler suggests as much. The high priest Jehoiada had to repair the temple and appoint priestly divisions after Athaliah was deposed (2 Chr 24:13). Chronicles even reports that Athaliah's children had "breached" (Heb. *parats*) the temple and "had used ... its sacred objects for the Baals" (2 Chr 24:7). The parallel account in Kings never mentions this "breach," an act that foreshadows the eventual breaching of Jerusalem's walls by the Babylonians. The post-exilic book of Nehemiah uses this verb (*parats*) to describe the state of Jerusalem's destroyed walls that needed repair (Neh 1:3; 2:13; 4:3, 7; 6:1).[26]

The Chronicler's account of King Joash's reign (2 Chr 24) also follows this incompatibility pattern. His reign can be divided into a period of temple loyalty (24:1–16) and temple disregard (verses 17–27), with the transition marked by the death of the high priest Jehoiada (24:14). Once Jehoiada died, Joash and his leaders "*abandoned* the temple of the Lord, the God of their ancestors, and worshiped Asherah poles and idols" (24:18), inviting divine wrath. His disregard for the temple became so severe that he eventually had the high priest's son Zechariah stoned in the temple courts (verses 21–22), which was eventually avenged by his death (verses 22, 25).

The story of Ahaz (2 Chr 28) and Hezekiah (2 Chr 29–32) illustrates the temple abandonment pattern most clearly. While Kings never calls Ahaz an idolator, Chronicles states clearly that he made illicit images, just like the kings of Israel (28:2–3), and he worshiped Aramean gods (28:23). He also shut down the temple entirely, destroyed the temple vessels, and made altars all around Jerusalem (28:23–24). In so doing, Ahaz "forsook" Yahweh, just like Jeroboam had done (2 Chr 13:11). By disregarding the temple and stealing its vessels, Ahaz anticipated the exile, when temple worship ceased and foreign rulers took the temple's vessels (2 Chr 36:7, 10, 18).

Hezekiah, by contrast, grieved his father's sins and the fact that the people had turned their faces away from the Lord's dwelling place and turned their backs on him. They had also shut the doors of the portico and put out the lamps. They did not burn incense or present any burnt offerings at the sanctuary to the God of Israel (2 Chr 29:6b–7).

Serving idols and serving Yahweh were wholly incompatible. Embracing foreign gods was like "entering a foreign land, away from the temple." By contrast, seeking Yahweh "constituted a mini return from exile."[27] To convey this, Chronicles portrays the reopening ceremony as the loyal king's very first act: "In the first month of the first year of his reign, he opened the doors of the temple of the Lord and repaired

[26]   The following section draws from my book, *Monotheism and Institutions*, 75–102.
[27]   Lynch, *Monotheism and Institutions*, 92.

them" (29:3). Hezekiah also appointed priests, purified the temple, and celebrated the temple's restoration.

Our last example of the incompatibility pattern comes from the reign of Manasseh and, like the other examples, it has no parallel in Kings. Manasseh's sins were flagrant. He built altars to foreign gods in the temple and its courts (2 Chr 33:3–5) and put an idolatrous image in the temple (verse 7). Manasseh eventually repented and began reforms after his own brief exile in Babylon. His reforms include detail that Kings never mentions, including the reinstatement of Yahweh's altar (2 Chr 33:16). In other words, when worshipping other deities, Yahweh's altar had been abandoned (cf. 2 Chr 15:8). It isn't until Josiah begins major reforms that we notice another aspect of the incompatibility pattern at work. In 2 Chronicles 35:3 we're told that Josiah ordered his priests to return the ark to the temple! We're never told that Manasseh had removed the ark, but its return suggests as much. Yahweh worship remained utterly distinct from non-Yahwistic worship.

By using this incompatibility pattern, the Chronicler reinforces the theological point that the temple reflected Yahweh's supremacy over other gods. Yahweh does not play second fiddle to other deities. Sara Japhet is one of the few scholars to note this pattern. She notes the Chronicler's aversion to the idea that syncretism is even possible:

> This principle of exclusivity, which governs the [Chronicler's] entire concept of divine worship, operates in two directions. Just as one cannot worship YHWH and recognize other gods, so, too, it is impossible to serve other gods and still worship YHWH ... pagan ritual had a direct adverse effect on the worship of God, to the extent that the Temple was closed and YHWH worship abolished.[28]

To this extent, Yahweh refused to compete with other gods, and retained his distinctiveness even when Israel failed to recognize it. Moreover, the pattern helps us recognize that turning to Yahweh involved forsaking all other loyalties and returning to the temple in worship.

CHRONICLES' USE OF SCRIPTURE

Chronicles is immersed in Scripture. Not only are major chunks of the book derived from its sources in Samuel–Kings, but it also draws

---

28 Sara Japhet, *The Ideology of the Book of Chronicles its Place in Biblical Thought* BEATAJ 9 (New York: Peter Lang, 1997), 216.

extensively from the Law, Prophets, and Psalms, the three major divisions of Scripture mentioned by Jesus on the Emmaus Road:

> [Jesus] said to them, "This is what I told you while I was still with you: Everything must be fulfilled that is written about me in the Law of Moses, the Prophets and the Psalms." (Luke 24:44)

It's impossible in this essay to capture the many ways that Chronicles draws from the deep well of Israel's Scriptures. In what follows, I will illustrate by several examples how Chronicles engages its sources.[29] Our first example shows how Chronicles retells a story from Kings by making the temple its main character. The second example shows one of the ways that Chronicles engages Psalms. The final example displays the influence of the tabernacle on Chronicles' thinking.

Jehoiada Overthrows Athaliah (2 Chr 23)

One way to notice the finer details of how Chronicles uses Scripture is by setting texts side by side. Sometimes the small details carry major significance. Let's note some of the major differences between Chronicles and its sources in this story about the high priest Jehoiada's plan to overthrow Queen Athaliah and install the young Joash as king.

Example 1 – Instructions to the Guards and People	
Samuel–Kings	Chronicles
In the seventh year Jehoiada sent for the commanders of units of a hundred, the **Carites** and the **guards** and had them brought to him at the temple of the LORD. He made a covenant with them and put them under oath at the temple of the LORD. (2 Kgs 11:4, NIV)	In the seventh year Jehoiada showed his strength. He made a covenant with the commanders of units of a hundred: [the following are all **priests**] Azariah son of Jeroham, Ishmael son of Jehohanan, Azariah son of Obed, Maaseiah son of Adaiah, and Elishaphat son of Zikri. ... [Then] the **whole assembly** made a covenant with the king at the temple of God ... "and all the others are to be **in the courtyards of the temple of the** LORD." (2 Chr 23:1, 3, 5, NIV)

---

[29] An excellent resource for studying Chronicles' use of Scripture is Gary Edward Schnittjer's *Old Testament Use of Old Testament: A Book-by-Book Guide* (Grand Rapids, MI: Zondervan, 2021), which devotes 149 pages to Chronicles (pp. 697–846).

In this example, Chronicles ensures that priests (not Carites, who were likely non-Israelites)[30] exercise leadership and that the people remain in the courts. The key here is that the proper authorities enter the temple. In addition, in Chronicles the whole assembly makes a covenant, signaling unanimous support for the cultic reform and the rule of Joash.[31]

Example 2 – Guard Responsibilities

Samuel–Kings	Chronicles
"**[You commanders]** Station yourselves around the king, each of you with weapon in hand. **Anyone who approaches your ranks** is to be put to death. Stay close to the king wherever he goes." **The commanders** of units of a hundred did just as Jehoiada the priest ordered. (2 Kgs 11:8–9a, NIV)	"**The Levites** are to station themselves around the king, each with weapon in hand. **Anyone who enters the temple** is to be put to death. Stay close to the king wherever he goes." **The Levites and all the men of Judah** did just as Jehoiada the priest ordered. (2 Chr 23:7–8a, NIV)

Here the Chronicler emphasizes the need to guard the temple's sanctity. Notice that in 2 Kings 11:8–9 the guards were to protect against infringement on the ranks of soldiers, whereas in Chronicles the Judeans, led by Levites, were to guard against anyone entering the temple. To be sure, Kings does mention the need to guard the temple as well (2 Kgs 11:7), but Chronicles puts this concern front and center and emphasizes the guardian role of the Levites. Earlier in 1 Chronicles, David appointed Levites as *guards* (1 Chr 26:1–19), an idea that Chronicles weaves into this story. Sara Japhet summarizes these differences well:

> In Kings the trespasser is to be slain for political reasons, because of the danger he may pose to the success of Jehoiada's coup d'état. In Chronicles the same penalty has religious motives – to prevent the desecration of the Temple.[32]

Finally, Chronicles also focuses on the iconoclastic afterparty. After ousting Athaliah, Joash and the people destroyed a Baal temple, and

---

[30]   The question of whether or not Carites were non-Israelite is debated.
[31]   Klein, *2 Chronicles*, 324.
[32]   Japhet, *I & II Chronicles*, 832.

Jehoiada assigned proper care for the temple to the Levitical priests and stationed Levitical gatekeepers to keep out the impure (2 Chr 23:18–19). In so doing, Jehoiada restored temple worship in keeping with the laws of Moses and David.

Chronicles' Allusions to Idol Critiques in Psalms (Ps 115, 135)

I sometimes describe the book of Chronicles as a priestly retelling of Samuel–Kings with Psalms as its soundtrack. For instance, 1 Chronicles 16 draws from Ps 105, 96, and 106, while 2 Chr 6:41–42 draws from Ps 132. Other sections of Chronicles use the "loyalty refrain" ("his love endures forever") prominent in Psalms in various places (2 Chr 5:13; 7:3, 6; 20:21). Elsewhere, David alludes to Ps 39:13 in his prayer (1 Chr 29:15), and his blessing in 1 Chr 29:10 is strikingly similar to blessings in Psalms (e.g., 41:13; 72:18; 89:52; 106:48).

I want to look at an example of how Chronicles seems to draw from the anti-idol Psalms 115 and 135 in 2 Chronicles 2:5. I've already mentioned this text, but not the connections to Psalms. Notice how Psalm 135:5 focuses on Yahweh, while 2 Chr 2:5 focuses on the temple and Yahweh:

> For I am certain that **Yahweh is great** / and [great is] **our Lord beyond all gods**. (Ps 135:5)

> The **temple** that I am going to build will be **great** / for great is **our God beyond all the gods**. (2 Chr 2:5)[33]

Solomon's words in Chronicles substitute temple for Yahweh in the first part of the quote, and retain the emphasis on God's supremacy over the gods in the second part of the quote. According to Chronicles, the temple reflects God's grandeur and power, and so we shouldn't be surprised that Solomon draws from this anti-idol psalm, as if to say, "This temple is an icon of the supreme God who is far greater than any of the nations' gods."

The Chronicler likely drew from this psalm not only because of its statement about God's power over the gods, but also because of its focus on the house of Aaron and house of Levi (verse 19–21) as well as its use of the loyalty refrain (verse 3).

We should also note that immediately after emphasizing the temple's greatness, Solomon acknowledges that "even the highest heavens" can't contain Yahweh (2 Chr 2:6). In response to Solomon's words, King

---

[33]   Translation mine for both quotations.

Hiram of Phoenicia responds with words that are strikingly similar to the only other anti-idol psalm in the book of Psalms:

Blessed are you by Yahweh, **maker of heaven and earth**. (Ps 115:15)

Blessed is Yahweh, God of Israel, **who made the heavens and the earth**. (2 Chr 2:11a)[34]

Hiram's blessing may be responding to Solomon's statement in 2 Chronicles 2:6 that "even the highest heavens" cannot contain him. He gets it! Though Yahweh's temple is great and reflects Yahweh's greatness, it in no ways reduces him. God *made* heavens and earth, after all!

Tabernacle and Temple

As a final example, let's look at how Chronicles draws inspiration from the tabernacle when talking about the temple. There are too many examples to explore here, so I'll just mention a few. First, when David prepared for the temple's construction, we're told that God gave him the "**pattern**" for the temple (1 Chr 28:11–12, 18–19). Kings never mentions a divinely given pattern. However, we do know that God had instructed Moses as follows: "Then have them make a sanctuary for me, and I will dwell among them. Make this tabernacle and all its furnishings exactly like the **pattern** I will show you" (Exod 25:8, emphasis mine).

Second, Chronicles states that Huram-abi, King Huram's servant, was full of wisdom and understanding and would create any design assigned to him (2 Chr 2:13–14). This description of Huram-abi sounds like the tabernacle designers Oholiab and Bezalel, who were full of wisdom and understanding to craft the tabernacle (Exod 31:2–3; 35:30–35). Moreover, Huram-abi came from the tribe of Dan (through his mother) like Oholiab in Exodus (Exod 35:34; 2 Chr 2:13–14).

Third, Solomon sacrificed at Gibeon on the altar that Bezalel made for the tabernacle in Exodus (Exod 31:2–11; 2 Chr 1:5–6; 4:1; 7:7). Kings never mentions this connection.

Fourth, just as the people donated their wealth willingly and generously for the tabernacle's construction, so too they donate willingly and generously in Chronicles for the temple's construction (1 Chr 29:5; 2 Chr 24:6–10; 29:31; 31:4; cf. Exod 35:21–29).

Finally, and perhaps most obviously, Chronicles tells us that the Levites and priests served at the tabernacle before the temple was built (1 Chr 6:31–32). After moving the ark to Jerusalem, David placed Zadok

---

34   Translation mine for both quotations.

the priest along with other priests at the tabernacle in Gibeon, where the altar still remained (1 Chr 16:39–40; cf. 21:29; 2 Chr 1:5)

Together, these bonds between the tabernacle and temple helped the people discern the links between their present worship at the temple in Jerusalem and the olden days when God had dwelled among his people in the wilderness. For those who returned from exile but longed for connection to the great God of Israel's past, Chronicles' stories likely proved to be a great comfort.

CONCLUSIONS

Chronicles is a rich and complex work of narrative art and history. Appreciating its literary merits requires us to set aside some of our modern expectations about how a good story begins, how it proceeds, and how it retells. Chronicles *begins* with a long genealogy, one that asks us to share the joy of "all Israel" as they find their place among God's people and the nations, and to anticipate some of the key themes and emphases in Chronicles (e.g., worship and the promises to David's house). Chronicles *proceeds* by use of patterns established in the past. These patterns provide great hope that just as God had done in the days of David, Solomon, Hezekiah, and Josiah, so he would do again for those among the post-exilic community and beyond. Chronicles *retells* by interpreting, quoting, and alluding to Israel's sacred Scriptures. Paying careful attention to how seemingly identical stories reflect differences in context and perspective can open up an exciting world for those of us who seek to engage these ancient texts in our context today.

10 The Genesis of Jesus in the Narrative of Matthew

SCOTT S. ELLIOTT

At first blush, the Gospel According to Matthew may not seem to offer readers the most fascinating or intriguing of narratives from among the canonical gospels. It does not have the same intricate juxtapositions and provocative narrative rhetoric as Mark's gospel. It lacks the scope of Luke's travel and adventure. And it is missing the deep, complex characters and characterization of John. However, upon closer inspection, one finds in it a different sort of narrative. It is a narrative that is deeply infused with Jewish storytelling techniques, and reflects an image of early followers of Jesus characterized by a particular way of reading, interpreting, and understanding the Old Testament in relation to Jesus and vice versa,[1] one that embodies and enacts a certain sense of divine presence and of time. Notwithstanding the so-called great commission that concludes the narrative, the feeling that Matthew's gospel evokes is less grand in scope than the epic-like tale of Luke–Acts. It is subtle, at times even sublime. Its episodic structure, which is assembled partly around conflict and partly around clusters of teachings ascribed to Jesus, results in a kind of collage that presents the reader with the sort of implicit narrative that one might derive from a list. Even with the longstanding traditions from which it takes its lead, there is something about it that borders on the experimental: despite the rising conflict, the narrative on the whole is rather sedate as the narrator foregrounds dialogue over action.

NARRATOLOGICAL APPROACHES TO MATTHEW

As one would imagine, there is a glut of material on Matthew's gospel, but relatively little that focuses on narratological elements. When there has been an interest in narrative, it often has often centered on the

---

[1] While it is standard academic practice (and my preference) to refer to this body of literature as the Hebrew Bible, I think it is fitting (for a variety of reasons that I hope will be clear from what follows), in a discussion of Matthew as narrative, to refer to it as the Old Testament.

narratives of distinct episodes (e.g., the infancy narrative, the passion narrative, the resurrection narrative), which suggests a formalist (if not form-critical) approach to narrative and neglects Matthew's narrative as a whole. The earliest explicitly narratological study of Matthew is Jack Dean Kingsbury's *Matthew as Story*, published amid the early heydays of New Testament narrative criticism.[2] Although it is primarily built on a redaction-critical foundation, Kingsbury focuses equally on the story and the discourse of Matthew's gospel, recognizing the inextricable relationship between form and content. He reads Matthew holistically and on its own terms, prioritizing the characterization of Jesus vis-à-vis various titles ascribed to him, while also attending to matters of plot, dialogue, and so forth, in a manner that highlights the impact of the story's unfolding on the imagined reader.

Another significant work is Warren Carter's *Matthew: Storyteller, Interpreter, Evangelist*,[3] though Carter's focus is much more historical-critical in its objectives and exegetical in its mode. His audience-oriented approach seeks to delineate the effects that Matthew has on its readers' identity and lifestyle. Hence, he's attuned to the narrative as a rhetorical device. Nevertheless, he retains an interest in the author's intentions and imagines the ideal audience to approximate the actual audience, which contemporary readers themselves should strive to emulate with respect to their own understanding of the gospel.

The work of Kingsbury and Carter illustrates the false start that New Testament narrative criticism experienced at its early stages when traditional historical-critical approaches resisted the implications of fully embracing narrative theory.[4] But as Michal Beth Dinkler has demonstrated, narrative itself is a mode of persuasive discourse: "Telling a story is a rhetorical act; narratives create rhetorical effects *as narratives*."[5] To wit, taking narrative seriously requires treating it as something other and more primary than mere packaging or an arrow in an author's quiver. It entails, among other things, appreciating (i.e., in the

[2]   Jack Dean Kingsbury, *Matthew as Story* (Philadelphia: Fortress, 1975).

[3]   Warren Carter, *Matthew: Storyteller, Interpreter, Evangelist* (Peabody, MA: Hendrickson, 1996).

[4]   Stephen D. Moore, *Literary Criticism and the Gospels: The Theoretical Challenge* (New Haven: Yale University Press, 1989). See also, Scott S. Elliott, *Reconfiguring Mark's Jesus: Narrative Criticism after Poststructuralism* (Sheffield: Sheffield Phoenix, 2011).

[5]   Michal Beth Dinkler, "New Testament Rhetorical Narratology: An Invitation toward Integration," *Biblical Interpretation* 24 (2016): 216, emphasis original. See also her book, *Literary Theory and the New Testament* (New Haven: Yale University Press, 2019).

sense of both comprehending and valuing) the fundamentally formative dynamics of narrative discourse whereby we world ourselves and others through story. The length and nature of this chapter does not allow for extended analysis of any one narratological dimension of Matthew's gospel. Therefore, what follows are some relatively general observations, suggestions, and notes concerning themes, motifs, tropes, plot, structure, settings, the dynamics of time, characters and characterization, dialogue, the narrator, point-of-view and focalization, and so forth. The hope is that they will serve as an invitation to further investigation.

THE GENESIS OF JESUS

The writer of Matthew is eminently attuned to writing and to story. His narrator begins the gospel with, "The *book* of the genealogy of Jesus Christ" (1:1, emphasis mine).[6] As we shall see, scripture is a central motif throughout Matthew, together with various associated themes. The proximity of "book" to "genealogy" is befitting insofar as Matthew's Jesus is a product of writing as much as he is a product of heredity. Indeed, Matthew's Jesus is an open book, a bookish reader even though he is never pictured among the library stacks. Matthew's genealogy plays in two ways. On one hand, Matthew 1:1 refers to the family tree that immediately follows in 1:2–16 which traces Jesus's lineage through David to Abraham. The writer would have us believe that this story begins neither *ex nihilo* nor *in medias res* but rather at the very beginning of all things – or at least at the beginning of things that matter most in the eyes of the narrator, namely the saga of God's chosen people, the Jews. On the other hand, it evokes both the book of Genesis and the generativeness of narration, thus simultaneously grounding both Jesus and Matthew's story in an older, much larger story, as well as gesturing toward the dynamics of creation and curation that are fundamental to narrative.

In his translation and commentary on the Pentateuch, Robert Alter notes that "nothing reveals the difference of the biblical conception of literature from later Western ones more strikingly than the biblical use of genealogies as an intrinsic element of literary structure."[7]

---

6   Unless otherwise indicated, all quotations of the biblical text are taken from the *Revised Standard Version* (Division of Christian Education of the National Council of Churches of the United States of America, 1971).

7   Robert Alter, *The Five Books of Moses: A Translation with Commentary* (New York and London: W. W. Norton and Company, 2004), 34. Citing J. P. Fokkelman, he notes the way that genealogies distinguish narrative units.

According to Alter, "repetition of formula dominates the genealogical list stylistically ... and when there is a divergence from the formula ... it is very significant."[8] Matthew follows suit by first imitating the genealogical form and structuring device, and second by diverging from it at verses 3, 5, 6, 11–12, and 16. Four of these divergences highlight women – namely Tamar, Rahab, Ruth, Bathsheba (referred to only as "the wife of Uriah"), and Mary. For Matthew, these literary forks reflect moments of grafting his narrative onto another, of writing himself and his story into the fabric of the Old Testament textual tapestry, interweaving the two so as to both establish and expand his story. Perhaps it is not so surprising that, later, the writer will quote Jesus as saying that "no one puts a piece of unshrunk cloth on an old garment, for the patch tears away from the garment, and a worse tear is made" (9:16).

Matthew's use of a structuring device within his genealogy (1:11–12, 17) also imitates Hebrew narrative style, and this mechanism does more than simply provide an arrangement or an aid to memory: it evokes a sense of significance and meaning. Speaking again of Genesis, Alter notes that "formulaic numbers as well are characteristically used by the biblical writer to give order and coherence to the narrated world."[9] Narratives impose connotation, causation, and clarity, and genealogies are one of many formal elements that writers use to accomplish this. Moreover, they lend gravitas to the story. Alter writes, "part of the intention in using the genealogy is to give the history the look of authentically archaic documentation," and later adds that "genealogy is adopted as a means of schemetizing complex historical evolution, and thus the terms 'father of' and 'begot' are essentially metaphors for historical concatenation."[10] Hence, Matthew's narrator presents the story not as something altogether new or invented but rather as a continuation, a sequel of sorts. This is one of the primary reasons for *and effects of* Matthew's gospel enjoying pride of place as the first gospel in New Testament canonical order.[11] Reading Matthew first, if one were reading the New Testament from start to finish in the order presented, frames everything that proceeds and follows in such a way as to suggest to the reader that *this* is what it all means and is all about (i.e., the Old Testament and New Testament alike).

---

8   Alter, *Five Books of Moses*, 34.
9   Alter, *Five Books of Moses*, 34.
10 Alter, *Five Books of Moses*, 35 and 54.
11 Other reasons include the clarity of the author's presentation and the emphasis on Jesus's teachings, which together result in a work that reads almost as a sort of narrative catechism.

From the genealogy, Matthew cuts to one more essential preliminary: Jesus's birth and all the drama and pageantry surrounding it. The
birth of Jesus serves a number of functions: it characterizes the story's
protagonist, Jesus; it characterizes the narrative itself; it provides an
element of setting and tone; and it initiates the story's plot, which is
marked foremost by conflict and fulfillment. The scandalous pregnancy
of Mary, visitations of an angel to Joseph in dreams before and after
Jesus is born and of Zoroastrian priests to the young family following
Jesus's arrival, the scheming and murderous actions of King Herod, and
the family's flight to and return from Egypt all combine to signify a
series of omens both auspicious and ominous. Everything that will follow – the unfolding, revelation, recognition, and conflict – is both lit
and shaded by this staging.

Amid this prelude, the reader is repeatedly told that one thing
or another came about "in order to fulfill what was spoken by the
prophet(s)." Instances of this formula, or some variation thereof, are
peppered throughout Matthew's narrative.[12] The first one to occur is
in 1:22–23 and it is, in some respects, illustrative of the role and meaning of this refrain everywhere it appears in Matthew. Here the narrator
cites Isaiah 7:14 in order to explain Mary's conception and to imbue it
with magnitude. But the citation includes a reference to the child being
called Emmanuel, which Matthew glosses for his readers as "God with
us." This raises the question: to whom does "us" refer? And by extension, for whom and in what manner are the words of the prophets "fulfilled"? Jesus is nowhere referred to as Emmanuel within the narrative
(i.e., at the story level), nor is he anywhere directly equated with God.
Hence, readers are invited on a quest to discern for themselves how it is
that Jesus "fulfills" the writings with which, presumably, they are intimately familiar, to divine God's presence both in the things portrayed
and in the workings of the narrative itself. It is akin to what Alter says
regarding the nature of the plagues that afflicted Pharaoh and his household because of Sarai in Genesis 12:17: "in the laconic narrative art of
the Hebrew writer, this is left as a gap for us to fill in by an indetermi-
nate compound of careful deduction and imaginative reconstruction."[13]
These citations evoke and reanimate the narratives of which they are a

---

[12]   See 1:22–23; 2:15, 17–18, 23; 4:14–15; 8:17; 12:17–21; 13:14–15, 35; 21:4–5; 26:56;
       27:9–10. Cf., 2:5; 3:3, 15; 5:17; 26:54. Lists of where this motif occurs are typically too
       confined by a focus on the formula. To be sure, the writer *is* doing something rhetori-
       cally by using the formula, but in terms of meaning and function, the reach is far more
       pervasive.
[13]   Alter, *Five Books of Moses*, 65.

part. As prophetic texts, they are not narratives in the traditional sense, but they are both set against the backdrop of an historical narrative and reflective of a particular narrative conceptualization in the mind of the prophet. For the narrator of Matthew and his audience, they function as both scripture and script. Likewise, with respect to Matthew's gospel, Jesus is scripted: a "paper person"[14] that is inextricably entwined with writing, a textual tapestry that takes shape in the interwoven words of Old Testament prophets and Matthew's story. To say that "it is written" is always to indicate a destiny, a fait accompli.

Afterward, the narrator will leap over the entirety of Jesus's childhood and early life to his baptism by John the Baptist, and this is where the focal story begins to unfold. Here, Matthew adopts another "common convention of biblical narrative: when a speaker addresses someone and the formula for introducing speech is repeated with no intervening response from the interlocutor, it generally indicates some sort of significant silence – a failure to comprehend, a resistance to the speaker's words, and so forth."[15] But this technique has unsettling consequences. John berates the Pharisees and Sadducees, but the only words allotted to them are those of an authoritative ventriloquist: John, who has been explicitly characterized as a prophet just prior to this, places on their lips words that are technically unspoken and quite possibly only imagined. The danger is twofold. First, the readers' introduction to the Pharisees and Sadducees is one of negative indirect characterization, which then colors the readers' view of them throughout the remainder of the narrative. Second, John is effectively putting into the minds of the Pharisees and Sadducees the very words he is admonishing them not to think, and by extension, the narrator is doing the same in the minds of the readers. In the end, his injunction is potentially undercut, and the negative characterization is ironically fulfilled.

MATTHEW'S GENRE, DESIGN, AND PURPOSE

Before proceeding any further with Matthew's story, a word should be said regarding what kind of story it is. Much ink has been spilled debating the genre of the gospels. Warren Carter explains that "a genre

---

[14] Elliott, *Reconfiguring*, 59–97, drawing on Mieke Bal, *Narratology: Introduction to the Theory of Narrative* (Toronto: University of Toronto Press, 1997). Not only is he a "paper person" (think "digital avatar") in the sense that all literary characters are, but he is especially so for Matthew who casts Jesus as a *scriptured* savior, one who is scholarly no less, even without formal training.

[15] Alter, *Five Books of Moses*, 51.

imposes limitations on an author and creates expectations of an audience," and argues that "to join the authorial audience ... requires a recognition of the gospel's genre and the roles and expectations appropriate to that genre."[16] This position is one that privileges authorial intent and aims to read historically, to read as a member of the implied audience. But while it may be true that writers imagine themselves to be writing a particular sort of thing and meeting the requirements of that thing in a particular way, there is little if anything to ensure that readers will follow the rules as prescribed. Moreover, and perhaps more importantly, genres are not rigid. There is fluidity and variance both among and within genres. Any designation or imposition of genre will inevitably bring to light certain elements of a text while casting others in the shadows.

That said, what Stephen Barton says regarding the genre of Matthew is representative: Matthew's gospel is "a life of Jesus, closest in literary genre to an ancient biography ... On this level, the dynamic of the narrative is to be sought in the innovations, tensions, surprises and conflicts generated by Jesus himself in his own time and place as Matthew tells it."[17] As most interpreters do, Carter notes that ancient biographies differ from those with which modern readers are familiar in terms of both their material and the purpose. Ancient biographies are neither comprehensive nor focused on interiority and motivation. Instead, they are concerned with the subject's character as it is revealed through actions with the aim of instructing readers in some fashion. These distinctions only further highlight the problem: how meaningful is it to designate Matthew a biography, for example, if what is meant by biography is something so different from what contemporary readers expect when they imagine themselves to be reading a biography? Once again, the focus of scholars like Carter is historical; they are interested in *ancient* readers and an imagined, ideal audience. Carter directly says as much when he writes, "naming the genre and identifying some of the text's expected features and functions assist us in taking another step toward joining the authorial audience."[18] What is overlooked, even when one is

---

[16]   Carter, *Matthew*, 35. Cf. Michal Beth Dinkler, "What is Genre? Contemporary Genre Theory and the Gospels," in *Modern and Ancient Literary Criticism of the Gospels: Continuing the Debate on Gospel Genre(s)*, ed. Robert Matthew Calhoun, David S. Moessner, and Tobias Nicklas (Tübingen: Mohr Siebeck, 2020), 77–96.

[17]   Stephen C. Barton, "The Gospel according to Matthew," in *The Cambridge Companion to the Gospels*, ed. Stephen C. Barton (Cambridge: Cambridge University Press, 2006), 123; cf. Carter, *Matthew*, 46–48.

[18]   Carter, *Matthew*, 48.

concerned with reading from within the context of an ancient reader, is the actual experience of reading and the affects of that experience, that is, the way the narrative moves the reader. To whatever extent the gospel of Matthew is a biography, a narrative life, it is ironically in the way that its "episodic and topical" construction reflects the kaleidoscopic collage of actual life and the effort to create meaning and order through the typical tendencies of life-*writing*.[19]

Barton identifies the chapters or milestones of this narrative "life" thus: the birth of the messiah (chapters 1–2); the testing of the messiah (4:1–11); the teaching of the messiah (chapters 5–7); the deeds of the messiah (chapters 8–9); the transfiguration of the messiah (17:1–9); and the resurrection of the messiah (28:1–20).[20] Kingsbury, calling it simply "a story about Jesus" (which, one could argue, is not quite the same as calling it a biography), divides it into three broad movements or acts: (1) the presentation of Jesus (1:1 – 4:16); (2) the ministry of Jesus to Israel (4:17 – 11:1) and Israel's repudiation of Jesus (11:2 – 16:20); and (3) the journey of Jesus to Jerusalem and his suffering, death, and resurrection (16:21 – 28:20).[21] Plenty of other options are available, as a quick perusal of various commentaries will readily show. Understandably, the focus of these outlines, in light of perceptions regarding the gospel's genre and purpose, centers on Jesus. However, while Jesus is indeed the protagonist of this narrative, the narrative *theme* (i.e., what the story is really about) from a narratological perspective is not Jesus, per se, but rather a particular understanding and characterization of Jesus, and that in relation to the Jewish scriptures.[22] The Gospel According to Matthew is a narrative reading of the Jewish Law, Moses, and Jesus that is focalized through the church as the author imagines it, which raises the issue of focalization.

FOCALIZATION, CHARACTERIZATION, DIALOGUE, AND TIME

Mieke Bal uses the term focalization as a means of capturing the fact that "whenever events are presented, they are always presented from within a certain 'vision.' A point of view is chosen, a certain way of

---

[19] Carter, *Matthew*, 47.
[20] Barton, "The Gospel according to Matthew," 121–38.
[21] Kingsbury, *Matthew as Story*, 3–9.
[22] Mark Allan Powell identifies three major themes in Matthew: (1) the abiding presence of God, (2) Jewish law and Christian faith, and (3) people of little faith. *Fortress Introduction to the Gospels* (Minneapolis: Fortress Press, 1998), 75–83.

seeing things, a certain angle, whether 'real' historical facts are concerned or fictitious events."[23] It is what Manfred Jahn refers to as "the submission of (potentially limitless) narrative information to a perspectival filter."[24] Focalization is distinct from point of view; it is more fundamental and much broader in scope, influencing not only point of view but also time, dialogue, and every other aspect of the narrative.[25] For the writer of Matthew, everything portrayed in his gospel has already happened before its apparent emergence and unfolding in the narrative, both in the scriptures that the story fulfills and in the history of the church's corporate life. Narrative is a *mode* of discourse. As such, it shapes and determines everything therein differently than would other modes of discourse. It is not simply that Jesus's life is set to narrative, as it were. Rather, Jesus's life is a narrative life; it is a life consisting of, constituted by, words and literary images. In Matthew's gospel, narrator, narrative, and reader work in tandem to generate a particular Jesus.

One example of the way focalization impacts the reader's experience of Matthew's narrative is the explanation of why Jesus taught in parables in 13:10–17. To begin, Matthew subtly changes the explanation that Jesus provides in the Markan parallel (Mk. 4:10–12). The latter indicates that Jesus used parables *so that* "those outside" would not understand. But then Mark's narrative goes on to provocatively problematize assumptions about exactly who is inside and who is outside (e.g., depicting those who are supposed to "know the secrets of the kingdom of God," like the disciples, as lacking in insight, while portraying those presumed to be outsiders, like the Syrophoenician woman in Mark 7:24–30, as those possessing understanding).[26] Matthew's Jesus, on the other hand, says that he teaches in parables *because* "to them [to know the secrets of the kingdom of heaven] has not been given" and *because* they do not understand (Mt. 13:11–12). In other words, the writer's *perception* of the parables and of why Jesus used them differs from that of Mark's writer. The parables shift from being riddles to being illustrations. This is seen further in the way that Matthew extends the explanation by including a more expansive quote from Isaiah and adding a

---

[23] Bal, *Narratology*, 142.

[24] Manfred Jahn, 'Focalization', in *The Cambridge Companion to Narrative*, 94–108, ed. David Herman (Cambridge: Cambridge University Press, 2007), 94.

[25] See Christy Cobb, *Slavery, Gender, Truth, and Power in Luke-Acts and Other Ancient Narratives* (London: Palgrave Macmillan, 2019), 63–68.

[26] Matthew's gospel includes the story of the Syrophoenician woman as well, but in his version the woman is rewarded for her faith rather than her wit (Mt. 15:28; cf. Mk. 7:29).

blessing on the disciples, which together set in sharper relief the identities of insiders and outsiders and the consequences of occupying those respective positions. Moreover, they merge the embedded narratives of the parables with the frame narrative of Matthew's gospel in such a way that the subplots of the parables function as microcosms of the frame story. As a result, the reader is less challenged by the parables than affirmed by them.

While Matthew largely follows the contours of Mark's gospel and supplements Mark with material from Q,[27] some of the most notable changes he makes to Mark's gospel are matters of characterization.[28] Mark Allan Powell notes, for example, that Matthew polishes Mark's Jesus by excluding questions that imply limitations to Jesus's knowledge, eliminating any indication of insufficiency in Jesus's ability or authority, eliding depictions of affect on the part of Jesus, and expunging episodes that portray Jesus as a sort of magician. Similarly, Mark's negative characterization of the disciples is softened such that the misunderstanding we see in Mark is tempered and reversed by Jesus's explanations (see esp. Matt. 13:51), and the crass ambition of James and John is transferred to their mother. But Matthew's characterological revision works the other way, as well: he paints the Jewish leaders more harshly, changing a scribe praised by Jesus into an opponent intent on testing Jesus, and stripping Jairus and Joseph of Arimathea of their descriptions as Jewish leaders.[29]

Furthermore, while the narrator uses a variety of modes and techniques to create and shape characters, chief among them is dialogue. Speech was commonly associated with character in antiquity insofar as one's speech was a reflection of one's *ethos*. Here, the idea is that speech is an expression of the self and therefore it exhibits one's nature, constitution, temperament, and so on. Some of this carries over into narrative characterization and literary characters, but it also extends beyond that to the dialogue taking place in and through the space of the

---

[27]   "Q" is an abbreviation for the German word *Quelle*, which means "source." New Testament scholars use it to identify the hypothetical document behind material that the gospels of Matthew and Luke share in common but that is absent from Mark's gospel.

[28]   See, e.g., Kari Syreeni, "Peter as Character and Symbol in the Gospel of Matthew" and Talvikki Mattila, "Naming the Nameless: Gender and Discipleship in Matthew's Passion Narrative," in *Characterization in the Gospels: Reconceiving Narrative Criticism*, 106–52 and 153–79, ed. David Rhoads and Kari Syreeni (Sheffield: Sheffield Academic Press, 1999).

[29]   Powell, *Gospels*, 64–65.

narrative itself.[30] A cacophony of voices are intermingling and vying for attention throughout Matthew, alternately bolstering or blustering in a lively exchange. It is important to keep in mind that narratorial control of this dialogue is tenuous at best. Every voice, including those of the readers, reverberates perpetually across the surface of the narrative.

Dialogue first enters the narrative at 1:20–21 with the words of "an angel of the Lord" speaking to Joseph in a dream, which occurs again in 2:13 and 2:19–20. We have already noted the way that one-sided dialogue functions with respect to the Pharisees and Sadducees being given no lines in response to John the Baptist's tirade. Here, Joseph is the one permitted no verbal reply or expression. Instead, the omniscient third-person (and presumably trustworthy) narrator only reports Joseph's thoughts, feelings, and seemingly passive obedience. Dialogue also occurs at 2:1–12 where everyone but Herod (e.g., "wise men from the East," the "chief priests and scribes" in Jerusalem) seems to be in the know regarding "the king of the Jews" and the portents that mark his arrival.

All of this serves as backdrop to the most critical dialogue running throughout the narrative, which is introduced in 3:15 with the first words of Jesus. God speaks two verses later (3:17), affirming the reliability of the narrator's point of view, and then the devil and Jesus exchange words throughout 4:1–11 by way of quotations of what is written (4:4, 6, 7, and 10). Meanwhile, the limited public at Jesus's baptism is interspersed with a private temptation and then followed by an increasingly greater public from 4:17 onward, and this speaks to an even more fundamental dialogue: that of the writer and his interlocutors. It is worth noting that Jesus's learning, authority, source of information, and so forth are unclear and unidentified prior to chapters 5–7, the first of five teaching discourses in the narrative, where Jesus expatiates on various topics unquestioned and without interruption. The build-up of 4:18–22 and 23–25 is summary in nature. Hence, Jesus's authority is merely an assertion on the part of the narrator via the pen of the writer and the lips of the crowd (another of Matthew's characters). Jesus's words at 4:17 and 19, as is often the case throughout the narrative, are met with *narrative* silence (though the latter garners an action-response on the part of those he called to follow him).

So much of the dialogue in the early part of Matthew is *around* or *about* Jesus rather than *by* or *through* him. Therefore, when that shifts in earnest at chapter 5, the reader is positioned to receive and accept the

---

[30]   See Cobb, *Slavery, Gender, Truth, and Power*, 63–68.

words of Jesus, affirmed in their reading of both him and the scriptures of the Old Testament, which functions as a voice for both God and the writer. The crux of Matthean dialogue concerns Jesus as a site of contest over how to read and understand the Old Testament.

From chapter 5 onward, Jesus takes center stage in terms of action, focus, and voice. The so-called Sermon on the Mount stages a collection of Jesus's teaching as an episode, a moment in the plot of Jesus's life as portrayed in this particular narrative, an assemblage or sampling of his presumably dispersed teachings folded into a delivery that emphasizes not solely the teaching as such, or its content, but its discursiveness vis-à-vis Matthew's narrative *and* Jesus's character, which is defined by or as an authoritative voice.[31] So how is this manner conveyed within the teaching itself? The heart of it occurs in the repeated refrain peppered throughout 5:21–48 (with variations): "You have heard that it was said … But I say to you …" It is also conveyed through Jesus's demanding tone: his exhortation to perfection, his vehement assertion that he has come not to abolish the law but to fulfill it, his warnings against empty performances and those who practice differently, and his insistence on prioritizing matters pertaining to the kingdom of heaven – all of which is laced with blessings of the marginal and rejected, assurances of God's provision, and a promise of safe harbor amid the tempest. The "I" that speaks here and in the remaining four teaching discourses that follow is not the historical Jesus but a literary character who speaks about these things in this manner in service to this or that end. The tendency among readers and many interpreters when considering Jesus's teaching discourses (especially the Sermon on the Mount), just as with the parables (the short stories Jesus narrates within the overarching story that narrates him), is to focus on the content of the teaching independent of the story world and its narrative presentation. But a narratological analysis requires one to think about them in relation to characterization, plot, setting, time/pace/duration, narrative rhetoric, and so forth. How are the story content and the discourse mutually affected and inflected by one another?[32]

Pausing our discussion of dialogue and its relationship to Jesus's characterization for a moment, the first scene depicting Jesus as a

---

[31] Note, in particular, 7:28–29. Whereas the response of the crowds to Jesus's teaching in the Markan parallel (Mark 1:22) is premised upon action, in Matthew it is the teaching itself.

[32] See, e.g., Jack Dean Kingsbury, "The Place, Structure, and Meaning of the Sermon on the Mount Within Matthew," *Interpretation* 41 (1987): 131–43.

healer (aside from the general description of him teaching, preaching, and healing in 4:23–24 – and note that it is the healing that receives the greatest attention through elaboration there) illustrates the way Matthew prioritizes the authority of Jesus and his identity as a prophet grounded in his embodiment of God's voice through the scriptures. There is a note of deference in the leper's words, "if you will" (8:2).[33] This deference toward Jesus is in turn reflected in Jesus's deference toward the Jewish Law insofar as the episode concludes with Jesus instructing the man to show himself "to the priest and to offer the gift that Moses commanded, for a proof to the people" (8:4). What is being proved? It is unconvincing to say that the healing is in view. Instead, what is proved is tied to the narrator's characterization of Jesus: he upholds the Law. What's more, the reader will see in 9:1–8; 12:1–8, 9–14; and elsewhere that Jesus enacts the essence of the Law, its proverbial spirit, as Matthew understands it. This brings us to the role of time in Matthew's gospel.

Time is, first of all, a structuring device in Matthew that signals transitions between the major parts of Matthew's story.[34] Barton points out that "the encounter between old and new gives to Matthew its *dynamic*. In Matthew's story of Jesus there is continuity with the past and discontinuity, profound indebtedness to the scriptures and traditions of Judaism, but also rupture and innovation."[35] For Barton, the point of convergence is God, the same God of the Old Testament, who is "with us" in the person of Jesus (1:23; cf. 18:20; 28:20). But the ambiguity of God's presence, where and in what manner God is present, in Matthew has already been noted. As Powell rightly observes, God's presence "may assume unlikely guises so as to go unrecognized by the righteous and the wicked alike (25:31–46)."[36] The important thing is that the writer presumes that he and his imagined audience do not fail to recognize it but in fact see it with eminent clarity. Moreover, it is not God who is doing something new but rather the gospel itself that is novel. Barton concludes that Matthew is weaving old and new together, referencing 13:52, which is unique to Matthew's gospel and

---

33 Deference of various sorts is also reflected in the two healing episodes that immediately follow. In 8:5–13, the centurion says to Jesus, "I am not worthy to have you come under my roof." And in 8:14–15, Peter's mother-in-law is healed without any indication that she or anyone else has requested it.

34 Note Matthew's use of the phrase, "From that time," at 4:17 and 16:21. See Kingsbury, *Matthew as Story*, 40.

35 Barton, "The Gospel according to Matthew," 121; italics original.

36 Powell, *Gospels*, 71.

reads, "Therefore every scribe who has been trained for the kingdom of heaven is like a householder who brings out of his treasure what is new and what is old."

Perhaps, however, the real key is to be found in 13:51, especially when coupled with the parable of the net that precedes it in 13:47–50. In Matthew 13:51, Jesus asks his disciples if they've understood "all this," and they confidently reply, "Yes." Unlike Mark's presentation of the disciples as dimwitted dolts, Matthew presents them as enlightened, obedient students. Here is where another element of time comes into play: generational time. The writer of Matthew occupies a position wherein the events that his narrator describes as either now or yet to come are already past. They have come to him by oral tradition and the written works of others, that is, Mark and Q. This is reflected in the theme of the church (esp. in 16:17–19 and 18:15–20) and the repeated use of "Lord" in reference to Jesus, among other things. However, it also surfaces more subtly in the writer's use of certain linguistic forms such as the pluperfect and future perfect.[37] The complex temporality at play highlights the tensions between focalization and point of view. It is not simply that the reader is positioned in such a way as to look backward and forward in alternating glances, or to consider the past from the vantage point of now. The writer focalizes, from the future, the narrator's forward-looking point of view such that what is promised is guaranteed by virtue of having already happened.[38]

MATTHEW'S AGONISTIC PLOT AND THE MOTIF OF DOUBT

In commenting on the writer's apocalyptic vision of the world, that is, one in which everything is divided into two diametrically opposed

[37] Occurrences of the pluperfect denote a sense of past completion once and for all. See, especially, Matt. 7:25; 12:7; 24:43; 25:26; 27:18, where all but one of the pluperfect verbs have to do with knowing and therefore suggest, together with the pluperfect "founded" (i.e., established, built upon) in 7:25, connote intimate, integrated, deeply understood knowledge. The future perfect, meanwhile, is frequently achieved by way of a periphrastic construction and indicates that the thing referenced or described will have been completed by a future point in time. Both instances of the future perfect in Matthew (Matt. 16:19 and 18:18) appear in the context of discussions regarding the church, reflecting the superimposition of the writer's context on to the world of the story.

[38] Alter writes of the use of the pluperfect in Gen. 13:14 amid the story of Lot's parting with Abram, "the definition of temporal frame is pointed and precise ... The utterance of the promise [to Abram] is already an accomplished fact as Lot takes up settlement in the plain to the east" (Five Books of Moses, 68).

"spheres of divine or demonic influence," Powell, referencing the parable of the weeds among the wheat (13:24–30, 36–43), makes the point that Matthew goes further than either Mark or Luke in imagining "that some human beings were put in this world by Satan." He goes on to argue that "the metaphors used in this parable seem to exert a controlling influence over the story," because the narrator elsewhere portrays Jesus implicitly referring to the Pharisees as wild plants not cultivated by God that will be rooted up in due course, as blind guides stumbling toward an inevitable fall into a pit, and as serpents inescapably destined for hell. Therefore, the disciples are cautioned against them and told to leave them alone. Powell suggests that "the effect of this apparently harsh characterization is to cast much of the story into a symbolic sphere that allows it to work on more than one level. Seemingly trivial disputes between Jesus and the Pharisees become representative of the ultimate conflict of good and evil, the cosmic clash between God and Satan."[39]

This agonistic plot is hovering in the backdrop from the story's outset with the mysterious foreboding resulting from a combination of divine activity (celestial omens, angelic pronouncements, dreams and visions) and the prescience of both the narrator and certain characters within the story on one hand, and the real-world violence of 2:16–18 that aims to resist and threaten (albeit futilely) God's inbreaking, on the other. What begins coming into focus with John the Baptist's scathing, vitriolic tirade against the Pharisees and Sadducees discussed earlier (3:7–12) courses throughout the narrative and erupts in every moment of conflict between characters, ultimately reaching its pinnacle in chapter 23 where Jesus urges his followers not to be like the scribes and Pharisees (verses 1–12), declares a series of "woes" against the scribes and Pharisees (verses 13–36), and mourns Jerusalem for "killing the prophets and stoning those who are sent" to it (verses 37–39). Later, it is the "chief priest and the elders of the people" who make plans and arrangements to kill Jesus, setting in motion the passion narrative, where these two spheres converge most saliently. "Literary critics invariably identify the death and resurrection of Jesus in Matthew as the climax of the narrative's plot, as the goal toward which most of the action is directed throughout the book."[40] But it is also where the scribes, Pharisees, chief priest, elders, and the Jewish crowd are all depicted as fully embracing, embodying, and enacting all of what has been ascribed to them when they say, in response to Pilate literally

[39]   Powell, *Gospels*, 70.
[40]   Powell, *Gospels*, 65.

washing his hands of Jesus's blood and professing innocence with regard to the horrific events about to follow, "His blood be on us and on our children!" (27:25).

Historically oriented interpreters regularly argue that this reflects an intrafamilial dispute, that the focus is on the Jewish leadership rather than on the Jews in general, that Rome alone is responsible for Jesus's death, and that early Christians were scapegoating in order to avoid drawing unwanted attention themselves. But, as Robert Allen Warrior famously remarks in his analysis of the conquest story in Joshua, "history is no longer with us. The narrative remains."[41] The *narrative* of Matthew blames the Jews for Jesus's death, attributes evil motivations to their machinations, and portrays them as acting with full cognizance of who they are and what they are doing. Not only does Matthew's explanation not hold up historically; it is ethically problematic and dangerous. So what is to be done? Warrior later goes on to say that "the text itself will never be altered by interpretation of it, though its reception may be."[42] Historical-critical exposition certainly makes a contribution in this regard. How might narratological study do so? Might we read Matthew as a cautionary tale against holding too tightly any reading?

In an effort to take one step toward answering this question, let us note two other characteristic aspects of Matthew's narrative style in addition to the fulfillment motif already discussed earlier: the writer's fondness for organizational patterns and his habit of doubling. The former is seen foremost in his grouping of Jesus's teaching into five distinct discourses ending with words along the lines of, "When Jesus finished these things" (see 7:28; 11:1; 13:53; 19:1; 26:1).[43] Throughout Matthew, events, actions, dialogues, and texts are interwoven and work together as a tool of characterization whereby Jesus is cast as a new Moses. In the same manner as the Moses of the Torah, Jesus writes and is written; he produces and is produced by narrative; he fulfills the scriptures and he embodies the script. His is the writing not of pen and ink but of the oral, the prophetic, the apocalyptic.

---

[41]   Robert Allen Warrior, "A Native American Perspective: Canaanites, Cowboys, and Indians," in *Biblical Studies Alternatively*, 400–05, ed. Susanne Scholz (Upper Saddle River, NJ: Prentice Hall, 2002), 402.

[42]   Warrior, "A Native American Perspective," 404.

[43]   The five teaching discourses are typically referred to as the Sermon on the Mount (chs. 5–7), the missionary discourse (ch. 10), the parables of the kingdom (ch. 13), the community discourse (ch. 18), and the eschatological discourse (chs. 24–25). Benjamin Bacon (cited in Powell, *Gospels*, 65) outlined the gospel on the basis of these discourses, noting that "narrative material preceding each of the speeches often deals with the same theme addressed in the subsequent discourse."

Meanwhile, the writer's habit of doubling, whereby, for example, two demoniacs are healed in 8:28–34 (cf. Mark 5:1–20; Luke 8:26–39), two blind men are healed in 9:27–31, two more blind men are healed in 20:29–34 (cf. Mark 10:46–52; Luke 18:35–43; also, the episode itself doubles what occurred in Mt. 9:27–31), most assuredly presumes to verify and solidify the events recounted. But a curious and illustrative incident of this doubling transpires in 21:1–9 (cf. Mark 11:1–10; Luke 19:28–38; John 12:12–19), which serves my argument. There, citing what unfolds as a fulfillment of Zechariah 9:9, the writer reads literally a parallelism of poetic verse, thereby depicting Jesus riding into Jerusalem on two animals simultaneously. The writer of Matthew holds so tightly to the text that he misreads it.

I have suggested already that at the heart of Matthew's narrative is a plot centered on reading, that the central conflict, at a fundamental level, is interpretive: a debate over *how* to read. In the end, Matthew's gospel with all its fulfillments is *not* an extension or sequel. The Old Testament is not simply the soil and a root structure out of and beyond which this story grows, or a trunk on to which this story is grafted; it is a palimpsest. In Matthew's gospel, the new overwrites the old, but it cannot and does not erase the latter completely. The dialogical dynamics borne of the tension between writings, characters, writers and readers reverberates over the surface story and in the deep structures of the narrative discourse. The retrospective portrayed as prophecy, even if it is "actual" memory, lends an air of control, purpose, and so on, imbuing happenstance with significance. But it is also a deflection, a sleight of hand.

It is an axiom of narrative theory to distinguish between the author of a narrative and its narrator. Arguably, biblical scholars have been doing this for a long time, even without taking explicit recourse to narrative theory insofar as they recognize that the gospels are effectively written anonymously. We cannot ascertain the actual author of Matthew; we can only reconstruct an implied author on the basis of clues we find and interpret in the narrative and the discourse. Customarily, critics identify the "Matthew" behind this story as an educated Jew.[44] The author/writer/narrator shares the interests of characters within the story, namely how to interpret the Old Testament

---

[44] "His biblical quotations are not all drawn from the Septuagint ... but sometimes appear to represent his own translations from the Hebrew. His style of writing and approach to argumentation have suggested to some that he might be a converted rabbi or former Pharisee" (Powell, *Gospels*, 72).

scriptures and the Jewish Law. But this author's reliable narrator holds within it a certain conceit: that he holds the keys to the interpretive kingdom, that his is the only and right way to read and understand both the scriptures and Jesus. The scene depicting the temptation of Jesus in 4:1–11, where both the tempter and Jesus cite verses from the Old Testament, modeling a rabbinical debate, functions as a sort of microcosm of the gospel as a whole. Scripture is set against scripture in a realm and setting that are at once both cosmic and earthly. While Jesus certainly does hold his ground in the wilderness, whether or to what extent he did so by besting the devil is not as clear as it may seem. The scene concludes with the narrator saying only, "Then the devil left him" (4:11). Indeed, the debate concerning how to read scripture that precedes the temptation continues after its conclusion as writer, narrator, characters, ideal audience, actual readers, and unintended interlocutors wrestle together to ascertain its meaning, thereby resisting its crystallization and perpetually animating it instead.

Matthew's gospel ends with an ascension (28:16–20). Just as the camera swept from a wide-angle lens to a close-up view of Mary, pregnant with Jesus, now it pans upward to watch the resurrected Jesus leave earth after commissioning the remaining eleven disciples, on the basis of "all authority in heaven and on earth" having been given to him, to "make disciples of all nations" through baptism and instruction, and promising to be with them always "to the close of the age."

It is interesting to note the narrator's remarks in 28:17 that upon seeing Jesus the disciples worshipped him, "but some doubted." The word "doubt" occurs three times in Matthew. In Matthew 14:22–33, the disciples are in a boat far from shore, being tossed about on the waves of a tumultuous and tempestuous sea, when Jesus approaches them walking on the water. They cry out in terror and disbelief, thinking he is a ghost, an apparition. When he attempts to calm their fear by assuring them it is he, Peter puts him to the test, saying, "Lord, if it is you, bid me come to you on the water." Jesus invites him to come and for a moment he, too, is walking on water. However, once he notices the fierce wind his concentration wavers, his fear returns, he begins to sink, and he cries out for Jesus to save him. Jesus complies and asks, "O man of little faith, why did you doubt?"

The next instance where doubt is mentioned is in 21:18–22. A hungry Jesus happens upon a fruitless fig tree and curses it with perpetual barrenness, causing it to wither immediately. The shocked disciples wonder aloud about why the tree withered, and Jesus answers, "Truly, I say to you, if you have faith and never doubt, you will not only do what has been done to the fig tree, but even if you say to this mountain, 'Be taken up and cast into the sea,' it will be done. And whatever you ask in prayer, you will receive, if you have faith." In both of these episodes, doubt is juxtaposed to faith and essentially cautioned against, discouraged, and dismissed. But there is a degree of forcedness to the version of faith that is promoted here.

Meanwhile, the occurrence of doubt at Matthew 28:17 is a bit different. Here, it is set over against worship. Moreover, whereas the first two scenes suggest that the doubt is somehow overcome, the final act of Matthew allows it to stand. It is merely stated as a matter of fact, a kind of reality effect. The words of Jesus that follow appear to be directed equally to those who worship and to those who doubted, and they are not words that urge the sort of faith we see in the earlier examples. Hence, the presence and persistence of doubt in the narrative's denouement resists closing the door on meaning. It leaves open the possibility of alternative readings that fruitfully trouble Matthew's troubling perspective. In so doing, it exposes the certainty of understanding expressed by the disciples in 13:51 as potentially fictional in the truest sense – namely, as a space between truth and falsehood that permits uncertainty, empathy, and wonder.

SELECTED FURTHER READING

Alter, Robert. *The Five Books of Moses: A Translation with Commentary*. New York: W. W. Norton & Co., 2004.

Bal, Mieke. *Narratology: Introduction to the Theory of Narrative*. Toronto: University of Toronto Press, 1997.

Barton, Stephen C. "The Gospel according to Matthew." In *The Cambridge Companion to the Gospels*, 121–38. Edited by Stephen C. Barton. Cambridge: Cambridge University Press, 2006.

Carter, Warren. *Matthew: Storyteller, Interpreter, Evangelist*. Peabody, MA: Hendrickson, 1996.

Cobb, Christy. *Slavery, Gender, Truth, and Power in Luke – Acts and Other Ancient Narratives*. London: Palgrave Macmillan, 2019.

Dinkler, Michal Beth. "New Testament Rhetorical Narratology: An Invitation toward Integration," *Biblical Interpretation* 24 (2016): 203–28.

Dinkler, Michal Beth. *Literary Theory and the New Testament*. New Haven: Yale University Press, 2019.

Elliott, Scott S. *Reconfiguring Mark's Gospel: Narrative Criticism after Poststructuralism*. Sheffield: Sheffield Phoenix Press, 2011.

Howell, David B. *Matthew's Inclusive Story: A Study in the Narrative Rhetoric of the First Gospel*. SNTSS 42. Sheffield: Sheffield Academic Press, 1990.

Kingsbury, Jack Dean. *Matthew: Structure, Christology, Kingdom*. Philadelphia: Fortress Press, 1975.

Kingsbury, Jack Dean. *Matthew as Story*. Minneapolis: Fortress Press, 1986.

Kingsbury, Jack Dean. "The Place, Structure, and Meaning of the Sermon on the Mount Within Matthew," *Interpretation* 41 (1987): 131–43.

Mattila, Talvikki. "Naming the Nameless: Gender and Discipleship in Matthew's Passion Narrative." In *Characterization in the Gospels: Reconceiving Narrative Criticism*, 153–79. Edited by David Rhoads and Kari Syreeeni. London: T&T Clark, 1999.

Powell, Mark Allan. *Fortress Introduction to the Gospels*. Minneapolis: Fortress Press, 1998.

Rhoads, David. "The Gospel of Matthew: Two Ways – Hypocrisy or Righteousness." *Currents in Theology and Mission* 19 (1992): 453–61.

Syreeni, Kari. "Peter as Character and Symbol in the Gospel of Matthew." In *Characterization in the Gospels: Reconceiving Narrative Criticism*, 106–52. Edited by David Rhoads and Kari Syreeni. London: T&T Clark, 1999.

11 Fear and Grief

Emotions at the Endings(s) of Mark's Story

ELIZABETH E. SHIVELY AND
KARA J. LYONS-PARDUE

If you've read the Gospel of Mark, you know that it begins, quite literally, with a beginning. The first line broadcasts, "The beginning of the
good news of Jesus Christ, the Son of God" (Mark 1:1).[1] You know that
Mark quickly introduces both human and superhuman characters who
engage each other in consequential words and actions as they move
through time and space. There is geographical movement from the
wilderness to Galilee and through Judea towards Jerusalem, and back
towards Galilee again. There is spatial movement, through the constant
interconnection of heaven and earth. And there is temporal movement,
both through a cultic year and to the eschatological end (Mark 3:26;
13:7, 13).

Mark's decision to begin and end as he does intimates choices in
the composition and **narration of a story**.[2] Mark was the first (as far
as we know) to select and arrange raw material about the words and
works of Jesus to narrate the "good news" in written form. The apostle Paul had earlier reminded his readers of the elements of the "good
news" when he proclaimed "that Christ died for our sins in accordance
with the scriptures, and that he was buried, and that he was raised on
the third day in accordance with the scriptures, and that he appeared
to Cephas and then to the twelve" (1 Cor 15:3–5). Paul's narration

---

[1] All quotations are from the NRSV unless otherwise noted.

[2] In narratological terms, "a *narrative* text is a text in which an agent or subject con-
    veys to an addressee ('tells' the reader) a story in a particular medium" (Mieke Bal,
    Narratology: Introduction to the Theory of Narrative, 3rd edition [University of
    Toronto Press, 2009], 5). A rhetorical definition elaborates on the narratological to
    account more fully for person-level communication between writers and readers:
    a narrative is "the act of somebody telling somebody else on a particular occasion
    for some purpose that something happened" (James Phelan, *Narrative as Rhetoric:
    Technique, Audiences, Ethics, Ideology* [Columbus: Ohio State University Press,
    1996], 218).

includes characters and action and sequencing, but that does not make it a story. To make it so also requires the depiction of those characters with actions and events in a cause-and-effect sequence.[3] This is what Mark does.

In this essay, we explore, in three movements, what it means to read Mark as a coherent narrative text.[4] First, we look at various ways scholars have interpreted Mark as a narrative, culminating in the proposal of an eclectic approach that joins historically informed narratological, rhetorical, and cognitive theories. Second, we discuss key narrative elements that enable readers to recognize Mark as a coherent narrative text. Finally, we advance the study of characterization, a lasting interest of Markan scholarship, by interpreting the emotions of the women and the disciples at Mark's short and longer endings, in narrative and cultural context.

INTERPRETING MARK AS NARRATIVE

Readers have interpreted "Mark as story" since the literary turn reached biblical studies in the 1970s and generated the development of narrative criticism.[5] In its conception, it insisted that Mark is an autonomous and unified text. In its use, narrative criticism has yielded author-oriented, text-oriented, and reader-oriented hermeneutics, or some combination.[6] Whatever the vantage point, the *sine qua non* of narrative criticism is the determination of the text-internal process of communication between the implied author or narrator and the implied audience.[7] Narrative analysis thus enables the interpreter to scrutinize

---

3 Marie-Laure Ryan comments: "a temporally ordered sequence of events could be a list rather than a story," in *"Towards a Definition of Narrative,"* in Cambridge Companion to Narrative, ed. David Herman (Cambridge: Cambridge University Press, 2007), 23. The point is that the cause-and-effect element of a narration. The point is that the cause-and-effect element of a narration is what makes it a story. Programmatically, Aristotle articulated the unified structure of a plot as that which represents the events or "the arrangement of the incidents" in a causal sequence (*Poet.* 1450a; 1452a).

4 For an argument that Mark is a coherent narrative text, see Elizabeth E. Shively, "The Eclipse of the Markan Narrative: On the (Re)Cognition of a Coherent Story and Implications for Genre," *EC 12* (2021): 369–87. For an opposing view, see Matthew D. C. Larsen, *Gospels Before the Book* (Oxford, Oxford University Press, 2018).

5 David Rhoads coined the phrase "narrative criticism" in "Narrative Criticism and the Gospel of Mark," *JAAR* L/3 (1982): 411–12.

6 See Mark Allan Powell, "Narrative Criticism: The Emergence of a Prominent Reading Strategy," in *Mark as Story: Retrospect and Prospect*, eds. Kelly R. Iverson and Chris R. Skinner, SBLRS 65 (Atlanta: SBL, 2011), 19–44.

7 Powell, "Narrative Criticism," 22–23.

the text and its elements; however, alone it does not afford the inter-preter a means to account for the activity of real writers and real read-ers in their socio-historical contexts. Historically informed literary approaches and rhetorical criticism go some way in helping to address this gap by contextualizing narrative analysis and attending to literary conventions common to Mark and his earliest reading communities. Reader-response criticism goes farther, by attending to text-effects on readers. Recognizing these developments, *Mark as Story*, the premier narratological textbook on Mark, exhibits a shift from a solely text-oriented approach in its first edition to a historically informed, reader-oriented approach in its second and third editions.[8]

Cognitive narratology[9] goes further still towards bridging the gap between literary and historical-cultural interpretations by explaining the activity of real writers and real readers in their contexts. Cognitive narratology builds on insights of cognitive science that show we com-prehend texts using the same sort of thinking we do every day. That is, when we encounter a concept or activity in a social or textual context, we form a mental model (imagine a cartoon thought bubble) as an aid to make sense of it. We populate mental models with prototypical knowl-edge held in long-term memory ("top-down" processing), and revise our understanding in real time based on new information from the textual or social world ("bottom-up" processing). Cognitive narratology ampli-fies prior interpretive approaches by insisting that reader-response can-not be divorced from the author's implicit and explicit textual cues (textual information) or from the cultural context of production and reception (extratextual information).

RECOGNIZING MARK'S TEXTUAL CUES IN CONTEXT

Hearing or reading Mark as a coherent narrative text is an intuitive, dynamic activity of top-down and bottom-up processing by which we integrate *textual information* with *extratextual information*. We do this naturally and quickly, without awareness. While we cannot account fully for diverse situations and aims that readers of various times and places bring to their reading of Mark's narrative, we can hypothesize Mark's (the historical, writing author's) communicative intentions

---

8   David M. Rhoads, Donald Michie, and Joanna Dewey, *Mark as Story: The Introduction to the Narrative of a Gospel*, 3rd edition (Philadelphia: Fortress, 2012).

9   For an accessible introduction, see Peter Stockwell, *Cognitive Poetics: An Introduction*, 2nd edition (London and New York: Routledge, 2019).

towards the intended audience and how some members of the earliest actual audience may have responded by attending to textual cues in context.[10]

Regarding extratextual information, cultural frames inevitably informed both what and how Mark wrote, and how members of Mark's earliest reading communities comprehended it. For instance, Mark and his earliest audience inhabited a world shaped by textual and social factors, especially the Greek scriptures with the political, economic, and religious elements of the Greco-Roman world. Moreover, they shared cultural frames informed by recent events. Specifically, Mark's telling reflects the scar of Jesus's public execution and the fresh wound of the Jewish War against Rome. How should early Christ-followers explain such catastrophe and the traumatic impact on their lives? Mark did it by producing a narrative text within a historical-cultural moment that tells of the suffering and death of Jesus and the subsequent suffering of his followers as the story of the good news of God's coming reign, according to the Jewish scriptures. Mark's act of telling *this* story in *this* way is thus not merely to report or regale; it is to perform an act of narrative imagining that reflects the memory and shapes the identity of a group of early Christ-followers.[11] All subsequent readers may participate in Mark's imaginative act by taking the role of the intended audience even as we acknowledge the perceptions and experiences that inform our readings. Below, we make a start by identifying textual cues that facilitate the comprehension of Mark as a coherent narrative text:[12] style, rhetoric, intertextuality, and character development.

Style

Mark's narrative is marked by paratactic style (parataxis, "arrange alongside"), in its simple, coordinate sentences joined with *kai*, "and."[13] Mark's style seems to suggest a rapid play by play: "And then ... and

---

[10]   We use the word "hypothesize" intentionally, because we recognize that we come to Mark informed by our own cultural frames, which may make certain choices relevant to us that might not be relevant to others. The *intended audience* is the hypothetical or authorial audience for which Mark orchestrated textual data to write the narrative rhetorically and comprehensibly for members of an *actual audience*, with whom he shared certain conventions of speaking and writing.

[11]   For further discussion, see Sandra Heubenthal, *Reading Mark's Gospel as a Text from Collective Memory* (Grand Rapids: Eerdmans, 2020); Helen K. Bond, *The First Biography of Jesus: Genre and Meaning in Mark's Gospel* (Grand Rapids: Eerdmans, 2020), 90–96.

[12]   Walter Kintsch, *Comprehension: A Paradigm for Cognition* (Cambridge: Cambridge University Press, 1998), 206.

[13]   More than 400 of Mark's sentences begin with the word *kai*.

then ... and then ..." This already somewhat urgent tone of the paratactic narration is amplified by another of Mark's favorite terms: *euthys*, "immediately."[14] Contrastingly, Greek writing tends to use a hypotactic style (hypotaxis, "arrange under"), marked by complex sentences joined by various conjunctions and subordinate clauses. Mark's style, however, imitates the paratactic style of Hebrew prose narrative, which uses the coordinate conjunction *waw* ("and"). In this case, Mark's frequent use of *kai* and *euthys* signals cohesion between scenes and an invitation to the reader/hearer to infer the meaning and the relationship between sentences and episodes from the context. Mark's textual cues facilitate such inferences by offering information about how one episode relates to the next (and to the whole).

Rhetoric

Mark also imitates rhetorical conventions of Hebrew narrative to facilitate narrative cohesion. To be sure, many of the conventions are not unique to Hebrew narrative. These rhetorical devices and structuring elements overlap and develop in diverse cultural contexts, and so, for instance, appear in Greek narrative. The *synkrisis* ("comparison") of Plutarch's *Lives* resembles the character juxtapositions of the Pentateuch (e.g., Jacob and Esau).[15] While we may be tempted to attribute common rhetorical conventions to classical sources, Mark's pervasive use of the Jewish scriptures suggests it as the primary source of influence. Three areas of rhetorical convention stand out.

First, like Hebrew prose narrative, Mark mixes chronological structuring (causal ordering) and non-chronological structuring (summary statements, intercalation [one story "sandwiched" by another], framing, foreshadowing, and flashbacks).[16] For instance, the *flashback* to John the Baptist's death (6:17–29) is *intercalated* into Jesus's sending out of the Twelve (6:7–13) and their return (verses 30–31).[17] In Mark's most famous intercalation, the healing of a woman with a hemorrhage (5:24b–34) is nested within the story of the healing of Jairus's daughter (5:21–24a, 35–43). Key terms shared between the narratives ("daughter,"

---

14   The terms *kai* and *euthys* are paired together twenty-eight times in the New Testament, twenty-five of them in Mark's Gospel alone.

15   See Helen Bond's discussion of Greco-Roman rhetoric in *First Biography*, 78–120, and *synkrisis* on p. 86.

16   For a discussion of these structuring devices in Hebrew narrative, see Jerome T. Walsh, *Style and Structure in Biblical Hebrew Narrative* (Collegeville, MN: Liturgical press, 2001).

17   Tom Shepherd, *Markan Sandwich Stories* (Berrien Springs, MI: Andrews University Press, 1993), 172–209.

5:34–35; "faith" and "believe," 5:34, 36; "twelve years," 5:25, 42) rein-force the interpretive relationship between the healing episodes and indicate that Mark's placement is intentional rather than merely acci-dental or sequential.

Second, like Hebrew narrative, Mark is replete with analogical patterning on the micro and macro levels, including repetition, paral-lelism, *inclusio* (a framing device), juxtaposition, and chiasm.[18] Such patterning affords the recognition of a coherent narrative. For example, the term *euangelion*, "good news," frames the prologue (1:1; 1:14–15), and the healings of blind men uniquely frame the section in which Jesus predicts his passion (8–10). Framing invites readers to understand the internal content in light of the "bookends." Also, *chiasm* structures Jesus's announcement of the good news in 1:14–15, and the cycle of conflicts in 2:1–3:6. Chiasm creates *parallel* sayings and events and invites reflection on the central part (the imminence of God's reign, 1:15; the removal of the bridegroom, 2:18–22; see also 1:14–15).[19] Moreover, *repetition* through *doubling and tripling* evokes a sense of progressive intensity as it creates narrative coherence through pattern-ing. Doubling appears on the micro-level, with two-step progressions in which the second word or phrase explains the first more specifically (1:32, "That evening, at sunset"; and 7:26, "The woman was a Gentile, of Syrophoenician origin"). On the macro-level, doubling occurs with the two feeding accounts (6:30–44 and 8:1–10; see also 4:35–41 and 6:45–52; 7:31–37 and 8:22–26). Significant examples of tripling include groupings of characters in threes (Peter, James, and John; Jesus, Moses, and Elijah; chief priests, scribes, and elders; Mary Magdalene, Mary, and Salome); Jesus's three passion predictions (8:31; 9:30–31; 10:33–34); Jesus's return to find sleeping disciples three times (14:37, 40, 41); and Peter's threefold denial of Jesus (14:66–72).

Third, like Hebrew narrative, Mark's use of *irony* requires read-ers to join the position of the intended audience to grasp textual cues against cultural frames and scripts.[20] Mark prefers dramatic irony, in which the significance of a character's words or actions are unknown to them but clear to the reader. For instance, some scribes question Jesus's authority to forgive the sins of a paralytic, saying, "Who can forgive sins

[18]   Meir Sternberg, *Poetics of Biblical Narrative: Ideological Literature and the Drama of Reading* (Bloomington, IN: Indiana University Press, 1985), especially 365–440.

[19]   Joanna Dewey, "The Literary Structure of the Controversy in Mark 2:1–3:6," *JBL* 92 (1973): 394–401.

[20]   See further Jerry Camery-Hoggatt, *Irony in Mark's Gospel*, SNTSMS 72 (Cambridge: Cambridge University Press, 1991).

but God alone?" (2:7). Underlying the scribes' protest is a shared belief that the "one God" of Israel singularly holds this authority (Deut 6:4; Isa 43:25). In response to the protest, Jesus demonstrates the coherence of his activity with that of the one God by extending forgiveness and healing as the self-designated Son of Man (2:10). This verbal allusion to Daniel 7:13–14, where one like a son of man receives authority and power from the Ancient of Days, implies that Mark's Jesus similarly receives divine authority to forgive sins on the earth. Attentive readers will thus recognize the truth in the scribes' words, of which they themselves are unaware, that *only God can* forgive sins, implying Jesus's divine identity.

In another case, the Roman soldiers who beat and mock Jesus prior to his crucifixion perform a parody of royalty (15:17–19) and call him "King of the Jews" (15:18). Jewish authorities have declared unanimously that Jesus is a blasphemer for his explicit messianic self-reference (Mark 14:62–64). Then at his crucifixion, Jesus is mocked as "king" by passers-by (15:29–30), chief priests (15:31–32a), and those crucified alongside him (15:32b). Even the charges inscribed above Jesus on the cross repeat the sarcastic honorific (15:26). Yet, readers progressively processing the narrative understand Jesus's Davidic descent (cf. 10:47–48; 11:10) and messianic status (cf. 1:1; 8:29; 14:61–62), and so grasp the honor of this title. The irony is twofold because Jesus really is king, installed in death.[21]

Intertextuality

As already indicated, Mark facilitates narrative coherence through use of the Jewish scriptures. He joins elements of Israel's scripture and tradition with raw material about people and events to narrate the written proclamation of the good news of God's reign through his Messiah (Mark 1:1, 14–15).[22] At the outset, Mark positions his intended readers to take their place in God's ongoing (hi)story by explaining his opening announcement of "good news" with a mixed citation (verses 2–3; Isa 40:3; Exod 23:20; Mal 3:1). This citation stands in the opening position as the narrator's only quotation, explicitly credited to "the prophet Isaiah" (1:2–3; cf. 7:6). These noteworthy features suggest that Mark

---

21 "For Markan Christology it is *in the moment of suffering, insult, humiliation, and finally death* that Jesus is king" (Francis J. Moloney, *The Gospel of Mark: A Commentary* [Peabody, MA: Hendrickson, 2002], 317).

22 See Elizabeth E. Shively, "Israel's Scriptures in Mark," in *The Old Testament in the New: Israel's Scriptures in the New Testament and other Early Christian Writings*, ed. D. N. Lincicum and M. Henze (Grand Rapids: Eerdmans, forthcoming).

intentionally tunes both the set of texts and the whole narrative to the key of Isaiah. Readers' opening encounter with scripture introduces a narrative and hermeneutical framework into which subsequent textual and scriptural information is integrated.

Mark composes a story based on Isaiah's "plot" about Israel's rejection of God and subsequent spiritual blindness and hardening (Isa 6:9–10 with Mark 4:12; Isa 29:13 with Mark 7:6–7; Isa 5 with Mark 12:1–9), and the announcement of the Lord's coming to redeem his people from captivity and sin (Isa 40:3 and Mark 1:2–3; Isa 42:29 and Mark 3:28; Isa 52–53 and Mark 10:45) with a view to God's universal reign (Isa 57; Mark 13). Mark modulates Isaiah's tune by incorporating other scriptures from Exodus, Daniel, Psalms, and Zechariah, which both share the tune and riff on it. In this way, Mark constructs a whole narrative as a national anthem for all God's people, by telling the good news of God's redemptive activity through his authoritative, suffering, and exalted Messiah, according to the scriptures (Mark 9:12; 14:21, 27–28, 49–50).[23]

Character Development

Markan scholars have long stressed the essential relationship between plot and character. For instance, in *Mark as Story*, Rhoads, Dewey, and Michie explain that "characters are agents in a plot" and "the actions of the plot are expressions of the characters."[24] Additionally, the human-likeness of characters contributes to their meaningful function in the plot by eliciting responses from readers. Consider the sympathetic fear and the faith expressed by the hemorrhaging woman in Mark 5:28–29, 33–34, the boldness of the Syrophoenician woman in 7:24–30, the desperation of the father who cries, "I believe; help my unbelief!" in 9:24, the unleashed devotion of the woman who anoints Jesus in 14:3–9, and the sorrow of Peter in 14:72.

Nevertheless, a general split exists between the use of historical analysis to view characters as mimetic, referring to real people in the world; and of narrative analysis to view characters as nonmimetic, a paradigm of traits based on words within the story.[25] As a result, any understanding

---

23   Shively, "Israel's Scriptures in Mark."
24   Rhoads, Dewey, and Michie, *Mark as Story*, 99 and 103, respectively. Elizabeth Struthers Malbon's contribution to Markan characters is significant, especially *Mark's Jesus: Characterization as Narrative Christology* (Waco, TX: Baylor University Press, 2009); and *In the Company of Jesus: Characters in Mark's Gospel* (Louisville, KY: Westminster John Knox Press, 2000).
25   Fotis Jannidis, "Character," in *Handbook of Narratology* 1, eds. Peter Hühn et al., (Berlin: De Gruyter, 2014), 32.

of characters' human-like qualities struggles between standing with the real-world referent on one side of a chasm or with the function of its linguistic or formal system on the other. Historically informed literary analysis aims to straddle the gap, contextualizing narrative analysis of characters by merging the historical-narratological world of the text with the contemporaneous world of its readers. A cognitive approach closes the gap further, amplifying a historically informed literary approach by viewing characters (like the narrative as a whole) as simultaneously *communicated* by actual writers and *constructed* by actual readers.[26] Under this view, characters are mental models of persons-in-a-world, and characterization is the operation by which actual readers build mental models of characters in the course of reading/hearing by the top-down and bottom-up processing of textual and extratextual data. As Ralf Schneider explains, characterization "happens through a complex interaction of what the text says about the characters and what the reader knows about the world in general, specifically about people and, yet more specifically, about 'people' in literature."[27]

In what follows, we employ our eclectic approach to understand how Mark and one of his earliest readers communicate integrated characters with emotions. We understand the author of the long ending (LE) to be an actual reader of Mark's Gospel, who responds, in part, to the emotions in the short ending (SE).[28] We explore how the progressive processing of extratextual information (cultural knowledge about emotions) and textual information throughout the narrative (progressive use of style, rhetoric, themes, and emotions) facilitates the construction of integrated character models of the women and disciples, with a focus on the two emotions that appear in at Mark's ends: fear (*phobos*) and grief (*lupē*).

Extratextual Information
Cognitive and cultural research shows that we recognize and ascribe character traits like emotions, not only because they are a natural part

---

[26] See further Jan Rüggemeier and Elizabeth E. Shively (eds.), "Cognitive Linguistics and New Testament Narrative: Investigating Methodology through Characterization," Special Issue of *Biblical Interpretation: A Journal of Contemporary Approaches* 29 (2021).

[27] Ralf Schneider, "Toward a Cognitive Theory of Literary Character: The Dynamics of Mental-Model Construction" *Style* 35 (2001): 608.

[28] We assume the priority of the SE while also believing that the LE is important to read as a *Markan* ending and a *canonical* ending. See further Kara J. Lyons-Pardue, *Gospel Women and the Long Ending of Mark*, LNTS 614 (New York: T&T Clark, 2020), 5–48.

of being human,[29] but also because they are culturally specific.[30] For instance, emotions will inevitably differ between someone who perceives a snake to be an adversary and therefore threatening, and another who perceives it to be food and therefore harmless. Alternatively, one might fear what is perceived to be a snake but which turns out only to be a stick. It is not the object or situation that generates the emotion of fear, but the appraisal (real or imagined) of that object in a situation. As a result, reappraisal (e.g., it was only a stick) can change a negative emotion.[31]

Ancient writers viewed emotion (*pathos*) similarly.[32] For instance, Aristotle defined fear (*phobos*) as response to a stimulus: "a kind of pain or disturbance deriving from an impression of a future evil that is destructive or painful."[33] Across Greco-Roman literature, the emotion of *fear* of enemies in battle is accompanied by bodily reactions of *trembling* (*tromos*) and the action of flight (*phyge*).[34] Similarly, classical texts normally describe the emotion of *grief* in response to death and accompanied by actions of weeping and mourning. Fear and grief are generally viewed as negative, irrational, or womanly emotions based on improper perception or assessment of an object.[35] Nevertheless, Aristotle believes that a negative emotion such as "fear makes people deliberative,"[36] and that "courage is not the absence of fear, but the right attitude toward the experience of fear."[37] In other words, reappraisal of the stimulus can change the emotion.

Jewish scripture and tradition similarly use the language of fear (*phobos*) and terror (*ekstasis*) to describe the emotional response to an enemy, pairing it with bodily sensations and the impulse to run.[38] For

---

[29]   Based on evolution or on neuroscience and psychobiology. For further discussion, see David Konstan, *The Emotions of the Ancient Greeks: Studies in Aristotle and Classical Literature* (Toronto: University of Toronto Press, 2016), 1–40.

[30]   See further Batia Mequita and J. Leu, "Cultural Influences on Emotion: Established Patterns and Emerging Trends," in *Handbook of Cultural Psychology*, eds. Dov Cohen and Shinobu Kitayama, 2nd edition (New York: Guilford, 2019), 292–318.

[31]   Keith Oatley and P. N. Johnson-Laird, "Cognitive Approaches to Emotions," *TICS* 18 (2014): 137.

[32]   For a comprehensive yet accessible treatment of emotions from a philosophical, theological, and cognitive perspective, see Samuel M. Powell, *The Impassioned Life: Reason and Emotion in the Christian Tradition* (Minneapolis: Fortress, 2016), 7–47.

[33]   Aristotle, *Rhet.* 2.3, 1382a21–25.

[34]   Homer's *Iliad* consistently equates fear of the enemy with flight.

[35]   Plutarch, *Cons. Apoll.* 22. For a similar statement, see Seneca, *Marc.* 7.3; *Lucil.*, 63.1–2, 12.

[36]   Aristotle, *Rhet.* 2.5, 1382a5.

[37]   *Eth. nic.* 3.7.1115b 11–13

[38]   Exod 15:15; Deut 2:25; 11:25; Judith 2:28; 15:2; 1 Macc 7:18; 4 Macc 4:10. Cf. the prayer for an enemy's fear and trembling (*saleuō*) in 1 Macc 4:32.

instance, the psalmist responds to the noise of their enemy's approach, saying that "fear [deilia] of death fell upon me, fear [phobos] and trembling [tromos] came upon me ... I have fled [pheugō] afar off" (LXX Ps 55:5b–6a, 8a [ET vv. 4b–5a, 7a]). And elsewhere the enemies of God's people experience a terror (ekstasis) from the Lord (2 Chr 14:14; 15:5; 17:10; 20:29; Zech 14:13).[39] As in classical texts, fear can be associated with womanly weakness (Isa 19:16; Jer 49:24; but cf. 4 Macc 15:18–19, 23, 30). Yet unlike classical texts, the overwhelming expectation is that the emotion of fear (phobos) is everyone's right response to God's presence and power, for "the fear of the Lord is the beginning of knowledge" (Prov 1:7). Moreover, fear and trembling are linked in the description of one's response to the Lord, for example, "Serve the Lord with fear [phobos]; rejoice/exult before him in trembling" (tromos; LXX Ps 2:11).[40] Additionally, the Jewish scriptures regularly use the language of grief without the negative connotation exhibited in classical texts. They describe open displays of grief over loved ones,[41] over the destruction of Israel,[42] and over one's own sin and threat of judgment;[43] and join "mourning and weeping."[44] Yet the Jewish scriptures expect a time when "you shall weep no more" (Isa 30:19; cf. Neh 8:9; Job 30:31), not because of death's inevitability (a Stoic view), but because of God's promise and power.

These texts reflect and inform what ancient people thought about emotions. In sum, emotions like fear and grief cannot simply be reduced to a feeling, nor are they "just physical, like a sneeze."[45] Instead, emotions are a process in which one responds to a stimulus by evaluating it (according to prior knowledge and experience within culture), assenting to it (or not), and acting as a result.[46] Armed with this extratextual information, we consider the textual information with which Mark maps the emotional terrain of "fear" and "grief" throughout the narrative, leading up to the ends.[47]

---

[39]   Cf. Ezek 26:16; 27:35; 32:10; phobos with ekstasis in Ezek 26:16.

[40]   Author's translation. For other descriptions of bodily agitation that accompanies fear in the presence God, see Job 4:6, 14–15; Hab 3:16.

[41]   Gen 23:2; 43:30; Tob 10:4, 7.

[42]   Cf. Jer 13:17; Lam 1:16; Isa 22:4; 30:19.

[43]   Isa 15:2; Ezek 24:16; 27:31; Joel 1:5.

[44]   2 Sam 19:2; Neh 1:4; 8:9; Sir. 7:34; Bar. 4:11, 23. See further Lyons-Pardue, Gospel Women, 103–104.

[45]   Oatley and Johnson-Laird, "Cognitive Approaches," 134.

[46]   See further, Konstan, Emotions, 129–33.

[47]   Because of the constraints of a short essay, we focus mostly on places where Mark explicitly uses language of fear.

Textual Information

Throughout Mark, *fear* and *grief* are emotional responses to *death* or to *evidence of God's reign* in Jesus's words and works.[48] Jesus consistently contrasts these emotions with *belief*. In light of our discussion above, we may view fear (improper or proper) and grief as emotions, and belief or unbelief as assent to an emotion leading to action, either acceptance or avoidance (e.g., flight; weeping and mourning).

Jesus's emphasis on belief throughout the narrative must be set within the larger context of his call to *believe* the good news about the eschatological imminence of God's reign (1:14–15). This initial call informs every subsequent call to believe. Jesus goes on to manifest the good news of God's inbreaking reign through his words and works, and people respond emotionally, with amazement (Mark 1:27; 2:12; 5:20, 42; 10:32; 12:17; 16:8) or fear (4:40; 5:15, 33, 36; 6:50; 9:32; 11:18) or both (10:32; 16:8). But Jesus calls for the sort of emotional response that results in belief. To respond otherwise is to fail to assess his presence and power as evidence of the inbreaking reign of God at the turn of the ages. Against Jesus's opening call to believe, we touch on episodes by which Mark maps the terrain of fear and grief.

First, when the disciples are caught in a storm and think they are about to die, Jesus asks, "Why are you afraid? Have you still no faith?" (4:40). The disciples' assessment of the deadly storm triggers their emotion of fear (*deilos*), which generates unbelief (cf. 6:50). But Jesus demonstrates that they have mis-assessed the storm as a threat because they have mis-assessed him. His act to calm the storm forces the disciples to reassess the situation. The change in language may prompt the audience to recognize the disciples' emotional shift from being *deilos* (afraid/cowardly)[49] to expressing *phobos* (fear/awe), as they wonder, "Who then is this?" (4:41). The audience may think at this point that the disciples will build a right assessment of Jesus, but subsequent episodes unfold how they become mired in the misunderstanding of his words and works.

Just after Jesus calms the storm, his reversal of death stimulates an emotional response of fear that leads to a clear action of avoidance (5:1–20). People from the Decapolis see a good-as-dead demoniac, whom no one could help, sitting clothed and in his right mind. They respond

---

48   Mark also ties fear to reverence (Herod fears John the Baptist and responds by protecting him, 6:20) and the threat of danger (the religious leaders fear the crowd and respond with inactivity in 11:18, 32; 12:12).

49   *Deilos* consistently means "cowardly" or "worthless" in classical and Koine texts. See, e.g., Rev 21:8.

to this demonstration of God's inbreaking reign with fear (*phobeō*) and ask Jesus to leave (5:15, 17). By contrast, when the healed man wishes to follow him, Jesus sends him instead to go and proclaim to his own "how much the Lord has done", and when he does, "everyone was amazed [*thaumazō*]" (5:19, 20).

This brings us to a central passage, in which the emotions of *fear* and *grief* appear together, where Mark intercalates the account of Jesus's healing of the hemorrhaging woman into the account of Jesus's raising of Jairus daughter (5:21–43). For Jairus, the threat of his daughter's death sparks actions that signify worship and trust in Jesus's power to restore. Prostrating himself, he places his hopes for his daughter's salvation (*sōzō*) and life (*zaō*) explicitly in Jesus's hands (5:23).

The outworking of this belief is interrupted by a touch Jesus receives (rather than bestows) mid-commute to Jairus's home. When the woman who touches him recognizes her healing, she approaches (*erchomai*) Jesus in fear (*phobos*) and trembling (*tremō*, verbal form of *tromos*), kneels before him, and tells him "the whole truth" (5:33; cf. Ps 2:11). This woman, in response to the stimulus of her miraculous healing, experiences the emotion of fear that propels her to move *towards Jesus* rather than to avoid or run. According to Jesus, her *faith* has healed her.

Against her story, the narration is refocused on Jairus when he hears of his daughter's death. The words of messengers from his own household offer Jairus an opposing logic: What more can "the teacher" offer now that his daughter is dead (5:35)? This disastrous news stimulates the sort of fear that threatens the steadfastness of the belief Jairus showed at first. Jesus overhears the messengers' assessment of death, and tells Jairus, "Do not fear, only believe" (5:36). The mourners at Jairus's home escalate the commotion by wailing as an emotional expression of grief, in response to this death (5:38). Against cultural norms, Mark's audience would expect such emotion; however, Mark's narration affords a reassessment. In light of God's inbreaking reign, Jesus says that Jairus's daughter might as well be sleeping (5:39). Yet the mourners' scoffing reaction reveals an entrenched mis-assessment of Jesus's presence and power (5:40). It is only at the conclusion, when Jairus and his wife respond in amazement,[50] that they join the ranks of the faithful woman who rightly assessed Jesus's saving power.

After this, Mark weaves the emotion of fear into the responses of Jesus's disciples to various stimuli, explicitly and implicitly. For

---

[50] Mark's description of their amazement is excessive, lit., "They were amazed (*exestēsan*) with great (*megalē*) amazement (*ekstasei*)" (5:42).

instance, when the disciples are in the boat again, after Jesus feeds the multitude, they see a form (Jesus) walking on the water. The narrator explains that they suppose he is a ghost. Their cry in response (*anakrazō*) is closely followed by a bodily response that accompanies fear: "for they all saw him and were terrified [*tarassō*]" until Jesus encourages them to take heart and not to fear (6:50). This cascade of textual cues indicates that terror is the likely (narratively and culturally available) emotion associated with the perplexing experience of encountering a beloved teacher in an unrecognizable state. This time, Jesus's self-revelation offers a new perception without altering their emotion, and the narrator explains why: "they were utterly astounded [or, confused] [*existēmi*] for they did not understand about the loaves, but their hearts were hardened" (6:51–52).

Then, in Mark 9:2–8, Jesus's innermost circle of three followers, Peter, James, and John, accompany him to the high mountain where he is transfigured (*metamorphoō*) before them. A combination of unnerving factors (Jesus's changed appearance, unearthly white clothing, Moses's and Elijah's presence) results in Peter's fumbling suggestion that they should set up tents for the three worthies (9:5). This response is inadequate, as the narrator explains with an aside: "He did not know what to say, for they were terrified [*ekphobos*]" (verse 6).

Later, after Jesus predicts his passion for a third time, his mere presence provokes an emotional response: "They were on the road, going up to Jerusalem, and Jesus was walking ahead of them; they were amazed [*thambeō*], and those who followed were afraid [*phobeō*]" (10:32).

When the disciples finally flee upon Jesus's arrest (14:50–52; cf. verses 26–31), Mark's readers would recognize a response of fear, due to cultural knowledge of "fear" and Mark's repetition of the disciples' imperception, hard hearts, amazement, and fear, leading up to this point.[51]

THE SHORT ENDING: MARK 15:40–16:8

The final episode properly begins in 15:40, where the narrator names women who act as characters for the first time:[52] Mary Magdalene, Mary the mother of James and Joses, and Salome. Into the account of

---

51   Another time it would be fruitful to explore other episodes in which cultural and textual knowledge would have stimulated Mark's readers to recognize fear even when the language does not explicitly appear.

52   Mark has named Mary, the mother of Jesus (6:3), but she does not act as a character. Also, Mark names Herodias (6:17, 19, 22) who is present in a tangential flashback sequence.

their activity (15:40–41, 47; 16:1–8), Mark intercalates the account of Jesus's burial (15:42–46). This "sandwich" reveals that Jesus's disciples fail to appear even now to bury their master (compare 6:29), while the women risk their safety to watch Jesus's crucifixion, albeit from a distance, and anoint his body at the tomb.

The narrator supplies details to characterize the women: they "used to follow [Jesus] and provided for him when he was in Galilee; and there were many other women who had come up with him to Jerusalem" (15:40–41). Textual cues alert us to integrate what we know from Mark's telling so far. First, this characterization reveals that the three are among a larger group of women who have been among Jesus's disciples all along. Those who reread the Gospel may now notice women in the margins (e.g., 3:31–35; 4:10; 8:34; 10:32, 46). But now the narrator singles out three (and names them three times!), just as he earlier and repeatedly singled out Peter, James, and John from among the Twelve. To recall these three disciples at the naming of the three women suggests how an audience can keep elements in mind over the course of a narrative. This analogical patterning suggests that the women take the role of the displaced disciples. The language that describes their actions reinforces this impression, for they have "followed" and "served" Jesus. This language would likely evoke a mental model of "disciple," since the word "follow" (akoloutheō) was used as stock language for discipleship in early Christian discourse and throughout Mark's narrative (1:18; 2:14, 15; 6:1; 8:34; 9:38; 10:21, 28, 32, 52). Moreover, their habit to "serve" (diakoneō) adds to this image if the reader recalls Jesus's teaching that service is the essence of followership (10:43–45, especially verse 45).

Because the description of the women and the disciples is analogous, the previous characterization of the Twelve provides additional data to characterize the women by comparison. We may remember how the disciples began following Jesus well, embracing his mission through initial opposition (1:16–3:30), receiving the secrets of God's kingdom with Jesus's special teaching (4:10–20), experiencing transformed fear when Jesus calmed the storm (4:35–40), and obeying his authorization to preach and cast out demons (3:14–15; 6:7–13, 30). Nevertheless, their understanding progressively diminishes until they openly resist Jesus's mission (8:27–10:45; esp. 8:32; 9:38–42; 10:13–14, 35–45), and finally abandon and deny him (14:50, 66–72; cf. 14:27–31). By contrast, the women follow Jesus from Galilee to Golgotha.

For a moment, the women raise our expectations that someone might assess Jesus rightly, that someone might follow him well; but their experience at the tomb exposes this misperception. Since the women have followed Jesus throughout Galilee and to Jerusalem, we surmise that they have heard him predict his suffering, death, and resurrection. Yet they go to the tomb expecting to find a dead body on the very day Jesus said he would be raised. When they find the stone rolled away and a young man with supernatural features, they are alarmed (*ekthambeō*, 16:6). Their agitation increases at the young man's announcement that the crucified Jesus is not there because he has been raised (verse 7). Finally, they receive the command to go and tell, but instead, they flee (*pheugō*) because "trembling [*tromos*] and astonishment [*ekstasis*] had seized them," and they say nothing "for they were afraid [*phobeō*]" (16:8). These conventional elements characterize the sort of fear/terror that classical and Jewish literature deplores and which Mark's prior narrative associates with unbelief. The combination of language reinforces their fear, so intense that their bodies convulse, and they are compelled to run. Instead of meeting our expectations, the women not only replicate the disciples' response but also escalate it (compare the description of their flight in 14:50).

Although the women's loyalty and service to Jesus make them sympathetic figures initially, our consideration of both extratextual and textual data confirms that they quickly join their shameful brothers in mis-assessing and, as a result, abandoning Jesus. Thus, in this one final scene, 15:40–16:8, Mark repeats the upward and downward progression of discipleship that has unfolded throughout the entire narrative.

Mark's narrative ends with a sense of completion, if not satisfaction, by drawing together Jesus's predictions that he would suffer, die, and *rise* with his scripture-based promise to meet his disciples in Galilee after he is *risen*, reinforcing the importance of *sight*. Yet the women's emotion-filled response to these stimuli leaves the audience with a sense of irresolution that may compel them to evaluate the women's roads of emotions and actions against the map of fear that has led up to this point.[53] This map includes not only the sort of fear/terror that generates unbelief and flight, but also the sort of fear/awe that generates belief and reverence in response to manifestations of God's reign. The experience of processing the emotions at the end of the narrative may have helped actual ancient audiences to interpret and

---

[53]   For arguments that ancient rhetoric and cognitive theory help explain Mark's abrupt ending, see Elizabeth E. Shively, "Recognizing Penguins: Audience Expectation, Cognitive Genre Theory, and the Ending of Mark's Gospel," *CBQ* 80 (2018): 273–92; Kelly Iverson, "A Postmodern Riddle? Gaps, Inferences and Mark's Abrupt Ending," *JSNT* 44 (2022): 337–67.

re-evaluate their own emotions in response to a crucified and risen Jesus whom they have never seen but whose improbable good news they are called to believe in the face of adversity. Such an audience might perhaps remember Jesus's words, "Do not fear, only believe," and respond, "I believe, help my unbelief!"

THE LONG ENDING: MARK 16:9–20

The writer of the LE responds to that fear and its accompanying action of flight which silences the proclamation that Jesus is raised. The passage moves through three parallel episodes that evoke a sense of progressive intensity, culminating in Jesus's rebuke and commission of the disciples.

First, Mary returns to the scene in the early moments of Sunday morning, but this time alone and is singled out as first ("he appeared first [prōtos] to Mary Magdalene," verse 9).[54] Her actions going forward show that she has abandoned her fear because she fulfils the requisite mission to "go, tell" (hypagete eipate, 16:7, 10). This narrator does not reveal Mary's emotional response to Jesus's appearance but focuses instead on her immediate action of sharing with Jesus's disciples the news of her encounter ("they heard that he was alive and had been seen by her," verse 11). An audience that reads this as a *Markan* ending might see Jesus's appearance as the thing that compelled Mary to reassess the object of her fear so that she no longer avoids her call.

The disciples receive Mary's report while they are "mourning and weeping" (penthousin kai klaiousin; verse 10). As we have noted, Jewish scripture and tradition describe grief as appropriate to dire circumstances, and Mark's Gospel includes instances of grief, such as Peter in the courtyard ("he broke down and wept [klaiō]," 14:72) and Jesus in Gethsemane and on the cross (14:34; 15:34). From a certain perspective, then, the disciples' grief might be viewed as the appropriate reaction to a death. But the combined phrase, "mourning and weeping," recalls Jesus's response to those who mourned and wept at the death of Jairus's daughter, reinforcing the recognition that the disciples' grief is entirely misplaced in response to *Jesus's* death. Their emotional response stands in resistance to the good news of God's promised reign, according to which Jesus said he would rise (8:31; 9:31; 10:33–34). Despite Mary Magdalene's message, which could have

---

[54]   For an extended discussion of Mary Magdalene's characterization, see Lyons-Pardue, *Gospel Women*, 49–75.

changed the disciples' assessment of the object of their grief, they reject her testimony to Jesus's resurrection: "they would not believe it [*ēpistēsan*]" (16:11).

In the second scene, two disciples from among the larger grieving and unbelieving group encounter Jesus "in another form [*en hetera morphē*]" (v. 12), one that resonates with two prior episodes. Earlier, in 6:47–52, the darkness and windy conditions combined to present Jesus in an altered form when he walked on the sea, and his disciples failed to recognize him for fear. Then, in 9:2–8, Peter, James, and John accompanied Jesus to the high mountain where he was transfigured (*metamorphoō*) before them, and they were terrified (*ekphoboi*) (verse 6).[55] Readers building an integrated character model of the disciples, afforded by the preceding narrative, might expect them to respond in fear. But the LE does not repeat the expected emotion. Instead, the two simply fulfill the prescribed response to the proof of Jesus's resurrection: they go (*apelthontes*) and tell (*apēngeilan*) (16:13).

Third, Jesus appears to the eleven disciples and reproaches them for their unbelief (*apistia*) and hardheartedness (*sklērokardia*), *because* they did not believe (*ouk episteusan*) the witnesses to his resurrection (16:14). By the time we get through Jesus's censure, references to unbelief pile high: "they would not believe [*ēpistēsan*]" Mary's report (16:11); "neither did they believe (the two witnesses)" (*oude ekeinois episteusan*; 16:13); Jesus chides them for "their lack of faith" (*tēn apistian autōn*) and, specifically, the fact that "they had not believed" (*ouk episteusan*) the eyewitness testimony (16:14). Moreover, the three scenes of the LE build on the SE by showing that *everyone* responds to witnesses with unbelief and failure to act (Mary with the other women, the two disciples, and the larger group). But when they *see the risen Jesus*, they abandon improper emotions, they believe (we surmise), and they tell the good news. The actual audience of the LE, like that of the SE, has not seen the risen Jesus, and so the repetition of unbelief leading up to Jesus's rebuke could seek to combat any continuing resistance to believing *without* seeing (cf. John 20:29).

Finally, the secrecy that Jesus so frequently commanded across the Gospel (e.g., 1:25, 34, 44; 3:12; 5:43), with rare exceptions (i.e., 5:19–20), is now unequivocally reversed in the LE's expansive commission. Even followers who had redoubled their disbelief and obduracy, manifesting

---

[55]   Cf. Synoptic parallels in which the disciples' emotional response follows the overshadowing cloud, rather than the change in Jesus's appearance (Matt 17:4–6; Luke 9:32–34).

hard hearts and imperception, are commissioned to proclaim the good news. At Jesus's concluding commission and promise, the disciples' future is forecast into the whole creation, new and distant spaces wherein potential dangers lurk. The "signs" that accompany those who believe will replicate those that Jesus's followers previously performed, like exorcising demons (16:17; see 3:15; 6:7, 13; cf. 9:18) and healing the sick (16:18; see 6:13). But other signs cross into new and even deadly territory, like speaking in new languages (16:17), drinking poison, and handling snakes (16:18). We may again hear echoes of Jesus's encouragement to Jairus: "Do not be afraid; only believe" (5:36). Finally, the Eleven's prospective actions align directly with the patterns established and reinforced by the first three witnesses to the resurrected Jesus: they go and tell.

CONCLUSION

Emotions influence audiences. Aristotle speaks of the role of emotions in persuasion: "The emotions are all those affections which cause men to change their opinion in regard to their judgements."[56] Similarly, cognitive science research shows that literature enhances emotions through identification.

> We put aside our day-to-day concerns and insert the protagonists' goals into our own planning processors – we take on their intentions as our own – and experience emotions related to what happens in the story. The emotions are empathetic.[57]

Similarly, the experience of identifying emotionally with the women in the SE can help all actual audiences understand and interpret their own emotions with their accompanying actions and consequences. The LE suggests how one later reading community did it. But the narrative with its endings will have a different metacognitive significance for today's readers, because of differences in situation, culture, values, and practices. Nevertheless, both ancient and modern audiences may share in the implications of Mark's key challenge, which is that the good news of Jesus's resurrection is to be met not with emotions that generate unbelief and inaction, but with emotions that elicit reverence, belief, and proclamation.

---

[56]   Arist. *Rhet.*1378a.
[57]   Oatley and Johnson-Laird, "Cognitive Approaches," 136.

SELECTED FURTHER READING

Bal, Mieke. *Narratology: Introduction to the Theory of Narrative*. 3rd edition. Toronto: University of Toronto Press, 2009.

Bond, Helen K. *The First Biography of Jesus: Genre and Meaning in Mark's Gospel*. Grand Rapids: Eerdmans, 2020.

Camery-Hoggatt, Jerry. *Irony in Mark's Gospel*. SNTSMS 72. Cambridge: Cambridge University Press, 1991.

Dewey, Joanna. "The Literary Structure of the Controversy in Mark 2:1–3:6." *JBL* 92 (1973): 394–401.

Heubenthal, Sandra. *Reading Mark's Gospel as a Text from Collective Memory*. Grand Rapids: Eerdmans, 2020.

Iverson, Kelly. "A Postmodern Riddle? Gaps, Inferences and Mark's Abrupt Ending." *JSNT* 44 (2022): 337–67.

Jannidis, Fotis. "Character." Pages 30–45 in *Handbook of Narratology* 1. Edited by Peter Hühn et al. Berlin: De Gruyter, 2014.

Konstan, David. *The Emotions of the Ancient Greeks: Studies in Aristotle and Classical Literature*. Toronto: University of Toronto Press, 2016.

Kintsch, Walter. *Comprehension: A Paradigm for Cognition*. Cambridge: Cambridge University Press, 1998.

Larsen, Matthew D. C. *Gospels Before the Book*. Oxford: Oxford University Press, 2018.

Lyons-Pardue, Kara J. *Gospel Women and the Long Ending of Mark*. LNTS 614. T&T Clark, 2020.

Malbon, Elizabeth Struthers. *Mark's Jesus: Characterization as Narrative Christology*, Waco, TX, Baylor University Press, 2009.

Malbon, Elizabeth Struthers. *In the Company of Jesus: Characters in Mark's Gospel*. Louisville, KY: Westminster John Knox Press, 2000.

Mequita, Batia and J. Leu, "Cultural Influences on Emotion: Established Patterns and Emerging Trends." Pages 292–318 in *Handbook of Cultural Psychology*. Edited by Dov Cohen and Shinobu Kitayama. 2nd edition. New York: Guilford, 2019.

Moloney, Francis J. *The Gospel of Mark: A Commentary*. Peabody, MA: Hendrickson, 2002.

Oatley, Keith and P. N. Johnson-Laird. "Cognitive Approaches to Emotions." *TICS* 18 (2014): 134–140.

Phelan, James. *Narrative as Rhetoric: Technique, Audiences, Ethics, Ideology*. Columbus: Ohio State University Press, 1996.

Powell, Mark Allan. "Narrative Criticism: The Emergence of a Prominent Reading Strategy," Pages 19–44 in *Mark as Story: Retrospect and Prospect*. Edited by Kelly R. Iverson and Chris R. Skinner. SBRLS 65. Atlanta: SBL, 2011.

Powell, Samuel M. *The Impassioned Life: Reason and Emotion in the Christian Tradition*. Minneapolis: Fortress, 2016.

Rhoads, David M. "*Narrative Criticism and the Gospel of Mark*," *JAAR* L/3 (1982): 411–34.

Rhoads, David M., Donald Michie, and Joanna Dewey *Mark as Story: The Introduction to the Narrative of a Gospel*. 3rd edition. Philadelphia: Fortress, 2012.

Rüggemeier, Jan and Elizabeth E. Shively (eds.). "Cognitive Linguistics and New Testament Narrative: Investigating Methodology through Characterization."

Special Issue of *Biblical Interpretation: A Journal of Contemporary Approaches* 29 (2021).

Ryan, Marie-Laure. "Towards a Definition of Narrative." Pages 22–35 in *Cambridge Companion to Narrative*. Edited by David Herman. Cambridge: Cambridge University, 2007.

Schneider, Ralf. "Toward a Cognitive Theory of Literary Character: The Dynamics of Mental-Model Construction." *Style* 35 (2001).

Shively, Elizabeth E. "Israel's Scriptures in Mark." Pages 236–62 in *The Old Testament in the New: Israel's Scriptures in the New Testament and other Early Christian Writings*. Edited by David N. Lincicum and Matthias Henze. Grand Rapids: Eerdmans, forthcoming.

Shively, Elizabeth E. "The Eclipse of the Markan Narrative: On the (Re) Cognition of a Coherent Story and Implications for Genre." *EC* 12 (2021): 369–87.

Shively, Elizabeth E. "Recognizing Penguins: Audience Expectation, Cognitive Genre Theory, and the Ending of Mark's Gospel." *CBQ* 80 (2018): 273–92.

Shepherd, Tom. *Markan Sandwich Stories*. Berrien Springs, MI: Andrews University Press, 1993.

Sternberg, Meir. *Poetics of Biblical Narrative: Ideological Literature and the Drama of Reading*. Bloomington, IN: Indiana University Press, 1985.

Stockwell, Peter. *Cognitive Poetics: An Introduction*. 2nd edition. London and New York: Routledge, 2019.

Walsh, Jerome T. *Style and Structure in Biblical Hebrew Narrative*. Collegeville, MN: Liturgical Press, 2001.

12 Luke's Gospel as a Narrative of Reconciliation

RAJ NADELLA

Addressed to a recipient with a Greek name, Theophilus, the book of Luke is the longest document in the New Testament, and presumably written to a predominantly Gentile audience. The gospel is the story of a Jewish messiah who lived and ministered primarily within the Jewish context, but with implications for all people. This essay discusses key aspects of Luke's narrative, and especially the parable of the prodigal son that forms the centerpiece of the central section of Luke's narrative (chapters 10–19). A literary analysis of this parable inquires if the history of Israel (with the tropes of inheritance, rebellion, exile in a distant land, and restoration) is refracted in the account of the younger son, and if, likewise, the story of all people is evocatively portrayed in this multilayered section of the book of Luke.

INTRODUCTION

The gospel of Luke stands out for its literary artistry and sophisticated storyline. Readers of the gospel quickly notice that it is an engaging narrative that draws them into its story world and keeps them engaged until the end. The gospel features complex and interesting characters, lively depictions of their actions and interactions with each other, and a well-crafted plot. Individual stories in the gospel move the plot forward at a brisk pace and reveal the various dimensions of characters. The narrator knows the characters well, is attentive to their emotions, and gives readers a window into their inner world, allowing them to connect with characters on a deeper level. The gospel often juxtaposes the actions of various central characters in ways that highlight their character traits for the readers.[1] Luke might not exactly read like a page-turner, but there are few dull moments in the gospel.

---

[1] Charles H. Talbert, *Reading Luke: A Literary and Theological Commentary on the Third Gospel* (Macon: Smyth & Helwys Publishing, 2013), 15–16.

Despite such fascinating literary aspects that make Luke a great candidate for narrative-critical analysis, historical critical approaches have been the prism through which biblical scholars analyzed Luke's gospel, as well as other canonical gospels, for much of the nineteenth and twentieth centuries. In his groundbreaking book *Literary Criticism and the Gospels: The Theoretical Challenge*, Stephen D. Moore calls attention to the sway historical criticism held on the gospel studies for centuries in the field of biblical studies as a whole.[2] Some scholars like Marianne Bonz have noted that Luke's gospel and the book of Acts resemble Greco-Roman epics such as Homer's *Odyssey* and Virgil's *Aeneid* in literary aspects such as travels undertaken by the protagonist, divine mission, and reversal of fortunes.[3]

Historical critical methods focus primarily on the social, cultural, and political contexts in which biblical texts were written, as well as on questions of authorship and authorial intent. They seek to reconstruct the world of biblical texts, or the world behind the text, with the goal of shedding light on various aspects of that world, the factors that facilitated the writing of the book, and potential intentions of author(s) who produced the texts. Related to these methods are approaches such as text criticism that explore textual variations and ideological and theological implications of those variations. In a similar way, redaction criticism analyzes editorial changes from one gospel to the next in a chronological fashion. Since these approaches examine developments and changes in biblical texts over a period of time, such analyses of texts are referred to as diachronic approaches. Until recently, and still to this day in some circles, these methods have been considered the hallmark of sophisticated biblical scholarship.

NARRATIVE CRITICISM: AN EXPLORATION OF THE WORLD WITHIN THE TEXT

In the last thirty years, however, there has been growing interest in literary approaches to biblical texts. Narrative criticism, a subset of literary approaches, has increasingly gained traction, especially in gospel studies.[4]

---

[2]   Stephen D. Moore, *Literary Criticism and the Gospels: The Theoretical Challenge* (New Haven: Yale University Press, 1989), xiii.

[3]   Marianne Palmer Bonz, *The Past as Legacy: Luke-Acts and Ancient Epic* (Minneapolis: Fortress, 2000).

[4]   Although scholars like Powell consider narrative criticism a subset of reader-response criticism. See Mark Allan Powell, *Chasing the Easter Star: Adventures in Reader-Response Criticism* (Louisville: Westminster John Knox, 2001), 63.

Narrative criticism focuses on aspects within biblical texts such as the plot, characterization, point of view, narrator, and irony. Narrative criticism takes the gospel narrative and its various components on their own terms and attempts to derive meaning from the text itself. It analyzes various characters in the story and their interactions with each other and treats the story within the text as a complete and self-sufficient world. Within this approach, the text is "presumed to be the unique and privileged source of meaning, with 'meaning' available to the interpreter only by means of careful attention to its language and structure."[5] Attention also shifts from authorial intent to meaning within biblical texts and implications of the text(s) for current contexts. Although narrative critics set aside historical-critical questions, their exploration of biblical texts at times relies upon knowledge of historical contexts in which texts were written. As Mark Allan Powell has noted, "narrative criticism does not seek to determine what the story teaches about the world that produced it but rather uses knowledge about that world to determine the effect the story is expected to have on its implied readers."[6] The focus is no longer on who wrote the text, why, and in which contexts, but rather on what is occurring within the world of the text and what the text means to readers. There is, however, an implicit acknowledgment of subjectivity that the reader brings to the text in the construction of meaning.

While many of the questions explored by historical critical approaches might be essential for understanding the various contexts that engendered gospel texts, narrative critics ask different questions of biblical texts and open up new possibilities for exploring them. The focus is primarily on what the text means rather than on what the author intended. Narrative critics explore how characters interact with each other within the story world rather than how individuals within a specific historical context might have interacted with each other. They are attentive to the ways a story insists that we enter its story world and engage it on its terms. As Teresa Bridgeman puts it, "the rules that govern those structures may or may not resemble those of the readers' world."[7] Rather than compare gospel accounts with earlier ones in order to trace the development of traditions, as redaction critics might do, narrative critics read each gospel as an independent entity with its

---

[5] Joel B. Green, "Narrative Criticism," in *Methods for Luke*, ed. Joel B. Green (Cambridge: Cambridge University Press, 2010), 74–75.

[6] Powell, *Chasing the Easter Star*, 117.

[7] Teresa Bridgeman, "Time and Space," in *The Cambridge Companion to Narrative*, ed. David Herman (Cambridge: Cambridge University Press, 2007), 52.

own meaning and significance. Since these narrative critical approaches treat biblical narratives as complete units with their own meaning and without needing to be analyzed vis-à-vis other books, they are often referred to as synchronic approaches.[8]

Gospel texts, however, are not the sole proprietors or producers of meaning. Meaning emerges when readers encounter and respond to texts and is often shaped by the specific contexts and unique points of view that readers bring. The unique questions each reader or reading group brings to the text invariably influence interpretations and their implications for communities who interpret them in modern contexts. More recently, gospel narratives are being read in light of current issues of our time in ways that bring texts alive in powerful ways and shed new light on those issues. Sharon Jacob's analysis of birth narratives that explores the character of Mary as a surrogate mother in the Indian context is especially illustrative.[9]

Moore skillfully describes the recent popularity of literary criticism in biblical studies, its impact on the field, and the new avenues it offers for explicating texts. He laments the outsider treatment literary criticism continues to receive, despite recent strides, and notes that it is deemed not scholarly enough because of its insufficient attention to historical critical issues. As Joel Green notes, some scholars might describe narrative critical approaches as "the flight from history" because of their proclivity to deemphasize questions of historicity.[10] Such a characterization presumes the priority of historical critical approaches and the questions they pose of biblical texts. Moore points out that literary approaches were actually part of gospel studies long before the dominance of historical methods. As he notes, literary criticism "has been a component of biblical criticism almost since its inception,"[11] and the questions raised by literary critics have always been an integral part of biblical exploration. He further argues that, ironically, it was historical criticism that used to be foreign territory to biblical studies when literary criticism was the defining paradigm. In that sense, biblical scholars who were drawn to historical critical methods and abandoned literary approaches had gone astray from home, much like the younger son in the parable of the prodigal son (Luke 15). As Moore puts it, "great

---

[8] However, the two sets of methodologies – diachronic and synchronic – do overlap at times.

[9] Sharon Jacob, *Reading Mary Alongside Indian Surrogate Mothers: Violent Love, Oppressive Liberation, and Infancy Narratives* (London: Palgrave Macmillan, 2015).

[10] Joel B. Green, "Narrative Criticism," 86.

[11] Moore, Literary Criticism and the Gospels, xv.

famine has arisen in that land,"[12] resulting in a resurgence of interest in literary critical readings thereby returning biblical interpretation closer to its original methodological home. Seen this way, biblical scholars returning to narrative criticism is analogous to the prodigal son's return to his parental home. The son was lured away but returned home when he came to his senses.

NARRATIVE CRITICISM AND THE GOSPEL OF LUKE

Since the 1980s, the gospel of Luke has become a fertile ground for narrative critics exploring biblical texts. Jack Dean Kingsbury's *Conflict in Luke: Jesus, Authorities, Disciples* and Robert Tannehill's *The Narrative Unity of Luke-Acts* were among the earliest examples of narrative critical approaches to Luke. Kingsbury's reading of Luke as a narrative explored how the conflict between Jesus and the elite drives the plot in the gospel and gets progressively worse.[13] Tannehill's two-volume work was a full-fledged narrative critical exploration of the gospel of Luke and the book of Acts, but it also highlighted how the gospel and Acts are connected to each other as a single narrative by themes, plot, point of view, and a coherent narrative.[14] Stories in Luke often refer to and build upon stories from the Hebrew Scriptures. Luke deftly weaves in narrative elements from Greco-Roman literary traditions but also presents the gospel narrative as a historical account contemporaneous with Roman history in ways that have theological implications. Luke presents the story of Jesus as a parallel, albeit a superior one, to the story of the Roman Empire.

Luke's gospel contains key narrative features such as reversals, complex characters, conflicts, divergent perspectives, and unresolved stories. Many of the stories stand out not so much because of what they reveal about characters or for resolving the plot, but because of what they leave open-ended. The gospel features disparate, and at times contradictory, perspectives on various issues that occur prominently in the gospel. These complex characters, unpredictability of plot, lack of a singular voice, and the unfinalizable nature of many stories make Luke a sophisticated narrative and a fascinating read. Much of the gospel, especially the central section, is characterized by

---

[12]   Moore, Literary Criticism and the Gospels, xiv.
[13]   Jack Dean Kingsbury, *Conflict in Luke: Jesus, Authorities, Disciples* (Minneapolis: Fortress, 1991).
[14]   Robert C. Tannehill, *The Narrative Unity of Luke-Acts: A Literary Interpretation, Vol. 1: The Gospel According to Luke* (Minneapolis: Fortress, 1991).

the motif of travel. The gospel often contains prolepsis – a foreshadowing of what is yet to occur – and analepsis – a look back at what has already occurred.[15]

REVERSALS

Luke's gospel contains a number of stories in which characters experience reversal of fortunes, at times with life-changing implications. The first chapter of the gospel highlights a reversal of fortune for Zechariah and Mary. Zechariah, a priest and a person of privilege, loses his ability to speak because of his unwillingness to believe an angelic proclamation about John's birth. On the contrary, Mary, a person of lowly social and economic status, is exalted based on her positive response to an angelic proclamation about the birth of Jesus. The "Magnificat" attributed to Mary anticipates a reversal of fortunes on a universal scale by calling for a downfall of the mighty and elevation of the lowly. Along those lines, Mitzi Smith's reading of Mary's song highlights how Mary, a doula at the very margins of society, becomes the mother of the savior and God's son.[16] Mitzi Smith and Yung Suk Kim highlight how Luke's narratives present the various reversals as part of the phenomenon of the impossible becoming possible.[17]

The reversals have life-changing political and economic implications for the characters involved, and the gospel presents them as harbingers of the new movement initiated by Jesus, the central character in Luke's story. This motif of reversal becomes evident in several other parts of the gospel, such as the Beatitudes (Luke 6) that proclaim relief for the oppressed and woes to the elite. The parable of the great banquet (Luke 14) highlights how the elite, the originally invited guests, failed to participate in the great banquet, forcing the host to extend it to those at the margins of society. Perhaps the most dramatic reversal in Luke's gospel occurs in the story of Lazarus and the rich man (Luke 16), where the grand reversal of fortunes occurs after the death of both central characters and extends into the heavens and the netherworld.

[15]   R. Alan Culpepper, *Anatomy of the Fourth Gospel: A Study in Literary Design* (Minneapolis: Fortress, 1987).

[16]   Mitzi J. Smith, "Abolitionist Messiah: A Man Named Jesus Born of a Doule," in *Bitter the Chastening Rod: Africana Biblical Interpretation after Stony the Road We Trod in the Age of BLM, SayHerName, and Me Too*, eds. Mitzi J. Smith, Angela N. Parker, and Ericka S. Dunbar Hill (New York: Fortress Academic, 2023), 55–56.

[17]   Mitzi J. Smith and Yung Suk Kim, *Toward Decentering the New Testament: A Reintroduction* (Eugene: Cascade Books, 2018), 143–46.

Mikhail Bakhtin, a twentieth-century Russian literary critic, explicated the motif of carnivalesque in the sixteenth-century world of Francois Rabelais, where kings and clowns traded places for a short period of time.[18] During these carnivals, kings and royals were ridiculed as fools, but those at the margins were celebrated as royals and seated on thrones. Such reversals that often feature roles blur boundaries between the mighty and the lowly, albeit for a day. Bakhtin applied the concept of carnival, or topsy-turvy world, to literature to shed light on the reversals that occur in the story world. Many of the reversals in Luke's gospel are similar to Bakhtin's concept of carnivalesque, but they are also different in significant ways. The carnival reversals in the world of Rabelais were temporary, had few definitive implications for existing power structures, and were often performed with the permission of those in power with the result that oppressive structures remained firmly intact. On the contrary, the reversals in Luke are permanent, undermine the interests of those in power, and are often carried out against their wishes.

PLOT, CHARACTERS, AND CONFLICT IN LUKE

Jack Dean Kingsbury reads the gospel of Luke primarily as a narrative that is characterized and driven by conflict. He explores how the conflict in Luke plays out between Jesus and the political and religious elite and moves the plot of the gospel forward.[19] There is a close interplay between plot and characters in this gospel. The plot reveals the various dimensions of characters and the various facets of characters in turn add to the complexity of the plot and move it forward. Readers of Arundhati Roy's The God of Small Things might remember how the omniscient narrator allows the readers a window into the complex emotions of joy, confusion, and anger experienced by main characters like Velutha, the carpenter.[20] In a similar fashion, Luke frequently narrates characters' emotions such as anger and compassion that move the plot forward. The gospel runs primarily on the strength of plot and characters.

Narrative critics typically divide characters into two types based on their traits: flat characters and round characters. Flat characters are those that exhibit fairly consistent traits throughout the narrative and

[18]   Mikhail Bakhtin, Rabelais and His World (Bloomington: Indiana University Press, 1984), 197–98.

[19]   Jack Dean Kingsbury, Conflict in Luke, 34–36.

[20]   Arundhati Roy, The God of Small Things (New York: Random House, 2008).

have little proclivity or even capacity for change as the story unfolds. Flat characters tend to be predictable in how they might respond in a given situation or conversation. Round characters, on the other hand, have complex character traits that evolve and change as the story unfolds. In his narrative critical reading of Mark's gospel, David Rhoads observes that the disciples in Mark are round characters, given the ways in which they evolve during the course of the narrative, but the authorities are flat characters.[21] Akin to characters in the novels of Charles Dickens, especially Ebenezer Scrooge, Luke's characters are complex, evolve in the course of the story, and refuse to be defined in simplistic terms. Dickens' characters often act unpredictably in ways that surprise the readers and define the trajectory of the novel. Many of the characters in Luke are round characters that act in complex, ambiguous ways and evolve during the course of the narrative.

MOTIF OF TRAVEL IN LUKE'S NARRATIVE

The motif of travel that occurs prominently in the parable of the prodigal son is a key aspect of Luke's narrative that moves the story forward. In one of the opening stories, Mary travels from Nazareth in Galilee to the hill country of Judea to visit her cousin Elizabeth. Joseph and Mary travel from Nazareth to Judea to participate in the Roman census. Later, in one of the infancy accounts in the gospel, Jesus travels to Jerusalem with his parents to participate in temple worship according to his Jewish religious traditions.

Luke, more than any other gospel, depicts Jesus as a figure who often travels and offers his disciples instructions about what to carry and what not to carry with them when they travel. The central section in the gospel – chapters 9–19 – narrates Jesus traveling from Galilee to Jerusalem. The centerpiece of that central section – the parable of the prodigal son – prominently features the younger son leaving his homeland and traveling to a distant land before returning to his homeland. As Bonz has aptly observed, Luke's depiction of the travels of Jesus, the central figure in the gospel, resemble the travels of Aeneas, the central figure in *Aeneid*, as well as that of Odysseus in Homer's *Odyssey*.[22] Luke's Jesus also frequently participates in meals in a variety of settings, often with individuals outside his typical social circles. In Luke's

---

[21] David Rhoads, *Reading Mark: Engaging the Gospel* (Minneapolis: Augsburg Fortress, 2000), 80–83.

[22] Marianne Bonz, *Past as Legacy*.

depiction of Jesus, the act of breaking bread is a metaphor for breaking social barriers. It also signifies challenging political and economic
structures, a point to which I will return later.

JUXTAPOSITION AND DIALOGUE OF DISPARATE PERSPECTIVES

Luke's gospel juxtaposes characters from various social locations in
ways that highlight their disparate attributes and responses in given situations. It often contrasts male and female characters. Zechariah and
Mary are juxtaposed at the beginning of the gospel to highlight the vastly
different ways in which they respond to angelic announcements about
the births of John and Jesus. The story of the centurion and the story of
the widow who lost a son occur next to each other in Luke 7 and contrast the two characters' different social locations and the very different
ways they engage, or do not engage, with Jesus. Toward the end of chapter 24, female and male disciples exhibit vastly different responses to
the news about the resurrection of Jesus. At times, the gospel contrasts
characters of the same gender and social locations. Mary and Martha
stand out for the different ways they engage with Jesus in Luke 10. The
two brothers in Luke 15 relate to their father and family inheritance in
opposing ways.

Luke's gospel presents an array of perspectives on issues, such as
the identity of Jesus, poverty and wealth, and the importance of hearing
vs doing, that are expressed by various characters. Such perspectives
exist throughout the gospel and accentuate the complexity of the plot.
Mikhail Bakhtin introduced the concept of polyphony to articulate the
literary phenomenon of competing perspectives that manifest themselves in a novel or story. Bakhtin presented Dostoevsky's novels, especially *The Brothers Karamazov*, as an example of polyphonic literature
that generates characters with varied perspectives and places them in
dialogue with each other. The concept of polyphony does not suggest a
lack of explicit theological or ideological commitments on the author's
part. Rather, despite any commitments, the polyphonic author popu-
lates the novel with characters representing diverse perspectives on key
issues and places them in conversation with each other. Bakhtin's concept of polyphony is aesthetically profound and liberative, but is not
sufficiently attentive to potential power imbalance between different
characters. One cannot expect a character from a peripheral location
to enter into dialogue with a character from a dominant location as an
equal conversation partner.

OPEN-ENDED ENDINGS

In literary critical readings of the gospels, Mark is often highlighted as the gospel with an unresolved ending that does not provide a closure to the story.[23] Mark's ending, in the "shorter version" of 16:1–8, is ambiguous as it abruptly ends with the story of women who went to anoint Jesus's body on the first day of the week. However, Luke's gospel has numerous open-ended sections that offer no closure or resolution to a conflict, allowing for varied interpretations. Such ambiguous nature of Lukan narratives is evident in stories such as the parable of the Samaritan and the parable of the prodigal son. In his conversation with a lawyer in Luke 10, Jesus narrates a parable about a man who was robbed and beaten by bandits on the road to Jericho. In response to Jesus's question, "Who was a neighbor to the person who was beaten?" the lawyer appropriately responds by saying, "The one who helped the victim." Jesus asks the lawyer to go and do likewise. Readers might be curious to know whether the lawyer does go and do likewise, as he is advised. The narrator, however, leaves the story unresolved. Similarly, toward the end of the parable of the prodigal son, the father tries to assuage the feelings of the older son who resents the grand welcome accorded to his brother. Luke does not say whether the older brother eventually joins the party to celebrate his brother's return from a distant land but leaves it open-ended.

Such ambiguous endings defy readers' attempts to arrive at straightforward and simplistic interpretations of stories. Readers might be tempted to suggest that the lawyer likely does not go and do likewise or that the older brother does not join the party, but the stories themselves caution against such simplistic readings. Building upon Bakhtin's concept of unfinalizability, one can suggest that these characters are capable of acting in surprising ways and have yet to give their final word on the matter. Since the characters have not spoken their final word, the gospel readers – ancient or modern – should be careful not to define them in finalizing terms that fail to acknowledge their complexity.

Employing insights from reader-response criticism, one can suggest that such an open ending to these texts is an invitation to the readers to participate in the story. Reader-response criticism explores what kind of response the author might have been expecting from readers in a given story. Accordingly, the unresolved nature of parables shifts the focus from the characters in the parable to the first-century listeners

---

[23]   Donald H. Juel, *A Master of Surprise: Mark Interpreted* (Minneapolis: Fortress, 2002).

of Jesus and subsequently to the readers engaging with the gospel. Consequently, the question is no longer whether the older brother joins the party but whether readers will act graciously in similar situations. Similarly, readers should no longer judge characters in the parable of the Samaritan or the lawyer but instead are expected to decide for themselves how they might respond if they were asked to do likewise.

THE PARABLE OF THE PRODIGAL SON WITHIN THE LARGER LUKAN NARRATIVE

The parable of the prodigal son features many of the aforementioned narrative aspects in the gospel of Luke: travel motifs, round characters, contrasts, conflict, reversal of fortunes, open-endedness, and dialogue of disparate perspectives. Travel is a common theme in the gospel, and Luke sets this parable in the context of Jesus's travel from Galilee to Jerusalem in the central section of the gospel. The parable begins with the motif of travel when the younger son demands his share of the property from his father and goes to a distant land. It ends with the younger son experiencing famine and deprivation in the foreign land and traveling back to his home. It is not the travel itself but the theme of travel back home to one's family and community that characterizes this parable. Abraham Smith reads Lanston Hughes's *Not Without Laughter* in light of the parable of the prodigal son and notes powerfully that the parable offers a basic model for blues singers who travel away from home, experience harsh realities in big cities, and return home.[24]

CHARACTERIZATION AND CONFLICT IN THE PARABLE OF THE PRODIGAL SON

Mikhail Bakhtin observes that Dostoevsky knows his characters well but does not arrive at any conclusions about the actions or motives of characters like Rodion Raskolnikov, the protagonist of *Crime and Punishment*. Bakhtin's motif of unfinalizability suggests that characters have the innate ability to evolve as round, complex characters and refuse to be defined in finalizing terms.

The complexity of various characters comes to the fore as the parable of the prodigal son unfolds. In particular, the closing scene – the

---

[24]   Abraham Smith, "A Prodigal Sings the Blues: The Characterization of Harriett Williams in Langston Hughes's 'Not Without Laughter,'" in *Yet With a Steady Beat: Contemporary U.S. Afrocentric Biblical Interpretation*, ed. Randall C. Bailey (Atlanta: SBL Press, 2002), 151.

younger son's return to his home – brings out traits of various characters hitherto unseen and at odds with what has been revealed to readers. The younger son emerges as a multidimensional character with great depth to his personality. He previously acted in a rebellious and impetuous manner when he demanded his share of his father's wealth, but now turns out to be a savvy and calculative person when he realizes his predicament in a foreign land. As Levine notes, he calculates and carefully articulates in his mind how best to approach his father.

The older son also turns out to be a complex character. He has previously been obedient to the father but now challenges the father's decision to welcome the younger son and therefore his authority itself. At the start of the parable, the older son seems nonchalant about his share of the property, even as his younger sibling demands a share, but now he wants assurance that his share is intact. He has previously seen himself as the heir but now feels insecure about his status in the family.

The father character evolves in surprising ways during the course of the narrative as well. He appears to be insouciant at the start of the parable, showing few emotions even as the younger son rebels, but he expresses strong emotions toward the end when his lost son returns home.

In short, just about every character in the parable demonstrates an ability and proclivity to evolve and act in surprising ways. To build upon insights from David Rhoads, many of the characters turn out to be round characters.[25]

Conflict characterizes the parable and remains a constant throughout. The story begins with a conflict when the younger son makes a demand of the father, leading to a rupture in the relationship. To build upon H. Porter Abbott's insights, it is this conflict that sets the plot in motion and moves the story forward.[26] Sharon Ringe aptly observes that the younger son's demand for his share of the property while the father is still alive as well as his decision to go a distant land would have been deeply respectful to the father.[27] It would have been seen as a violation of the family's honor and rebellion against existing social norms and the father himself. Just as the story begins with a conflict, it also ends with a conflict between the father and older son who disapproves of the father's generous welcome of his younger brother.

[25]   Rhoads, *Reading Mark*, 80–83.
[26]   H. Porter Abbott, "Story, Plot, and Narration," in *The Cambridge Companion to Narrative*, ed. David Herman (Cambridge: Cambridge University Press, 2007), 43.
[27]   Sharon H. Ringe, *Luke* (Louisville: Westminster John Knox, 1995), 207.

The parable stands out not only for the younger son's rebellion and subsequent dire predicament in a foreign land, but also for his eventual return home. The younger son's act of "coming to himself" and the spatial dimension of returning to the father has metaphorical significance. It has the connotation of repairing and restoring personal relationships. As Scott Spencer noted, the fact that the father "orders his slaves to serve 'this son of mine' (15:24) shows that he in no way disavows the young man's filial status because of his rebellion but seeks to restore it."[28] Spencer also helpfully observes that the image of father running toward the younger son, throwing his arms around him, and kissing him upon his return reminds readers of similar actions by Esau at his reunion with Jacob (Genesis 33:1–15) and, together with the presence of sandals, robe, ring, and fatted calf, signal celebration of a restored relationship.[29] The narrator observes that the father's decision to accept his son is driven by compassion. There are other examples of compassion in Luke's gospel. The Samaritan's act of attending to the needs of the dying man is driven by compassion. Such observations about the inner feelings of characters are characteristic of Luke's omniscient narrator who establishes a rapport with readers by sharing intricate details about the emotional state of characters in the gospels.

CONTRASTS AND DIALOGUE OF DISPARATE PERSPECTIVES IN THE PARABLE

There are several contrasts in the parable. The older son's proclivity to maintain the status quo is contrasted with the younger son's decision to rebel. The two sons represent competing approaches to inheritance and competing visions of how to engage their traditions, community, and wealth. The older son who has worked closely with the father maintains family structures and contributes to the family wealth. The younger son who pursues his own dreams defies traditions and conventions, possibly challenging existing familial structures. Ringe aptly notes that the introductory statement, "There was a man who had two sons," sets the stage for the double plot line in the parable.[30] The two sons occupy two different places in the family and society, take different approaches to their status, and relate vastly differently to their father. Their decisions place them on two very different trajectories. While the older son

---

[28]   F. Scott Spencer, Luke (Grand Rapids: Eerdmans, 2019), 394.
[29]   Spencer, *Luke*, 395.
[30]   Ringe, Luke, 207.

maintains the status quo, the younger demands his share of the property and goes off to a distant land. The father does not explicitly endorse or discredit either son's approach. Akin to the polyphonic narrator in Dostoevsky's novels, the narrator, too, does not side with any of these approaches or perspectives.[31]

Ringe further helpfully notes the contrast between the promptness with which the younger son manages to have his demands granted by the father and the slow pace at which his fate plays out in a foreign land. The slow pace of the younger son's unfolding predicament away from home and every detail in it reminds readers of his prior status at home and his decision to jeopardize it. The famine the younger son experiences in the distant land stands in stark contrast to the feast and abundance at his father's home. The father's forgiveness and celebration of the younger son upon his return is contrasted with the judgmental attitude of the older son and his refusal to forgive his sibling. Such contrasting approaches and responses reflect not only the characters' varied approaches to given situations but also the author's invitation to the readers to consider the issues from various points of view and social locations.

A bigger and unresolved conflict is between the father and the older son toward the end of the story, and it pertains to their competing responses to the younger son's return. The parable contrasts the father's desire to forgive the younger son and accord him a grand welcome with the older son's complaints about such an extravagant welcome. The two disparate responses to the younger son – father and older son – represent two approaches to rebellion – forgiveness and retribution.

REVERSALS IN THE PARABLE

The younger son's return also sets in motion a series of reversals in the parable. There is a reversal in the fortunes of the younger son, but also in the older son's relationship with the father and family. The younger son was in conflict with the father and has now apparently made peace with him. In a grand reversal, the father loses his son but gains him back. However, he seemingly loses the obedient older son who now initiates a conflict with his father. The outsider, the younger son, who was distant from the father (literally and metaphorically) has now grown closer to his father. The older son who has hitherto been the insider has

---

[31]   Mikhail Bakhtin, *Problems of Dostoevsky's Poetics* (Minneapolis: University of Minnesota Press, 1984).

become the outsider, both metaphorically and literally. Toward the end of the story, the younger son is literally in the house partying, but the older son is outside the house refusing to go in.

The one who was lost has been found, but the one who has always been here is now lost. The one who was preparing to be treated as an enslaved person receives a grand welcome, but the supposedly true inheritor of the father's wealth sees himself as an enslaved person. For much of the story, a potential question on the readers' mind is whether the younger son will return to his father, but at the end of the story, an unresolved question is whether the older son will make peace with his father, go into the house, and join the party. To borrow an insight from Saddat Hassan Manto, the late Indo-Pakistani writer, the parable features a series of reversals as well as characters that blur the lines between opposites, seemingly irreconcilable components.[32]

THE PARABLE OF THE PRODIGAL AS AN OPEN-ENDED STORY

The parable ends without any closure to the story. The reconciliation between father and younger son quickly engenders a conflict between father and older son who is now protesting the father's decision to celebrate his brother's return. The story resolves one conflict – the one between the father and the younger son – but creates a new one – between the father and the older son. Will the older son respond positively to the father's attempts to mollify him and join the party? Will he see past his grievances about his younger brother and reconcile with his father and brother? Luke is silent about these questions. The omniscient narrator who knows the inner feelings of characters and often lets the readers know them does not seem to know how the story ends, or perhaps does not let the readers know.

The narrator provides closure for one story (that of the younger son) but creates a new gap (of the older son who is now protesting the father's decision). As Porter Abbott insightfully notes, a narrative "at one and the same time fills and creates gaps."[33] Building upon Lockwood's insight, Abbot asks, "What type of story [or plot] is in this gap?" and notes, "In those gaps lie the whole worlds that the art of narrative invites us either

---

[32]   Saddat Hassan Manto never wrote about this parable or any of the gospel texts, but his insights from his short stories can be helpful in interpreting gospel texts. His short story "Khol Do" is especially relevant for this parable's motif of characters that blur boundaries between contrasts.

[33]   Abbott, "Story, Plot, and Narration," 44.

to actualize or leave as possibilities."[34] The unresolved nature of this parable might not be an anomaly but the point of the story. It creates a gap, an opening, and invites readers to enter the story world and join the conversation.

Reader-response criticism, a subset of narrative criticism, focuses on how readers might be expected to respond to a specific story. Specifically, the goal of reader-response critics is to determine what response the narrator or author might have anticipated from their original readers and what strategies they might have employed to elicit such a response. If one applies reader-response criticism to this parable, Jesus's audience in Luke's narrative were invited to decide how they might respond if they were in the place of the older brother. By extension, Luke's readers – ancient and modern – are invited to consider their response in similar contexts. Seen this way, unfinalizability happens in this story on many levels – at the level of characters in the parable, in Luke's narrative world outside the parable, and finally at the level of reading the parable – and the focus gradually shifts from one plane to another.

THEOLOGICAL SIGNIFICANCE: THE YOUNGER SON'S STORY AS ANALOGOUS TO GOD'S RELATIONSHIP WITH ISRAEL

The parable of the two sons is often interpreted as an allegory in which the older son is analogous to Jewish religious leaders and the younger son to Gentiles and other outsiders in the first-century context of Jesus. More often than not, interpreters argue that, just as the younger son receives grace and forgiveness from the father figure, Gentiles and other outsiders too receive grace from God. They further note that, just as the older son in the parable is judgmental toward the younger son, resents father's celebration of his return, and acts entitled to inheritance, Jewish religious leaders in the first century were critical of Gentiles who were included in the Jesus movement. Many of these readings caricature first-century Judaism as a religion obsessed with rigid laws and unwillingness to make any room for grace.

In her fascinating analysis of the reception history of the parable, Amy-Jill Levine notes that "common is the view that the older son is an allegorical representation of the Jews, who slavishly serve God the father in order to earn a reward while Jesus proclaims salvation by

---

[34]   Abbott, "Story, Plot, and Narration," 50.

grace."[35] Levine challenges such deeply problematic readings and negative stereotypes about Judaism. At the risk of understatement, such readings have contributed to negative depictions of the Jewish community in the first century and beyond. They have perpetuated antisemitic trajectories in Christian interpretation of scriptures and have deeply problematic implications for Jewish–Christian relations. Arguing that such readings are anachronistic, Levine helpfully suggests that the parable should be read within the first-century Jewish context in which Jesus ministered. In her reading, the parable's message is about "finding the lost, of reclaiming children, of reassessing the meaning of family."[36]

What would it look like if one were to move past problematic interpretations that are antisemitic in nature and to read the parable as a story within the first-century Jewish context? Who might the two sons be analogous to, and what might the two characters signify? It is difficult to make an exact determination of how the parable would have been understood in its original context but, in light of our knowledge of the first-century Jewish context in which it was written, the younger son, rather than the older son, would be analogous to Israel. Parables, by nature, are open to multiple interpretations and defy easy categorizations or interpretations. Given the complex nature of parables, as well as the spatial and temporal distance from which most of the modern readers interpret them, we cannot be certain that this parable is indeed about Israel's relationship with God. However, to the extent it is interpreted within the first-century Jewish context, it is the younger son who is analogous to Israel. The story of the younger son, at its core, encapsulates the story of Israel – with inheritance, rebellion, exile, and restoration – and Israel's relationship with God. The younger son moves away from home and lives in a foreign land, just as Israel in its history moved into exile and had a rupture in its relationship with God. Ultimately, the story of Israel ends with reconciliation and restoration of relationship with God. The parable, with its focus on rupture, return, and reconciliation, captures the complex relationship between the father and the son but, on a deeper level, it calls attention to the story of the relationship between God and Israel. And it celebrates the complex but strong and irreparable bond between them.

On a different level, one could suggest that Luke's depiction of the conflict between the father and the older son toward the end of the

---

[35] Amy-Jill Levine, *Short Stories by Jesus: The Enigmatic Parables of a Controversial Rabbi* (New York: Harper One, 1989), 30.
[36] Levine, *Short Stories by Jesus*, 30.

parable signifies a tension between two understandings of the divine – one that highlights the perception of God as judgmental and another that depicts and celebrates God as forgiving. Theologically, the father's forgiveness of the younger son challenges any stereotypes about understanding God as one who is only interested in vengeance. Furthermore, as Levine helpfully argues, the notion that the father's welcoming of the younger son violates Jewish cultural standards of Jesus's time amounts to a stereotype, a deeply problematic one.[37] It depicts the Jewish culture of Jesus's time as uncaring and steeped in legalism, and it reflects the proclivity on the part of some interpreters to highlight the older son's response as reflective of the Jewish cultural standard while discounting the father's gracious response as a strong strand within the Hebrew tradition.

LUKE'S FINAL PLOT SUMMARY

The gospel of Luke ends with the story of Jesus making his first post-resurrection appearance to disciples on the road from Jerusalem to Emmaus. It weaves together several key themes in Luke's story – travel, breaking bread, and open-ended narratives – that invite readers to participate in the story, akin to the parable of the good Samaritan and the prodigal son.

The road to Emmaus story is both anticlimactic and open-ended. The disciples had high hopes that Jesus would challenge the Romans successfully, redeem the nation, and rise from the dead triumphantly. In the end, all of it turned out to be a tragic story, at least from their perspective. Jesus meets the grieving disciples on the road to Emmaus, hears their tragic narrative about him, corrects it, and even offers a sign of resurrection, but does so in an anticlimactic manner. Readers might expect the story to end with Jesus, the central protagonist, making a grand and triumphant appearance to his disciples. Instead, he makes a low-key appearance to two disciples, who are not among the Twelve, and joins them as they are going to a fairly unknown town. They do not even recognize him until much later. Mark's longer ending has a much shorter version of this story wherein Jesus appears to two disciples as they are walking in the countryside, and they do recognize him. Others do not believe their account of seeing Jesus, but that is a different story.

Luke, on the other hand, makes it clear that the two disciples repeatedly miss opportunities to recognize Jesus. Luke uses the

37   Levine, *Short Stories by Jesus*, 32.

imperfect Greek verb *suneporeuto* to suggest that Jesus walks with them for a good bit of time, but the disciples still cannot recognize him. Later, Jesus corrects their narrative of despair about him and offers a lengthy interpretation of everything that is in the Scriptures about him. They still do not recognize him until they reach the house and are seated around the table.

Luke's audience would have been familiar with stories of *theoxenia* – divine beings appearing in the form of a stranger. Zeus was known to appear in the guise of a guest to see how well people would welcome strangers, but this stranger does not seem content with being the guest. He breaks the bread instead of the host. Luke, who takes pride in writing an orderly account of Jesus's life, does not say how Jesus ends up in that role – whether the disciples invite him to play the host and break the bread or if he completely takes over the host role. Luke simply states that their eyes are opened and they recognize him when he takes the bread, blesses it, breaks it, and gives it to them. As the two disciples tell the story later, it is specifically in the breaking of the bread that they recognize him. What is it about the breaking of bread that gives away his identity? Is it the way he handles the bread? Does he have a special way of breaking it? Is he especially skilled at breaking the bread perfectly down the line? Again, Luke offers no details.

Resurrection, a significant event in Luke's narrative, does not become evident in lengthy discussions or interpretation of scriptures. Rather, the ultimate sign of that significant moment of resurrection occurs in the seemingly mundane act of breaking bread that comes to define Jesus's identity.

Readers of the gospel know well that bread, specifically the action of breaking bread, is transformative in the ministry of Jesus. As Sharon Ringe notes, the motif of breaking bread that appears in the Last Supper recalls key aspects of Jesus's ministry.[38] In the feeding stories, breaking bread is a metaphor for challenging existing economic structures and extending resources to the poor. Meal stories in Luke are about breaking social barriers, restoring relationships, disrupting established norms, and even crashing exclusive parties, like the "sinful" woman in Luke 7. Many barriers have already been broken in this story itself. Post-resurrection appearance happens in an unlikely place, two unknown disciples take the center stage in the story, and a stranger ends up at the head of the table.

[38]   Ringe, *Luke*, 207.

CONCLUSION

In Luke's narrative, that moment of breaking bread confirms for the disciples that it is indeed Jesus, and that he has risen from the dead, but it quickly shifts attention from resurrection to the significance of the action. Jesus's identity and legacy are closely tied to the practice of breaking bread, which in Luke is a metaphor for challenging oppressive structures, breaking barriers, and restoring relationships. Legacy matters in Luke's account because it has a descriptive function as well as a prescriptive function. It prescribes for the disciples their commitments, ethos, and priorities. Luke Timothy Johnson calls attention to a key detail in this story. In the feeding stories and in the Last Supper, Jesus takes the bread, blesses it, breaks it, and gives it to others. Luke is using the same set of verbs in this story but replaces *didomi* (to give) with *epididomi* (to hand over).[39] By using the compound verb *epididomi*, Luke is suggesting that Jesus does not simply give the bread to the disciples but hands it over to them so that they too can break barriers and challenge oppressive structures.

With its open-ended nature, the story invites the disciples not to seek power but to continue Jesus's mission of breaking barriers. The Emmaus story reminds them that the burden of confronting powers should not lie solely with their messiah and that they, too, have an obligation and agency to challenge the Empire. Will the disciples continue the mission of breaking bread? Luke leaves open-ended the question of how the disciples responded to Jesus in this story and shifts the attention to readers. Will the readers continue the mission of breaking bread?

SELECTED FURTHER READING

Bakhtin, Mikhail. *Problems of Dostoevsky's Poetics*. Minneapolis: University of Minnesota Press, 1984.

Bakhtin, Mikhail. *Rabelais and His World*. Bloomington: Indiana University Press, 1984.

Bonz, Marianne Palmer. *The Past as Legacy: Luke-Acts and Ancient Epic*. Minneapolis: Fortress, 2000.

Culpepper, R. Alan. *Anatomy of the Fourth Gospel: A Study in Literary Design*. Minneapolis: Fortress, 1987.

Green, Joel B. "Narrative Criticism." Pages 74–112 in *Methods for Luke*. Edited by Joel B. Green. Cambridge: Cambridge University Press, 2010.

Herman, David. *The Cambridge Companion to Narrative*. Cambridge: Cambridge University Press, 2007.

[39] Luke Timothy Johnson, *Luke* (Collegeville: Liturgical Press, 1991), 396.

Jacob, Sharon. *Reading Mary Alongside Indian Surrogate Mothers: Violent Love, Oppressive Liberation, and Infancy Narratives.* London: Palgrave Macmillan, 2015.

Johnson, Luke Timothy. *Luke.* Collegeville: Liturgical Press, 1991.

Juel, Donald H. *A Master of Surprise: Mark Interpreted.* Minneapolis: Fortress, 2002.

Kingsbury, Jack Dean. *Conflict in Luke: Jesus, Authorities, Disciples.* Minneapolis: Fortress, 1991.

Levine, Amy-Jill. *Short Stories by Jesus: The Enigmatic Parables of a Controversial Rabbi.* New York: Harper One, 1989.

Moore, Stephen D. *Literary Criticism and the Gospels: The Theoretical Challenge.* New Haven: Yale University Press, 1989.

Powell, Mark Allan. *Chasing the Easter Star: Adventures in Reader-Response Criticism.* Louisville: Westminster John Knox, 2001.

Ringe, Sharon H. *Luke.* Louisville: Westminster John Knox, 1995.

Roy, Arundhati. *The God of Small Things.* New York: Random House, 2008.

Spencer, F. Scott. *Luke.* Grand Rapids: Eerdmans, 2019.

Smith, Abraham. "A Prodigal Sings the Blues: The Characterization of Harriett Williams in Langston Hughes's 'Not Without Laughter.'" Pages 145–58 in *Yet With a Steady Beat: Contemporary U.S. Afrocentric Biblical Interpretation.* Edited by Randall C. Bailey. Atlanta: SBL Press, 2002.

Smith, Mitzi J. "Abolitionist Messiah: A Man Named Jesus Born of a Doule." Pages 53–70 in *Bitter the Chastening Rod: Africana Biblical Interpretation after Stony the Road We Trod in the Age of BLM, SayHerName, and Me Too.* Edited by eds. Mitzi J. Smith, Angela N. Parker, and Ericka S. Dunbar Hill. New York: Fortress Academic, 2023.

Smith, Mitzi J. and Yung Suk Kim. *Toward Decentering the New Testament: A Reintroduction.* Eugene: Cascade Books, 2018.

Talbert, Charles H. *Reading Luke: A Literary and Theological Commentary on the Third Gospel.* Macon: Smyth & Helwys, 2013.

Tannehill, Robert C. *The Narrative Unity of Luke-Acts: A Literary Interpretation, Vol. 1: The Gospel According to Luke.* Minneapolis: Fortress, 1991.

13 Signs Cultivating Imperfect Belief in the Fourth Gospel

TYLER SMITH

INTRODUCTION

While all four canonical gospels present Jesus performing astonishing deeds – healing the sick, raising the dead, feeding multitudes, exercising dominance over winds and waves, casting out demons, and more – the Fourth Gospel stands apart from its gospel neighbors in several important respects.[1] While the Synoptic Gospels Matthew, Mark, and Luke prefer the language of "miracles" (δυνάμεις) to describe many of Jesus's astonishing actions, the term "miracles" is never used in the Fourth Gospel, a complex text that probably took shape around the end of the first century CE and later than the Synoptics. Some, but not all, of the Synoptics' miracle stories are paralleled in John.[2] The Fourth Gospel, a highly symbolic text, seems to prefer the language of "signs" (σημεῖα) to describe Jesus's astonishing deeds, and these signs are tightly associated with the Johannine motif of believing (πιστεύειν) in Jesus.[3] There is a

---

[1] The terms "Gospel of John" and "Fourth Gospel" are used interchangeably in this essay. The terms "John" or "the evangelist" are used interchangeably in reference to the implied author of the narrative, without making any claims about the real-world author(s) and editor(s) responsible for bringing the text into its ultimate form. Unless otherwise noted, all translations follow the NRSV. Where a chapter-and-verse reference is given without indicating a source book, the reference is to the Fourth Gospel.

[2] Whether John knew some or all of the Synoptic Gospels remains a difficult question. At the very least, the evangelist was familiar with synoptic traditions. Among scholars who hold that John did know the Synoptics in some form, there is a further disagreement concerning the nature of the relationship: did he set out to supplement them, to replace them, or something else? For a survey of the possibilities, see Harold W. Attridge, "John and Other Gospels," in *The Oxford Handbook of Johannine Studies*, eds. Judith M. Lieu and Martinus C. de Boer (Oxford: Oxford University Press, 2018).

[3] On Johannine symbolism as it relates to the signs, see Dorothy Lee, "Symbolism and 'Signs' in the Fourth Gospel," in *The Oxford Handbook of Johannine Studies*, eds. Judith M. Lieu and Martinus C. de Boer (Oxford: Oxford University Press, 2018). The present essay does not attempt to identify what is symbolized or signified by each of the Johannine signs. Such efforts may in fact be doomed to frustration; the argument has been made that at least in the case of the first two major signs

curious disconnect, however, between characters' professions of belief and their ability to understand the object of their belief. Both belief and understanding are highly thematized features of the cognitive dimension of the Fourth Gospel's narrative.[4] This essay traces the play of belief and understanding in and around the Johannine signs narratives, from characters' anticipatory gestures of belief to the reinforced but still imperfect belief that emerges in the wake of Jesus's signs.[5]

SIGNS AND BELIEVING

Now Jesus did many other signs [σημεῖα] in the presence of his disciples, which are not written in this book. But these are written so that you may come to believe [πιστεύητε] that Jesus is the Messiah, the Son of God, and that through believing [πιστεύοντες] you may have life in his name. (John 20:30–31)

These two verses offer a purpose statement and first conclusion for the Fourth Gospel, and characterize the gospel as a series of narrated acts whose significance transcends the face value of the acts themselves.[6] Specifically, these verses suggest that the signs – or rather, the writing down of a select set of signs, which is not necessarily the same thing – were meant to produce or sustain a certain sort of belief. The belief has a propositional component, but to believe in Jesus, for John, also involves what might better be captured by terms like "faith" or

---

narratives, deliberate ambiguity may be in play. See Harold W. Attridge, "Ambiguous Signs, an Anonymous Character, Unanswerable Riddles: The Role of the Unknown in Johannine Epistemology," *New Testament Studies* 65 (2019): 267–88; Harold W. Attridge, "How Johannine Signs Signify (or Don't)," in *Anatomies of the Gospels and Beyond: Essays in Honor of R. Alan Culpepper*, eds. Mikeal C. Parsons, Elizabeth Malbon Struthers, and Paul N. Anderson, BibInt 164 (Leiden: Brill, 2019), 335–47.

4 The refocusing of scholarly attention on the gospel's final form owes its greatest debt to Alan Culpepper, particularly his *Anatomy of the Fourth Gospel: A Study in Literary Design* (Philadelphia: Fortress, 1983). Among the many Culpepper-inspired investigations of literary dynamics of the Gospel of John to have appeared in the last three decades, several have focused in particular on the "cognitive dimension" of the narrative, alongside or in dialogue with the literary dynamics bearing on the "pragmatic dimension." See in particular Kasper Bro Larsen, *Recognizing the Stranger: Recognition Scenes in the Gospel of John*, BibInt 93 (Leiden: Brill, 2008); Tyler Smith, *The Fourth Gospel and the Manufacture of Minds in Ancient Historiography, Biography, Romance, and Drama*, BibInt 173 (Leiden: Brill, 2019).

5 On the "imperfect" aspect of Johannine believers, see Susan Hylen, *Imperfect Believers: Ambiguous Characters in the Gospel of John* (Louisville: Westminster John Knox, 2009).

6 Chapter 21 is widely regarded as a secondary addition to the narrative, and thus a second conclusion.

"trust."[7] Here we see clearly that the hoped-for belief answers a question about Jesus's identity (i.e., that the man Jesus, whose story the Fourth Gospel narrates, was "the Messiah, the Son of God") and that holding this belief has high-stakes consequences (i.e., "life in his name," recalling the promise of "eternal life" from earlier in the gospel [3:16, 36]). The purpose statement seems to promote a favorable view of the Johannine signs: at least part of their significance lies in their ability to bring readers or hearers into this state of belief. But this view of signs stands in tension with the way signs and signs-based belief function in the narrative of the Fourth Gospel itself.

At the beginning of his ministry, the Johannine Jesus finds himself in Jerusalem at the time of Passover, where, the evangelist explains:

> many believed [ἐπίστευσαν] in his name because they saw the signs [σημεῖα] that he was doing. But Jesus on his part would not entrust [ἐπίστευεν] himself to them, because he knew all people and needed no one to testify about anyone; for he himself knew what was in everyone. (2:23–25)

While these verses reinforce a causal link between Jesus's signs and belief, they also show that there is something "within" these new believers that makes them untrustworthy: Jesus refuses to reciprocate their trust.[8] The gospel leaves this tension unresolved.[9] The belief that results from seeing signs, it would appear, is less than ideal.

Moreover, signs in the Fourth Gospel do not inevitably lead to belief. Near the center of the gospel, a seemingly exasperated Jesus is forced to hide from the crowd, for, as the narrator explains, "Although he had performed so many signs [σημεῖα] in their presence, they did not believe [οὐκ ἐπίστευον] in him" (12:37). A similar dynamic is at work in the aftermath of Jesus's feeding of the five thousand (6:15). And near

---

[7] For the semantic range of John's πιστεύειν language, see chapter 10 of Teresa Morgan, *Roman Faith and Christian Faith: Pistis and Fides in the Early Roman Empire and Early Churches* (Oxford: Oxford University Press, 2015), 394–443.

[8] On the reciprocity motif in the Fourth Gospel, with particular attention to its interplay with the recognition and mutual indwelling motifs, see Kasper Bro Larsen, "The Recognition Scenes and Epistemological Reciprocity in the Fourth Gospel," in *The Gospel of John as Genre Mosaic*, ed. Kasper Bro Larsen, SANt 3 (Göttingen: Vandenhoeck & Ruprecht, 2015), 341–56.

[9] Chris Seglenieks argues that the rhetorical function of 2:23–25, read together with 20:31, is to challenge readers to reflect on the (in)adequacy of their faith response to Jesus and to strive to take on genuine belief. Christopher Seglenieks, "Untrustworthy Believers: The Rhetorical Strategy of the Johannine Language of Commitment and Belief," *NovT* 61 (2019): 55–69.

the end of the gospel, immediately before the purpose statement, is the story of "doubting Thomas" (20:24–29), which concludes with Jesus saying to Thomas, "Have you believed [πεπίστευκας] because you have seen me? Blessed are those who have not seen and yet have come to believe [οἱ μὴ ἰδόντες καὶ πιστεύσαντες]" (20:29). The reference to "many other signs" directly following this verse (20:30) suggests that Jesus's offering his body to Thomas for inspection should be understood as one of the many belief-stimulating "signs" Jesus performs in the Fourth Gospel. Jesus does not reject this belief, but he nevertheless contrasts it with a (more?) blessed mode of believing on the part of those who have not seen.

On the one hand, then, Jesus's signs cause some people to believe; on the other, Jesus does not unambiguously celebrate this belief or reciprocate it by "entrusting" himself to those who have it. The gospel also creates space for believing apart from witnessing signs. Attempts to resolve these tensions have largely been propelled in the twentieth and twenty-first centuries by the conviction that a "signs source" lies behind the received, final form of the gospel, and that careful attention to literary seams and aporias in the gospel will allow scholars to distinguish between this source and John's appropriation of it.[10] While attempts to get behind the gospel to its sources or to the social history of its author and authorizing community have stimulated important conversations, the present essay is concerned with the Johannine signs narratives in the final form of the gospel. But first, we need to lay out some parameters for the discussion: What exactly are the Johannine signs and just how many of them are there?

---

[10] The theory is most often associated with work by Rudolf Bultmann and Robert Fortna, but it also intersects with the hugely influential "developmental approach" to the Fourth Gospel associated with work by J. Louis Martyn and Raymond Brown. The developmental approach attempts to find clues in the text of the Fourth Gospel to reconstruct the origins, trials, and travails of a "Johannine community." Both the source- and form-critical work in search of an otherwise-unattested signs source and the quest to reconstruct a Johannine community have faced considerable scrutiny in recent years. See Rudolf Bultmann, *The Gospel of John: A Commentary*, trans. G. R. Beasley-Murray, R. W. N. Hoare, and J. K. Riches (Philadelphia: Westminster, 1971), 113 and passim; Robert T. Fortna, *The Gospel of Signs: A Reconstruction of the Narrative Source Underlying the Fourth Gospel*, MSSNTS 11 (Cambridge: Cambridge University Press, 1970); Robert T. Fortna, *The Fourth Gospel and Its Predecessor: From Narrative Source to Present Gospel* (Edinburgh: T&T Clark, 1988). For critique, see Gilbert Van Belle, *The Signs Source in the Fourth Gospel: Historical Survey and Critical Evaluation of the Semeia Hypothesis*, BETL 116 (Leuven: Leuven University, 1994). For a more recent attempt to approach the gospel diachronically, see Urban C. Von Wahlde, *The Gospel and Letters of John*, 3 vols. (Grand Rapids: Eerdmans, 2010).

WHICH SIGNS? FINDING THE PARAMETERS

Scholars routinely speak of there being seven signs in the Fourth Gospel: the changing of water to wine at Cana (2:1–11); the healing of a royal official's son (4:46–54); the healing of the man at the pool by Jerusalem's Sheep Gate (5:1–18); the feeding of the five thousand (6:1–15); walking on the Sea of Galilee en route to Capernaum (6:16–21); the healing of the man born blind (9:1–41); and the restoration of Lazarus to life (11:1–53).[11]

On closer inspection, however, this list is not as straightforward as one might expect. If, instead of beginning with theories about a hypothetical signs source or a privileging of the number seven, we take these narratives as they appear in the final form of the Fourth Gospel, we find that signs language is used specifically in connection to only five of the traditional seven narratives (at 2:11; 4:54; 6:14; 9:16; 12:18), and Jesus's act is only formally designated a sign in the first two.[12] Neither the healing of the man at the pool (5:1–18) nor the walking on water (6:16–21) is described specifically as a sign. Those who wish to count these among the signs narratives point to general and retrospective references to signs in 6:2 and 7:31. Nor is the miraculous appearance of the boat at Capernaum (6:16–25) identified specifically as a sign, though some lists of seven signs identify it as one.[13] In lists where the boat event is treated as one of the signs, scholars will sometimes either combine the feeding of the five thousand (6:1–15) and the walking on water (6:16–21) or combine the arrival of the boat (6:16–25) and the walking on water (6:16–21) to keep the list at seven. More often, however, the arrival of the boat (6:16–25) is not considered a sign at all. Different configurations of sets of seven signs highlight the difficulties inherent in trying to nail down just how many signs feature in John's Gospel. One can find more than seven or fewer than seven, depending on the criteria employed.

---

[11] With slight variations in labeling, Raymond E. Brown, *The Gospel According to John I–XII: A New Translation with Introduction and Commentary*, AB 29 (Garden City: Doubleday, 1966), cxxxix; Franz Zeilinger, *Die sieben Zeichenhandlungen Jesu im Johannesevangelium* (Stuttgart: Kohlhammer, 2011); Andrew T. Lincoln, *Truth on Trial: The Lawsuit Motif in the Fourth Gospel* (Peabody: Hendrickson, 2000), 14; and many others.

[12] On this last point, Attridge, "Ambiguous Signs, an Anonymous Character, Unanswerable Riddles," 270.

[13] E.g., Udo Schnelle, "The Signs in the Gospel of John," in *John, Jesus, and History, Volume 3: Glimpses of Jesus through the Johannine Lens*, eds. Paul N. Anderson, Felix Just, and Tom Thatcher, ECL (Atlanta: SBL, 2016), 233–34.

To wit: just because an action of Jesus is not explicitly labeled a sign need not preclude its functioning as one in the larger narrative context. While the five episodes that unambiguously function as Johannine signs narratives – the changing of water to wine at Cana (2:1–11); the healing of a royal official's son (4:46–54); the feeding of the five thousand (6:1–15); the healing of the man born blind (9:1–41); and the raising of Lazarus (11:1–53) – should of course be counted among the signs that were (as the purpose statement has it) done in the presence of the disciples and written down so that the reader of John might believe in Jesus, it is clear from John's many general references to signs (cf. 2:23; 3:2; 4:48; 6:2, 14, 26; 7:31; 9:16; 11:47; 12:37; 20:30) that other acts of Jesus qualify as well. In addition to the healing at the pool and the marvelous transportation miracles on the Sea of Galilee, we might consider such events as Jesus's activity in the temple (2:13–22), Jesus's conversation with the Samaritan woman (4:5–42), the foot-washing (13:3–20), the crucifixion (19:14–30), the empty tomb (20:1–10), and the post-resurrection appearances (20:11–29; 21:1–22).[14] Like the five unambiguous episodes, these all involve an extraordinary, surprise-inducing action by Jesus that reveals his glory. Some of these are extraordinary not because they are "miraculous" in a post-Enlightenment sense, but rather because they mark departures from the ordinary order of things.[15] To ask a drink of a Samaritan woman is extraordinary because, as the narrator explains, "Jews do not share things in common with Samaritans" (4:9; cf. the disciples' astonishment in 4:27). Similarly, the foot-washing entails a surprising inversion of roles in the master–disciple hierarchy (13:6, 8, 14–16). Astonishment in response to the extraordinary is also

---

[14] The linen wrappings and the cloth in the tomb (John 20) are considered as Johannine signs by Jörg Frey, "From the Sēmeia Narratives to the Gospel as a Significant Narrative: On Genre-Bending in the Johannine Miracle Stories," in *The Gospel of John as Genre Mosaic*, ed. Kasper Bro Larsen, SANt 3 (Göttingen: Vandenhoeck & Ruprecht, 2015), 226. The resurrection appearances are considered as signs by Gilbert Van Belle, "The Resurrection Stories as Signs in the Fourth Gospel. R. Bultmann's "Interpretation of the Resurrection Revisited," in *Resurrection of the Dead: Biblical Traditions in Dialogue*, eds. Geert Van Oyen and Tom Shepherd (Leuven: Peeters,2013), 249–64. Girard, followed by Grassi, drops the walking on water episode and takes the "great hour of Jesus: his mother, the cross, and the issue of blood and water from Jesus' side" (19:25–37) as a seventh sign. Marc Girard, "La composition structurelle des sept « signes » dans le quatrième évangile," *SR* 9 (1980): 315–24; Joseph A. Grassi, "The Role of Jesus' Mother in John's Gospel: A Reappraisal," *The Catholic Biblical Quarterly* 48.1 (1986): 67–80.

[15] In framing the matter this way, I disagree with those who would characterize the Johannine signs as supernatural. E.g., Peter Riga, "Signs of Glory: The Use of 'Sēmeion' in St. John's Gospel,"*Interpretation* 17.4 (1963): 402–24.

thematized explicitly at 5:20 in connection to the works (ἔργα) that the Father will show the Son (cf. 5:28; 7:15, 21).[16]

So, while John explicitly identifies five acts of Jesus as signs, other extraordinary acts of the Johannine Jesus – whether narrated in the gospel itself or playing out off stage – are presented as similar kinds of work. The "how many signs" question, however, is less interesting than the question of how the signs individually and collectively function in the cognitive dimension of the Fourth Gospel's narrative – the domain of (mis)understanding, (mis)identification, and (dis)belief. To that end, let us take a closer look at the purpose statement and then at the five unambiguous signs narratives.

THAT YOU MIGHT BELIEVE

A famous crux in the purpose statement (20:30–31), cited earlier, concerns the verb, which appears in some manuscripts as an aorist subjunctive (πιστεύσητε) and in others as a present subjunctive (πιστεύητε). The former could be construed as suggesting that the gospel is intended to bring readers to an initial expression of belief ("so that you may start believing" or similar). The latter might imply that the gospel is intended to encourage current believers to persevere in their belief ("so that you may keep on believing" or similar). The former suggests an audience of community outsiders who are not (yet) believers; the latter suggests that the gospel is directed at community insiders, whom the author sees as imperfect believers. It may be that the aorist subjunctive was the earlier reading (either in an earlier editorial layer of the gospel itself, or in a source) but was replaced by the present subjunctive at a later stage in the text's history.[17] These questions could quickly take us beyond the world of the narrative into diachronic analysis of the text, or into attempts to reconstruct authorial intentions, or into the reception of the gospel by its initial readers. At the same time, these questions have important implications for understanding the function of the signs within the Fourth Gospel.

One way of addressing the question without leaving John's narrative world is to consider characters' responses to the signs, on the

---

[16] On signs and works, see most recently Harold W. Attridge, "Signs Working and Works Signifying," in *The Semeia Narratives in John – Form, Function, and Theology*, eds. Jörg Frey, Margareta Gruber, and Christos Karakolis, WUNT (Tübingen: Mohr Siebeck, forthcoming).

[17] Harold W. Attridge, "A Textual Problem and a Gospel's Purpose: A Reflection on Current Johannine Studies," *Toronto Journal of Theology* 36 (2020): 150–58.

view that the various Johannine characters illustrate different potential belief-responses to the signs.[18] Such a survey reveals that the signs
work to cultivate an incipient, imperfect belief in some characters,
while simultaneously alienating other characters, pushing them further
away. Among the characters who respond positively, three conspicuous
characteristics bear noting: first, there is often an anticipatory gesture
of belief precipitating the sign;[19] second, the sign itself is de-emphasized
so as to focus on what the sign signifies and the inability of those present to fully appreciate its significance; third, the belief that follows
from seeing or hearing about the sign is consistently imperfect in various ways. While the Johannine Jesus never outright rejects these imperfect expressions of belief, he frequently ignores characters when they
endeavor to express their belief and, even at the end of the narrative,
will not "entrust" himself (cf. 2:24) to any of these imperfect believers.

WINE AT CANA AND THE BELIEF OF THE DISCIPLES

The first mention of signs in the Fourth Gospel comes in a narrative
aside following the episode it describes: in 2:11, after changing the water
into wine at Cana, the narrator observes that "Jesus did this, the first of
his signs [ἀρχὴν τῶν σημείων], in Cana of Galilee, and revealed his glory;
and his disciples believed [ἐπίστευσαν] in him," establishing a clear link
between the signs and belief. Furthermore, the narratorial aside establishes "Jesus's signs" as a category of special interest for making sense
of John's vision of Jesus's modus operandi in the world. A function of
the sign is the revelation of Jesus's glory, anticipating the "hour" (ὥρα)

---

[18]   The scholarship on characterization studies in the Gospel of John is enormous. Two
       important collections in recent years are Christopher W. Skinner, ed., *Characters
       and Characterization in the Gospel of John*, LNTS 461 (London: Bloomsbury, 2013);
       Steven A. Hunt, D. Francois Tolmie, and Ruben Zimmermann, eds., *Character
       Studies in the Fourth Gospel*, WUNT 314 (Tübingen: Mohr Siebeck, 2013). The ques-
       tion of whether Johannine characters represent a range of potential faith-responses to
       Jesus's revelation is much older. See the influential articles by Raymond F. Collins,
       "The Representative Figures of the Fourth Gospel. Part I," *DRev* 94 (1976): 26–46;
       "The Representative Figures of the Fourth Gospel. Part II," *DRev* 94 (1976): 118–32.
       For a different view of Johannine characters, critical in some respects of Collins's
       work, see Cornelis Bennema, *Encountering Jesus: Character Studies in the Gospel of
       John* (Milton Keynes: Paternoster, 2009).

[19]   The anticipatory gesture of belief is often overlooked, leading some commentators
       to contrast the Synoptics (where miracles [δυνάμεις], especially "healing miracles,"
       are often preceded by faith) and John (where believing in Jesus follows the sign). See,
       e.g., Jo-Ann A. Brant, *John*, Paideia Commentaries (Grand Rapids: Baker Academic,
       2011), 94.

of his glory (i.e., on the cross). The actual transformation of water into wine is not emphasized; instead, John emphasizes what leads up to and what follows the sign.

Jesus's mother observes that their hosts have run out of wine. Is this a request that he do something about it? Jesus seems to treat it as such, asking, "Woman, what concern is that to you and to me? My hour [ὥρα] has not yet come." Despite the initial rebuff, Jesus's mother, having identified an opportunity for Jesus to reveal his glory, now offers an initial gesture of faith, saying to the servants at the wedding, "Do whatever he tells you." In response to this anticipatory gesture of faith, Jesus instructs the attending servants to fill six stone jars with water, and then has them draw some out and take it to the chief steward. They do so, the chief steward tastes it, and the narrator notes that, in contrast to the servants, he "did not know where it came from."

This disparity between some characters "knowing" and others "not knowing" develops into a Johannine motif, including especially in the events surrounding the man born blind and the raising of Lazarus. Low social status characters like these servants, some among the crowds, and the disciples themselves seem to "see" or "know" more than higher status characters like the chief steward, the chief priests, or the Pharisees. Here, the disciples, who have apparently seen all of this unfold, from the running out of wine to the misunderstanding, amazed response of the chief steward, respond to the sign with belief. The evangelist does not specify who is in this group of disciples, but it presumably includes those called by Jesus in the previous chapter (Andrew, an anonymous disciple of John the Baptizer, Simon Peter, Philip, Nathanael) and perhaps also the whole group of "the twelve" (cf. 6:67). Here, the group "Jesus's disciples," like "crowds" elsewhere in the gospel, is amorphous and nonhomogeneous. Many of them, the evangelist reports, "turned back and no longer went about with him" after hearing his shocking, apparently pro-cannibalistic remarks in 6:53–65. It is clear that the belief of the disciples in 2:11 does not prevent the disciples, individually or as a group, failing to understand the person who is the object of the belief. In this light, perhaps it is not surprising that the Johannine Jesus neither rejects nor endorses the belief they exercise in 2:11.

Whether or not Jesus's mother, who noticed the opportunity for Jesus to reveal his glory and offered the anticipatory gesture of faith, is among the group of disciples that believes in 2:11 is unclear. Nevertheless, she is with Jesus and the disciples in the next scene as they travel to Jerusalem (2:12) and she is mentioned again at the end of the narrative (19:25) with no indication that she has ever been far removed from her son in the interim. She may, therefore, offer an exception that proves the rule. Whereas the post-belief failures and misunderstandings of other characters are highlighted, no indication is given from first (2:1) to last (19:25–27) that Jesus's mother's belief is anything but ideal.

THE OFFICIAL'S SON AND THE BELIEF OF THE OFFICIAL

The second unambiguous signs narrative (4:46–54) involves similar language and cognitive dynamics: "Now this was the second sign (σημεῖον) that Jesus did after coming from Judea to Galilee." Like the first sign in Cana, belief and the signs-belief relationship figure prominently. The belief motif punctuates the episode at three points: following the initial request, Jesus says to the man, "Unless you [pl.] see signs and wonders you [pl.] will not believe [οὐ μὴ πιστεύσητε]." This remark, like Jesus's initial rebuff of his mother (2:4), is often read as disapproving or condescending. If there is disapproval or condescension, however, the official brushes it off and persists in his petition: "Sir [κύριε], come down before my little boy dies." By persisting, and perhaps also by recognizing Jesus with the title κύριος, even if he does not (yet) understand this term's significance as a Johannine christological title, the man demonstrates his nascent belief in anticipation of the sign.[20] This time, Jesus responds directly to the man's request: "Go; your son will live." The result is, "The man believed [ἐπίστευσεν] the word that Jesus spoke to him and started on his way." This belief, however, is not an instance of the belief produced by the performance of a sign. That comes later, after the man learns from his slaves that his son began to recover at the precise hour Jesus spoke to him. Now he and his whole household believed (ἐπίστευσεν). As in the case of the marvelous wine, emphasis falls not on the sign itself but on the responses triggered by the sign. Unlike the first sign, where the belief of the disciples repeatedly proves imperfect in the course of the subsequent narrative, the fate of the royal official and his family and the nature of their belief lies beyond the narrative horizon; this is the last readers hear of them. As before, however, their belief is neither celebrated as well conceived nor condemned as insufficient; it simply is.

---

[20]   The term κύριος is multivalent. It can function as a polite form of address – "mister" or "sir," as the NRSV translates here – or it can function in a higher register – "lord" or even "Lord" as a christological title.

THE FEEDING OF THE FIVE THOUSAND AND THE BELIEF OF THE CROWD

The third unambiguous signs narrative (6:1–15) opens with the observation, "A large crowd kept following him, because they saw the signs [σημεῖα] that he was doing for the sick." Probably among these healing signs should be included the healing of the man at the pool (5:1–18), although, as noted earlier, John does not explicitly identify that act in context as a sign. Surveying the crowd, Jesus asks Philip, "Where are we to buy bread for these people to eat?" The narrator explains that this question was less than candid: "He said this to test him, for he himself knew what he was going to do." Philip – who, as one of the disciples, has already "believed" in Jesus at Cana – apparently fails this test when he answers, "Six months' wages would not buy enough bread for each of them to get a little." Then fellow disciple Andrew observes a boy present with five barley loaves and two fish. This initially suggests that Andrew believes Jesus will be able to do something with these – the anticipatory gesture of faith – but Andrew's belief also comes up short, as demonstrated by what he says next: "But what are they among so many people?" These failures notwithstanding, Jesus takes the loaves, gives thanks, and distributes them. The disciples gather the leftovers, filling twelve baskets. The narrator focuses attention on the effects of the sign: "When the people saw the sign [σημεῖα] that he had done, they began to say, 'This is indeed the prophet who is to come into the world.'"[21]

Although there is no explicit indication that belief is produced by this sign, the feeding together with the signs Jesus has been doing for the sick has the effect of leading the crowd to identify Jesus as "the prophet who is to come into the world," a reference to the "prophet like Moses" promised in Deuteronomy 18:15–22.[22] Like the other signs, however, it is not clear that their belief rises to the level hoped for in the Johannine purpose statement (20:30–31). To believe in Jesus as the prophet is not the same as to believe in Jesus as "the Messiah, the Son of God." The crowd of followers continues to waver in its ability to make sense of Jesus; their belief is fragmented and imperfect. As in his

[21] Although it would seem most natural to consider the feeding of the five thousand as a single sign (thus the NRSV translation), the plural σημεῖα is used here at the end of the episode. This has the effect of linking the feeding to the healing signs mentioned in 6:2.

[22] On this important Johannine motif, see Wayne A. Meeks, *The Prophet-King: Moses Traditions and the Johannine Christology*, NovTSup 14 (Leiden: Brill, 1967).

previous encounters with crowds, Jesus does not reciprocate the trust
of these new believers. There is no positive acknowledgement of their
belief; on the contrary, Jesus "realized that they were about to come
and take him by force to make him king," so "he withdrew again to the
mountain by himself." This note, recalling Jesus's preternatural ability
to know "what was in everyone" (2:25), also reinforces the notion that
the crowd persists in misunderstanding. The Johannine Jesus is not just
a prophet and not just a king; for the evangelist, he is the Christ and the
Son of God.

THE MAN BORN BLIND AND BLINDNESS OF JESUS'S JEWISH ANTAGONISTS

The fourth unambiguous signs narrative (9:1–41) is also one of the most
elaborate. It begins when Jesus sees "a man blind from birth," a description that immediately evokes two important Johannine motifs: seeing
and blindness function as cognitive metaphors in the Fourth Gospel for
understanding and misunderstanding what Jesus reveals, and the language of "from birth" (ἐκ γενετῆς) recalls the need to be born "again"
or "from above" that emerges in Jesus's night-time conversation with
Nicodemus in chapter 3. The disciples ask Jesus a question that illustrates their failure to understand the nature of blindness: "Rabbi, who
sinned, this man or his parents, that he was born blind?" Jesus answers
the question directly:

> Neither this man nor his parents sinned; he was born blind so that
> God's works [τὰ ἔργα τοῦ θεοῦ] might be revealed [φανερωθῇ] in him.
> We must work the works of him who sent me while it is day; night
> is coming when no one can work. As long as I am in the world, I am
> the light of the world. (John 9:3–5)

The reference to the works of God being revealed (φανερωθῇ) recalls 2:11,
which linked the performance of a sign to the revelation of glory. The
language of God's works (τὰ ἔργα τοῦ θεοῦ) establishes a link between the
sign (σημεῖον) that Jesus is about to perform and the "works" that he does
throughout the gospel, opening the door to consider all of Jesus's works
as significant in his campaign of revelation. Jesus will elsewhere speak
of his "works" (ἔργα) leading to belief (14:11–12), just as signs can lead
to belief, and of finishing the "work" (ἔργον) that God gave him to do as
a means of glorifying God on earth (17:4), which is reminiscent of how
the doing of the σημεῖα is thematized as the revealing of Jesus's glory (cf.
2:11). The language of sending and the day–night binary in 9:3 recalls

the night-time visit of the misunderstanding Nicodemus in chapter 3. Nicodemus's opening salvo – "Rabbi, we know that you are a teacher who has come from God [ἀπὸ θεοῦ ἐλήλυθας]; for no one can do these signs [σημεῖα] that you do apart from the presence of God" (3:2) – is dissembling but, for the evangelist, ironically true.[23] The night–day binary, furthermore, corresponds to binaries that either have already been established or are being established in this episode: darkness–light, blindness–seeing, misunderstanding–understanding, and disbelieving–believing.

Jesus proceeds to spit on the ground and make mud with the saliva and spread the mud on the man's eyes, saying to him, "Go, wash in the pool of Siloam." The man does so and gains his sight. But neither he nor those who see him understand the significance of the healing. At this point, the neighbors and those who have seen him before as a beggar bring him to the Pharisees, who investigate in vain. When they ask the newly sighted man what he has to say about the one who "opened his eyes," the man says, "He is a prophet," recalling the misunderstanding of the five thousand to the earlier signs (6:14). The man's words provoke a response:

> The Jews did not believe [οὐκ ἐπίστευσαν] that he had been blind and had received his sight until they called the parents of the man who had received his sight and asked them, "Is this your son, who you say was born blind? How then does he now see?" (John 9:18–19)

The man's interlocutors, initially identified as Pharisees, are now identified as "the Jews."[24] The shift may indicate that joining the Pharisees are the man's erstwhile "neighbors and those who had seen him before as a beggar" who had already expressed doubts about his identity (cf. 9:8). This act of "not-believing" about the origins of the man born blind anticipates later acts in the Johannine narrative of "not-believing" about the divine origins of Jesus. It is the negative corollary of the anticipatory believing of the royal official in 4:50.

The man's parents affirm that the man is their son and that he was born blind, but they claim not to know how he came to see or who brought it about. They deflect: "Ask him; he is of age. He will speak for

---

[23] On Nicodemus as dissembler, see Michael R. Whitenton, "The Dissembler of John 3: A Cognitive and Rhetorical Approach to the Characterization of Nicodemus," *JBL* 135 (2016): 141–58.

[24] The identification of and role played by the Ἰουδαῖοι ("the Jews" or "the Judeans") in the Fourth Gospel is a charged and highly fraught question. For a recent treatment, see Adele Reinhartz, *Cast Out of the Covenant: Jews and Anti-Judaism in the Gospel of John* (Lanham: Lexington Books / Fortress Academic, 2018).

himself." The narrator intercedes to explain that "his parents said this because they were afraid of the Jews; for the Jews had already agreed that anyone who confessed Jesus to be the Messiah [Χριστόν] would be put out of the synagogue" (9:22). The narrator seems to suggest that if the parents were to answer, "How it is that now he sees?" and, "Who opened his eyes?" without equivocation, their answer could be interpreted as a confession that Jesus is the Christ and result in their expulsion from the synagogue. Both the Jews and the parents seem to be operating with the understanding that the healing, if substantiated, constitutes a sign indicative of Jesus's messianic identity. While the disbelief of the Jews is explicit, the belief-status of the parents is left ambiguous. At any rate, their fear of the Jews aligns them with other furtive Johannine characters, including the Passover crowds in Jerusalem, Joseph of Arimathea, and even the core group of disciples on the evening of Jesus's resurrection (7:13; 19:38; 20:19).

The Jews in this signs narrative swivel their attention back to the newly seeing man and engage him in a heavily ironic back-and-forth, culminating in the man's saying, "If this man were not from God, he could do nothing," and being answered by the Jews, "You were born entirely in sins, and are you trying to teach us?" The Jews then "drove him out," recalling the narrative aside in 9:22 that Christ-confessors would be thrown out of the synagogue.

When Jesus finds the man and asks him if he believes in the Son of Man, the man answers, "And who is he, sir [κύριε]?"

Jesus now reveals himself: "You have seen him, and the one speaking with you is he." This precipitates the climactic moment: "He said, 'Lord [κύριε], I believe [πιστεύω].' And he worshiped him."

As in the case of the royal official, an anticipatory identification of Jesus as κύριος is the prelude to the revelation of Jesus's glory and a fuller expression of understanding Jesus's identity and belief on the part of the sign's beneficiary.

This climactic scene is juxtaposed in the following verses, however, with a very different outcome. In response to the man's profession of belief, Jesus says, "I came into this world for judgment so that those who do not see may see, and that those who do see may become blind." The man born blind clearly figures in this summary statement as representative of the first type; the representatives of the second type, however, are about to reveal themselves: "Some of the Pharisees near him heard this and said to him, 'Surely we are not blind, are we?' Jesus said to them, 'If you were blind, you would not have sin. But now that you say, "We see," your sin remains.'" The fallout from the sign is polarizing: on the one hand is the man born blind, who now "sees" with his physical eyes and has at least a partial perception of the identity of the doer of the signs; on the other hand are those who claim to be able to see but, from the perspective of the evangelist, cannot. Their failure to see what the man born blind can see pushes the gospel's ideal belief-response further out of their reach.

THE RAISING OF LAZARUS, THE BELIEF OF MARTHA, AND THE DISBELIEF OF JESUS'S JEWISH ANTAGONISTS

The final Johannine signs narrative for us to consider (11:1–53) is in many respects the most sublime. As in previous cases, Jesus associates the sign at the outset with the motif of the revelation of God's glory: "This illness does not lead to death; rather it is for God's glory" (11:4; cf. 2:11; 9:3). The sign is specifically linked to the belief motif: clarifying that Lazarus is not sick but actually dead and that he plans to go to him now, Jesus explains to his disciples, "For your sake I am glad I was not there, so that you may believe." Thomas's response reveals that he still fails to comprehend what is obvious to Jesus and the implied reader, but that he nevertheless trusts Jesus: "Let us also go, that we may die with him." This is one of several anticipatory gestures of belief in this signs narrative.

When Jesus and the disciples arrive at Bethany, Jesus speaks with Lazarus's sister Martha, who offers another anticipatory gesture of faith: "Lord [κύριε], if you had been here, my brother would not have died. But even now I know that God will give you whatever you ask of him."

Jesus announces the sign that he is about to perform, but she does not understand, or rather exhibits only a partial understanding: "Your brother will rise again," he says, to which she responds, "I know that he will rise again in the resurrection on the last day." Like the royal official, she has recognized Jesus as κύριος, and expressed anticipatory belief that Jesus can accomplish whatever he asks God for, although she stops short of asking Jesus to raise her brother here and now.

Jesus riffs on her assertion by revealing an important dimension of his identity: "I am the resurrection and the life. Those who believe [ὁ πιστεύων] in me, even though they die, will live, and everyone who lives and believes [ὁ ζῶν καὶ πιστεύων] in me will never die. Do you believe [πιστεύεις] this?"

Martha responds by saying, "Yes, Lord [κύριε], I believe [πεπίστευκα] that you are the Messiah [ὁ χριστός], the Son of God, the one coming into the world." This remarkable confession, employing the perfect tense

of πιστεύειν, comes closer to the belief ideal of the purpose statement
("... that Jesus is the Messiah, the Son of God, and that through believing you may have life [καὶ ἵνα πιστεύοντες ζωὴν ἔχητε]") than any other
christological confession or statement of belief in the Fourth Gospel:
not only does Martha recognize Jesus as the Messiah and the Son of
God, but she also articulates this belief in response to Jesus asking a
question about life and death.

And yet, upon arriving at the cave where the body has been laid,
Martha's belief seems to falter as she objects to Jesus's instructions to
remove the rock sealing the tomb: "Lord [κύριε], already there is a stench
because he has been dead four days" (11:39). Again, this illustrates the
ongoing misunderstanding that seems to afflict even the most ardent
and articulate of Johannine believers (cf. Andrew in 6:9).

Jesus responds, "Did I not tell you that if you believed [πιστεύσῃς],
you would see the glory of God?" (11:40). If this is in reference to their
earlier conversation, it suggests an identification between the "glory
of God" that is being revealed in Jesus's signs (cf. 11:4) and the "life"
that is made possible for those who believe. Martha offers no further
objection, and Jesus proceeds with the sign. After praying, highlighting his desire for the assembled crowd to "believe that you sent me,"
Jesus calls out to Lazarus. The dead man emerges, wrapped in burial
clothes, and Jesus has the crowd unbind him. This has the now-familiar
result: "Many of the Jews therefore, who had come with Mary and had
seen what Jesus did, believed [ἐπίστευσαν] in him." But, as in previous
encounters with crowds and "the Jews," the result is division.

"Some of them went to the Pharisees and told them what he had
done." The Pharisees and the chief priests gather to voice their concerns:
"What are we to do? This man is performing many signs [σημεῖα]. If we
let him go on like this, everyone will believe [πιστεύσουσιν] in him, and
the Romans will come and destroy both our holy place and our nation."
As in previous signs narratives, the performance of signs is tied to the
production of belief in Jesus. The chief priests and Pharisees are right,
from the perspective of the evangelist, to see that Jesus is performing
signs and that these signs prompt belief in those who see them. They
themselves, however, do not draw the same conclusion. The raising
of Lazarus has led to an inchoate belief in Martha and in "many of the
Jews," and to a further hardening and alienation on the part of the Jews
represented at the council of the chief priests and Pharisees. This divide
is underscored in the final references to the sign of Lazarus (12:9–19),
where the chief priests extend their homicidal designs to encompass
Lazarus too, "since it was on account of him that many of the Jews were

deserting and were believing in Jesus" and subsequently in Jerusalem, when a crowd gathers to hear Jesus "because they heard that he had performed this sign [τὸ σημεῖον, i.e., the raising of Lazarus]," which results in the Pharisees despairing: "You see, you can do nothing. Look, the world has gone after him!"

The Lazarus affair concludes when Jesus departs and hides from the crowds that continue to demonstrate their misunderstanding (12:36). This recalls his post-signs departures earlier in the gospel from misguided new believers (2:23–24; 6:15; cf. also 5:13; 7:10). John then refers to a pair of passages in Isaiah (Isa 53:1; 6:9–10) by way of explanation for why the people "did not believe in him," despite his performing "so many signs in their presence" (12:37). These prophetic verses offer the evangelist a rationale for how and why the preponderance of the Jews in the story reject Jesus: "They could not believe," John writes, "because Isaiah also said, 'He has blinded their eyes and hardened their heart, so that they might not look with their eyes, and understand with their heart and turn – and I would heal them" (12:39–40; citing Isa 6:9–10). John then returns to the glory motif with which the signs motif has been entwined from the start of chapter 2: "Isaiah said this because he saw his glory and spoke about him" (12:41; cf. 2:11). That pessimistic note notwithstanding, John reports that "many, even of the authorities, believed in him. But because of the Pharisees they did not confess it, for fear that they would be put out of the synagogue; for they loved human glory [δόξαν] more than the glory [δόξαν] that comes from God" (12:42–43). John does not explicitly link this skittish belief to the performance of signs, but its position in the narrative at the culmination of the Lazarus episode supports a connection. Their secret belief, however, counts for little. It is neither acknowledged nor celebrated by Jesus, who again withdraws into hiding (12:36; cf. 2:23–24; 6:15; 7:10). These fearful believers demonstrate their disordered priorities insofar as they value human glory (δόξα) above divine glory (δόξα). Jesus will have nothing more to do with them and turns his attention, in the second half of the gospel, to his immediate circle of disciples.

CONCLUSION

In all of the signs narratives we have discussed, an act of Jesus is identified as a sign after the fact. When by contrast a character asks Jesus for a sign (2:18; 6:30), Jesus deflects, defers, or ignores the request, perhaps because he knows "what [is] inside everyone" (2:25) and therefore senses the unreceptivity of requestors, knowing that the sign will push them further away than they already are. And yet, when certain characters (Jesus's mother, the royal official, the hungry crowd, the disciples, Martha) create or identify opportunities for Jesus to reveal his glory, the Johannine Jesus is apt to do something that the narrator and some in the Johannine cast of characters recognize as a sign. These acts are preceded in the narrative by anticipatory gestures of belief. Although the Johannine signs never seem to elicit the ideal belief response hoped for in the gospel's purpose statement – those who come to belief almost without exception go on to show shortcomings in their understanding of Jesus – they are nevertheless a key dynamic in the interplay between Jesus and those to whom he reveals himself.

What, in the end, are we to make of the tensions identified at the start of this essay? In the first place, there is the simple (simplistic?) and positive valuation of the signs as generative of belief in Jesus. This is amply borne out in the story John tells. Then again, it is clear that belief in Jesus arising from the signs does not preclude misunderstandings of Jesus, and may even lead to Jesus's withdrawal, Jesus's refusal to reciprocate new believers' imperfect trust. Perhaps the solution is that we are not to distinguish between an "adequate" or "introductory" belief that comes from signs and a "solid" or "persevering" belief which is the goal.[25] John does not distinguish between two kinds of belief. There is only belief, and it is always imperfect.

At this point, we might return to the question posed in connection to the gospel's purpose statement. When John writes "these ... that you might believe" or "... continue to believe," is the evangelist speaking to outsiders in hopes that they will come to believe? Or to insiders, expressing his hope that exposure to these written signs will strengthen their existing belief? Our survey of signs and their effects on the cognitive dimension of the narrative supports the second option, with the caveat that neither the before-signs faith nor the after-signs faith is necessarily ideal. The evangelist expects that exposure to these signs will cultivate the belief of those who – like Jesus's mother, the royal official, the disciples, or Martha – are receptive to Jesus's revelation of his glory and are willing to offer an initial, anticipatory gesture of belief. This is not moving from no belief to perfect belief, nor is it the maintenance of a perfect belief in a perfect state. It treats the reader's faith as something akin to gardening. Gardening may lead to a flourishing garden, but there

---

[25]   These terms are taken from Keener, though the position is ubiquitous in Johannine scholarship. Craig S. Keener, *The Gospel of John: A Commentary*, 2 vols. (Peabody: Hendrickson, 2003), 1215–16.

is no guarantee that the work will result in a perfect harvest, nor does gardening necessarily imbue gardeners with an accurate understanding of the forces that allow their plants to grow and thrive (germination, photosynthesis, cell growth, mitosis, etc.). As gardeners work and see their gardens flourish in response, their faith in the value of the gardening may be reinforced. Ultimately, however, these cultivators rely on forces beyond their own willingness to work – nutrients in the soil, the rain, the sun, or, in the Fourth Gospel's parlance, the Spirit – for these gardens to yield a life-giving harvest.

SELECTED FURTHER READING

Bennema, Cornelis. *Encountering Jesus: Character Studies in the Gospel of John*. Milton Keynes: Paternoster, 2009.

Frey, Jörg. "From the Sēmeia Narratives to the Gospel as a Significant Narrative: On Genre-Bending in the Johannine Miracle Stories." Pages 209–32 in *The Gospel of John as Genre Mosaic*. Edited by Kasper Bro Larsen. SANt 3. Göttingen: Vandenhoeck & Ruprecht, 2015.

Frey, Jörg, Margareta Gruber, and Christos Karakolis, eds., *The Semeia Narratives in John – Form, Function, and Theology*, WUNT. Tübingen: Mohr Siebeck, forthcoming.

Hunt, Steven A., D. Francois Tolmie, and Ruben Zimmermann, eds. *Character Studies in the Fourth Gospel*. WUNT 314. Tübingen: Mohr Siebeck, 2013.

Hylen, Susan. *Imperfect Believers: Ambiguous Characters in the Gospel of John*. Louisville: Westminster John Knox, 2009.

Moloney, Francis J. *Signs and Shadows: Reading John 5–12*. Minneapolis: Fortress, 1996.

Reinhartz, Adele. *Cast Out of the Covenant: Jews and Anti-Judaism in the Gospel of John*. Lanham: Lexington Books / Fortress Academic, 2018.

Salier, Willis Hedley. *The Rhetorical Impact of the Sēmeia in the Gospel of John*, WUNT II/186. Tübingen: Mohr Siebeck, 2004.

Seglenieks, Chris. *Johannine Belief and Graeco-Roman Devotion: Reshaping Devotion for John's Graeco-Roman Audience*, WUNT II/528. Tübingen: Mohr Siebeck, 2020.

Skinner, Christopher W., ed. *Characters and Characterization in the Gospel of John*. LNTS 461. London: Bloomsbury, 2013.

Smith, Tyler. *The Fourth Gospel and the Manufacture of Minds in Ancient Historiography, Biography, Romance, and Drama*. BibInt 173. Leiden: Brill, 2019.

Thompson, Marianne Meye. "Signs and Faith in the Fourth Gospel," *Bulletin for Biblical Research* 1 (1991): 89–108.

Whitenton, Michael R. "The Dissembler of John 3: A Cognitive and Rhetorical Approach to the Characterization of Nicodemus." *JBL* 135 (2016): 141–58.

14   The Acts of the Apostles

MATTHEW L. SKINNER

READING THE ACTS OF THE APOSTLES AS A NARRATIVE

Among all the narratives collected in the Bible, none tells a story quite like the Acts of the Apostles. In Acts, readers travel along with the action over very long distances and visit a range of cultural settings. Not only does the book tell a geographically expansive tale, but it also brings a wide spectrum of people onto the narrative stage: as Jesus' followers respond to his command to bear witness to him near and far, they encounter nameless people who rely on begging to survive and powerful Roman officials, zealous converts and insidious apostates, a seamstress and a fabric dealer, virtuous military officers and violent mobs, as well as audiences both superstitious and sophisticated. The sheer scope and variation within the plot mark Acts as a complex story that rewards those who interpret it with attention to its narrative dynamics.

The narrative of Acts is also distinctive because it has no kindred literature in the New Testament. No other canonical book tells the same stories Acts tells, although parts of Paul's writings may refer, in vaguely similar ways, to events also narrated in Acts (e.g., Gal 1:11–17 and Acts 9:1–22; Gal 2:1–10 and Acts 15:1–29; 1 Cor 1:14–17; 2:1–5 and Acts 18:1–18). Biblical interpreters frequently compare the four Gospel narratives with one another to learn more about those books' source materials and the distinctive aspects of each one's narrative rhetoric. Reading Deuteronomy alongside Exodus yields significant comparisons and contrasts, as does reading 1 and 2 Chronicles in concert with 1 and 2 Kings. But interpreters' ability to inquire into the source and redaction histories behind Acts is much more limited, in terms of the relevant literary materials available to them. It is not simply *possible* to investigate the ways in which Acts functions as a self-contained narrative; it is a *necessary* piece of making sense of this book.

(It must be noted that Acts is not unique or entirely isolated literature. The biblical text read as Acts today was not the only version of the book that emerged from the ancient world. A collection of similar versions, usually collectively called the "Western Text" or "D-Text," were created probably after the original author had died. Those versions are about ten percent longer than the earlier [canonical] version of Acts. They tend to add more details and in some cases they offer more severely critical depictions of individual Jewish characters and Judaism in general. It is also the case that Acts is hardly the only ancient literature devoted to recounting the achievements of significant individuals. The Greek term for "acts" [*praxeis*] was employed to describe other literary works about extraordinary figures, even though the book of Acts never uses the that term. Also, other Christian writings from the mid or late second century focused on the *praxeis* of certain followers of Jesus. It is possible, then, to compare Acts to similar narrative works.)

As a narrative and as an account of the activities conducted by some of Jesus' earliest followers after his death, resurrection, and ascension, the basic story of Acts does not stand entirely disconnected from other narratives. Nearly all critical scholars agree that the same author – traditionally called Luke – wrote both the Third Gospel and Acts. Even those who read the books in translation and without close regard for themes and tendencies can see the connections in the books' prefaces (Luke 1:1–4; Acts 1:1–2). Acts presents itself as a sequel to Luke, picking up and continuing the story begun in the Gospel, with overlap in the books' respective accounts of Jesus' ascension (Luke 24:44–53; Acts 1:3–11). Although both books tell the story of the ascension, they do not tell it in the same way. Furthermore, in Luke the ascension appears to occur on the same day Jesus' empty tomb is discovered, while Acts 1:3 stipulates that it happens forty days later.

Scholars over the last century have found it profitable to read the books together as a united (although hardly uniform) whole, referring to both volumes together as "Luke-Acts." That nomenclature highlights the ways both books share certain theological themes and narrative tendencies, but it should not lead one to assume that Acts lacks distinctive foci and narrative dynamics. Acts is, of course, a book that describes – through storytelling – Jesus' significance and even his direct influence continuing in the experiences of his followers (e.g., Acts 1:1–2, 8; 2:32–33; 4:29–30), but it also takes its rhetorical bearings from various kinds of ancient narrative. Acts bears similarities to narratives in the Old Testament, ancient Jewish historiography, and Greco-Roman historiography. Literary conventions from Greek and Roman epics and Greek novels also left their mark on Acts. This is no surprise, for ancient authors were not bound by the lines that sometimes divide modern

notions of fact and fiction, especially when recounting historical events
or extolling historic figures. Ancient historians knew that any history
worth its salt had better be entertaining to read.

There was a time when biblical interpreters considered Acts more
useful for knowing history than for learning theology. In other words,
they viewed the purpose of Acts as mostly concerned with chroni-
cling travel itineraries, preserving important speeches and sermons
from luminaries in the early church, recording significant events to
exemplify the church's expansions and struggles, and remembering
notable deaths. If the author ever made the shift from *reporting* the
story to *testifying* about the God at the center of the activity, that
older line of interpretation reasoned, those theological testimonies
emerge when certain characters in Acts – usually Peter, Stephen, or
Paul – step to the fore of the narrative stage and deliver a speech that
makes claims about God, Jesus, the good news, resurrection hope,
and related topics. In other words, the *speeches* were taken to be the
occasions when Acts explained the *events* of the narrative and their
ongoing importance, especially relating to theological matters. It was
when the narrative essentially paused that a character, or the author
speaking through the character, would make the most noteworthy
confessional claims.

More recent interpreters have successfully corrected those assumptions and focused on the ways in which Acts is a theological narrative;
the story constructs a theological world – a world animated by God and
people who seek to be responsive to their understanding of that God.
The speeches are only a piece of the narrative's theological rhetoric.
Also, the plot of Acts, the storytelling techniques, the narrative patterns
and surprises, and even the unexplained and enigmatic parts of the story
implicitly and sometimes explicitly prompt readers to imagine God as
a discernible presence or agent in the narrated world. Paying attention
to the story Acts tells and how it tells it is, therefore, more than just
an exercise in analyzing literary aesthetics. It is a way of engaging in
the question of how reading Acts – whether in the ancient world or the
modern – might prompt people to reflect on topics such as the nature of
God, the Christian message, humanity, and the purpose of the church.

Acts has a particular flair for the spectacular. This goes beyond
accounts of healings, exorcisms, and resuscitations that resemble episodes in other biblical literature, especially the Gospels. The story
ratchets up the suspense through its heroes' narrow escapes: three
miraculous jailbreaks, courtroom drama with behind-the-scenes machinations, a massive public demonstration in a city center, a shipwreck,

and a bite from a venomous snake that proves harmless. Characters hear from God through visionary experiences and prophecies. In one instance, the Spirit of God disappears a person, inexplicably moving him from one geographical location to another. The miraculous activity, the dialogues between main characters and high-ranking Roman officials, and the deliverances from peril – with their startling *deus ex machina* flourishes – fuel ongoing debates among Acts scholars about historicity. For many readers, the larger-than-life story elements test how much one is willing to believe about what might have really happened in the first decades of the church.

The narrative's artistic pageantry, to say nothing of its carnivalesque delight in villains' come-uppances and its reliance on romantic novelistic literary tropes, injects both thrill and disgust into experiencing the story. As mentioned already, it distorts the understanding of what it means to tell "history" when one draws a thick line between fact and fiction in ancient historical literature. Ancient history-writers – or historiographers – were obviously interested in conveying the significance of historical figures and developments; they were likewise interested in delighting their audiences and transporting those audiences into the action and its attendant emotions. A key tool for doing that was the rhetoric of narrative. When modern interpreters set aside preoccupation with questions about "What really happened?" and focus instead on how the story is told, they are able to focus attention on how this story might have moved audiences in ancient times, as well as how it still might today. Studying the narrative character of Acts is not the only way to study the book, but it is a necessary piece of other kinds of analysis, including historical scrutiny of Acts.

As with any story, there is no single way to read Acts as a narrative, in terms of tracking how the plot develops and shifts. The opening verses of Acts invite readers to consider the geographic framework of this story about the Christian movement's expansion. That occurs explicitly when Jesus declares to his followers, "You will receive power when the Holy Spirit has come upon you; and you will be my witnesses in Jerusalem, in all Judea and Samaria, and to the ends of the earth" (1:8). The rest of the narrative makes good on that introductory thumbnail sketch, with the action located in Jerusalem in chapters 1–7 (with most of the action in chapters 3–7 occurring specifically within or with reference to the temple). It then expands to Samaria and other parts of Judea in chapters 8–12. Paul of Tarsus occupies center stage beginning in chapter 13 and figures in the expansion of the gospel in the wider majority-gentile world into chapter 21. The final quarter of the book (chapters 21–28) follows Paul as he, now in Roman custody, finds his way to Rome as a prisoner seeking an audience before the emperor.

Taking geography as an organizing aspect of the narrative is not especially controversial, but things become more complicated when we consider what to make of all the travel and transfers in Acts. Is the story trying to relocate the landscape of God's expressed fidelity to the world from Jewish Jerusalem to imperial Rome? Or is there a subtle challenge to the empire residing in the impressive opportunities for someone like Paul to declare the power of the good news to Roman governors (Felix and Festus) and a Roman-installed client king (Herod Agrippa II) and then eventually, beyond the bounds of Acts itself, to the Roman emperor?

There are other choices for readers who seek a cohesive way of navigating the narrative, beyond the geographical framework. One outlook considers how the plot moves forward in unforeseen ways because of various discoveries or decisions that occur, usually leading to an expanding understanding of the implications of the good news about Jesus. For example, the arrival of the Holy Spirit (Acts 2) creates a sense of new possibilities and reunion brought by the Spirit of God indwelling all people. When opposition to the young church and its spokespeople turns deadly, a sense of risk attends the rest of the narrative (Acts 7). When Samaritans, an Ethiopian court official, an archenemy named Saul, and a gentile centurion all embrace the good news (Acts 8–11) the church learns that it will be changed through the discovery of just how universal the gospel's scope really is. When Paul discerns that he must return to Jerusalem (Acts 19–21), his part of the story changes permanently, with an apparently deadly outcome awaiting him.

Another way that readers might apply an organizational scheme to Acts, as a way of interpreting the narrative, is to consider prominent characters and their experiences. Peter first and then Paul receive the lion's share of attention. Their experiences mirror those of Jesus in the Gospel according to Luke, in that all three of these men confront the power of satanic forces, heal people who cannot walk on their own, raise people from the dead, and find themselves arrested and interrogated. Acts limits the comparisons among them by refusing to narrate Peter's and Paul's deaths, but the point nevertheless remains that their ministry picks up and continues the same ministry Jesus began. Other characters fade into the narrative shadows, suggesting that Acts of *the Apostles* is probably not the best title for this book. Non-apostles such as Stephen and Philip (Acts 6–8) receive much more attention that most of the apostles, but their ministries very much resemble what the apostles do, which is to continue Jesus' controversial work in public spaces. Furthermore, there are numerous other characters – men and women – who, even though they receive little explicit attention from the narrator, nevertheless clearly contribute to the vitality of the church insofar as they do what the church is commissioned to do back in Acts 1:8 – namely, bear witness to Jesus. The prominent characters in Acts are prominent precisely because they call attention to what is a central emphasis in Acts: the ability of the word of God – the embodied, corporate message about Jesus and salvation through him – to persist despite setbacks and opposition.

Like any story that purports to describe how people exist in the world or how a movement grows, adapts, and survives, Acts exhibits its share of ambiguity and inconsistencies. Those things make the narrative more realistic, not less. No decent narrative about human interactions speaks without a degree of internal contradiction or a capacity for expressing multiple voices and ideas. It seems that readers should expect nothing less, especially from a narrative that intends to describe how the presence and activity of God is transformative and able to set lives in new directions. A key first step for any interpretations of Acts that try to describe its potential for shaping audiences is to engage the story it tells, in all of its potential for both messiness and order.

How might tending to the narrative dynamics of Acts illuminate certain aspects of this intriguing book? An overview is a good way to begin.

ACTS 1–2

Jesus stays on the visible narrative scene long enough to tell his followers what they can expect when the "power" of the Holy Spirit comes upon them, recalling aspects of Luke 24:48–49 and establishing the Spirit as a significant (though often unmentioned) agent entwined in the plot of Acts. The focus on the Spirit's presence and activity, as well as the Spirit as an indication of God's promises coming to fruition, in Acts 1–2 may recall explicit mention of the Spirit in the events of Luke 1–4. In a similar vein, Acts calls attention to Mary, Jesus' mother, among the 120 people who wait in Jerusalem for the fulfillment of Jesus' promise. With the ascension of the resurrected Jesus, the arrival of the Spirit, and the collection of familiar characters – including Judas Iscariot who meets a grisly demise – Acts begins as a story in continuity with the story told in Luke.

Another significant piece of characterization at the outset of Acts comes with Peter's leadership. In Luke he was last seen denying Jesus

(22:54–62), observing the empty tomb (24:12), and having an unnarrated encounter with the risen Jesus (24:34). Suddenly in Acts he is leading the group, which appears to be something Jesus predicted or ordained in Luke 22:31–32. Peter discerns the need for a new twelfth apostle and interprets scripture to make his case. Once Pentecost arrives in Acts 2, he will emerge as the story's most prominent apostle. Most of the other eleven, including the newcomer Matthias, fade into the narrative background, making it appear that Acts regards their significance as a group in more of a symbolic than functional vein. They will accomplish things, as brief references to them in the next few chapters will indicate, but they will never be the only members of the new, emerging church who perform those actions.

On the Day of Pentecost Peter continues to be the central character, for his public sermon occupies the majority of Acts 2. He is hardly alone, however, for Acts depicts a Spirit-filled community coming to the fore. The praying community of 120 people becomes a Spirit-infused prophesying community, speaking miraculously about "God's deeds of power." The event becomes a reunion of sorts, with Jews and converts to Judaism representing a wide array of locations – a broad representation of what was in the first century a multi-national (or multi-ethnic, given the word *ethnos* in 2:5) religious identity. Given the prominence of Jerusalem in both Luke and Acts, it is vital to notice the way that Peter's first sermon describes a kind of regathering in the power of the Holy Spirit. The Spirit knits together discrete Jews but also addresses Judaism in all of its geographic and ethnic varieties. Jerusalem remains one place, a crucial place for Jewish identity and the promises of God, but it also becomes a more expansive place in this scene's depiction, for it hosts a diverse Jewish audience from all over. When the Day of Pentecost ends, at the conclusion of Acts 2, a unified and hospitable community has been established, reminding readers that Acts is not merely a story to celebrate heroic and gifted individual public figures like Peter. The narrative implies that the Holy Spirit also brings the power to create community that manifests an ethos of generous belonging.

ACTS 3–5

When Peter and John meet a man who cannot walk at the beginning of Acts 3, it begins a series of stories centered mostly on the Jerusalem temple. When Peter pronounces the healing of the man "in the name of Jesus Christ of Nazareth," readers may detect an echo of Luke 5:17–26 and a foreshadowing of a similar deed by Paul in Acts 14:8–11. The work Jesus commenced in Luke continues in Acts, in the work of his followers.

As for the public sermon in the part of the temple named Solomon's Portico, Peter explains why the name of Jesus possesses so much power, referring to the blessings associated with Jesus' death, resurrection, and glorification. In the process he indicts the people of Jerusalem for their role in Jesus' execution, building on a similar claim he made in Acts 2:23. Although Peter explains that Jesus' demise was a consequence of ignorance – on the part of both the people and their leaders – the accusation nevertheless has significant implications. Speeches in the early chapters of Acts spread the blame for Jesus' death widely; in similar ways, the Gospel of Luke indicts Jerusalem as a whole for the rejection of Jesus (Luke 13:34; 19:41–44; 23:13–25), even as it recognizes the distinct blame borne by the ruling authorities (Luke 23:35; 24:20). This is a significant detail in how Acts characterizes early opposition to the church from people in Jerusalem. The leaders – the elite group of Jewish authorities that Luke describes prosecuting the case against Jesus in Luke – act to curtail the apostles' influence and complain that the apostles' preaching assigns blame to them for Jesus' death (Acts 5:28). In that complaint the leaders show themselves to be missing the larger story told in the speeches of Acts 2–5. In any case, the group of these particular leaders shows itself to be more interested in displays of power, threats, and violence than open debate. Acts portrays the official assembly or "council" (sunedrion) as hotheaded and dangerous.

The characterization of Jewish opponents has significant consequences for how readers make sense of what Acts is trying to say about the early church and its connections to God's promises. There are many Jewish characters in Acts who are violent and recalcitrant in response to the church's preaching about Jesus. At the same time, most of the church's members in Acts are themselves Jewish. The hostility of the council in Acts 4–5 (see also 6:8–15; 7:54–60), as well as the self-condemning wisdom of Gamaliel (5:38–39), can be read as paradigmatic, exaggerating this kind of opposition to the church as the kind of thing that "the Jews," generally speaking, are bound to do. Indeed, there are more than thirty occasions later in Acts when the general expression "the Jews" appears as an unspecific identifier of a group, often an antagonistic one. The narrative risks – or, regrettably, succeeds in – creating a corporate, composite character that appears to associate Judaism with strict opposition to the church. At the same time, individual Jewish characters continue to listen to the church's message and respond positively through to the last scenes of the book (Acts 28:24, 30–31). The narrative is not clear about whether it condemns Judaism in sweeping terms or whether it depicts vehement disagreement about Jesus within a Jewish context, meant to spur people toward repentance. The ambiguity may be part of the point.

As for the church in these chapters, it grows in boldness, protected from its vulnerability by a powerful God who is stronger than the authorities' attempts to incarcerate individuals. The church, represented by its most visible leader, is also able to see through the satanic deceptions that insiders such as Ananias and Sapphira might perpetrate. A community of "one heart and soul" (Acts 4:32) resides at the center of the story and embodies a sense of Christian identity and the lived well-being that comes as a part of God's salvation. The church's popularity is as impressive as its power to heal others (Acts 5:12–16). The future looks rather bright at this point.

ACTS 6–7

The plot of Acts shifts dramatically in these chapters. First, the good times appear likely to continue when inequities in the ministry of food distribution lead to an administrative shake-up and the creation of new offices or roles for people in the church. In Acts 6:1–7, a serious problem is addressed and the outcome is a great increase in the church's membership, including the inclusion of some priests. Some interpreters see here a denial of women's opportunities to exercise leadership in a public way, if it is widows who are the ones in charge of distributing food before the apostles appoint seven men. Others see an attempt to ensure that hungry widows remain the recipients of needed charity. The narrator runs so quickly through the scene that it is difficult to tell. A less controversial observation is that this is a scene in which the twelve apostles insist they have a special role in prayer and "serving the word" instead of having to "wait on" (diakoneō) others. They seem unimpressed that Jesus himself boasted of his role as one who serves (diakoneō) in Luke 22:27. The narrative may here be reasserting the apostles' unique role and prime importance; it may also be showing them to be cavalierly unaware the God can and will work though anyone to conduct noteworthy public ministry.

Stephen, one of the seven chosen to "wait on tables," ends up looking like Peter, John, and other apostles because he does what they did in previous chapters: he displays power through the impressive signs and wonders he performs and speaks boldly to defend himself from accusations. Stephen acquits himself well from the perspective of the narrative. In the story's longest speech, he retells aspects of Israel's scriptural history to insist that God has never been confined to one place, a temple. He also seizes the opportunity to accuse his opponents of resisting God's Spirit and killing prophets. Those opponents do not acquit him.

The narrative presents the death of Stephen in comparison to Jesus' crucifixion. Not only does Jesus' ministry of compassion and healing continue in the experience of the church; so too does his suffering and trust. Both Jesus and Stephen die after calling out in a loud voice (Luke 23:46; Acts 7:60). Both ask for their killers to receive forgiveness (Luke 23:34; Acts 7:60). Both offer an expression of trust before they die (Luke 23:46; Acts 7:59). Stephen dies in the confidence that God can be encountered in places other than the Jerusalem temple. Acts will demonstrate something similar, because Jesus' followers will soon have to flee Jerusalem and bear witness elsewhere. Persecution has its obvious costs, as Stephen attests, but in this narrative it also spurs expansion.

The persecution begins at the beginning of Acts 8, after readers learn about a man named Saul, who will later be known as Paul. He approves of Stephen's death. When he returns to the narrative in Acts 9 as a leading figure in the persecution effort, he will learn about what God has in store for him. Acts has a tendency of briefly introducing characters who will subsequently return and play more substantial roles later in the story. This happens most notably with Saul but also with Philip (Acts 6:5; 8:5) and Barnabas (Acts 4:36; 9:27; 11:25).

ACTS 8–12

Jesus' followers leave Jerusalem not as a matter of choice or strategy but apparently as a matter of survival. This hardly precludes the possibility of God influencing the plot and creating ways not only for the church to expand its reach but for it to come into new understandings of what God has in store in terms of who will belong to this nascent community. Recall, in 5:38–39, that Gamaliel raised the question of whether the apostles and their movement were proceeding according to a human or a divine plan.

Philip, one of Stephen's colleagues in food distribution, takes center stage in Acts 8. Like the apostles and Stephen, he proclaims the good news in public and performs signs and miracles. Through him the testimony about Jesus extends into Samaria and finds a conduit leading the way to "the ends of the earth" (Acts 1:8) when he baptizes an Ethiopian court official traveling back to Africa. Even more incredible, Saul the archenemy encounters Jesus while traveling to commit violence against the church in Damascus and then begins proclaiming the good news himself. Peter performs more miracles, even raising a woman named Tabitha (also known as Dorcas) from the dead, before God leads him to preach to a gentile centurion and his household, marking the beginning of gentile inclusion in the church. Peter then experiences a miraculous escape from prison and restoration to his fellow believers.

Over the course of these chapters, readers encounter several of the most awe-inspiring and consequential scenes in the whole book. It appears that there are no dead-ends when God's Spirit leads the way. There are setbacks, of course, as seen in the execution of the apostle James, but on the whole the word of God, embodied in the story's protagonists, continues dramatically on its trajectory "to advance and gain adherents" (Acts 12:24).

In addition to being an unseen agent in these scenes, God and God's will become recognizable to characters in the Holy Spirit. The arrival of the Spirit among the Samaritans, within Saul (implied in the words of Ananias but unnarrated), and among Cornelius and his household makes a declaration that these people belong. In Acts, witnesses from the wider church play a part in discovering that belonging: Peter and John experience the Spirit's manifestation among the Samaritans; Ananias – who was supposed to be Saul's prey in Damascus – likewise places his hands on Saul and calls him "brother"; Peter and his companions recognize the Spirit among Cornelius and his associates as a sure sign of God's full embrace of a gentile household. Acts is careful to describe conversions as more than individual personal experiences but as entry into a larger community. That community also undergoes change, as a result. Ananias experiences a conversion in his appraisal of what is possible with the persecutor Saul. Peter converts to a new way of thinking about what or who is "unclean" in God's sight, and his friends in Jerusalem likewise see that God has initiated something new among gentiles. These extraordinary scenes depict the church living into new understandings of what is possible in the aftermath of Pentecost.

The narrative rhetoric in this part of Acts depicts God at work in multiple directions or within multiple characters to bring new realities to pass. It is not enough for the Samaritans to believe and submit to baptism; this new development, accomplishing a sort of reconciliation between Samaritans on one hand and Judeans and Galileans on the other, involves the experience of apostles from Jerusalem as well. Philip's extraordinary encounter with the Ethiopian court official is full of odd coincidences and serendipitous details, suggesting divine orchestration at work. Saul's encounter with Jesus on the road to Damascus does not give him all the answers; Ananias is summoned, like a reluctant prophet questioning the wisdom of God's calling, to finish the work and commission Saul. Peter and Cornelius need some time, and each needs the other to tell his own story from his point of view, before it becomes clear what is going on and Peter determines he needs to preach the good news. No one has a blueprint. No one sees exactly where the story is headed. Everyone tries to be responsive to what the Holy Spirit is orchestrating or simply making possible. The narrative proceeds in a way to make readers delight in the frequent discoveries.

This section of Acts also continues a theme from chapters 4–7 in the interaction with authorities. The Ethiopian whom Philip meets is both a eunuch and an influential man with significant political power. Cornelius is no mere soldier but a centurion in the Italian Cohort, indicating his elevated status. King Herod Agrippa, who executes James and tries to do the same to Peter, represents the other end of the spectrum. Acts portrays him as God's enemy, one who would try to oppose the spread of the good news but who suffers humiliation and death for his vain sacrilege. He stands in Pharaoh's biblical legacy.

Speaking of villains, Simon the Samaritan magician comes across as especially appalling, in light of ways that Acts signals certain characters' depravity. He seeks control over the power of God and assumes that money is part and parcel of that power. His greed recalls Judas, who died in the field he purchased with his blood money in Acts 1. With a heart that "is not right before God," Simon recalls Ananias and Sapphira in Acts 5. He illustrates the ways that Acts draws connections among greed, manipulation, and opposition to God, as seen also in the magician Bar-Jesus (Acts 13:4–12) and the repentant magicians of Ephesus (Acts 19:18–19). By contrast to several of these villains, those aligned with the Way of Jesus are characterized by works of charity and a willingness to liquidate and share assets (Acts 4:32–37).

There is an element of wonder and revelry in Peter's escape from incarceration in chapter 12. Previously, in chapter 5, an angel opened doors and directed the apostles to resume preaching in the temple. In this scene, Peter's threat is more lethal and so his escape results in him fleeing to another place. Later, in Acts 16, Paul and Silas will be able to walk out of their imprisonment but they will be uneager to run away. The escapes are all miraculous but none is like the others in terms of how it happens or what its consequences are. In all three instances, however, humor is part of the narrative rhetoric, for the scenes depict the power of God

surpassing, and even humiliating, the power that the authorities wield
to stem the influence of Jesus' followers. Acts is hardly subtle about the
ways in which imperial might is no match for the power of God.

ACTS 13–15

The geographical horizons of Acts begin to expand dramatically in chapter 13, when Saul and Barnabas board a ship and take their message and
Spirit-given powers to Cyprus and beyond, finding audiences both receptive and resistant. The narrative includes a brief reminder of Pentecost
when it highlights an ethnically diverse crowd of prophets and teach-
ers – although all are men – in the church of Antioch. They discern the
Spirit speaking in the midst of their worship and the result is travel and
expansion: Saul – henceforth referred to as Paul – and Barnabas set sail.

Their initial encounter with a powerful Roman official (Sergius
Paulus) and a "son of a devil" (Bar-Jesus, also known as Elymas) continues familiar themes. Bearing witness to Jesus repeatedly brings
characters in Acts in front of some of the most powerful men in their
contexts, and it also attracts sinister opposition. Paul – who, like Bar-
Jesus, has two names in this scene – pronounces the blindness that
engulfs his foe. It recalls the experience that Paul (then known as Saul)
had on the road to Damascus in Acts 9.

When they reach Antioch of Pisidia, Paul preaches to an audience
in a Jewish synagogue. It resembles oratory from Peter and Stephen in
the first quarter of the book, tracing scriptural narratives, focusing on
Jesus' death and resurrection, and promising forgiveness in Jesus. There
is a strong theological continuity between Paul's ministry and that of
his predecessors. At the same time, Acts uses this scene to introduce
a severe rebuke of Jews who are not persuaded by the sermon. In Acts
13:46–47 the missionaries declare that their opponents are "unworthy
of eternal life" and announce their intention to preach to gentiles. Paul
makes similar statements elsewhere, in 18:6 and 28:25–28. The narrative repetition raises questions, since Paul returns to speaking to Jewish
audiences after the first two instances (see 14:1; 19:8–10). It is unclear
if Paul's ire wears off after each pronouncement or whether there is a
cumulative, snowballing effect that makes the final denunciation in
Acts 28 all the more final. In any case, the narrative suggests that Paul's
focus on gentile audiences is born partly from frustration with and disgust for Jewish audiences that do not accept his message.

Ministry continues at a rather rapid pace through Iconium, Lystra,
Derbe, and elsewhere before returning to Antioch. A pattern of preaching,

violence, and flight emerges. The narrative pauses in Lystra to highlight the confusion experienced by ignorant locals who too quickly assume Barnabas and Paul to be Greek deities (compare Cornelius' response to Peter in Acts 10:25–26). Paul's message to them is not about Jesus and his death and resurrection but simply about the goodness of "the living God." The narrative implies that preaching within different cultural settings demands different messages. Although there are patterns of confusion, curiosity, acceptance, and rejection in these and subsequent chapters, in the narrative not all people hear or experience the preaching in the same way, due to their various cultural and religious assumptions.

The conference in Jerusalem in Acts 15 fulfills multiple functions in the plot. It recalls the encounter between Peter and Cornelius in Acts 10:1–11:18, underscoring the reality that welcoming gentiles into the church without expecting complete law obedience from them was a significant shift in the early church's expectations and a challenge for them to live out. One previous conversation between Peter and his associates in Acts 11:1–18 did not satisfy everyone's concerns. The scene also returns Paul and Barnabas to the church in Jerusalem, reminding readers that their ministry is not a separate, parallel movement but something integrated with the church of the twelve original apostles. Acts is careful to infuse the narrative with a sense of general unity and cooperation under apostolic guidance. At the same time, the narrative never entirely erases people's old memories of Saul the persecutor (see Acts 22:4–5; 26:9–11).

ACTS 16–21

The focus returns to Paul, now traveling without Barnabas, as he turns to venture further afield. In Acts 16–19 he visits a range of prominent cities. In many of these places Paul or his associates become the target of an accusation leveled against them in public. Not all of the charges are formal in a juridical sense, and they vary from advocating anti-Roman customs (Philippi), to disobeying the emperor and proclaiming a rival king (Thessalonica), to promoting "foreign divinities" (Athens), to advocating worship that violates either Roman or Jewish law (Corinth), to denigrating the goddess Artemis and her devotees (Ephesus). Although the charges are exaggerated in some settings or stem from curiosity instead of hostility in others, they all describe opposition to the Christian message. These are vital scenes for understanding how Acts depicts the church and its work in light of its imperial setting. Those outside the Christian movement see it as threatening to a range of political, cultural, and economic values. The implication is that this movement has the power to turn "the world upside down" (Acts 17:6) and upend the Roman prerogatives embedded in the status quo.

In traveling alongside Paul, occasionally drawn into the action when the narration inexplicably switches from a third-person narrator to a first-person-plural narrator (we/us), readers experience the distinctive character of some of these cities. Philippi, as a Roman colony, values its Roman character. Some of its influential residents do not respond favorably when Paul casts out a spirit of divination whom the Philippians might associate with the god Apollo and his powers. The philosophically minded and religiously inquisitive Athenians are mocked for devoting themselves to "nothing but telling or hearing something new." Representatives of the civic pride and wealth of Ephesus, connected in large part to the micro-economy attached to devotion to the goddess Artemis, have reason to worry when a church comes into being there and causes people to renounce their previous religious practices. None of these scenes is the same, but they all underscore the risk that Paul and others face. The public action, the ignorance of the opponents, and the thrilling escapes undercut the power of the empire and intimate that God will prevail, even if suffering and hardship remain realities.

These chapters also remind readers that the story is about more than Paul and his sidekick Silas. Less-visible characters such as Lydia (Acts 16), Jason (Acts 17), Priscilla and Aquila (Acts 18), Apollos (Acts 19), and the elders of the Ephesian church (Acts 20) add more than local color. They situate the more visible Paul within a larger organism of narrative activity. Paul remains important not for his own sake but for how he represents larger communities that band together, show hospitality, conduct ministry, take risks, and even suffer.

In Acts 19:21 the trajectory of the plot changes: Paul announces his intention to go to Jerusalem, presumably in response to the Holy Spirit's guidance. This recalls the moment in Luke 9:51 when Jesus "set his face to go to Jerusalem" and began his final journey. Paul and others recognize that danger awaits him in Jerusalem (Acts 20:22–25, 38; 21:12–14). None of this shakes his resolve. It will turn out to be his final journey as a free man.

ACTS 21–26

When Paul arrives in Jerusalem he appears isolated. The other believers there have suspicions about him. Soon he will find himself arrested and without companions or advocates. His arrest is no surprise, given previous foreshadowing (e.g., Acts 21:11). What is surprising is how his custody, stretching all the way to the end of the book, is not especially onerous for him, even though others have been expecting him to suffer. Throughout his Roman custody, Acts depicts Paul as exercising significant control over his settings. He is able to dictate some of the terms of his treatment, and he continues to proclaim the good news as a prisoner, but now to more limited – and more elite – audiences. Paul's calling to bear witness to Jesus continues, but custody gives him different and more exclusive avenues to follow that calling.

Courtroom drama was as thrilling and suspenseful to many ancient audiences as it can be today. These chapters narrate an extended juridical contest, in which Paul deftly responds to charges against him and uses his Roman identity and privileges to his advantage (Acts 22:25–29; 25:10–12). Jewish officials from Jerusalem pursue a case against Paul, and their allies try underhanded ways of ambushing him, but the Roman officials who incarcerate him end up protecting him and allowing him to survive and eventually travel to Rome.

The narrative emphasizes Paul's skills as an orator. He does not argue for his legal innocence as much as he contends that he has been faithful to a divine commissioning. He twice retells the story of his experience of meeting Jesus, in Acts 22 and 26, emphasizing the importance of that event as an outgrowth of and not a departure from of his own Jewish fidelity. The descriptions of these juridical scenes strike a balance between courtroom drama and evangelistic opportunity, further suggesting that the word of God will continue to advance, even when it is confined to custody. Like a tenacious weed, the church's ministry can apparently sink roots into any setting.

The Roman officials in these scenes find themselves caught in a bind that they did not entirely engineer for themselves. They are less interested in Paul's religious beliefs and more interested in him as an asset in their ability to partner with the Jewish aristocracy of Jerusalem. After building the suspense and level of risk for several chapters, finally Acts stages a spectacular hearing in which Paul addresses the Roman governor Festus alongside the Jewish client king Herod Agrippa II, his sister (and reputed lover) Bernice, and the elites of Caesarea, which was the Roman provincial capital. Paul indeed fulfills his calling to bring the name of Jesus "before Gentiles and kings and before the people of Israel" (Acts 9:15). All that remains for him to do is to see Rome, which he announced in Acts 19:21 and Jesus reaffirms when he appears to Paul in Acts 23:11. Paul makes sure that will happen when he plays his trump card just before it appears he is doomed: he appeals his case to the emperor himself (25:11–12). Paul may be in deep trouble as a prisoner, but the narrative continues to depict him as the one who controls his fate, although attentive readers detect that the narrative understands that control as ultimately belonging to God.

ACTS 27–28

Acts displays some of its most vivid literary artistry in its depiction of Paul's sea voyage and shipwreck in Acts 27. The extended narrative builds suspense for Paul's arrival in Rome and expands the sense of Paul on trial. Not only are the Romans imperiling him and assessing whether he deserves to live; it seems the forces of nature are, too. Paul continues to exercise control over his surroundings. Although still a prisoner escorted by Roman soldiers, he gives commands about how to tend the ship. He distributes the food supplies. He warns against allowing people to flee the battered vessel. The centurion guarding him protects him. Shipwrecked on Malta, Paul survives what looks to the local islanders like divine judgment against him when a viper bites his hand. Paul heals the ruling official on the island and thus ensures the possibility of continuing to Rome. He looks more like a conquering hero than an imperiled prisoner.

The story ends in Rome, the destination Paul needs to see, according to Jesus in Acts 23:11. Paul meets believers there and also Rome's Jewish population, which has a divided response to his preaching. Acts declines to narrate Paul's death, even though the narrative has given multiple indications that it is certain (Acts 20:17–38; 21:13–14). Acts ends midstory, then, without complete resolution. By refusing to describe the deaths of its two most prominent characters, Peter and Paul, Acts concludes with the message that the real focus of the story all along is the perseverance of the word of God, not the heroism of those who bear witness to that word.

SELECTED FURTHER READING

Aarflot, Christine H. *God (in) Acts: The Characterization of God in the Acts of the Apostles*. Eugene, OR: Pickwick, 2020.

Alexander, Loveday C. A. *Acts in Its Ancient Literary Context: A Classicist Looks at the Acts of the Apostles*. Early Christianity in Context. Library of New Testament Studies, 298. London: T&T Clark, 2005.

Bauer, David R. *The Book of Acts as Story: A Narrative-Critical Study*. Grand Rapids: Baker Academic, 2021.

Bonz, Marianne Palmer. *The Past as Legacy: Luke, Acts, and Ancient Epic*. Minneapolis: Fortress, 2000.

Dupertuis, Rubén René. "The Acts of the Apostles, Narrative, and History." Pages 330–40 in *The Oxford Handbook of Biblical Narrative*. Edited by Danna Nolan Fewell; New York: Oxford University Press, 2016).

Jennings, Willie James. *Acts. Belief: A Theological Commentary on the Bible*. Louisville: Westminster John Knox, 2017.

Marguerat, Daniel. *The First Christian Historian: Writing the "Acts of the Apostles."* Society for New Testament Studies Monograph Series 121. Cambridge: Cambridge University Press, 2002.

Matthews, Shelly. *The Acts of the Apostles: Taming the Tongues of Fire*. T&T Clark's Study Guides to the New Testament. London: Bloomsbury T&T Clark, 2017.

Reimer, Ivoni Richter. *Women in the Acts of the Apostles: A Feminist Liberation Perspective*. Minneapolis: Fortress, 1995.

Shauf, Scott. *The Divine in Acts and in Ancient Historiography*. Minneapolis: Fortress, 2015.

Shepherd, William H. *The Narrative Function of the Holy Spirit as a Character in Luke-Acts*. Society of Biblical Literature Dissertation Series 147. Atlanta: Scholars Press, 1994.

Skinner, Matthew L. *Intrusive God, Disruptive Gospel: Encountering the Divine in the Book of Acts*. Grand Rapids: Brazos, 2015.

Spencer, F. Scott. *Journeying through Acts: A Literary-Cultural Reading*. Peabody: Hendrickson, 2004.

Tannehill, Robert C. *The Narrative Unity of Luke-Acts: A Literary Interpretation*, vol. 2: *The Acts of the Apostles*. Minneapolis: Fortress, 1990.

15 Stories from Letters

Paul's Correspondence and the Narrative Approach

LYNN H. COHICK

INTRODUCTION

Humans love stories, share stories, create stories, and make sense of the world through stories. Sometimes these stories take shape as epic poems, or as novels, or as biographies. Other times, stories run in the background, like a computer program that allows an author to write an essay. Scholars using and evaluating the narrative approach to Paul's epistles start at several different points, which both reveal their understanding of narrative and determine to a certain degree their conclusions. These starting points fall into at least four camps. First, some begin with individual epistles and examine narratives on the surface of or within the text itself, for example, Paul's stories about himself (Gal 1:13–24). Second, other scholars look below the surface to the stories implied or retold, for example, from Israel's history. For these scholars, each epistle has its own story, and readers compare each epistle's story. Third, other scholars examine the epistles together as a whole and build an overarching narrative that structures and supports Paul's specific arguments for the different situations within each epistle. Fourth, some scholars grant that narrative operates in Paul's letters as he reflects on the story of Israel, his own story, and that of the churches based on the Christ event. However, they suggest that the Christ event stands outside a narrative model because it is a singular (redemptive) moment, not a series of related events that move towards a climax. They stress discontinuity within the biblical narrative with regard to the inbreaking of the Christ moment.

Each of these positions will be discussed before we analyze Philippians through the narrative method. I will suggest that letters inhabit stories, and stories inhabit letters, grounding the exchange with shared experiences, intertextual references, and identity-making claims. Paul's letters reflect the larger narrative of God's redemptive work in Christ for the church and for the world. Paul's own story fits within this larger narrative, and Paul makes sense of his life through experience and reflection on the story of Jesus Christ.

DEFINITIONS OF NARRATIVE AND EPISTLE

A narrative is a story and, indeed, the terms are often used interchangeably. A narrative includes a plot, characters, and events, while letters argue, persuade, or encourage readers to a particular point of view or action. An epistle or letter is an occasional document, written to a specific audience in particular circumstances. Ancient letters typically included (1) a greeting and wishes for the recipients' good health, (2) the body of the text which informed or gave instructions, and (3) the closing. Paul's letters follow this pattern. Rowe explains that narrative is "the substructure of nonnarrative texts."[1] The narrative is not a separate cognitive structure alongside doctrines or propositions; rather, "in a crucial sense, to know the story is to know the thing itself."[2] As Melanie Johnson-DeBaufre states, "Paul was also in the business of thinking big stories about God, justice, peoples, and salvation."[3] Paul's story was contested by others, as is clear in his letters. The epistle format is especially suited to address the false or misguided theology and ethics carried in his opponents' stories.

NARRATIVE CRITICISM AND READING LETTERS

Within biblical studies, narrative criticism developed in the latter half of the twentieth century as a method to explore the literary qualities of the Gospels. It grew from a sense that we should read the Gospels as stories as we do other ancient literature such as Homer's epics or Plutarch's biographies. An important work for New Testament scholars was Robert Alter's *The Art of Biblical Narrative*.[4] Alter focuses on the Hebrew Bible (Old Testament), demonstrating the value of "trying to look carefully into the literary art of a biblical text."[5] He suggests a literary analysis of the Hebrew Bible similar to that which one would

---

[1] C. Kavin Rowe, *One True Life: The Stoics and Early Christians as Rival Traditions* (New Haven: Westminster John Knox, 2016), 201.
[2] Ibid., 199.
[3] Melanie Johnson-DeBaufre, "Narrative, Multiplicity, and the Letters of Paul," in *The Oxford Handbook of Biblical Narrative*, ed. Danna Nolan Fewell (Oxford: Oxford University Press, 2016), 364.
[4] Robert Alter, *The Art of Biblical Narrative* (New York: Basic Books, 1981).
[5] Ibid., 12.

render to Shakespeare's plays or Dante's poetry, or Tolstoy's novels.[6] Attention to characters, their dreams, desires, and faults, and to events and dramas unfolding, reveals the Bible's central tenet that humans "must live before God, in the transforming medium of time."[7]

Historical Criticism and Narrative Criticism

Narrative criticism confronted the dominant approach at the time in biblical studies, historical critical method, that examined the history revealed in the text, to apprehend the ancient world of the author and readers. In the case of Paul's letters, the historical critical method focused on the specific problems and issues of each community, and Paul's response. Often those using the historical critical approach viewed biblical books as "a compilation of direct imprints from the past, providing direct evidence for events and ideas contained in the discourse or for the life situation of the author (or authors) and the first audience of the text."[8] This method tended to view Scripture as communicating propositions and doctrines. The historical critical method helpfully provided historical context for Paul's letters and highlighted specific, sometimes called "contingent," issues each recipient faced.[9]

The narrative approach to Paul's letters arises in part from a frustration in not reaching a consensus of a central core idea in Paul's thought. Michael Gorman observes, when we speak of center, such as the sun with its orbiting planets, we do not see the connection or integration between these discrete elements. The strength of a story, however, is that it does not have a center; stories have a plot, characters, and a climax. "A narrative suggests action and movement not merely around an immovable central feature but *within* the central phenomena of the story."[10]

---

[6] Ibid., 13. Alter continues, 21, that "the literary approach is actually a good deal less conjectural than the historical scholarship that asks of a verse whether it contains possible Akkadian loanwords."

[7] Ibid., 22.

[8] Mark Reasoner, *Five Models of Scripture* (Grand Rapids: Eerdmans, 2021), 54.

[9] J. Christiaan Beker, *The Triumph of God: The Essence of Paul's Thought*, transl. Loren T. Stuckenbruck (Minneapolis: Augsburg Fortress, 1990), 15–38, outlines the coherence (enduring) and contingency (context-specific) of Paul's gospel, and promotes the apocalyptic nature of his message.

[10] Michael J. Gorman, *Cruciformity: Paul's Narrative Spirituality of the Cross* (Grand Rapids: Eerdmans, 2001), 370. See also Ben Witherington III, *Paul's Narrative Thought World: The Tapestry of Tragedy and Triumph* (Louisville: Westminster/John Knox, 1994).

Postmodernism, Ethics, and the Narrative Approach

The narrative approach grew within the postmodern landscape, as scholars became convinced that stories shape our worldview. Questions quickly emerged around the question of meta-narrative. Though emphasizing story, the liberationist and postmodern approaches may resist both a sense of stable realities and meta-narrative, because these lack particularity. Said another way, the dominant voice in a meta-narrative can drown out minoritized voices. Particularity is especially important for minoritized readers, those at the margins of society whose voice and experience have been silenced and dismissed. Analyzing Paul's letters from a narrative perspective should attend to the multiple characters, named and unnamed, past and present, to allow for the rich texture of Paul's own story and the grand story of God to have full effect.

Narrative method developed from a desire to understand identity-making and ethics in Paul and was energized by a dissatisfaction over systematic theology's claims of universalism and abstract reasoning as sufficient for theological reflection. Narrative theology embraces "non-rational tradition (symbols and myth), particular lived experience, and the self as person."[11] Moreover, narrative shapes communities, and humans are embedded in communities.

Narratives frame and give meaning to the propositions (doctrines) that any community holds. As an example of this claim, C. Kavin Rowe examines Christianity and Stoicism, arguing that the ideas within each tradition (1) are inseparable from expected practices exhibited by a Stoic or Christian and (2) are mutually incompatible. In the end, Stoics inhabits reason, pulling into themselves, and become "solitary, self-sufficient fortresses of right judgment."[12] The Christian, by contrast, is drawn into a community based on the life, death, and resurrection of Jesus Christ, in whose resurrected life they participate within their local church communities. As such, Rowe declares, "Christianity is prima facie a narrative way of life."[13]

Underneath the question of whether to use narrative or systematic theology, and historical critical or narrative method, is a question of how one perceives truth. What counts as true? An added question for those who read the Bible is how we ascertain its truth claims. Addressing the first question, James Cone asserts the promise of story for testifying to

---

[11] John Klaasen, "Practical Theology and Narrative: Contours and Markers," *STJ* 3.2 (2017): 459.

[12] Rowe, *One True Life*, 215.

[13] Ibid., 215.

the truth of God's redemption: "For in the Christian story, truth is not an object but is the project of freedom made possible by the presence of God in the midst of the people."[14] He continues that in "black religion, the people tell the story of their lives as they walked and talked with Jesus,"[15] and as they lived into Jesus's resurrection, creating a theology of hope based on their "encounter with the crucified and risen Lord in the context of American slavery."[16] Here we see personal and community experiences as crucial components of knowing and believing; this contrasts with convictions that theology could be gained through abstract, rational argument and universal categories.

YES, THERE IS A NARRATIVE IN PAUL'S LETTERS

Richard Hays, in his ground-breaking work first published in 1983, *The Faith of Jesus Christ*, focuses on "narrative elements that undergird Paul's thought."[17] He proposes that Paul's theological teachings assumed a story about Jesus Christ that provided a narrative substructure to his letters.[18] Hays points to the "centrality of *narrative* elements in his [Paul's] thought" that express the story of Jesus Christ, which acts "as a constraint governing the logic of Paul's argumentation."[19] As Hays argues, "*a story about Jesus Christ is presupposed by Paul's argument … and his theological reflection attempts to articulate the meaning of that story.*"[20] This story reaches back into the Old Testament, the narrative and promises to God's people (Israel). The story propels forward towards a climax in Jesus as God's messiah, and to the end of the current age, and to the arrival of the new heavens and new earth.

Hays stresses that the narrative approach not only expresses Paul's argument, but also emphasizes the expected way of life exhorted by Paul, which is summed up in his oft-repeated phrase, "in Christ." Followers of Jesus are "in Christ," and participate in new life in the Holy Spirit. The narrative hinge is the death of Jesus on the cross, and

---

[14] James H. Cone, *God of the Oppressed*, revised edition (Maryknoll: Orbis Books, 1997), 114.

[15] Ibid., 114.

[16] Ibid., 117.

[17] Richard B. Hays, *The Faith of Jesus Christ: The Narrative Substructure of Galatians 3:1–4:11*, 2nd edition (Grand Rapids: Eerdmans, 2002), xxiii.

[18] Ibid., 7.

[19] Ibid., 6.

[20] Ibid., xxiv. See also Matthew W. Bates, *The Hermeneutics of the Apostolic Proclamation: The Center of Paul's Method of Scriptural Interpretation* (Waco: Baylor University Press, 2019).

his resurrection, which becomes Paul's story as he declares that he has been crucified with Christ, and no longer lives, but Christ lives in him (Gal 2:20). Hays concludes, "Paul's gospel *is* a story, and it *has* a narrative structure, but it is not *a* narrative except when it is actually narrated, as in Phil 2:6–11."[21]

N. T. Wright has developed his narrative approach over several decades, drawing on narrative studies, and reacting against the implicit (and explicit) anti-Jewish bias that infiltrated much of New Testament scholarship in the first half of the twentieth century. Wright emphasizes the story of Israel, found in the Bible and in Second Temple Jewish literature, as integral to understanding the story of the New Testament.[22] Wright finds a total of three levels of narrative within Paul's epistles. He argues for two levels of narrative within Paul's letters: a *poetic sequence* and a *referential sequence;* the former is "the order of things as they appear in the text itself," while the latter is "the assumed and/ or reconstructed order of events within the total narrative world of the letter."[23] Wright admits that the *poetic sequence* is very much how historians read texts, but the *referential sequence* involves the narrative world of the text.

Alongside the poetic and referential sequence, there is a third level, Wright maintains, a larger Christian story that "gave narrative depth to Paul's worldview, which formed an irreducible part of his symbolic university."[24] This deeper story, rooted in Israel's story, is not at the surface of Paul's letters, but forms the base and provides the content of his worldview.[25] Wright asserts that Paul's worldview has at its center the sweeping story of God and creation of the cosmos, with attending subplots. One sub-plot tells the story of humanity's creation, disobedience, redemption, and future immortal life in Christ. A second tells the story of Israel, the patriarchs and matriarchs, the Law, the temple, the nation, the exile, the promises of restoration. Israel's story, the Jewish story, is reimagined and reinterpreted by the Christ story. A third, the climax

---

[21] Hays, *The Faith of Jesus Christ*, 19.

[22] N. T. Wright, *The New Testament and the People of God* (Minneapolis: Fortress, 1992), 338, continues that the Jews of Jesus's day were hopeful of God's faithfulness to his people, and, concerning Jesus, "it was to this same people that ... [a] prophet came, announcing in the villages of Galilee that now at least Israel's god was becoming king." (Note: god is not capitalized in the original.)

[23] Wright, *The New Testament and the People of God*, 404.

[24] Ibid., 404.

[25] Ibid., 405, contends that "we can only understand the more limited narrative worlds of the different letters if we locate them at their appropriate points within this overall story-world, and indeed within the symbolic universe that accompanies it."

in history, is Jesus's story. This story for Paul is "always the story of *how Jesus enables the other stories* to proceed to their appointed resolution."[26]

Michael Gorman pursues narrative in Paul with a focus on spirituality "that tells a story, a dynamic life with God that corresponds in some way to the divine 'story'."[27] This narrative spirituality is best described as "cruciformity," that is, "conformity to the crucified Christ."[28] The death of Jesus on the cross is the climax of God's redemptive story that began in creation and will reach its fullness in the new creation. Paul holds up Christ's death and resurrection as the narrative believers enter as they are "in Christ." Christ's story becomes the community's narrative. Hays and Gorman highlight a key point, namely the idea that way of life and belief go hand in hand. The phrase "in Christ" unlocks this participatory focus of the Christian life.

Scot McKnight argues that Paul tells stories of himself that parallel the story of Christ as told in Philippians 2:6–11: "Paul shaped his own self-identity and story as an expression of Christoformity."[29] McKnight means by this term the goal of being conformed to Christ. McKnight concentrates on story as well in his book on Romans. He states that "story forms both identity and community."[30] He expounds on the different stories that ground gentiles, found in the ancient myth of Remus and Romulus, and epics of Homer and Virgil, and those stories found in Jewish Scripture – stories of Abraham and Sarah, Moses, David, and the prophets. Paul provides a unifying story for gentile and Jewish believers based on Christ's work on the cross, reading Israel's story through the lens of Christ's story. McKnight argues that "Paul's narrative in Romans 9–11 both articulates and legitimates the lived theology of Christoformity of 12–16. The story Paul tells is the symbolic universe he wants the Strong and the Weak to inhabit together."[31] McKnight modifies Gorman's cruciformity slightly to focus on Christoformity, Paul's emphasis on Christ being formed in believers, but the overall emphasis in both scholars is participating in Christ. In Romans, Paul

[26] N. T. Wright, *Paul and the Faithfulness of God*, Book I, Parts 1 & 2 (Minneapolis: Fortress, 2013), 517.
[27] Gorman, *Cruciformity*, 4.
[28] Ibid., 4.
[29] Scot McKnight, *Pastor Paul: Nurturing a Culture of Christoformity in the Church* (Grand Rapids: Brazos Press, 2019), 140.
[30] Scot McKnight, *Reading Romans Backwards: A Gospel of Peace in the Midst of Empire* (Waco: Baylor University Press, 2019), 59.
[31] McKnight, *Reading Romans Backwards*, 59.

applies Christoformity to the specific problem of disunity between Jewish and gentile followers of Jesus: "For Paul, Christoformity was the only way Jewish and gentile believers could live in peace, love, and reconciliation."[32]

McKnight's emphasis on reconciliation and the social implications of Paul's gospel message is of primary concern to Corneliu Constantineau, who reflects "seriously on the inability of Christian communities to incarnate the message of reconciliation."[33] He finds promise in the possibility of a narrative substructure to Paul's thought, which informs Paul's discourses in his letters. Narrative proves a way to link theology and ethics, with the epistles "reflecting, and contributing to, a narrative myth which constructs a particular symbolic universe ... This myth, enacted in ritual, is an identity- and community-forming narrative which shapes both the world-view (the 'is') and the ethos (the 'ought') of the adherents."[34] Constantineau looks for "narrative features" that call to mind the full story.[35] He points to Stanley Hauerwas, a leading theologian and ethicist who champions narrative for moral formation and identity construction. Hauerwas stresses story as the place of community and character formation.[36]

NO, WE CANNOT CONSTRUCT A META-NARRATIVE FROM PAUL'S LETTERS

Not surprisingly, not all scholars believe the narrative method is the most effective approach to reading Paul's letters. The hesitancy primarily revolves around the following four issues. First, some scholars do not discern a basic story or "all-encompassing" story within Paul's letters.[37] Similarly, some argue that a meta-story might silence aspects of individual letters or hide the possibility that Paul has a different story of God in his various letters; in other words, diminish particularity.[38]

---

[32] Ibid., 59.

[33] Corneliu Constantineau, *The Social Significance of Reconciliation in Paul's Theology: Narrative Readings in Romans*, LNTS 421 (London: T&T Clark, 2010), 2.

[34] Ibid., 97–8.

[35] Ibid., 18.

[36] Stanley Hauerwas, *A Community of Character: Toward a Constructive Christian Social Ethic* (Notre Dame: University of Notre Dame Press, 1981), 9–35.

[37] Edward Adams, "Paul's Story of God and Creation: The Story of How God Fulfils His Purposes in Creation," in *Narrative Dynamics in Paul: A Critical Assessment*, ed. Bruce W. Longenecker (Louisville: Westminster John Knox,2002), 42.

[38] Ibid., 42. See also R. Barry Matlock, "The Arrow and the Web: Critical Reflections on a Narrative Approach to Paul," in *Narrative Dynamics in Paul: A Critical Assessment*, ed. Bruce W. Longenecker (Louisville: Westminster John Knox, 2002), 51–52.

Second, scholars hesitate to read an implied story, and therefore focus only on the story within the letter itself. For example, Edward Adams concludes, "It seems wise to me, therefore, in narratological analysis of Paul's writing, to treat 'narrative' as a textual phenomenon rather than a mental phenomenon, and to use 'story' as a tool for analysing [sic] what Paul said on a given occasion rather than as an instrument for probing the innermost workings of his mind."[39] Andrew Lincoln agrees that narrative is "first of all a *literary* category" and thus is concerned with "the world of the text."[40] While Lincoln holds that "Paul's letters reflect a symbolic universe that has narrative qualities," he also cautions that when speaking about Paul's use of Abraham in Galatians, one should not use the term "story" because Paul's comments are better viewed as "applied commentaries on the scriptural story of Abraham," and best described as "creative exegesis of the Jewish scriptures."[41] Third, some point to the misuse of meta-narrative as reason not to use it. Grand stories have been used to justify persecution and domination. Fourth, those who read Paul from an apocalyptic perspective view Paul's gospel as non-narratival. They emphasize God's singular inbreaking event of Christ's cross and resurrection and de-emphasize the gospel as linear story. Francis Watson observes that Paul tells stories in his letters; however, the gospel itself is not a story because it is not a linear or timebound reality: "What Paul does *not* do is to incorporate his gospel into a linear story of creation and Israel as the end and goal of that story."[42]

Morna Hooker addresses the implicit critique against reading Paul through narrative, namely the apparent lack of consistency in his telling of the grand narrative. She cites two problems with this critique. First, the critique wrongly assumes that a substory of the larger narrative of God's purposes revealed in the world can stand on its own without reference to the larger story. This myopic view tends to skew the meta-narrative. Hooker points out that this tendency is not new, for Paul and his antagonists in Galatia both read the same promises in the Jewish Scriptures that God would redeem Israel. Paul saw that as accomplished in Christ and including gentiles. His opponents read the

---

[39] Adams, "Paul's Story of God and Creation," 42.

[40] Andrew T. Lincoln, "The Stories of Predecessors and Inheritors in Galatians and Romans," in *Narrative Dynamics in Paul: A Critical Assessment*, ed. Bruce W. Longenecker (Louisville: Westminster John Knox, 2002), 202.

[41] Ibid., 173, 199.

[42] Francis Watson, "Is There a Story in These Texts?" in *Narrative Dynamics in Paul: A Critical Assessment*, ed. Bruce W. Longenecker (Louisville: Westminster John Knox, 2002), 234.

story as God promising redemption of Israel and its ruling over gentiles.[43] Second, one assumes that with a single story, we find the entire narrative behind it. In this case, we discover that Paul rarely tells the whole story of God's purpose in any one spot. Even Philippians 2:6–11 does not mention resurrection. This "failure" does not worry Hooker, because she does not expect Paul to give every detail of the gospel whenever he speaks about it.[44] He draws on aspects of particular stories to answer the specific questions and problems faced by the recipients of his letter. Hooker concludes, "the different ways in which Israel's story is handled in Romans and Galatians, therefore, are not due to 'unstable' elements in that story but are rather the result of the different circumstances underlying the letters."[45] The key question for Hooker is whether Paul is interested in what God is doing in history. If we answer "yes" to this question, then for Hooker, "it is clear that his interpreters should not ignore the role of 'narrative.'"[46]

STORY IN PHILIPPIANS

As we turn to explore Philippians from a narrative approach, we will not follow the order of chapter and verse but will explore the stories that undergird Paul's message. We must remember that Paul spent a few weeks with the Philippian church years earlier (see Acts 16), and they had some contact in the intervening years. Through Paul and his coworkers (including Euodia and Syntyche, Phil 4:2–3), the gospel message in its grand fullness had been discussed and enacted by the new community. We will look first at the Old Testament hints and allusions to this grand story of God's purpose in Christ for the church and the world. Then we will turn to the immediate controlling narrative for the epistle, namely the poem-like passage about Christ in 2:6–11. From there, we turn to Paul's personal story as it reflects and embodies Christ's story. A deeper dive into Philippians would include exploring the main characters, including Timothy and Epaphroditus, as well as the impact of key events, such as Paul's imprisonment as he writes the letter, but we are unable to explore these areas in this essay.

---

43 Morna D. Hooker, "'Heirs of Abraham': The Gentiles' Role in Israel's Story: A Response to Bruce W. Longenecker," in *Narrative Dynamics in Paul: A Critical Assessment*, ed. Bruce W. Longenecker (Louisville: Westminster John Knox, 2002), 87.
44 Ibid., 88.
45 Ibid., 95.
46 Ibid., 96.

GOD'S GRAND NARRATIVE AS EXPRESSED IN PHILIPPIANS

The full story of redemption begins with creation of the world and of humanity, the fall, the calling of Israel and its history, leading to the work of Christ, and now the moment of the church, anticipating the full new creation of the new heavens and new earth. The full story supports Paul's joyful letter to the Philippians. Paul emphasizes the future when speaking of the "day of Christ Jesus" (1:6) and more specifically, the return of the Savior, Jesus Christ (3:20). This thought is nuanced in Paul's confident claim that the Philippians will be saved, while their enemies who persecute them will be destroyed (1:28). Paul personalizes the promise in his confidence that when he dies, he will be with Christ, a state of being far superior to his present condition (1:21–24).

ISRAEL'S SCRIPTURE AND STORY IN PHILIPPIANS

Both the master-story of Christ and Paul's story discussed later rest in part on Israel's Scriptures and story. In some cases, one has the sense that Scripture permeates Paul's understanding such that he draws on its language and concepts reflexively. For example, as he describes his imprisonment (1:19), he pulls from the Greek translation of Job 13:15–16, that the ordeal "will turn out for my deliverance." Job declares that his deliverance/salvation will be that God does not allow the godless to come before him. Indeed, God vindicated Job as a righteous man, and Paul may be drawing on this teaching. Alternatively, this passage in Job occurs just after Job's faithful declaration that though God slay him, yet still will he praise him (13:15). Paul might be reflecting on this testimony of faithfulness, for his imprisonment could end with his death. The options are not mutually exclusive; the point is that Paul draws on Job's situation of suffering to interpret his own.

In expressing God's exaltation of Christ (Phil 2:9–10), Paul includes Isaiah 45:22–23, wherein God declares that there are no other gods like God, righteous and a savior; every knee will bow and every tongue will swear to this claim. Paul shifts the focus from God the Father to the Lord Jesus Christ, highlighting Christ's honor in addition to God the Father's glory (Phil 2:11. Interestingly, Paul cites this same verse in Romans 14:10–14, warning believers not to judge each other, for God will ask each to give an account of their life to him. Earlier in the Philippians passage, Paul leans on Isaiah's presentation of the suffering servant as he describes the suffering and slave status of Christ (Isa 52:13–53:12). Isaiah speaks of this servant being humiliated by a lack of justice (53:8) and poured out unto death (53:12); Jesus experiences humiliation and death on a cross (Phil 2:8).

Paul alludes to other Scripture passages obliquely. His injunction to obey God in 2:12–16 draws on several common phrases or well-known stories in Jewish Scripture. In 2:12, Paul encourages the demeanor of "fear and trembling" as the Philippians live out their beliefs. Israel is called to fear and tremble before the Almighty (Exod 15:16; Ps 2:11). We find that they tremble before human enemies (Ps 55:5) or will have their own enemies tremble before them (Deut 2:25; 11:25). Paul uses this phrase to describe his humility before the Corinthians and (more problematic for us today), in asking slaves to obey their owners (1 Cor 2:3; Eph 6:5).[47] In 2:14, Paul warns against grumbling or murmuring. The prohibition against grumbling calls to mind the wilderness wanderings of the Israelites and God's judgment against them when they bellyached. For example, Miriam and Aaron grumbled against Moses because he married a Cushite woman, and God chastised them (Num 12:1–15; see also 11:1–34). This passage might resonate with Paul as he enjoins the Philippians to unity (2:1–4) and seeks to have two of his coworkers, Euodia and Syntyche, be of the same mind (4:2–3). In 2:15, Paul encourages the believers to be without fault or blemish among their "crooked and perverse generation," and to "shine like stars." Paul pulls from Moses' castigation of Israel for its unfaithfulness when he describes the wider social context of Philippi as a "crooked and perverse generation" (Deut 32:5). Jesus uses this phrase when describing his disciples' and the community's lack of faith (Matt 17:17). Paul continues to encourage the Philippians to shine like stars among their willful and wicked society. The phrase is found in Daniel, although the prophet promises the righteous that they *will* shine as stars in the sky (Dan 12:3). Interestingly, in the following verse, Daniel speaks of the deliverance of all those whose name is written in the book (Dan 12:4). Paul speaks of all those whose names are found in the book of life in 4:3. Perhaps Paul has in mind the Daniel passage, with its focus on the current suffering and the coming redemption of the righteous, as he composes this letter.

CHRIST'S STORY IN PHILIPPIANS 2:6–11

One of the most well-known passages of this short epistle is found in 2:6–11. Yet many do not think about these verses as story, because

---

[47] For a discussion of slavery in Ephesians 6:5–9, see Lynn H. Cohick, *The Letter to the Ephesians*, NICNT (Grand Rapids: Eerdmans, 2020).

typically they are presented as a poem and often referred to as the "Christ hymn." Yet scholars emphasizing the narrative approach point to the story within these verses. Richard J. Weymouth summarizes much of scholarship in his statement, "Does not the recognition that in Phil 2:6–11 we are dealing with a story, the Christ-story, actually compel us towards using a narrative approach as an interpretative key to unlocking the treasures of this beloved passage."[48] Philippians 2:6–11 narrates Jesus Christ's incarnation and suffering, climaxing in his death on a cross, followed by his exaltation. The humiliation and exaltation of Christ are brought together, and "the two parts together yield a complete story corresponding to the pattern of exaltation following humiliation that permeates Hebrew wisdom literature and finds graphic expression in Isaiah's fourth servant song (Isa. 52:13–53:12)."[49]

The verses have been called the *kenosis* passage, highlighting the Greek term for "emptied." Michael Gorman explains the self-emptying of Christ with the formula: although [x], not [y] but [z].[50] Specifically, Christ, although in the form of God, did not use this status for his own advantage, but emptied himself and obediently died on a cross for the sake of humanity's redemption. God exalted Christ following his humiliation, not as a reward for suffering, but as evidence that such self-giving humility is in fact a lord-like thing to do.[51] Gorman concludes, "the two parts together yield a complete story corresponding to the pattern of exaltation following humiliation that permeates Hebrew wisdom literature and finds graphic expression in Isaiah's fourth servant song (Isa 52:13–53:12)."[52] He observes that the passage highlights themes around the cross found throughout Paul's letters, including "obedience, love, grace, sacrifice, altruism, grace, self-giving," as well as the humble suffering and death, followed by exaltation, and concludes that this passage might be "accurately described as *Paul's master story of the cross*."[53]

---

48 Richard J. Weymouth, "The Christ-Story of Philippians 2:6–11: Narrative Shape and Paraenetic Purpose in Paul's Letter to Philippi," PhD diss., University of Otago, 2015, 135.

49 Gorman, *Cruciformity*, 87. See also, Michael J. Gorman, *Inhabiting the Cruciform God: Kenosis, Justification, and Theosis in Paul's Narrative Soteriology* (Grand Rapids: Eerdmans, 2009).

50 Gorman, *Inhabiting the Cruciform God*, 11–15, argues that Philippians 2:6–11 is poetic narrative that expresses Paul's theology, including intertextual threads and social resonances woven throughout. He continues, 25, that "Christ's divinity, and thus divinity itself, is being narratively defined as kenotic and cruciform in character."

51 Ibid., 30.

52 Gorman, *Cruciformity*, 87.

53 Ibid., 88.

Melanie Johnson-DeBaufre agrees with Gorman that "numerous encapsulated personal stories throughout Paul's letters show signs of this pattern [although [x], not [y] but [z]]."[54] She raises an interesting question about how a person without status would enter into this paradigm. What might a slave's "although" look like since her life was a continual humiliation? Gorman recognizes that most of Paul's congregation are the "have-nots" and yet Paul maintains that every person can make choices and establish practices that embody Christ: "Moreover, if Christ took on the form of a slave, in some sense he dignifies the lowest run of society (i.e., persons there) and gives them the honor and privilege as slaves of being indwelt by him and being part of a Christ-infused, Christ-shaped community."[55] Gorman reminds us that Paul speaks to the Philippians as a community, not merely as a group of individuals. As such, the community should care for each other, embodying the cruciform life together.[56]

Paul speaks of his suffering in his current imprisonment and points to the Philippians' own suffering as in solidarity with his own (1:27–30). These sufferings participate in the suffering of Christ as narrated in 2:6–8. As Weymouth observes, "Significantly, the intersecting narratives of Philippians all revolve around one central story, that of Christ in 2:6–11."[57] Paul speaks of his and the Philippians' participation in Christ's exaltation by way of being transformed to be like his glorious body (3:21).

PAUL'S STORY IN PHILIPPIANS 3:4–11

Philippians 3:4–6 is one of a few passages in Paul's letters that provide a window into Paul's past as he sees it now (see also Gal 1–2). Paul describes himself as belonging to a sincere and active Jewish family who took their identity seriously. Paul continued that path by following one of the Jewish groups of the day, the Pharisees. He spent much time studying the law, including the Torah delivered to Moses on Mt. Sinai, which shapes Jewish self-understanding and practices to this day (Exod 19:1–20:21). Looking back, Paul does not regret any of this. Yet when he places these successes and privileges next to knowing the Messiah Jesus, Paul declares that all else pales in comparison.

Paul continues in 3:9–11 that he desires to know the power of Christ's resurrection and participation in his suffering. With this, Paul

54   Johnson-DeBaufre, "Narrative, Multiplicity, and the Letters of Paul," 367.
55   Michael J. Gorman in personal communication, 29 September 2021.
56   Ibid.
57   Weymouth, "The Christ-Story of Philippians 2:6–11," 48.

fills in the missing piece of Christ's story in the previous chapter. Recall that 2:8 ends with Jesus's death on the cross, and 2:9 tells of his exaltation. Does Paul assume the readers know of the resurrection? His declaration in 3:10 supports that supposition.

Paul provides this personal history to help the Philippians understand the relative importance of circumcision for the people of God. Paul maintains that the followers of Jesus can claim a spiritual circumcision identity, but the gentile men in the group should not undergo physical circumcision. Instead, both Jew and gentile in Christ share God's Spirit, and are therefore part of God's family. Paul's own story is not solely his own, but is the story of Christ, which gives life to Paul's story.

CONCLUSION

Paul offers glimpses into his relationship with the Philippian church and the coworkers with him. We discover a shared story, and Paul's views of events that shaped both their paths. As readers today, we reconstruct that story to better understand Paul's message. Paul's letters make sense within the larger narrative of God's purposes told in the Jewish Scriptures, in creation and the promised new creation, and most assuredly in the Christ story. The meta-narrative of God's redemptive work in the world through Christ includes several substories that animate Paul's letters. This story will do more than simply hold historical references such as past events or shared friends, because Paul and other biblical authors "*affirm a theological story* in their communication – the story of who God is and what God is doing in this world."[58]

SELECTED FURTHER READING

Adams, Edward. "Paul's Story of God and Creation: The Story of How God Fulfils His Purposes in Creation." Pages 19–43 in *Narrative Dynamics in Paul: A Critical Assessment*, edited by Bruce W. Longenecker. Louisville: Westminster John Knox, 2002.

Alter, Robert. *The Art of Biblical Narrative*. New York: Basic Books, 1981.

Bates, Matthew W. *The Hermeneutics of the Apostolic Proclamation: The Center of Paul's Method of Scriptural Interpretation*. Waco: Baylor University Press, 2019.

Beker, J. Christiaan. *The Triumph of God: The Essence of Paul's Thought*. Translated by Loren T. Stuckenbruck. Minneapolis: Augsburg Fortress, 1990.

Brown, Jeannine K. *Scripture as Communication: Introducing Biblical Hermeneutics*, 2nd edition. Grand Rapids: Baker Academic, 2021.

---

[58] Jeannine K. Brown, *Scripture as Communication: Introducing Biblical Hermeneutics*, 2nd edition (Grand Rapids: Baker Academic, 2021) 161.

Cohick, Lynn H. *The Letter to the Ephesians.* NICNT. Grand Rapids: Eerdmans, 2020.

Cone, James H. *God of the Oppressed,* revised edition. Maryknoll: Orbis Books, 1997.

Constantineau, Corneliu. *The Social Significance of Reconciliation in Paul's Theology: Narrative Readings in Romans.* LNTS 421. London: T&T Clark, 2010.

Gorman, Michael J. *Cruciformity: Paul's Narrative Spirituality of the Cross.* Grand Rapids: Eerdmans, 2001.

Gorman, Michael J. *Inhabiting the Cruciform God: Kenosis, Justification, and Theosis in Paul's Narrative Soteriology.* Grand Rapids: Eerdmans, 2009.

Hauerwas, Stanley, *A Community of Character: Toward a Constructive Christian Social Ethic.* Notre Dame: University of Notre Dame Press, 1981.

Hays, Richard B. *The Faith of Jesus Christ: The Narrative Substructure of Galatians 3:1–4:11,* 2nd edition. Grand Rapids: Eerdmans, 2002.

Hooker, Morna D. "'Heirs of Abraham': The Gentiles' Role in Israel's Story: A Response to Bruce W. Longenecker." Pages 85–96 in *Narrative Dynamics in Paul: A Critical Assessment.* Edited by Bruce W. Longenecker. Louisville: Westminster John Knox, 2002.

Johnson-DeBaufre, Melanie. "Narrative, Multiplicity, and the Letters of Paul." Pages 362–75 in *The Oxford Handbook of Biblical Narrative. Edited by Danna Nolan Fewell.* Oxford: Oxford University Press, 2016.

Klaasen, John "Practical Theology and Narrative: Contours and Markers," *STJ* 3.2 (2017): 457–75.

Lincoln, Andrew T. "The Stories of Predecessors and Inheritors in Galatians and Romans." Pages 172–203 in *Narrative Dynamics in Paul: A Critical Assessment.* Edited by Bruce W. Longenecker. Louisville: Westminster John Knox, 2002.

Matlock, R. Barry. "The Arrow and the Web: Critical Reflections on a Narrative Approach to Paul." Pages 44–57 in *Narrative Dynamics in Paul: A Critical Assessment.* Edited by Bruce W. Longenecker. Louisville: Westminster John Knox, 2002.

McKnight, Scot. *Pastor Paul: Nurturing a Culture of Christoformity in the Church.* Grand Rapids: Brazos Press, 2019.

McKnight, Scot. *Reading Romans Backwards: A Gospel of Peace in the Midst of Empire.* Waco: Baylor University Press, 2019.

Reasoner, Mark. *Five Models of Scripture.* Grand Rapids: Eerdmans, 2021.

Rowe, C. Kavin. *One True Life: The Stoics and Early Christians as Rival Traditions.* New Haven: Yale University Press, 2016.

Watson, Francis. "Is There a Story in These Texts?" Pages 231–239 in *Narrative Dynamics in Paul: A Critical Assessment.* Edited by Bruce W. Longenecker. Louisville: Westminster John Knox, 2002.

Weymouth, Richard J. "The Christ-Story of Philippians 2:6–11: Narrative Shape and Paraenetic Purpose in Paul's Letter to Philippi," PhD diss., University of Otago, 2015.

Witherington, Ben. *Paul's Narrative Thought World: The Tapestry of Tragedy and Triumph.* Louisville: Westminster/John Knox, 1994.

Wright, N. T. *The New Testament and the People of God.* Minneapolis: Fortress, 1992.

Wright, N. T. *Paul and the Faithfulness of God, Book 1, Parts 1 & 2.* Minneapolis: Fortress, 2013.

16 Reading Revelation for Its Plot

DAVID L. BARR

We all know what stories are, though it proves challenging to explain them to someone else.[1] This is due in part to the great variety of stories and in part to the difficulty of pinning down the meaning of any abstraction. As Augustine lamented, "What then is time? If no one asks me, I know what it is. If I wish to explain it to him who asks, I do not know" (*Confessions* 11.14).

DEFINING THE ISSUES

The Bible contains many narratives, as this volume so ably demonstrates, but it may surprise some to find essays on Paul's letters and the Book of Revelation in such a collection. Are they really narratives? It is not too much to say that a quiet revolution has taken place over the last thirty years, with the application of narrative theory to the Bible.[2] Paul's letters, for example, have most often been read as discussions of ideas or as exhortations to proper behavior. Letters are not stories. However, every letter supposes a story since we must imagine who is speaking, to whom, and why.[3] In a similar way, Revelation has often been considered as a collection of discrete visions, having little in common with each other except themes and ideas.[4] In the contemporary world it is most often read as a collection of cryptic symbols

---

[1] Thomas M. Leitch, *What Stories Are: Narrative Theory and Interpretation* (University Park: Pennsylvania State University Press, 1986).

[2] Mark Allan Powell, *What is Narrative Criticism?* (Minneapolis: Fortress, 1991); Norman R. Petersen, *Literary Criticism for New Testament Critics* (Philadelphia: Fortress, 1978).

[3] Norman R. Petersen, *Rediscovering Paul: Philemon and the Sociology of Paul's Narrative World* (Philadelphia: Fortress, 1985).

[4] Arthur Wainwright, *Mysterious Apocalypse: Interpreting the Book of Revelation* (Nashville: Abingdon Press, 1993).

to be decoded,[5] either as a guide to some future time or as theology in disguise.[6]

A few literary critics have had the temerity to apply narrative theory to the Book of Revelation,[7] with modest success. But even when literary analysis is uncertain, some interesting things begin to happen when we read the Book of Revelation as a story.[8]

For one thing, we begin to ask different questions. Put most simply: before the nineteenth century, most readers asked religious questions (What does the narrative mean to me?), but with the development of historical criticism a shift occurred as scholars asked after its original meaning (What *did* the text mean in its historical context?). Without neglecting these questions, narrative criticism focuses on the text and its construction (*How* does the text mean?). A storyteller has many choices to make, for any story could be told in a variety of ways. Narrative criticism seeks to consider consciously how the action is presented, how the characters are portrayed, how the storyteller is portrayed, how those who hear the story are imagined, how the time of the events in the story is measured, how the setting is located in space, how the story begins and ends, and much more.

This essay can only begin such analysis and will be limited to the specific aspect of narrative known as plot. I have chosen for my title "Reading Revelation for Its Plot." While this seems straightforward enough, every word in the title needs qualification.

Reading. While Revelation pronounces a blessing on its reader (1:3), it does not at all envision the modern reader silently deciphering the work in the privacy of their study. It is rather a public reader, a lector, who reads it aloud to the assembled audience who are probably largely illiterate.[9] The author of the Apocalypse assumes that meaning will be

---

5   Bruce M. Metzger, *Breaking the Code: Understanding the Book of Revelation* (Nashville: Abingdon, 1993).

6   Christopher C. Hong, *History of the Future: A Study of the Four Major Eschatologies* (Washington DC: University Press of America, 1981); Richard J. Bauckham, *The Theology of the Book of Revelation* (Cambridge: Cambridge University Press, 1993).

7   Harold Bloom, *Revelation of St. John the Divine* (New York: Chelsea House, 1988); Frank Kermode, *The Sense of an Ending: Studies in the Theory of Fiction* (New York: Oxford University Press, 1967).

8   David L. Barr. "John's Apocalypse in Light of Modern Narrative Theory," in *1900th Anniversary of Johns Apocalypse: Proceedings of the International and Interdisciplinary Symposium (Athens Patmos, 17–26 September, 1995)* (Athens: University of Athens, 1999).

9   Mary Beard, "Ancient Literacy and the Function of the Written Word in Roman Religion," in Mary Beard et al., *Literacy in the Roman World*. JRA Supplementary Series no 3 (Ann Arbor, MI: Journal of Roman Archaeology, 1991).

apprehended by ear: "The one who has an ear should listen" (2:7, 11, 17, 29; 3:6, 13, 22). The verb "listen" (ἀκούω) occurs more than forty times in John's writing. Most people in antiquity experienced literature as an oral event; even when they read for themselves, they read aloud.[10] Notice that the author of first Enoch explained both his reception of his visions and the transmission of those visions in a clearly oral mode: "I saw in my sleep what I will now say with a tongue of flesh and with the breath of my mouth: which the Great One has given to men to converse therewith and understand with the heart" (1 Enoch 14:2).

The role of authors was to make physical (tongue, breath, mouth) the meaning that they experienced. The role of readers was to make this word sound again so that those to whom it is read ("those who hear and who keep," Rev 1:3) might experience the meanings originally apprehended by the author.

This understanding of reading has many implications, for an author composing for the ear will employ distinctive techniques to enable the listener to follow the thread of the narrative.[11] One obvious technique is the numbering of scenes – almost always seven in the Apocalypse. Another widely favored memory technique in antiquity was to imagine certain images set in certain places, so that place, image, and meaning merge.[12] So in John's narrative the messages to the seven churches come in the order one would encounter them were one to follow a circuit from Patmos. It is significant (and memorable) that one beast comes from the sea and one comes from the land. Omens appear in the sky where the signs of the zodiac correspond to characters of John's story. These vivid images make this story unforgettable.

Perhaps the closest analogies today to the ancient experience of the Apocalypse would be a poetry slam or a one-person play. The reading of Revelation was a public event, meant to be experienced, not a puzzle meant to be solved. A puzzle, once solved, can be laid aside, for it offers little more satisfaction. A work of art can be (indeed must be) experienced over and over again, each time eliciting new insights. Encountered as an oral performance, the Apocalypse does not merely inform the reader of some ideas; it also allows the hearer to experience

[10] Walter J. Ong, *Orality and Literacy: The Technologizing of the Word* (New York: Methuen, 1982); Ann E. Hanson. "Ancient Illiteracy," in Beard et al., *Literacy in the Roman World*.
[11] David L. Barr, "The Apocalypse of John as Oral Enactment," *Interpretation* 40, (1986): 243–56.
[12] Classical memory techniques are discussed by Cicero, *Rhetorica Ad Herennium* (Harvard University Press).

what John experienced on the barren island of Patmos, an experience that transported him (and the audience) to heaven and back. Lourdes Garcia Ureña has shown that there are surprising insights that derive from a thorough analysis of Revelation in the categories of short stories.[13]

Revelation. In the modern world, John's writing travels under two names, known both as the Book of Revelation and as the Apocalypse of John. Both are appropriate, but both need qualification. The opening words of the Greek text are Ἀποκάλυψις Ἰησοῦ Χριστοῦ (*Apocalypsis Iesou Christou*), literally "Revelation of Jesus Christ." But an apocalypse is a certain kind of revelation, for its imagery is that of removing a veil, uncovering, laying bare – the root meaning of *apocalypsis*.

Unfortunately, to the modern ear, the word apocalypse suggests cataclysmic misfortunes, perhaps portending the end of the world. But an apocalypse in the ancient world was a work that claimed to see behind the everyday world, removing the veil that obscures our ordinary vision. So whether we call it by its Greek name (Apocalypse) or by its Latin derived title (Revelation), we should resist the all too common assumption that it is a prediction of the future. What is uncovered, and thus revealed, is the meaning the author sees in his or her present situation.

Its. Hidden in this small pronoun is an assumption that a story has but one plot, that the plot resides in the text, and that the reader's task is merely to discover it. This is, at best, a dubious proposition. We have all had the experience of rereading a story and understanding it in a new way.[14] Was that new meaning always there or did we bring new perspectives? As far as meaning is concerned, we are faced with a paradox: meaning resides in the text yet meaning depends on the reader. Just as different people looking at the starry heavens see the same points of light but draw different lines between them, so one person sees the Big Dipper and another sees the Plow. In the same way, every reading supposes two things: the words on the page that the author provides and the lines between them that the reader supplies. Said differently, the reading of the text is both an objective construction of the meaning of the words and a subjective experience of the reality those words construct.

---

[13] See especially Lourdes Garcia Ureña, *Narrative and Drama in the Book of Revelation: A Literary Approach* (New York: Cambridge University Press, 2019).

[14] Wolfgang Iser, *The Implied Reader: Patterns of Communication in Prose Fiction from Bunyan to Beckett* (Baltimore: Johns Hopkins University Press, 1974); Wolfgang Iser, *The Act of Reading: A Theory of Aesthetic Response* (Baltimore: Johns Hopkins University Press, 1978).

Since there is always this subjective experience of the reader/hearer, we should abandon any notion of simply finding one plot in a narrative. By "its plot" we should understand a plot that author and reader produce.

There is another way in which "its plot" must be qualified. While each literary work is unique, there are certain plots typical of certain kinds of writing. Critics as far back as Aristotle recognized two types of plots: the tragic and the comic. In a comic plot, the protagonist is a person of lowly status and the story begins in chaos. But through a series of unlikely and often humorous incidents, everything changes, often culminating in a grand banquet, sometimes including a wedding. A tragic plot is the complete opposite: a noble figure is set on an ill-fated course of action that results in disaster. The classic example of tragedy is Sophocles' *Oedipus the King*, the closing line of which has the Chorus explain the lesson to be learned: "Count no mortal happy till he has passed the final limit of his life secure from pain." These two plot types (sometimes called archetypes or meta-plots) dominated ancient aesthetics and were never mixed.[15] But seeing Revelation as a tragic (or comic) plot is not the same thing as following the plot of the story.

Plot. The English word "plot" is remarkably elastic. We use it to refer to a broad array of activity, from how we plant our vegetables (the garden plot), to how we might plan to overthrow the present social order (the Gunpowder Plot). The OED lists at least five meanings, including to refer to a relatively small piece of ground, particularly if used for a specific purpose such as a garden plot or a burial place). It might be used as a verb (to map, plan, or scheme), or refer to the result of scheming: a conspiracy. It can also graph the relationship between two variables. And, specifically for our concerns, it can refer to a plan or scheme of a literary work. We might construe these various uses as a progression from the physical to the theoretical.

> Plot of ground → map of such a plot → a scheme → a conspiracy → plan of a story

One useful way to understand the notion of the plot of a story is to see it as a conspiracy between an author and a reader to map out the ground on which we stand. Both author and reader/hearer are involved in laying out the plot. The author tells a tale in which certain things happen; the audience understands these events by the way they are presented.

---

[15]   Northrop Frye, *The Great Code: The Bible and Literature* (New York: Harcourt Brace Jovanovich, 1982).

The author has many choices to make in plotting a story. The author decides: What incidents are necessary to the story? What order should they be told in? Where do the events occur? Are they told simply or in detail? Who tells them? To whom?

The reader/hearer must imagine the plan behind these choices. As one scholar puts it: narrative criticism is like telling a story to a child who repeatedly asks: What happened next? Why?[16] But, of course, we can never know why; we can only imagine it. That is the indispensable role of the audience, who must join the author in the conspiracy of meaning.

CONCEPTIONS OF PLOT

The first (surviving?) literary critic to discuss the narrative aspects of theatrical performances was Aristotle, who wrote two books probing how plays worked – one on tragedy and one on comedy. Only the one on tragedy survives.[17] The *Poetics* differentiates the elements of the kinds of writings known to Aristotle (comedy, saga, satyr plays, mimes, and poems), comparing each to tragedy. The basic elements of such writings include: plot, characterization, meter, song, and thought. The most important element of a tragedy is said to be plot (*Poetics* 1450a 80).

For Aristotle, a plot consists of a unified action, one that has a beginning, middle, and end. The initial action sets in motion a series of events that culminate in a final event that resolves the action – one incident leading to the next by necessity or probability (*Poetics* 1450a 51). It is not just that one action follows another, but each action is triggered by a prior action and causes a subsequent action. In a tragedy, this chain of events typically occurs on one day: Oedipus rose that fateful morning as King of Thebes; he ended his day an outcast, blind, and alone. This focused time period results in a tightly connected plot. Other genres allow for elements that do not directly contribute to the plot, such as various subplots, character development scenes, reflections on meaning, and asides (*Poetics* 1459b 31). No one argues that the Apocalypse of John is as tightly plotted as a tragedy; nor is it as elaborate and diffuse as an epic. But there is as yet no agreement on the

---

[16] Elizabeth Struthers Malbon. "Narrative Criticism: How Does the Story Mean?" in *Mark and Method: New Approaches in Biblical studies* ed. Janet Capel Anderson and Stephen D. Moore (Minneapolis: Fortress, 1992).

[17] For an outstanding translation and commentary, see Leon Golden and O. B. Hardison, *Aristotle's Poetics: A Translation and Commentary for Students of Literature* (Englewood Cliffs: Prentice-Hall, 1968).

relationship between the various incidents portrayed. We can highlight
the various approaches to Revelation's plot by asking how one might
diagram the action; three suggestions have been made: as a straight line,
as a U-shaped line, or as a spiral line.

The traditional reading of the Apocalypse sees it as a linear progression portraying the transition from the (present) evil age to the (future)
kingdom of God. It is, as it were, history written backwards. The job of
the historian is to take the reader from some significant time in the past
and then to show how we got from then to now – with one thing leading
to another. The job of a prophet in this paradigm is to show the events
that will take us from now to some ideal future.[18]

James L. Resseguie adopts a basically linear conception of the plot:
how the people of God make the arduous journey from the loss of Eden
to the new promised land but with one all-important difference: the line
is not straight; it is U-shaped.[19] A U-shaped plot is a story that starts
with a stable social order, descends into chaos, only to climb again to
stability. Or the inverse: an upside-down U – a story that begins in
chaos, rises to stability, only to fall again into chaos. This inverted U is
the shape of tragedy; the upright U is the shape of comedy. Resseguie
argues that Revelation is an upright U-shaped plot, moving from the
vision of God enthroned (Rev 4), through chaos, to the vision of a new
kingdom of God (Rev 22).

Young Jang has taken this model a step further, using a five-part
plot model:

Setting (Rev 1:9–4:11)
Complication (5:1–11:19)
Resolution (12:1–16:1)
Evaluation (17:1–2:5)
Moral (22:6–21)[20]

Like Resseguie, Jang sees the events of the Apocalypse as a linear progression according to a predetermined pattern. We might visualize this
as a series of straight lines – perhaps a dashed line.

Elisabeth Schüssler Fiorenza was perhaps the first to suggest that the
action of the Apocalypse is neither a straight line nor simply U-shaped;

---

[18] See the careful overview in Grant R. Osborne, *Revelation* (Grand Rapids: Baker
      Academic, 2002).

[19] James L. Resseguie, *The Revelation of John: A Narrative Commentary* (Grand Rapids,
      Mich: Baker Academic, 2009).

[20] Young Jang, "Narrative Plot of the Apocalypse," *Scriptura: International Journal of
      Bible, Religion, and Theology in Southern Africa* 84 (2003): 381–90.

it is a spiral. It rises and falls, progresses and regresses, often repeating previous actions with new detail.[21] While her arguments are founded on conceptual rather than literary methods, this seems to me to be the most promising metaphor for appreciating the plot of Revelation. It is also the most flexible approach, not forcing the action of John's story into a predetermined form.

Lourdes García Ureña describes the plot using both a linear and a spiral metaphor, seeing the events portrayed as both repetitive (looking back) and novel (looking forward), with each repetition moving the story forward.[22] With extraordinary attention to detail, she presents the entire story of the Apocalypse unfolding from John's experience on Patmos.

With the above concerns in mind, the following offers one way of reading Revelation as a spiraling plot.

LISTENING FOR THE PLOT

Ideally, this endeavor would begin with an oral presentation of the Book of Revelation in its entirety. In my experience with students, two responses are common. First, in an oral performance there is no time to grasp all the details. The story rushes forward, carrying the audience along to the next action with an emotional intensity that causes one to feel satisfied, even without grasping all the details. Thus, and second, paradoxically the oral audience tends to report that they now understand not so much the induvial incidents as the meaning of the work as a whole. Why is this?

John is very careful in his opening to orient the audience to his writing. He first gives it a title (1:1–2), then a blessing that echoes the opening of a letter (1:3–8), then he begins an autobiographical account – a story of what happened to him on the island of Patmos (1:9). This is one of the oldest opening gambits of the storyteller: I was off by myself one day when something extraordinary happened (let me tell you about it). John frames his work with his personal attestation, in his own voice.

> I John … was on the island called Patmos on account of the word of God and the testimony of Jesus. I was in the Spirit on the Lord's day, and I heard behind me a loud voice like a trumpet saying,

21 Elisabeth Schüssler Fiorenza, *The Book of Revelation: Justice and Judgment* (Minneapolis: Fortress, 1998). Originally published in *Catholic Biblical Quarterly*, 1977.
22 García Ureña, *Narrative and Drama in the Book of Revelation*.

"Write what you see in a book and send it to the seven churches,
to Ephesus and to Smyrna and to Pergamum and to Thyatira and to
Sardis and to Philadelphia and to Laodicea." (Rev 1:9–11)

I John am he who heard and saw these things (Rev 22:8).

This is surely a clear assertion of narrative unity. And there are at least
ten other parallels between the opening and closing.[23] In fact, like a
tragedy, all the action of the Apocalypse happens on one day, artfully
labeled "the Lord's day." At this macro level the plot of the story is as
simple as if someone said: One day I fell asleep and dreamed I saw won-
drous things. Then I woke up. And, like a dream, the action between the
opening and closing of the Apocalypse is extremely diverse, with major
shifts in the action and characters. We will first examine the narrative
shifts and then ask how they fit together.

PLOT TWISTS

The first segment of John's narrative is clear, so clear that every com-
mentator recognizes Revelation 1–3 as a discrete unit. A majestic heavenly figure appears to John while he is "in the spirit" and commands
him to write to seven churches of Asia Minor. More like an oral exam
than a letter, these notes reveal the strengths and weaknesses of each
assembly. Then, as soon as the last message is transcribed, everything
changes (4:1). With the simple notation, "After this," the story shifts
completely.

All the action before this occurs on Patmos and involves John acting as recorder of messages to seven churches on the mainland of Asia
Minor, revealing their accomplishments and failures. But from 4:1 on
there is no mention of the churches; John himself becomes an actor in
the story, not just the recipient of the vision; Jesus is portrayed in the
striking new figure of a Lamb; the action now occurs in the divine throne
room in heaven, accessed through a door in the sky. John describes the
room in great detail and then reports an enthronement ritual wherein
a Lamb (alone) is found worthy to open a sealed scroll. He is given the
scroll and as each of seven seals is broken a new vision is seen. The connection between these short visions is sometimes clear (as the first four
seals show the progression from conqueror to war to famine to death)
and sometimes must be imagined (as seals 6 and 7). As the oral audience

---

[23]   David L. Barr, *Tales of the End: A Narrative Commentary on the Book of Revelation*
(Salem, Ore: Polebridge Press, 2012).

would hear the enumerated series, the expectation of a climax would no doubt increase. When a fourth series is deferred because there can be no further delay, these expectations are met: the last trumpet sounds and it is announced: "The kingdom of the world has become the kingdom of our Lord and of his Christ, and he shall reign for ever and ever" (11:15).

The enthronement ritual is complete. The plot in this section is a unified action with a beginning, middle, and end. But, except for the use of a series of seven, it has no obvious connection to the previous unit. Nor does it flow naturally into the rest of the narrative.

It is impossible to over-emphasize the dramatic shift that occurs at 11:19. No longer in the throne room, let alone on Patmos, the revealer stands in an indefinite space from which one can peer into the heavenly temple. Now the whole focus of the story shifts. All the earlier action was initiated by the God, but here the antagonist is Satan's Dragon. He attacks the woman and her child, and makes war on her other children (12:1–17).

The characters are new: two women (one a bride and the other a prostitute); three (perhaps four) new antagonists (a dragon, a sea monster, a land monster; Satan); and a warrior angel named Michael. John fades into the background, merely narrating the events. More is going on here than meets eye.

Eugene Boring was perhaps the first to recognize that the various actions and visions of the Apocalypse do not exist on the same narrative level.[24] He identified four levels. The first is the level of the narrative frame where the primary actors are John, the seven churches, and a heavenly messenger. The second level is a heavenly scene where John is both narrator and character. The third level portrays what happens as a result of the heavenly vision (what he calls the world's story). The fourth level is the larger story of Christian suffering which is presumed but not plotted in the narrative. While I do not see these levels in quite the same way, this is a valuable and original insight into John's narrative.

One way to clarify the narrative levels is to consider the role of John at each level. The first narrative level is a story John tells about himself: "I John was" (1:9). At this level, John is the major focus of the story. John continues to be a character in the second-level narrative, but a minor character. The real action is performed by the one on the throne and the slaughtered Lamb. John even admits that he (the character in

---

[24] M. Eugene Boring. "Narrative Christology in the Apocalypse" (paper presented at Catholic Biblical Association October 1992).

the story) doesn't understand what he sees (5:4–5). At the third narrative level, John ceases to be a character in the story and becomes simply a witness to what others are doing. Just as clear, and even more important, the portrayal of Jesus in each of these sections is unique. In story one he appears as the judge who pronounces blessings and curses on the seven churches. In story two he is a slaughtered Lamb worthy to open the scroll. In story three he is the heavenly warrior who brings justice and renewal to the cosmos. But it is not quite that simple.

In the narrative of Revelation these three stories are laid atop one another, blended, with the action of each affecting and interpreting the others. Take, for instance, the war in heaven (12:7–12) that opens the third story, a story filled with holy war motifs and actions. At one level, this incident belongs to the story of the origins of the war: the defeat of Satan by the angel Michael. But in summing up the scene, the victory is attributed to the Lamb and the martyrs. This is why the Lamb can open the scroll. Thus this action from level three of the narrative explains worthiness of the Lamb proclaimed in level two, and is presented as a past tense already in level one (3:21).

These new characters perform new actions only hinted at in the earlier narrative: birth and war. The Dragon pursues the woman into the wilderness, intent on murdering her newborn child. Failing at this, the Dragon turns to make war on the rest of her children (12:17). This holy war dominates the action for the rest of the story, finally climaxing in the complete destruction of the Dragon (20:7–10). This is the third complete action of John's drama. It has a beginning action (the Dragon's pursuit of war), a series of intermediate actions, one leading to another, until we arrive at a satisfying end.

While we can see the *story* in a linear fashion, the *telling* of the story (its plot) is far from a straight line. There is considerable redundancy, foreshadowing, and flashback. A prime example of redundancy is the series of seven bowls, which mirror the series of seven trumpets, which themselves mirror the ten plagues of the Exodus story (Exod 7–12). The Dragon is defeated by Michael and by the testimony of the martyrs (12:11), but he continues to act (always with the same result – his ultimate defeat). The primary motif of this section is holy war – a final conflict between the forces of good and the forces of evil in which the good prevail.[25] These incidents are not presented in a straight-line progression but rather like a spiral, with the story circling back on

---

[25]   Adela Yarbro Collins, *The Combat Myth in the Book of Revelation* (Chico: Scholars Press, 1976).

itself, repeating and reinforcing its meaning. There are, for example, at least five portrayals of the final battle (16:14; 17:14; 19:11, 19; 20:8). And the war against the faithful was foreshadowed in the Throne narrative without any explanation (11:7–8). Story-wise, the triumphant scene that closes the Throne narrative (the kingdoms of the world have become the kingdom of God; 11:17) is the end of the story; but it is only midway in the plot. Why?

THREE STORIES IN ONE VISION OR ONE STORY IN THREE VISIONS

John presents his work as a Revelation of Jesus Christ. We should take this seriously. The main actor in each of John's stories is Jesus, though presented in different guises.[26] While John includes an incredible variety of materials within the common frame of his vision on the Isle of Patmos, all centers on Jesus.

Jan A. Du Rand offers a very interesting musical reading of Revelation, with the various portrayals of Jesus acting as a kind of repeated and varied melody.[27] He sees the three acts of John's drama bound together by this melody. He details it thus:

Act 1 shows God's involvement *in the church* because of the Christ event (chapters 1–3).

Act 2 shows the unfolding of God's plan of salvation and judgment *in the cosmos* on the grounds of the Christ event (chapters 4–11).

Act 3 shows the final unfolding of God's salvation and judgment in *history* because of the Christ event (chapters 12–22).

This is a commendable attempt both to do justice to the radically different portrayals in the three acts and still to explain how they work together, giving full weight to the centrality of Jesus in John's story.

First we see Jesus in the theophany of the divine figure, who demands that John write his vision and send it to the seven churches. These messages clarify what John expects of the churches, put into the very mouth of Jesus. Why, the reader might ask, do John and Jesus have the authority to do this? This question is answered in the second stage of John's vision, where we see the enthronement of the Lamb who has earned the right

---

[26] David L. Barr. "Dis-guising Jesus: St(r)aying in Character in John's Apocalypse," in *Let The Reader Understand: Essays in Honor of Elizabeth Struthers Malbon.* ed. Edwin K. Broadhead (London: Bloomsbury T & T Clark, 2017).

[27] Jan A. Du Rand, "A 'Basso Ostinato' In the Structuring of the Apocalypse of John?" *Neotestamentica* 27.2 (1993): 299–311.

to open the scroll. The episodic visions that follow are unified by presenting them as a sequence of seals and a sequence trumpets. This culminates in the exalted declaration that the kingdoms of the world have
become the kingdom of God *and of his messiah* (italics added, 11:15).
This declaration begs the final question of how this could possibly be so.
John now tells the third story of the cosmic war between the forces of
good and evil, God and Satan, a heavenly warrior and a dragon.

These three stories are bound together by a series of literary devices,
including shared characters, foreshadowing and flashback, and the use
of common motifs, including the sevenfold series and the meanings
of colors and numbers. Each story has reminders of the other stories
embedded in it. The description of the heavenly warrior (19:11–16) is
foreshadowed in the description of the figure who dictates the seven
messages (1:12–16). The war of the Dragon against the people of God is
foreshadowed in a scene that portrays the death of the two witnesses
(11:7–13). And the Lamb who is enthroned in story two dominates the
action of story three, leading God's army and even marrying the bride at
the end of the struggle (21:9–14). And above all, these actions are bound
together by being found in the framework of John's Patmos vision. The
author makes no explicit connection between these events; that job is
left to the reader/hearer.

Building on the distinction between story and narrative, Jamie
Davies offers a reading of the Book of Revelation as a linear story
presented in a nonlinear narrative, much like some modern films. He
rehearses a whole series of story-events presented out of linear order in
the narrative. These anachronisms and redundancies in the audience's
experience of the narrative are both confusing and revealing, making
high demands on the audience.[28]

Consider the way John keeps deferring the ending of the story. For
example, the seven messages elicit a sense of an ending; seven being
a common symbol for a finished work (in the Genesis creation story,
for example). The audience for this story has no reason to think there
is more to it. This is true of each septet; the seventh member implies
completion, but the end is not yet. John even has a bit of fun with the
audience's expectation by reporting a series of seven thunders, which he
has been forbidden to explain because "there should be no more delay"
(10:1–7). Perhaps the reader is supposed to wink here, for the performance is only halfway done.

---

[28]   Jamie Davies. "Reading the Apocalypse with Christopher Nolan" (paper presented at
       Annual Meeting of the Society of Biblical Literature. San Antonio, 2021).

Surely the series of catastrophes that complete the throne vision, which culminate in the declaration that judgment has come and God's reign has begun, is the end of the story (11:15–17). But no. John peers into the heavenly temple and the story continues. A new series of seven is narrated, culminating in the bold declaration, "It is done" (16:17). But still the story goes on.

Numerous battles are set forth, each ending with the triumph of the Lamb and his followers and the seeming obliteration of the forces of evil. The two beasts initiate a reign of terror but are defeated and destroyed. Satan himself is captured and confined to the Abyss. But still the story goes on, for after a thousand years he must be released (20:7). He launches another battle and is finally consigned to the lake of fire. With the judgment of humanity and the appearance of a new heaven and a new earth, surely the end has come.

In one sense everything has changed. The coming of Jesus anticipated in the seven messages is realized. John even speaks in the voice of Jesus: "I Jesus have sent my angel to you with this testimony for the churches" (22:16). The promise made at the beginning (that the reader and hearer would be blessed) has been made real.

But in another sense, nothing has changed. The time is still near (22:10); the dogs are still outside (22:15); and they still await Jesus' coming (22:20). There seems to be more to the story.

CONCLUSION

Read as a narrative, the Apocalypse of John invites us to listen in on a hidden world – one far distant from ordinary reality. It is a world of monsters and mayhem, bloodied Lambs and spotless brides, of worlds vanquished and of worlds created anew. The full force of this narrative is best felt in an oral presentation, wherein the audience re-experiences John's visions. The plot of this narrative is quite complex. Three stories which on the face of it have little to do with each other are presented. But because they are presented together, the reader begins to imagine how they relate to each other – for relationship is at the heart of plot. One way to begin this process of reading Revelation for its plot is to raise the question of consequences. What will be the consequence of John taking these messages back to his churches? By what authority does John/Jesus make these demands and restrictions? What has the Lamb done to be worthy to open the scroll? John never answers such questions directly; he just tells another story.

SELECTED FURTHER READING

Barr, David L. "The Apocalypse of John as Oral Enactment." *Interpretation* 40 (1986): 243–56.

Barr, David L. *Tales of the End: A Narrative Commentary on the Book of Revelation.* 2nd edition. Salem, Ore: Polebridge Press, 2012.

Bauckham, Richard J., *The Theology of the Book of Revelation.* Cambridge: Cambridge University Press, 1993.

Bloom, Harold, *Revelation of St. John the Divine.* New York: Chelsea House, 1988.

Frye, Northrop, *The Great Code: The Bible and Literature.* New York: Harcourt Brace Jovanovich, 1982.

García Ureña, Lourdes, *Narrative and Drama in the Book of Revelation: A Literary Approach.* English ed., Society for New Testament Studies Monograph Series. New York: Cambridge University Press, 2019.

Jang, Young. "Narrative Plot of the Apocalypse." *Scriptura: International Journal of Bible, Religion, and Theology in Southern Africa* 84 (2003): 381–90.

Kermode, Frank. *The Sense of an Ending: Studies in the Theory of Fiction.* New York: Oxford University Press, 1967.

Malbon, Elizabeth Struthers. "Narrative Criticism: How Does the Story Mean?" Pages 23–47 in *Mark and Method: New Approaches in Biblical studies.* Edited by Janice Capel Anderson and Stephen D. Moore. Minneapolis: Fortress, 1992.

Powell, Mark Allan. *What is Narrative Criticism?* Guides to Biblical Scholarship. Old Testament Series. Minneapolis: Fortress, 1991.

Resseguie, James L. *The Revelation of John: A Narrative Commentary.* Grand Rapids: Baker Academic, 2009.

Schüssler Fiorenza, Elisabeth, *The Book of Revelation: Justice and Judgment.* Second ed. Minneapolis: Fortress, 1998.

Wainwright, Arthur, *Mysterious Apocalypse: Interpreting the Book of Revelation.* Reprint of Wipf and Stock, 2001. Nashville: Abingdon Press, 1993.

Index

www.ingramcontent.com/pod-product-compliance
Lightning Source LLC
Chambersburg PA
CBHW050303300125
21111CB00003B/3